CW00692887

# SENT BY THE IRON SKY

OSPREY
PUBLISHING

Almighty God, we kneel to Thee and ask to be the instrument of Thy fury in smiting the evil forces that have visited death, misery and debasement on the people of earth. We humbly face thee with true penitence for all of our sins for which we do most earnestly seek Thy forgiveness. Help us to dedicate ourselves completely to Thee. Be with us, God, when we leap from our planes into the dread abyss and descend in parachutes into the midst of enemy fire. Give us iron will and stark courage as we spring from the harnesses of our parachutes and seize arms to meet and defeat them in Thy name and in the name of freedom and dignity of man. Keep us firm in our faith and resolution, and guide us that we may not dishonor our high mission or fail in our sacred duties. Let our enemies who have lived by the sword turn from their violence lest they perish by the sword. Help us to serve thee gallantly and to be humble in victory.

Amen.

The 506th Parachute Infantry Regiment Prayer written by Captain James G. Morton

## Dedication
For my dad and mum – Dennis & Joan

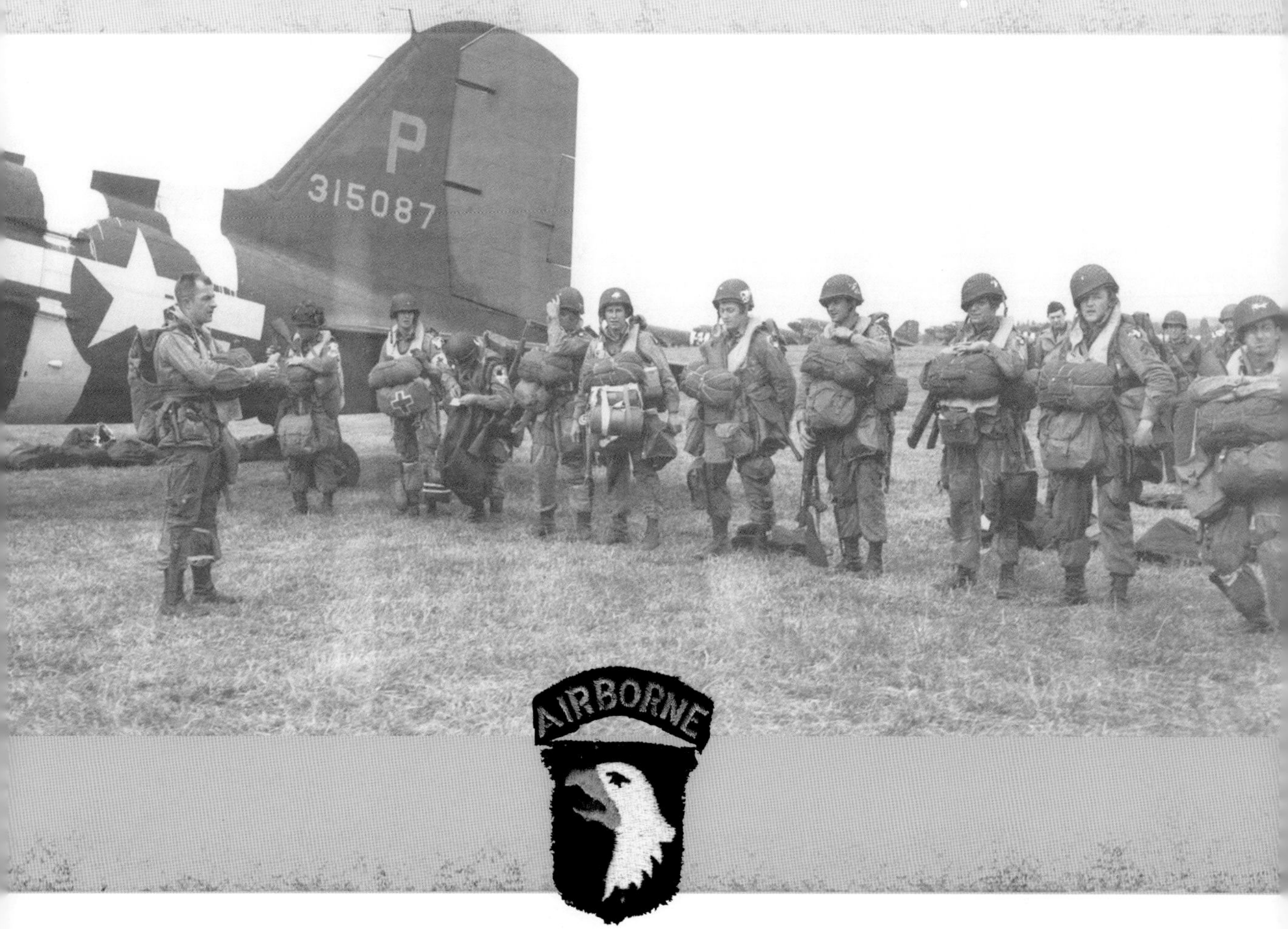
P
315087
AIRBORNE

# SENT BY THE IRON SKY

## THE LEGACY OF AN AMERICAN PARACHUTE BATTALION IN WORLD WAR II

22nd Dec 2019

IAN GARDNER

OSPREY PUBLISHING
Bloomsbury Publishing Plc
PO Box 883, Oxford, OX1 9PL, UK
1385 Broadway, 5th Floor, New York, NY 10018, USA
E-mail: info@ospreypublishing.com
**www.ospreypublishing.com**

OSPREY is a trademark of Osprey Publishing Ltd

First published in Great Britain in 2019

19 20 21 22 23   10 9 8 7 6 5 4 3 2 1

Maps by the author
Index by Alison Worthington
Originated by PDQ Digital Media Solutions, Bungay, UK
Printed and bound in India by Replika Press Private Ltd.

FRONT COVER: On June 4, for the benefit of the camera Lt Col Robert Wolverton checks his adjutant
Lt Alex Bobuck's equipment. In the background stands the 440th Troop Carrier Group C-47 aircraft 315087
"Lady Lillian," freshly painted in the black and white recognition stripes. (NARA colorised by Johnny Sirlande)
TITLE PAGE: 1st Lt Alex Bobuck (captured) checks a manifest on the morning of Sunday June 4 for the
benefit of Signal Corps cameramen. In the background stands C-47 "Lady Lillian" which carried Executive
Officer Maj George Grant's stick to Normandy. (Left to right): Pvt Anthony Wincensiak (KIA), Sgt Tom
Newell (captured), Pvt Ray Calandrella (captured), Pvt Jesse Cross (captured), Pvt John Rinehart (KIA),
Sgt Bill Pauli (captured), T/5 Jack Harrison (died of wounds), Pfc Harry Howard (captured), T/5 Charles
Riley (captured), and S/Sgt John Taormina (captured). (NARA)
All other images in the book that are not credited are from the Author's Own Collection.

Osprey Publishing supports the Woodland Trust, the UK's leading woodland conservation charity.
To find out more about our authors and books visit **www.ospreypublishing.com**. Here you will find
extracts, author interviews, details of forthcoming events and the option to sign up for our newsletter.

EDITOR'S NOTE
This book contains some material previously published in *Tonight We Die As Men*, *Deliver Us From Darkness*
and *No Victory in Valhalla*.

# CONTENTS

# ACKNOWLEDGMENTS

As usual this section has been one of the hardest parts of the book to complete, as so many people have contributed to *Tonight We Die as Men*, *Deliver Us From Darkness* and *No Victory in Valhalla*. Without this long list of amazing individuals, many of whom have since passed away, *Sent by the Iron Sky* could never have been put together. If anyone's name has been overlooked – and it has been a long time – I hope you will accept my sincere apologies. Individual thanks are extended by country to the following:

## United Kingdom

Laura Callaghan, Rosemary Connor, Marcus Cowper, Roger Day, Elsie Douglas, Rodge Dowson, Emily Holmes, Monique Jones, Patricia Howard, Peter Mills, Kate Moore, John Mundy, Doreen Ramsden, Rosemary and Sarah Pinches, Monica Tovey and Graeme Trim, Francis Wyndham.

## United States of America and Canada

Miles Allen, Jannie Anderson, Kathleen "Tachie" Anderson, Jacqueline Rickards Andrews Jim Bigley, Fred and Rick Bahlau, Mark Bando, Mike Baldinger, Doug Barber, Barbara Bartell, Manny Barrios, Ralph Bennett, Dave Berry, Lurie Berteau, Joe Beyrle, Joe Beyrle II, Denis van den Brink, Marcus Brotherton, Tom Bucher, Sharon Bunker, Roy Burger, Don Burgett, Ray Calandrella, Derwood Cann, Joan Chincarini, Merrick O'Connell, Denis and Donna Cortese, Dan Cutting, Louis DeNegre, Mario "Hank" DiCarlo, Carole and Harley Dingman, Joe Doughty, Bob Dunning, Mark Durivage, George Dwyer, Teddy and Bette Dziepak, Bud Estes, Bill Galbraith, Judy Gamble, John Gibson, Len Goodgal, Brian Gottlieb, George Grant Jr, Clark Heggeness, Randy Hils, Ben Hiner, Bob Izumi, Ken Johnson, Tom Kennedy, Brenda Kightlinger, John Klein, Laurie Kotsch, George Koskimaki, John Kutz, Gerry and Bobbie Lord, Alfred Lowe, Walter Lukasavage, Piet "Pete" Luiten, Pete and Mary Madden, Clair Mathiason, James "Pee Wee" Martin, Sid McCallum, Jim and Pat McCann, Earl McClung, Karen McGee, George McMillan, Jim Melhus, John Merkt, Eugene and Vada Montgomery, Tim Moore, Byron and Robby Moore, Dave and Neil Morgan, Gil Morton, Ray Nagell, Mary Lou Neally, Don Orcutt, Carolyn Packert, Bonnie Pond, Jake Powers, John Reeder, Rich Riley, Doyle Rigden, Bobbie Rommel, George Rosie, Ken Ross, Philip Russo, Barney Ryan, Bob Saxvik, John Shank, Ray Skully, Ed Shames, Bob Smoldt, Elsie and Nathan Spurr, Harold Stedman, Tom Stedman, Jay Stone, Ann Tanzy, Kathy Tozzi,

Lou Vecchi, John Vecchi, Geoff Walden, Aaron Walser, Bob Webb Jr, Bill Wedeking, Chad Weisensel, Harold Winer, Lee Wolverton, Don Zahn.

## France and Switzerland

Msr and Mme Brohier, Charles Carel, André Descamps, Charles Destrés, Michel DeTrez, Thérése Dieudonné, Msr and Mme Droin, Msr Dumoncel, Eugéne Enot, Thierry Ferey, Maurice de Folleville, Philippe Frigot, William Hébert, Nicole Laurence, Amand Laurent, Léon Lehay, Jean Pierre Lemesnil, Michel and Martine Léonard, Louis Letourneur, Paulette Menilgrente, Jean Mignon, Msr and Mme Poisson, Susan Rochat, Msr La Rue, Jean Savary and Henry Villand.

## The Netherlands

Dick Bakker, Henk Beens, Frits Berens, Donald van den Bogert, Hans den Brok, Jo van Dongen, Bernard Florissen, Gerda den Hartog, Johannes van den Hatert, Peter Hendrikx, Piet van den Heuvel, Gido Hordijk, Jenny and Jan Van Hout, Erwin Janssen, Wim and Jos Klerkx, Steph Leenhouwers, Vic van Lijf, Peter van der Linden, Frans Mientjes, Ronald Ooms, Wan van Overweld, Johannes Peerbolte, Tom Peeters, Gert and Clazien van Rinsum, Albert Roxs, Frits van Schaik, Jaap van Schaik, Frank and Chantal Slegers, Ronald Stassen, Willemien van Steenbergen, Jurgen Swinkels, Noud Stultiens, Tom Timmermans, Dirk van Tintelen, Frenk Derks van de Ven, Peter van de Wal.

## Belgium

Ivonne Dumont, Jean-Francois d'Hoffschmidt, Philippe d'Hoffschmidt, Reg Jans, Jean-Marie Koeune, Adjutant Eric "Rony" Lemoine, Maguy Marenne, André Meurisse, Robert Remacle, Joël Robert, Jules and Denise Robert, Philipe Wilkin.

## Germany

Florian Beierl, Gerhard Roletscheck.

A "Prop Blast" party held in November 1942 in the officers' mess. One ritual required that a concoction of spirits be consumed within 30 seconds from the "Sink Grail," which is still used on special occasions today by the 506th. 2nd Lt Ed Harrell is seen here cheered on by, among others, Bob Wolverton (partially obscured behind Harrell), Lt Salve Matheson (Regimental Personnel Officer – cigarette in hand), and next right George Grant, who went on to become Third Battalion's Executive Officer and was killed on D-Day. (Mark Bando Collection)

# INTRODUCTION

Countless words have been written on men at war, part of the innate human desire to explain the inexplicable, to comprehend the incomprehensible, to know what only those who have taken up arms can truly know: why do they do it? What compels human beings, whose existence is by its very nature so fragile and finite, to risk all? The answer, I believe, can be found in pages seldom seen. In the front of a regimental history compiled by the 101st Airborne's 506th Parachute Infantry Regiment is a collection of black-and-white photographs of the leaders of that elite unit, whose exploits turned the tide in Europe and World War II. If we want to understand what drove them, the explanation appears beneath the picture of my grandfather, Lieutenant Colonel Robert Lee Wolverton. He commanded Blue, the Third Battalion in the 506th, fulfilling a dream born when he was a boy in Elkins, West Virginia. He longed to lead men into battle and devoted himself to that pursuit. It guided his every step, from West Point to Ramsbury, England, to the moment he leapt on June 6, 1944 from a C-47 into the fiery darkness over Normandy. There is no better way to know him and the men of Third Battalion than by reading the simple, succinct inscription beneath his photograph in that old, faded regimental history: "Leader this man… He loved Blue, and Blue loved him."

War is defined by killing and killing is commonly defined by hate, the sort of which compels one race to seek systematic domination, subjugation or elimination of another. When one mass of people aligns to wipe away another, it can be stopped only by those willing to fight and give all. The men of Third Battalion did this in love for one another and love for what is right. "Greater love hath no man than this," Christ said, "that he lay down his life for his friends." Leading the battalion in prayer before the jump, the colonel said: "[I]f die we must, let us die as men would die, without complaining, without pleading and safe in the knowledge that we have done our best for what we believed was right." Those words were an expression of love for his men, part of his caring for them at the most perilous moment of their lives, guiding them, if necessary, to the ultimate sacrifice in the spirit and honor each of them so cherished and with the assurance that it was not in vain but for the good of humankind.

Ian Gardner's work, *Sent by the Iron Sky*, honors the Third Battalion in the manner those warriors so richly deserved. Families of that unit are indebted to him, just as each of us is indebted to them, not only for all they accomplished but for all they represented, for the lesson in love they left us and the remainder of humanity forever.

Lee Wolverton – October 2018

PROP BLAST PARTY #2   11-14-42

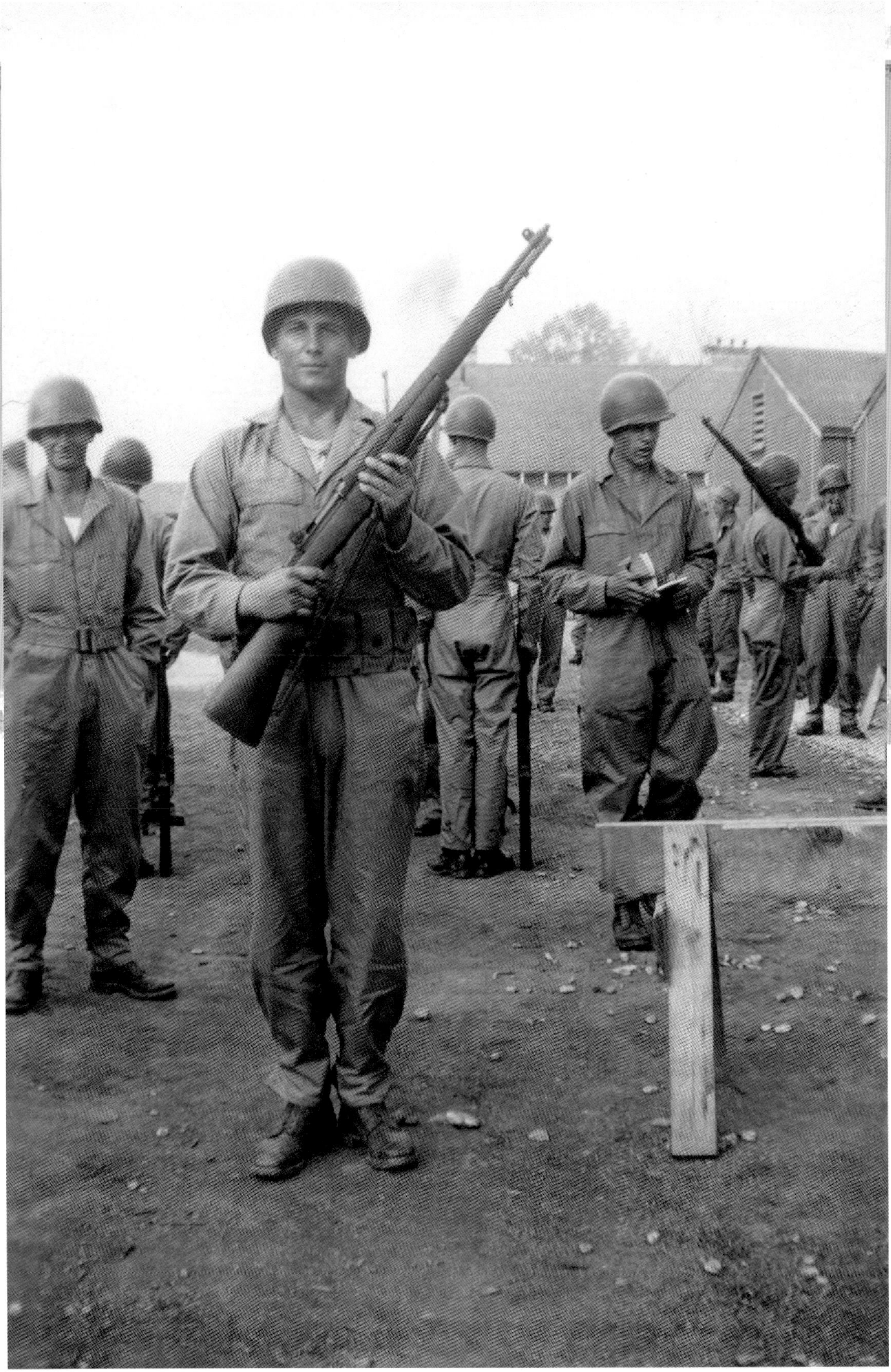

# Chapter 1
# GUIDING STAR

## Selection and Training

After a heavy night out on the town in March 1944, Lieutenant Colonel Robert Wolverton, commander of the Third Battalion, 506th Parachute Infantry Regiment (PIR), returned to his fashionable London hotel in Berkeley Square. While thumbing through some family photos, he allowed himself to consider the past, the present and the future, which as the commanding officer of a frontline parachute battalion seemed to be closing in at an alarming rate. Diminutive and bullish, Bob could be a man of few words but was gifted with a beautifully subtle sense of humor and when he did talk, he was always faultlessly clear, precise and very much to the point.

At a time such as this, he could not help thinking about his wife Kay and their two-year-old son Lachlan back home in West Virginia. A pad of hotel headed paper on the bedside table pricked his interest. Bob's planned series of letters to his family were long overdue but perhaps now the time was right as he set about jotting down a few thoughts, including advice for his son and what was expected of him when he eventually started school.

Members of 1 Platoon, H Company, practicing rifle drill at Toccoa. (Left to right): Lou Vecchi, Mario "Hank" DiCarlo and Fred Neill. Hank came from the small coastal resort of Wildwood-by-the-Sea, New Jersey. (Hank DiCarlo)

Still only 29 years old, Bob had an inner feeling, call it intuition, that his own "future" would not be that far away. Whatever the personal cost, he believed that it was his destiny to lead what he proudly considered one of the finest airborne units ever to be created. All too soon this unit would be tested in battle – a battle they had spent the previous two years preparing for.

\* \* \*

Kay and Lachlan (Lock) Wolverton, 1946. (The Wolverton Family)

Maj Bob Wolverton, Kay and their son Lachlan, standing outside his parents' house in Elkins, West Virginia in 1942. Lachlan was born at Fort Bragg in August 1941 during Bob's time with the 9th Infantry Division. The photo was taken on September 9, while Bob was on leave from a promotion course at Fort Leavenworth. (The Wolverton Family)

BELOW LEFT A southern boy from Lexington, North Carolina, and legendary commander of the 506th Parachute Infantry Regiment, Col Robert F. Sink had been an early pioneer of parachute tactics and organization at Fort Benning. With great energy and determination, Sink devised one of the most grueling training regimes ever experienced by any World War II American military unit. But along with rigor came fairness and concern. No problem was ever too small for his attention. This photo was taken at Zell am See in 1945.

BELOW RIGHT Thirty-one-year-old Col Charles Chase, the regiment's Executive Officer (XO), nicknamed "the Bantam Rooster," was originally from Portland and by 1942 had been married to Elizabeth (Beth) for almost six years. Steady, cool, funny and charming, Charlie was a graduate of the West Point Class of 1933 and fluent in four languages including French and Spanish. (NARA)

It did not take long for the 506th to become acquainted with Mount Currahee. At 1,753ft in height, the "zigzag" summit trail is almost 3 miles long and whatever the time of day, the candidates were expected to make it to the top and back well within the designated cut-off time of 1 hour and 10 minutes – with no exceptions. (Jim "Pee Wee" Martin)

Officially activated on July 20, 1942, the 506th was the brainchild of West Point trained 37-year-old Colonel Bob Sink. Back in North Carolina, Sink's father was active in state politics and ran a daily newspaper called *The Dispatch*, which over the next three years would report every move made by the regiment and, in turn, Bob Wolverton's Third Battalion. It was rumored at the time that the senior members of the War Department's civil service had the unprecedented idea of creating a "super unit" recruited directly from the civilian population to help boost morale stateside.

Upon its creation the 506th was divided into three battalions – the First, Second and Third – and each coded with the radio call sign of "Kidnap" followed by the color white, red or blue. Each battalion had four companies, and the Third's were designated HQ (Headquarters), G, H, and I. The place chosen by the government for the selection and training of this new independent regiment was Toccoa, Georgia. Camp Toccoa was 5 miles outside of town and nestled beneath the imposing shadow of the mighty Currahee Mountain. This feature marked the western edge of the Blue Ridge Range and over the next 13 weeks came to symbolize the fledgling unit. Several times per week the men would run the 6-mile round trip up and down, and "Currahee," which is Cherokee for "Stands Alone," eventually became the battle cry for the regiment.

Known as "A Stage" and vastly over-subscribed, more than 6,000 eager volunteers drawn from the length and breadth of the country were subjected to a particularly hideous 13-week basic training regime personally devised by Sink. Sink had specifically created the program to eliminate all but the very strongest. Even before stepping onto the parade ground, every man had already undergone an intense medical examination along with a qualifying IQ test that had a pass mark higher than that of the average Army officer candidate! Many had falsified birth certificates or simply lied about their age, and the youngest that we now know of was a mere 15.

All of the senior NCOs came from the regular Army and formed the initial nucleus known as the cadre. That first week the men were put through a program of calisthenics, drill and PT over on the nearby athletics field situated behind the parade ground in a shallow valley. The vast, sandy, oblong-shaped training area was dotted with a variety of apparatus including pull-up bars, a 40ft-high scramble net tower and mock-up aircraft fuselages. In addition, the trainees embarked on a series of 20-mile route marches coupled with field-craft lessons and combat training. Hundreds of people washed out during the first few weeks of that late, stifling, Georgian summer. By the final week nearly 5,000 recruits had melted away due to injury and physical exhaustion.

Closer to the parade ground was a makeshift parachute school complete with outdoor exit trainer, flight swings and a series of 10ft wooden ramps from which to practice parachute landing falls. Built into the steep hill adjacent to the creek was a bone-shattering obstacle course with both the start and finish points straddling the brackish water. Fenced on both sides like a racetrack, Colonel Sink's little folly ran through pinewoods up and down a steep hillside and featured among its many sadistic creations a 12ft-high log wall and 20ft-high jump platform. It is said that Sink made a bet with one of his old classmates from West Point regarding the severity of the course. His former classmate duly arrived with a platoon of Marines from Paris Island, intent on showing the so-called "civilians" just how quickly the professionals could smash the assault course. But despite the obvious bravado, the Marines failed to complete, citing certain aspects as being too risky for them to even attempt.

The accommodation for the new recruits was basic to say the least and built around a large grid system. It comprised 12 neat rows of single-story wooden huts, each row serviced by its own dedicated mess, which carried the slogan "TAKE WHAT YOU WANT – EAT WHAT YOU TAKE." Seemingly everything was to be done at the double, even going to chow.

Within a few weeks most of the battalion were completing Currahee in less than 50 minutes. The entire regiment was blossoming into Sink's vision, with every soldier now willing to take on any challenge firm in the belief that he could and would overcome. Weeks of 12-hour days were spent on dry firing and drills to familiarize everybody with their individual weapon, the mighty .30-caliber M1 Garand Semi-Automatic Rifle. Inter-company rivalry was high and each platoon would vie to produce the largest number of sharpshooters and marksmen.

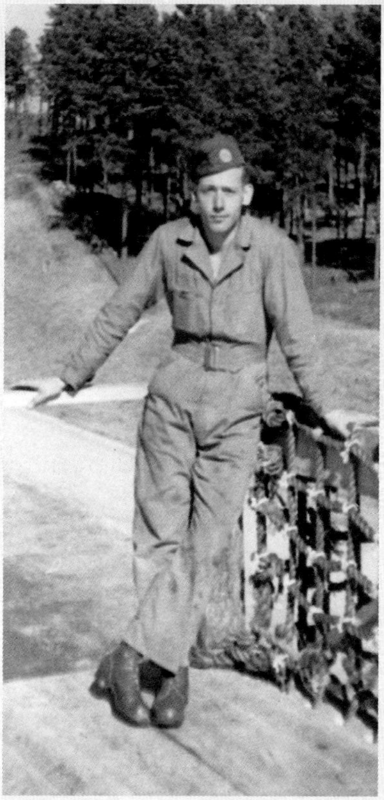

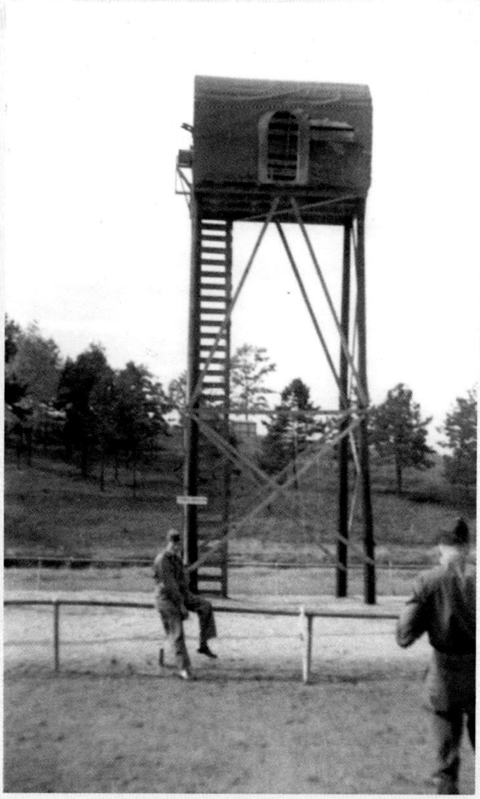

FAR LEFT Harvey Jewett from G Company standing on top of the scramble net tower overlooking the athletics field. (Harvey Jewett via Robin Vertenten)

LEFT Outdoor exit trainer. (Harvey Jewett via Robin Vertenten)

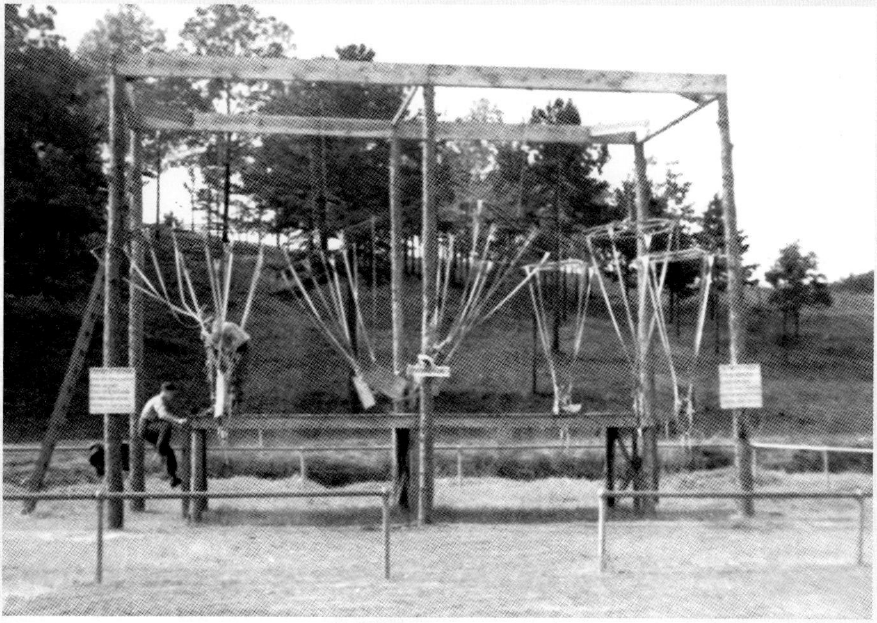

Flight swings. (Harvey Jewett via Robin Vertenten)

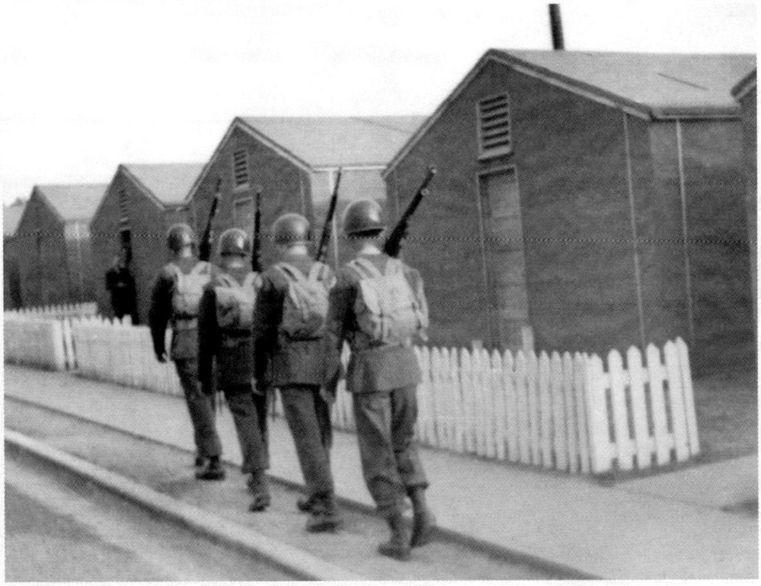

Members of 2 Platoon, G Company march along their "company street" en route for guard duty at Company HQ. (Jim "Pee Wee" Martin)

BELOW LEFT Members of the Machine Gun Platoon receiving instruction at Toccoa, 1942. (Judy Gamble)

BELOW RIGHT Eighteen-year-old Pvt Jimmy Martin from Ohio (wearing helmet) and members of 2 Platoon, G Company getting a "butch-cut." (Jim "Pee Wee" Martin)

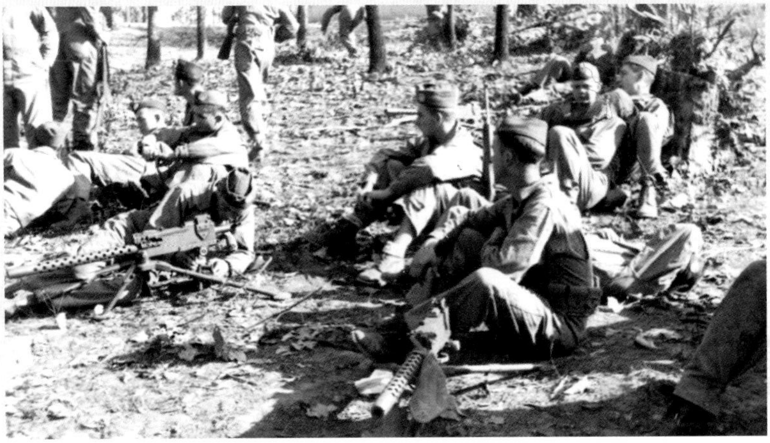

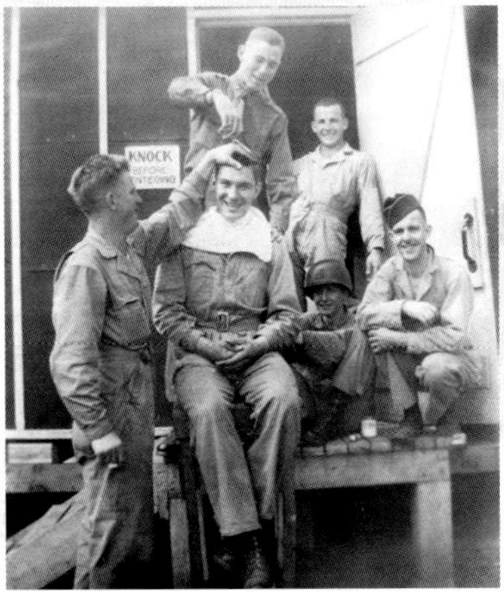
KNOCK

After First Battalion set a stratospheric standard during their skill at arms contest at the nearby Camp Croft ranges, Third Battalion were not about to be beaten. Bob Wolverton promised three-day passes for every man who scored "expert" and then, just to prove a point, decided that his soldiers would march 30 miles with full combat load across the state line into South Carolina to the Reserve Officer Training Corps (ROTC) ranges at Clemson University. The men spent the following week at Clemson, where some of the previously parachute-qualified officers and NCOs made a display jump in front of the young officer cadets. The return march on Sunday October 24 took 18 hours to complete and covered a total distance of 49 miles. Needless to say, Wolverton had started a precedent that would ripple through the regiment over the coming weeks.

Troops from G Company taking part in a battalion skill at arms competition at the Clemson University ranges. (Left to right): Lt Harold Van Antwerp, Sgt Wilbur Croteau, Pfc Don Austin and, in the background, Capt John Graham. Graham was G Company's first commander and a talented musician. He wrote "Song for the Paratroops" whose chorus was sung continuously by the company during the "Long March." Ironically it was during this record-breaking slog that Graham washed out and "Van" took over command. Van Antwerp and Croteau were both killed in Normandy and Austin lost an eye at the Battle of Bloody Gully on June 13, 1944.

Privates George "Doc" Dwyer (shorts) and Don Howenstein from the Machine Gun Platoon practicing self-defense moves on the athletics field. After becoming separated from his stick in Normandy, Dwyer was captured. Dwyer was among 700 other prisoners being transported by train when he saw an opportunity to escape. Together with Sgt Joe Gorenc, they jumped from their train near the town of Loches and swam the River Loire to make good their escape. "We hooked up and fought with the FFI [Free French Forces of the Interior] for a couple of weeks before making it back to American lines. We were taken for interrogation to Paris, which had only just been liberated. Once the US intelligence service had finished with us, we were flown to the UK where I was posted to the jump school at Chilton Foliat."

After missing out on the battalion's operations in Holland, Doc was returned to the machine guns as platoon sergeant and stayed with them from Bastogne to the end of the war. (Bob Webb Jr)

Throughout October and November, the officers and cadre were put through their paces at the Toccoa "jump school." The apparatus had been specifically designed and built as a one-off to prepare and condition the regiment for Fort Benning. By the end of November, the last few officers had completed their parachute-packing and ground training courses and were driven out to a nearby airport. The first jump onto Dicks Hill Drop Zone (DZ) went well but the other four had to postponed due to bad weather. Afterwards a "Prop Blast" party was held in the officers' mess where each newly qualified officer was required to consume a concoction of alcohol from the specially commissioned "Sink Grail." The grail was in fact a silver-plated propeller hub from a C-47 fitted with D-ring handles – the same type as those on the reserve parachutes.

Meanwhile the soldiers were going through an enhanced specialist program that included parachute ground training, courses in signals and demolition, basic hand-to hand combat and endless lectures, as well as the usual fitness regime of mountain and obstacle courses. As the first phase was drawing to a close and the weather started to get colder, the men anxiously began looking forward to jump school.

By early December, the regiment received its movement orders for Fort Benning, and in doing so became the first unit ever to go through as one complete organization. After First Battalion had departed by train, Major Robert Strayer, the commander of Second Battalion, was given permission from Sink to march his men from Toccoa to the railway station in downtown Atlanta, accompanied by half of the regimental Medical Detachment. They duly set off on Tuesday, December 1, and arrived three days later, having clocked up a marching time of 33 hours and 30 minutes and covered an astonishing 118 miles. Not to be outdone by Strayer, competitive as ever, Wolverton got permission to de-train at Atlanta and continue the rest of the journey on foot (estimated to be around 136 miles) to Fort Benning! The idea was to smash the Japanese Army's distance-marching record and in doing so generate extra publicity for the 506th PIR, who were still an independent unit looking for a home. The march turned into an endurance test nobody could have ever imagined and in turn became Third Battalion's crowning glory.

Regimental Headquarters Company joined Third Battalion for the event, along with the rest of the Medical Detachment. For the majority of the march the weather was misty and wet. The battalion group wore coveralls and helmets and carried weapons together with full packs as well as three days' rations. They ploughed through driving rain and kept up their morale by singing cadence songs and popular tunes of the day. Inevitably, dozens fell out along the way suffering from blisters but were quickly patched up by the medics. The battalion spent four days on the road, with Bob Wolverton leading and setting the pace. Due to badly swollen feet, the major was forced to remove his boots and continue on wearing three pairs of socks. It was only then that everyone really began to realize what a truly inspirational

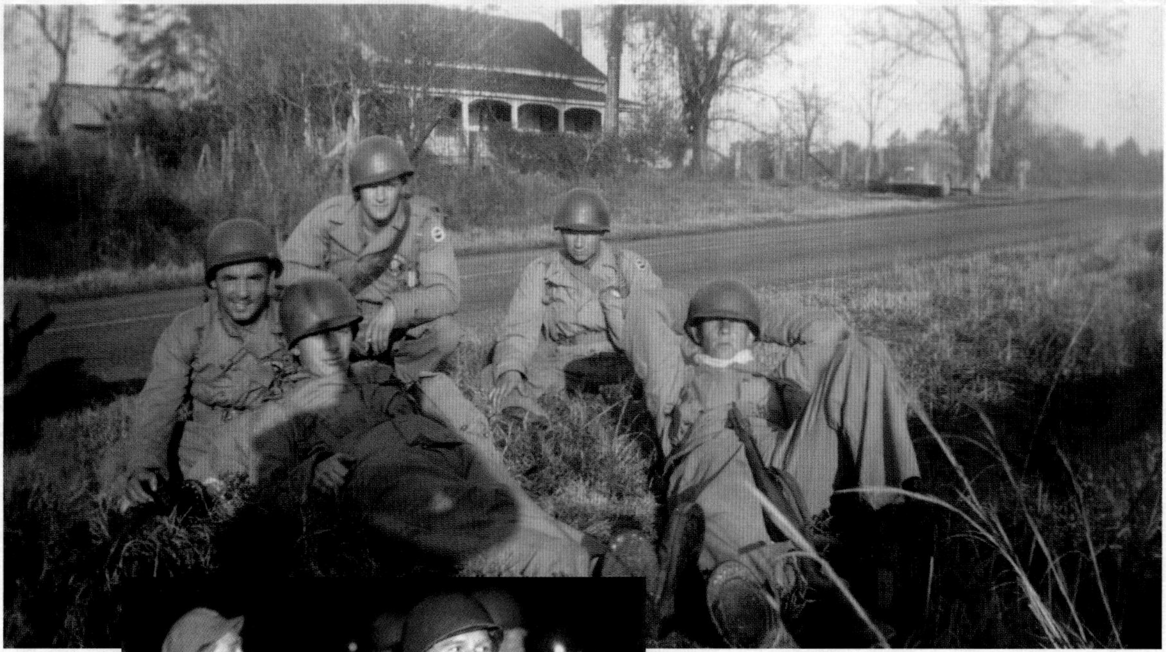

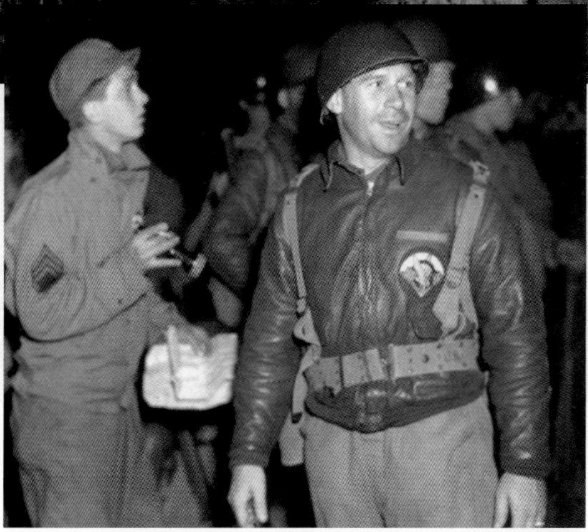

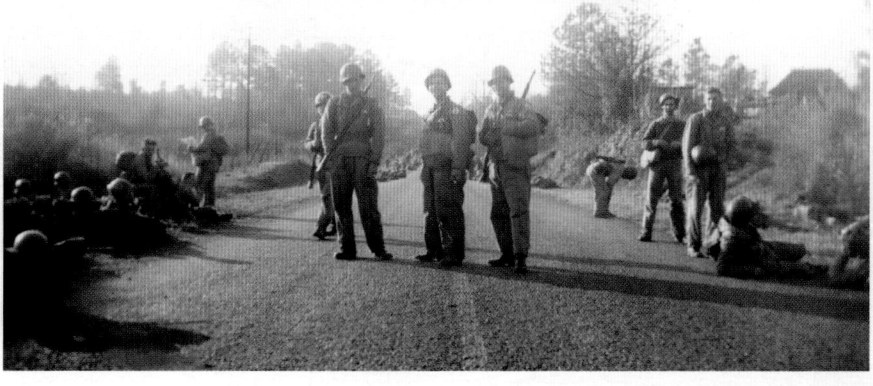

ABOVE (Left to right): Pvts Don Artimez, George Montilio, an unidentified soldier, Tom Beasley and Sonny Sundquist from H Company taking a short break during the "Long March." Artimez was seriously wounded on June 6, 1944 and tragically Montilio was accidentally shot dead by a nervous replacement on April 19, 1945. (Johnny Gibson)

Bob Wolverton (right) looking somewhat relieved after reaching Fort Benning. The man on the left is I Company Supply Sergeant Jimmy Police. (Wolverton Family)

Johnny Gibson (center) soaking up the morning sun before hitting the tarmac once again en route to Fort Benning. (Johnny Gibson)

TOP Southern Pines, 1943.
(Left to right): 1st Lt Joe Doughty (3 Platoon, G Company), Maj Bob Wolverton, Maj Carl Buechner (then Executive Officer), 1st Lt Howard Littell (then G Company, KIA June 7, 1944), 1st Lt Harold Van Antwerp (G Company Commander). Littell rejoined G Company in March 1944 before being transferred on May 17 to the 81mm Mortar Platoon which he took over for Normandy. When dawn broke on June 7, Littell was killed along with two other men while hiding in a hedge close to St-Côme-du-Mont. (K. Barickman via Mark Bando Collection)

MIDDLE Pvt Leo Knight from 2 Platoon, H Company pictured before a training jump in the Parachute Packing & Supply Area on Camp Mackall military airfield. A Hopi Indian from Eastern California, Leo was the ammunition carrier for 1st Squad's machine gun team crewed by Ken Johnson and Sam Porter. Knight and the boys were in Lt Ken Christianson's stick for Normandy and their jump went in fast and low but was at least accurate. The gun broke loose on the drop, fracturing Johnson's ankle, and Knight never made it to the rendezvous. A few days later his body was recovered from a field close to the battalion's main objective – the road and foot bridges over the Canal de Carentan at Brévands. (Johnny Gibson)

BOTTOM LEFT Maj Wolverton on the DZ at Camp Mackall, 1943. (Mark Bando Collection)

BOTTOM RIGHT Pvts Frank Lujan and Jim Millican from 3 Platoon, I Company, posing outside of their hut at Camp Mackall. Both Jim and Frank were from California and became great friends. At the time that this photo was taken Jim was only 16 years old. Frank was captured while on observation post (OP) duty in Holland and Jim killed on D-Day. This is how the young paratrooper tragically met his death: 1st Lt Jim Nye (I Company, 2 Platoon leader) and Cpl Elmer Gilbertson were closing in on their objective when they saw Millican waving. He was positioned in front of the first of three berms that separated them from the objective. Millican told Nye's group about the threat from a nearby 88mm gun and directed them to the bridge. It was being targeted by enemy mortar and artillery fire, most of which appeared to be coming from a factory up on the adjacent hill. To reach the bridge the new arrivals had to scramble over the first berm, then crawl along a ditch on the other side to relative safety. As they crept over the dyke, the German gun crew spotted them and opened fire. The shell hit a large tree and exploded, killing young Millican instantly.

TOP LEFT Pvt Bobbie Rommel from Modesto, CA, was 19 years old when he joined Third Battalion at Camp Mackall as a machine gunner. Incredibly, he was distantly related to Field Marshal Erwin Rommel, who commanded the German forces in Normandy at the time of the invasion.

TOP RIGHT G Company Executive Officer, 1st Lt Jim Morton, overseeing a platoon kit check at Camp Mackall, June/July 1943. Nicknamed "Jungle Jim," Morton broke his right ankle on the D-Day jump but refused to be evacuated. After being promoted to captain, Jim was given command of HQ Company, whom he led with distinction through Holland and into Bastogne. Morton's war ended on January 9, 1945 at Bastogne when he was severely wounded by shrapnel on "Hell Night." (Jim "Pee Wee" Martin)

MIDDLE Members of 2 Platoon, I Company at Camp Mackall, 1943.
(Left to right, rear): Pvt Bill Weber, Cpl Stan Zebroski (KIA June 6, 1944), Pvt John "Chuck" Abeyta (transferred out), Pvt Frank Cress (KIA September 24, 1944), Pvt Murton McCarty, Pvt Lloyd Rosdahl, Pvt Wilbur Fishel (Seriously Wounded in Action, January 13, 1945).
(Left to right, front): Pvt Ray Silvey (transferred out), Pvt John Edwards, Pvt Jim Brown (KIA January 13, 1945), Pvt Bill Galbraith (SWA September 18, 1944) and Pvt Jack Brown (POW June 8, 1944). Three dead, two wounded, one captured and two lost through training injuries – the figures speak for themselves. (Bill Galbraith)

BOTTOM LEFT Pvt Jim Brown breaking out the ammo for the .30cal at Camp Mackall, 1943. (Bill Galbraith)

BOTTOM RIGHT Mario "Hank" DiCarlo with his mom Anna while home on leave from Fort Benning in January 1943. Hank's parents were Italian immigrants and came to the States with nothing after World War I and by this point were the proud owners of the prestigious Trieste Hotel in Wildwood, New Jersey. DiCarlo would have been just 16 years old when this photo was taken. (Hank DiCarlo) leader Wolverton was. He could have easily got into one of the support wagons like Captain John Graham from G Company, who ironically wrote and published a "never give up" style marching song for the paratroopers!

Finally, on the fourth night, after almost 45 hours on the road, the battalion was on the final approach to Benning. With the red lights of the three massive jump towers clearly visible, Wolverton gave the order to double time. Colonel Sink and the remainder of the regiment, along with the parachute school's commanding officer, were open mouthed at the main gate as the soldiers ran by, annihilating the Japanese record by an impressive margin. Their feat would go down in history as the "Long March."

On December 12, 1942, following two days of recuperation, Third Battalion joined Second Battalion along with Regimental Headquarters (RHQ) Company, the Medical Detachment and Service Company and was assigned to Wings Course Number 49. The lean, mean parachute jump instructors had been completely unprepared for the level of fitness displayed previously by First Battalion during their first week on Benning's specialist pre-para program, known to all as "the Fort Benning Shuffle." Subsequently Course 49 skipped the usual regular Army "beat up" and went straight into the next phase, which consisted of ground training and landing drills. By Christmas Eve, after passing all the required training blocks, the men had reached C Stage and looked forward with a mixture of excitement and trepidation to the enormous jump towers. Originally built for the New York World Fair in 1939, each crane was 250ft high and fitted with four arms, each designated for a different aspect of parachuting, including controlled descents and free fall. While the men were going through C Stage most of the previously parachute-qualified officers and senior NCOs were learning to become jumpmasters. The two-week course covered aircraft inspection prior to emplaning, plus instruction drills, under-slung loads, equipment checks and the specific commands necessary to jump a "stick" of up to 20 men.

After successful completion of C Stage and before the students moved on to parachuting, they spent some time in the sweltering packing sheds learning how to pack the 'chutes that they were to be using before they finally made their first two jumps on New Year's Day. On January 2, 1943 the soldiers completed their three remaining descents to qualify. The men could now officially call themselves paratroopers. Uniforms pressed and jump boots polished, it was a proud day when they were awarded their metal military parachutist wings and given a two-week furlough.

The regiment returned to Fort Benning and spent the next two weeks preparing for the "house to house" fighting phase that was to take place across the Chattahoochee River in Alabama. After completion, the outfit headed by train to the town of Hoffman in North Carolina, 15 miles down the road from Fort Bragg. Over the next few months Camp Mackall, with its purpose-built barracks and wonderful dining halls, would become the battalion's new home, providing a nice contrast to the ramshackle accommodation they had become used to up to this point. The training intensified with plenty of two- and three-day field exercises. When off duty the men would often head to nearby towns such as Pinehurst or Rockingham. Conversely, many of the officers like Bob Wolverton hung out at the Country Club in Southern Pines.

In early May, the regiment's senior commanders visited Fort Bragg for a meeting with Airborne Command to learn more about the 506th's forthcoming role in the Tennessee maneuvers against the US Second Army. Subsequently training ramped up, with tactical night jumps, each more complex and convoluted than the last. The final stage, in South Carolina on June 3, was a command post exercise, which took place in pouring rain and began with a full regimental parachute insertion followed by an exhausting ground attack that lasted almost 24 hours. By June 6, the regiment had set up camp near Sturgis, Kentucky in readiness for the six-week-long exercise in Tennessee. A day or so later the men jumped into the mountains as reserve for the 101st Airborne Division. The drop was extremely low, under 350ft, and many were injured on the high rocky slopes.

On June 10, 1943, the 506th was finally recognized by the commander of the 101st Airborne Division, Major General Bill Lee, and unofficially attached to the division. Now the 506th had a potential home and on July 13 the regiment jumped into Tennessee's Lebanon training area. The purpose of the exercise was to learn how to establish roadblocks, demolish bridges and interrupt lines of communications. But at the very start, Third Battalion was misdropped and Wolverton and the rest of Company HQ landed in a "German"-designated bivouac area. Bizarrely, this random event would play out for real one year later. This was the last jump made on American soil. From here the regiment returned to Fort Bragg in preparation for overseas deployment. The time at Bragg was full of meetings and conferences trying to ensure that the regiment was prepared for wartime service in Europe. Between September 5 and 6, 1943, the regiment was ferried out to His Majesty's Troop Ship *Samaria* moored in New York Harbor. As the *Samaria* passed the burned-out hulk of cruise liner *SS Normandie*, the men took a long look at the Statue of Liberty and wondered whether they would ever see her again.

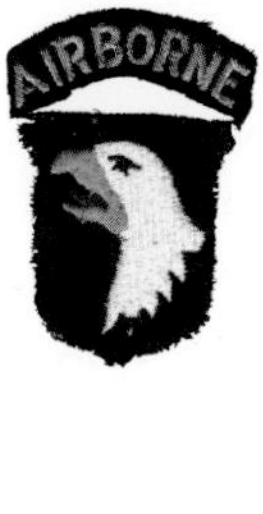
AIRBORNE

Cpl Don Francis, G Company lines, Camp Ramsbury, winter 1943/44. Don from 2 Platoon was mortally wounded on June 7, 1944 in the meadow directly behind the footbridge that was his platoon's D-Day objective. As dawn broke, S/Sgt Charlie Skeen and his group who included Francis were crossing a large field on the final leg of their journey to the bridge. Unknown to Skeen, 300 yards behind were two companies of German coastal artillerymen who were following the same course. From his position on the northern side of the bridge, Lt Santarsiero from I Company was looking in Skeen's direction through binoculars. Suddenly he noticed the rear of the German column. At almost exactly the same time as I Company opened fire, the Germans attacked Skeen's group. All hell broke loose and after a brief firefight the leading enemy company withdrew into the trees that bordered the edge of the field. A couple of Skeen's men made it into a tree-lined ditch but others, including Jimmy Martin and Don Francis, were stranded in the field with just grass for cover. "We were being raked with machine-gun and rifle fire," recalled Martin. "Don lay to my left and was hit in the right forehead by a bullet." Cpl Francis never regained consciousness and died the following day in the aid station at Fortin Farm. (Jim "Pee Wee" Martin)

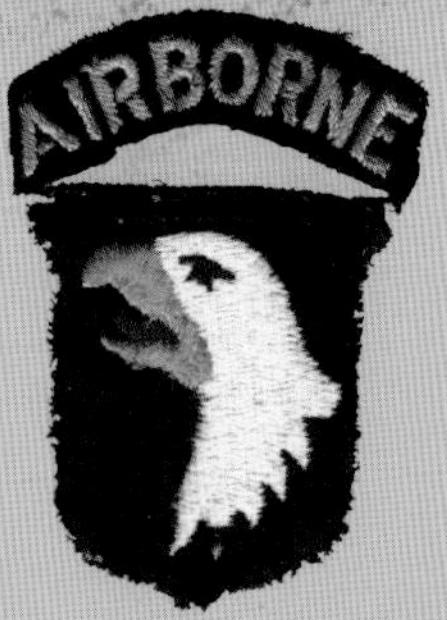
AIRBORNE

Chapter 2

# GET LOADED

## Deployment to the United Kingdom & Ramsbury

Following their arrival at Liverpool on September 16, 1943, the regiment unloaded and headed inland to the nearest operational railhead in readiness for transportation south. Early the next morning the paratroopers arrived at a Victorian-era station in the Kennet Valley, 68 miles east of London. In the half-light, a sergeant from the divisional advance party welcomed everyone to Hungerford – emphasizing the word "Hunger" – before directing each battalion to its designated trucks. From here the Third Battalion was driven a short distance to a small camp in the picturesque village of Ramsbury. The ancient rural village lies beside the river Kennet, which flows through beautiful water meadows that flourish in the valley below the airfield. Situated on the northern edge of town, beside Love's Lane, Camp Ramsbury consisted of 17 sparse wooden barracks and a Nissen hut, which became Colonel Wolverton's headquarters. Subsequently the building was subdivided into a number of separate rooms mostly belonging to the various clerical and technical departments such as Personnel, Intelligence, Planning and Operations, and Supply – known in the battalion respectively as S1, S2, S3, and S4.

Pfc Jim "Pee Wee" Martin, 2 Platoon, G Company, Camp Ramsbury, winter 1943/44. (Jim "Pee Wee" Martin)

Medic John Gibson using his barbershop skills on Cpl Jim Bradley of the 81mm Mortar Platoon. This picture was taken at Ramsbury in April 1944 outside of the camp's infirmary and aid station. Following the D-Day drop Gibson and Bradley were both captured by the Germans. Bradley remained in captivity until 1945, while Gibson was sent to look after Allied wounded in a German Evacuation Hospital at Mortain and then Stalag 221 in Rennes. He was liberated on August 4, 1944. After surviving the fighting in Holland, John's luck ran out during the Battle of the Bulge, when he was severely wounded near Foy on January 9, 1945. (Johnny Gibson)

Privates George Rosie, Phil Abbey and Leo Krebs from the 81mm Mortar Platoon standing next to their hut at Camp Ramsbury. Rosie and Krebs were captured along with John Gibson on D-Day near La Basse Addeville. During their capture Abbey was shot across the chest and died shortly afterwards. (George Rosie via Roger Day)

Adjacent to the camp's main entrance and connected by a tall hedge-lined footpath was Parliament Piece. The imposing 16th-century manor house had already been requisitioned as a billet, mess and club facility for the junior officers along with the old coach house, which became home for one platoon of troopers from C Company. Fifty-four-year-old widower Violet Wyndham was the lady of the house and was more than happy to share her spacious home with the Americans. Born in Paris, Violet had been a sophisticated debutante whose mother Ada Leverson was a popular writer and good friend of Oscar Wilde. Over the coming months the house became party central for the dashing young officers who were far from home and often in need of "Lady W's" sage-like advice.

Built during the reign of Charles I, Parliament Piece was utilized as a home away from home for most of Third Battalion's company commanders and junior officers. The numerous attic rooms accommodated the junior officers while the more spacious bedrooms on the second floor catered for company commanders and their XOs. Even today wartime graffiti can be found carved into the window frames, and bullet holes are still evident in the garden walls.

Colonel Wolverton, Major George Grant (Battalion XO) and Captain Charles Shettle (Battalion Operations Officer) were allocated rooms a couple of miles east of the village at Crowood House, which at the time was home to Mrs Robina Clifton Brown and her three teenage children. A month or two later the stables behind the house became home to 3 Platoon from I Company. Most of the camps allocated to the 101st Airborne Division were in the Kennet Valley between Reading in the east and Ramsbury in the west, a distance of about 30 miles. 101st Divisional HQ was midway between the two at Greenham Lodge near Newbury. The 506th Regiment established its command post (CP) at Littlecote House together with RHQ Company and HQ Company First Battalion. The entire Second Battalion went to the village of Aldbourne, about 3 miles north of Ramsbury, and was joined by companies A and B, while C Company found itself in the more than comfortable surroundings of Ramsbury Manor then owned by the wealthy Burdett family. Service Company, which was in charge of the regiment's motor pool, went to Manor Farm, Froxfield.

1st Lt Ken Christianson, 2 Platoon, H Company, seen here at Parliament Piece before Normandy. From California, Ken was tall and strong, but quiet with an intelligent, enquiring mind. Ken was the first officer to reach the battalion's primary objective on D-Day, an important vehicle crossing over the Canal de Carentan, and was instrumental in keeping enemy paratroopers away from the bridge on D-Day+2. However, his war ended one week later during the Battle of Bloody Gully when his shoulder was shattered by enemy machine-gun fire.

# STANLEY "DOC" MORGAN

Dr Stanley Morgan, the Battalion Surgeon, is seen here after Normandy in the rear garden of Kennet House looking toward the river. Morgan was from New Orleans and a graduate of Louisiana State University School of Medicine. He sprained an ankle on the jump and was captured but managed to establish an aid station in St-Côme-du-Mont to treat other injured POWs. After being liberated on June 9, Morgan returned to his duties.

He was captured for a second time in Holland at Opheusden. Due to a lack of stretchers, the medics had been unable to remove everyone from the H Company command post that had been established on the western outskirts of Opheusden adjacent to a small railway crossing. As a result, Morgan and Cpl Walter Pelcher, who had come forward to help, decided to stay at the signalman's house and look after the remaining wounded until the Medical Detachment could return. When it became apparent that the medics would not be coming back, Morgan sent Pelcher and H Company medic "Blackie" Baldinger back to Opheusden with the rest of 3 Platoon, opting to stay behind and look after Harry Clawson and Morris Thomas, whose injuries initially did not seem life threatening, as well as several others himself. Soon a rearguard action implemented by Sgt Ralph Bennett and Lt Alex Andros began to break down. Dr Morgan refused to leave when Bennett told him it was time to go. Instead he said that the Germans would not do him or the wounded any harm, so Bennett stood to attention, saluted, and told the doc that he would get back if he could. In a matter of minutes, the aid station was overrun, and despite his protests, Dr Morgan was marched away with the walking wounded to the nearby town of Ommeren, leaving Clawson and Thomas

behind. Morgan glanced back and saw a column of dense smoke rising from the signalman's house. At some point after the signalman's house was hit, the Germans moved Clawson and Thomas to a forward aid station on the southern side of the railway embankment. It is unclear if they were dead at that point but subsequently the corpses of the two Americans were buried across the tracks, presumably to keep them separate from the German dead. Over the weeks following the battle the shallow graves were covered by floodwater and any external sign of their existence washed away.

Between 1945 and 1966, the bodies of 27 American servicemen missing in action at Opheusden were eventually discovered and given proper burials; however, the remains of S/Sgt Harry Clawson and Pfc Morris Thomas were not discovered until 1971. When exhumed, they were each found to have a complete set of dog tags, but only Thomas' remains revealed any sign of fractures associated with being crushed.

Third Battalion's surgeon, Dr Stanley Morgan.
(Peter Mills)

Next morning the entire battalion formed up on the grass "parade ground." Colonel Wolverton explained that there were strict protocols governing how they should behave toward the local population. Everyone was issued a booklet entitled *A Short Guide to Great Britain* that outlined British customs and rationing and the complicated currency of pounds, shillings and pence. Each barrack hut could accommodate one platoon and had a row of double-tier bunks along either side of the room. Mattresses were stuffed with straw. The four lightbulbs in each block did not generate enough light to even read by and the two stoves provided just about enough heat to stop the water from freezing in the winter. As there was no furniture available the men had to keep their clothes and other possessions in barrack bags stored between the beds. Radios were installed to liven things up a little, but some who had brought their own short wave sets from the States soon tuned in to the likes of "Axis Sally" and her German propaganda channel which also played all the big band music of the time. After one week confined to camp the men were allowed off base to explore the delights of their new English home. At that time there were eight pubs in the village and the battalion made full use of them. When the bartenders called "time" the men learned to finish their drinks quickly.

Two squads from I Company's 2 Platoon were quartered in a stable block belonging to one of the more upmarket boozers called The Bell Hotel, while 1st and 2nd Squad were in the main stable and the NCOs, all four of them, were in a smaller one opposite. At the opposite end of the village The Bleeding Horse became home to the battalion's four supply sergeants.

The Square, Ramsbury

There were eight pubs in Ramsbury during the war. This 1930s view of the square from the High Street shows two of these watering holes – The Windsor Castle (left) and The Bell Hotel. Many marriage proposals were accepted while cuddling beneath the old elm tree including Moose Mehosky (H Company) and Yvonne, Vince Michaels (G Company) and Barbara, Darvin Lee (Machine Gun Platoon) and Molly, Tom Kennedy and Sheila, and Ralph Bennett (H Company) and June – who all eventually became GI Brides. At one point the paratroopers threatened to blow up "the pride of the village" if something was not done about the over inflated beer prices. Sadly, in 1983, after almost 400 years, the heavily diseased elm was condemned and removed. (Peter Mills)

Most of the senior NCOs were sent to homes around the village that had previously been billets for the British 34th Army Tank Brigade. Most, like Hills Grocery Store in the High Street, were still furnished with basic Government Issue beds and blankets. To encourage closer links with British families, local children were often invited to spend a day at the camp, playing soldiers with the Americans. The battalion also took out a short lease on a property in Oxford Street, which became the camp laundry and tailor's shop. One of the troopers who worked here, Manny Barrios, spent six months happily co-habiting with a married woman across the road whose husband was a prisoner-of-war in North Africa. This was by no means unusual.

The enlisted men's mess hall was situated just down the road from the camp in an old schoolhouse along Back Lane. Not far from the mess was another place owned by the church dubbed "The British Restaurant." These restaurants were run by local authorities and subsidized by the government. This self-service chain provided, for soldier and civilian alike, good, cheap snacks without the need for ration coupons.

Even though the Americans were reasonably well fed, poaching became very popular during the first few months. Double British Summer Time meant longer evenings. Often the smell of barbeques would waft across the entire camp, and despite numerous crackdowns and fines the practice continued right up until the battalion left for Normandy.

Midway along Ramsbury's High Street, just opposite The Burdett Arms, the American Red Cross set up a recreation club and Army Exchange (PX). The club was for enlisted men only and was housed within a large Nissen hut. The club was unofficially called the "Wolverton Donut Dugout" and run by Helen Briggs and Louise Shepard. Together Helen and Louise would organize quiz nights, bingo sessions, card games and sometimes outings by bus to Swindon, Reading or places of local interest. Dances and concerts were also held in the local village hall.

For soldiers on leave, Marlborough and Swindon were popular destinations, but London was the Mecca, and 48-hour passes to the capital were always the hardest to get a hold of – not that there was much time for that. No sooner had the Americans settled into their new home that there began a long period of intensified training. Colonel Sink called meetings with his battalion and company commanders, and in mid-September 1943, General Bill Lee, the 101st divisional commander, visited the unit and gave a sobering talk entitled, "The responsibility ahead of us."

The first full-field exercise undertaken by the regiment was scheduled to take place over two days in early October. The aim was to drive "enemy" forces from Ramsbury and then defend and hold the village against any possible counterattack. The countryside around the village consisted mainly of small fields and hedgerows which would prove to be not very different to northern France. The 506th began training day and night in every location imaginable prior to the exercise and continued after it was successfully concluded. Local people were often surprised to find soldiers running through their gardens and hiding in sheds and outbuildings. An area just north of Ramsbury near to Pentico Farm was allocated and reserved extensively for live firing exercises including bazooka, grenade and explosive demolition practice.

Tragically, on January 13, 1944, while G Company was making a demonstration jump for the Duke of Gloucester, Sergeant Homer Sarver was killed when his parachute failed to open. His death was the first suffered by the battalion as a direct result of jumping but was a painful reminder of the inherent dangers for all airborne troops. In March, due to ill health, General Bill Lee was replaced by General Maxwell Taylor as commander of the division. Nearly two weeks later Taylor, together with General Dwight D. Eisenhower and Prime Minister Winston Churchill, watched a massive demonstration jump by the Second and Third Battalions of the 506th. The First Battalion remained on the ground and was inspected by the visitors. In the days that followed General Taylor did his utmost to get to know his regimental and battalion commanders and soon started preparations for the division's final D-Day training phase.

Seen here in Paris, 1944, 29-year-old ex dental nurse Miss Helen Olivia Briggs, American Red Cross Representative to the Third Battalion who affectionately called her "Briggsy" and who adored her for the care she gave to them all. (Photo via the Gettysburg Museum of History)

So that the Allies could test their plans for assaulting Hitler's "Fortress Europe," a number of training areas were established along England's southern coast. It was essential that these stretches of coastline had similar features to the actual Normandy landing beaches. Slapton Sands in South Devon was chosen to represent "Utah" Beach. "Utah" was the codename given to the area at the base of the Cotentin Peninsula where "U" Force was to land on D-Day – one of two Normandy beaches designated as the responsibility of US forces, the other being, of course, Omaha. In total there were seven major exercises conducted within the Slapton Battle Training Area between December 1943 and May 1944.

All units of the 101st Airborne Division participated in Exercise Tiger in April 1944 as a full-scale dress rehearsal for the Normandy landings. Its overall commander was General Lawton Collins from VII Corps, which would ultimately be responsible for the main amphibious assault on Utah Beach. Security was taken very seriously and strictly enforced. Jumpsuits were not worn by airborne troops, as it was vitally important that the Germans were kept in the dark regarding the real purpose of the exercise.

TOP Third Battalion supply crew and technicians at Welford Airfield on March 23, 1944, when the battalion made a demonstration jump in front of Churchill and Eisenhower.
(Rear standing, left to right): S/Sgt Bob Webb (S4 supply), 1st Lt John King (S4 supply), T/5 Leslie Riley (I Company armorer, KIA Normandy), T/5 Warren Nelson (G Company armorer, KIA Normandy), Pfc Bruce Paxton (H Company). (Front kneeling, left to right): S/Sgt Fred Bahlau (H Company supply), S/Sgt Zolman Rosenfield (G Company supply), S/Sgt John Luteran (I Company supply), Pfc Eugene Darby (HQ Company), T/5 John Mihalko (HQ Company armorer). (Bob Webb Jr)

BOTTOM March 23, 1944, Ninth Air Force Commander Gen Lewis Brereton (who would later command the First Allied Airborne Army), Gen Dwight D. Eisenhower and Prime Minister Winston Churchill, relaxing on their podium overlooking the DZ while awaiting the big drop. Also present was BrigGen Tony McAuliffe who would subsequently command the 101st Airborne Division during the Battle of the Bulge. The DZ was located in a shallow valley just east of Welford Airfield situated about 8 miles from Ramsbury. (NARA)

OPPOSITE PAGE

TOP Around 1,400 men jumped on March 23; luckily injuries were light, but those who suffered broken ankles or legs on this and other exercises that followed did not make the D-Day jump. (NARA)

MIDDLE First Battalion remained on the ground and are seen here being reviewed by Generals Eisenhower and Taylor together with Churchill. (NARA)

BOTTOM A soldier lies injured on the DZ awaiting evacuation. During Exercise Eagle, which followed a couple of months later in May, the regiment suffered a total of 146 casualties on the jump. (NARA)

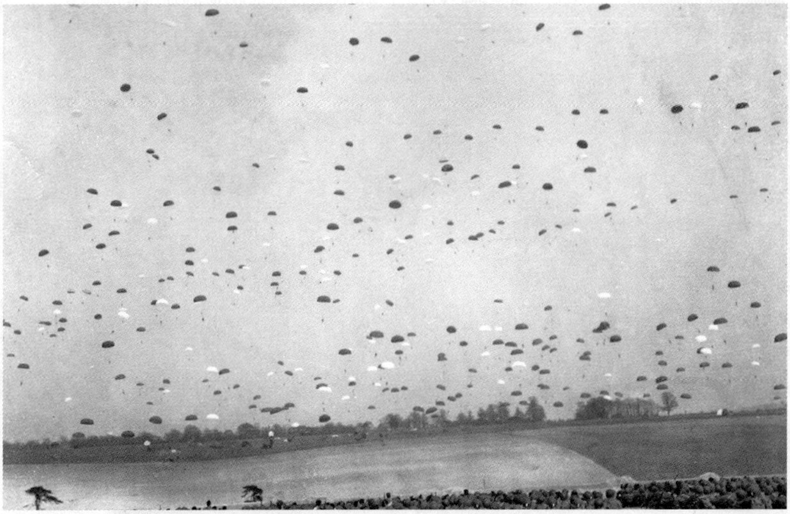

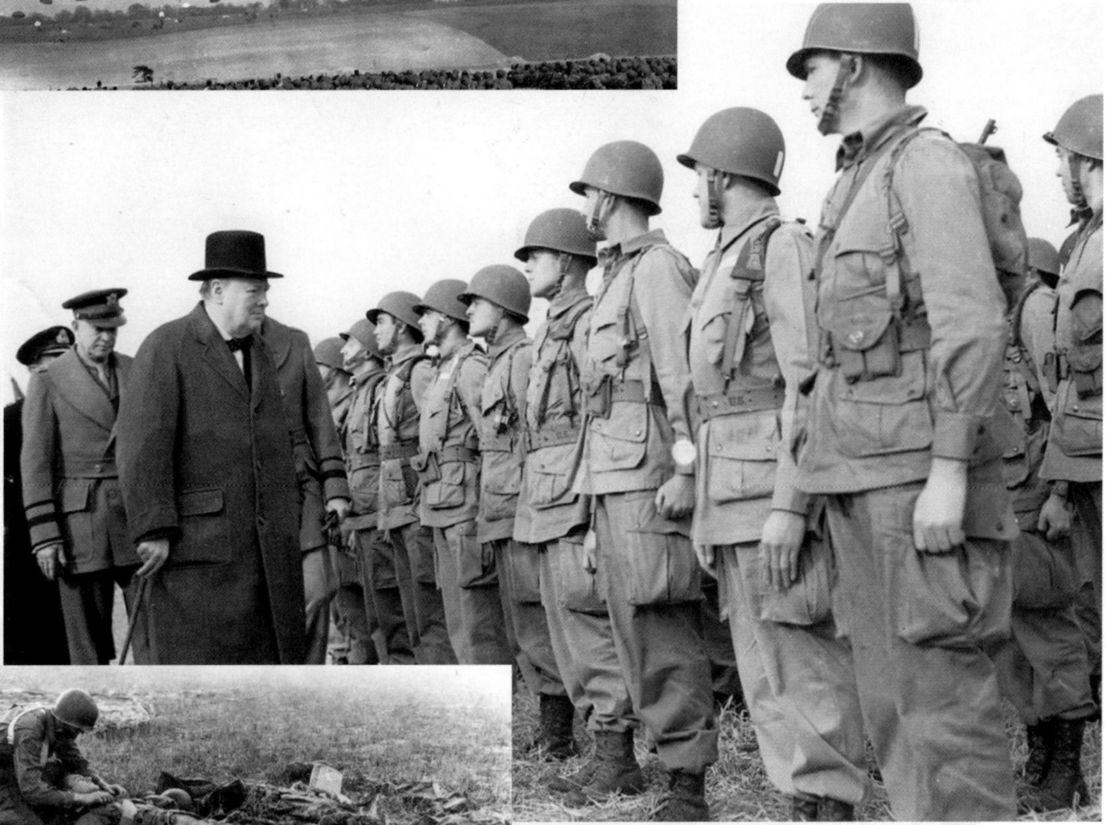

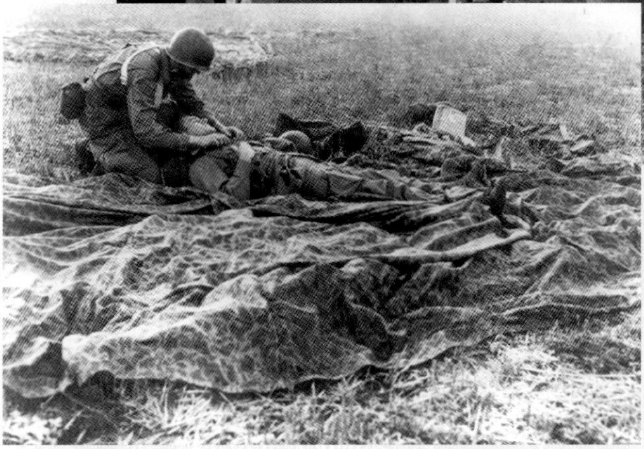

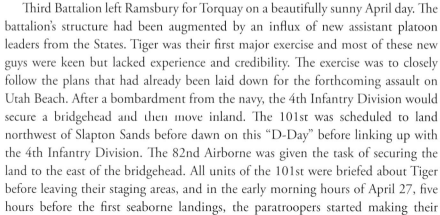

This picture sent home from England during April 1944 shows members of I Company's 3 Platoon 60mm mortar squad which is why the shoulder patch has been removed by the censor. (Left to right): Pvt Harold Stedman, Pvt Claud Tucker, and Pvt Frank Lujan. (Harold Stedman)

Third Battalion left Ramsbury for Torquay on a beautifully sunny April day. The battalion's structure had been augmented by an influx of new assistant platoon leaders from the States. Tiger was their first major exercise and most of these new guys were keen but lacked experience and credibility. The exercise was to closely follow the plans that had already been laid down for the forthcoming assault on Utah Beach. After a bombardment from the navy, the 4th Infantry Division would secure a bridgehead and then move inland. The 101st was scheduled to land northwest of Slapton Sands before dawn on this "D-Day" before linking up with the 4th Infantry Division. The 82nd Airborne was given the task of securing the land to the east of the bridgehead. All units of the 101st were briefed about Tiger before leaving their staging areas, and in the early morning hours of April 27, five hours before the first seaborne landings, the paratroopers started making their simulated jumps from trucks behind the beachhead.

On May 9, Third Battalion left Ramsbury and headed for Exeter Airfield, this time for a rehearsal of the division's movement in terms of parachute and glider. The men spent most of the next couple of days sealed into their marshaling area preparing for the appropriately named Exercise Eagle. Forty-eight hours after they had left Ramsbury, at 2100hrs the entire 101st took off in C-47s and were flown around for a couple of hours, roughly the same duration of time they would experience on the real thing. The moon was full and for the very first time the various carrier groups were guided onto their targets by lead aircraft fitted with GEE – a sophisticated radio system based on triangulation and devised by the RAF. Every group, no matter which airfield they had departed from, eventually found themselves over the town of Devizes in Wiltshire, which was their final turning point. Over 400 aircraft filled the sky, all heading east to Welford. Once the paratroopers had landed, the men quickly assembled in the darkness and moved off toward objectives such as bridges, road junctions and canals. Four hours later it was the turn of the glider riders to make an appearance, and just as day was breaking about

80 gliders loaded with jeeps, artillery and other equipment touched down at Welford Airfield.

For the next ten days the battalion took part in more intensified training culminating, on the night of May 22/23, in a jump, assembly and attack rehearsal. Afterwards the battalion began to prepare for its move back to Exeter Airfield and the tented camp that had been left in place since Tiger. Only the most senior men like Wolverton himself would have known for sure that this latest move signaled it was finally time for the invasion. But that did not stop the rest of the battalion guessing what was next – especially after a leaflet was distributed stating the severe penalties for desertion. For those stationed at Parliament Piece the night before the final movement order was given, a last-minute party was thrown and at the end of the evening a special toast raised by the girlfriends and wives present saying, "Here's to your dog tags and may they never part." At 0755hrs on the morning of May 27 the battalion boarded buses in readiness for the short 5-mile journey to Hungerford railway station. Unusually the weather had been exceptionally warm for May. Struggling under the weight of equipment and clothing, the men sweated profusely as they waited at Hungerford until 0845hrs and clambered aboard the train that would take them to Exeter. After arriving at the station one squad from 2 Platoon, I Company, led by 2nd Lieutenant John Windish, was told that they had been selected for a special mission with the Third Battalion Pathfinder Team based at North Witham, and were duly transferred to another truck in preparation for the long drive north to the Midlands.

Exeter Airfield was home to the 440th Troop Carrier Group and the 45 C-47 transport aircraft commanded by Colonel Frank Krebs. After a four-hour train journey, the main body checked into the marshaling area opposite the main gate and were shown back to the same tents they had vacated the week before. Encircled by barbed wire, the camp was under strict security protocols; no one could enter or leave without special permission and the perimeter was under constant patrol by Military Police (MP). Third Battalion's objectives for D-Day were two wooden bridges and a passenger ferry crossing the Canal de Carentan near the village of Brévands. The bridges were about 6 miles inland from Utah Beach and almost 2 miles east of St-Côme-du-Mont, providing a vitally important link between the two American D-Day beaches. The ferry was operated by a chain link pulley system that had been in use for many years. However, this method of crossing the river never really suited the Germans, and during the latter part of 1942 they had built the footbridge a few hundred yards away. One year later, a second bridge designed for vehicles was built about half a mile upstream from the ferry. Headquarters Company, supported by H Company, was to secure the road bridge, while G and I Companies were to hold the footbridge, which was a little easier to find as a large white poplar tree was growing nearby. In accordance with previous exercises, the battalion was to

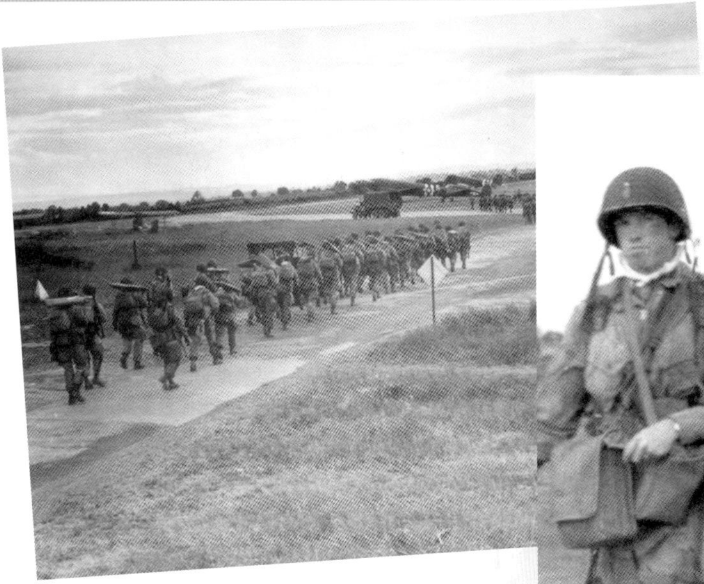

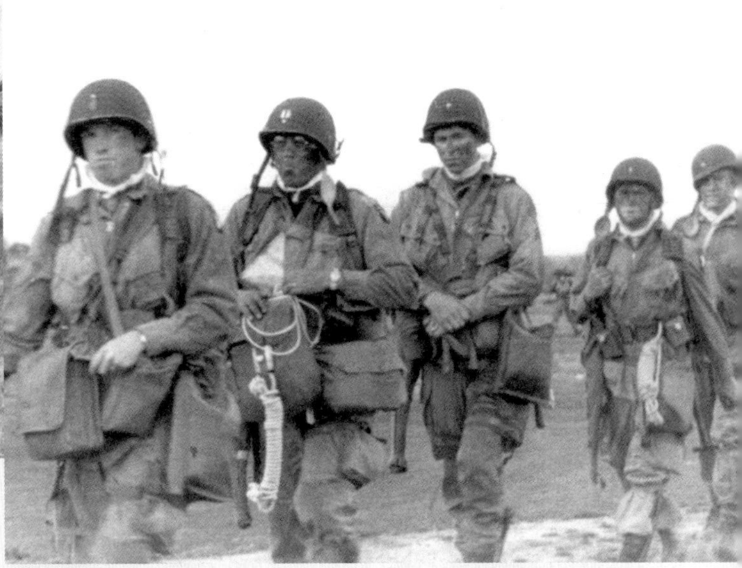

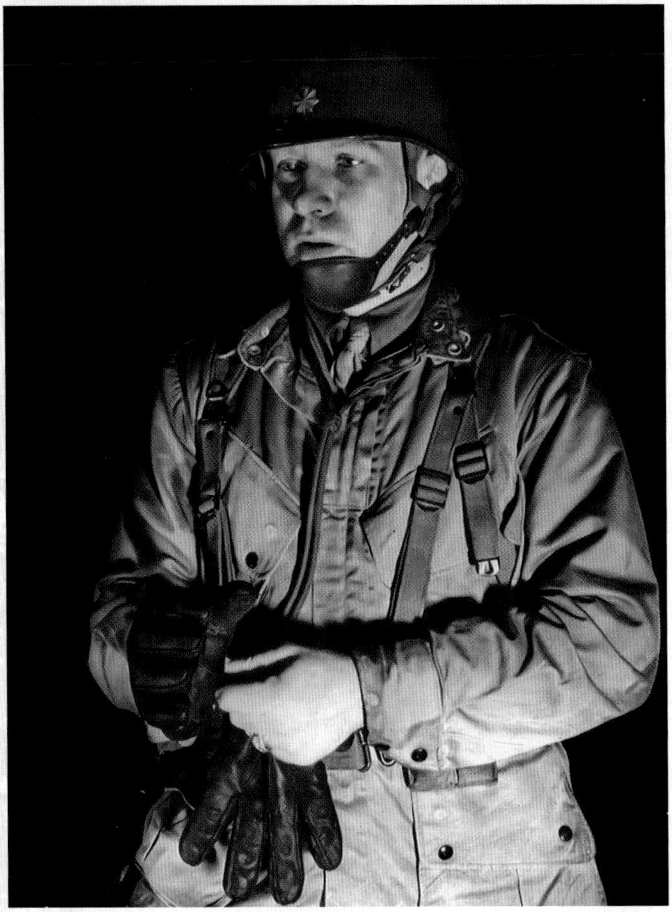

Moving onto the airfield – June 5, 1944. (NARA)

Twenty-eight-year-old Battalion XO Maj George S. Grant leading the number two stick out to their waiting aircraft. Grant was killed on June 6 after landing in the grounds of Rampan Manor near St-Côme-du-Mont. Grant came from Batesville, Arkansas, and was distantly related to Civil War Union hero and former US President Ulysses S. Grant. (NARA)

Bob Wolverton looking understandably nervous. Three or four hours after this photo was taken he was dead – killed while hanging helplessly from his parachute harness in St-Côme-du-Mont. Nearly three months later, the colonel's then unidentified body was found in an isolated grave and reburied at Blosville Cemetery with all known data placed in a bottle under his left arm. The dog tags were missing, and because of decomposition no fingerprints could be obtained. A jump jacket bearing the rank of LTC with the manifest for his stick in a rear pocket did narrow the search, but Wolverton himself was still listed as MIA. Bob was officially identified on December 12, 1944 by the laundry mark (W-1275) found in a front trouser pocket. Additional identical marks were also found in the collar of the shirt and on the waistband of his long woolen underwear. The status was officially changed to KIA on December 18, 1944. (NARA colorized by Johnny Sirlande)

The number one stick fitting equipment by the lead aircraft nicknamed "Stoy Hora." The two men in the foreground with their backs to the camera are Dr Stanley Morgan and Lt Alex Bobuck (both captured June 6). From there left to right are: Pvt Jesse Cross (captured June 6), Bob Wolverton (KIA June 6), S1 T/5 Bill Atlee (KIA June 6), Signaler Pfc Harry Howard (captured June 6), Pfc Don Ross (captured June 6), Medic Sgt Tom Newell (captured June 6) and Sgt Joe Gorenc (captured June 6). Also somewhere in the picture are S/Sgt John Taormina (captured June 6), Pvt Ray Calandrella (captured June 7), Pvt John Rinehart (KIA June 6), Sgt Bill Pauli (captured June 6), T/5 Jack Harrison (died June 25 in hospital at Rennes) and Pvt Anthony Wincenciak (KIA June 6). (NARA)

Twenty-year-old Sgt Joe Gorenc, from Sheboygan, Wisconsin, the assistant S3, climbing aboard the lead aircraft "Stoy Hora" on D-Night. The week before D-Day, Joe had won $2,000 in a card game. Unable to send his winnings home, Gorenc asked his immediate superior, Ed Shames (who was then S3 operations sergeant) to hide the cash in his private room above the grocery store at Ramsbury. Several weeks after being captured in St-Côme-du-Mont, Joe found himself on a prison train with "Doc" Dwyer. The two men managed to jump off and escape into the Loire Valley near Loches on July 20 and made it back to the battalion around the middle of August. A lot had changed since D-Day. Ed Shames had won a battlefield commission and been posted to 2/506. Joe tracked him down to Aldbourne and was relieved to find his winnings still safe and sound. After the war Gorenc used the money to set himself up in business as a refrigeration and heating engineer. Despite all he had been through, tragedy struck when he was critically injured in a boiler explosion and died two weeks later on October 30, 1957. Joe is buried at Greensdale Cemetery, Sheboygan. (NARA) hold these two crossing points until relieved by the US 4th Infantry Division arriving from Utah Beach. Two platoons from C Company, 326th Airborne Engineers, were to assist Third Battalion in holding the bridges and, if the need arose, prepare them for demolition.

The days were anything but quiet while the battalion waited at Exeter. Countless briefings took place and the men attended at least two platoon-strength lectures each day.

Most of these took place around a sand table which recreated the battalion's objective. Six farms ran along the road that led to the vehicle bridge, each lovingly recreated in miniature on the sand table. The farmhouse nearest to the junction leading to the bridge was earmarked as the battalion aid station and supply store. Unfortunately, intelligence could not tell how many of these properties were occupied by the enemy, so all had to be viewed as potentially hostile. Where known, the identity of the German units and their respective strengths were marked, although the actual bridges themselves were rather a gray area. The weather was on the turn and getting wetter; regardless, each day the men honed their battle skills, working from 0600hrs to at least 1700hrs.

As May gave way to June, the high pressure that had dominated the weather over the British Isles for the previous three weeks moved away and was replaced by a deepening depression. Any nagging doubts among the battalion about the operation planners being just another "dry run" were finally put to bed when General Taylor turned up to give a "get in there and fight" big team talk. He made a point of telling the men that on no account should they allow themselves to be taken prisoner or take prisoners. Final briefings were given and live ammunition issued. The parachutes and stores had already been offloaded from trucks and placed beside the waiting aircraft, only for the jump to be postponed by 24 hours due to the weather conditions. Earlier that day a group of war correspondents had visited the airfield and interviewed men from the Third Battalion. After a church service in the middle of the bivouac area the battalion held its final platoon-level sand table critiques. Live ammo was re-issued and faces blackened. Around 2000hrs on June 5 Colonel Wolverton ordered everyone to gather. Standing on an earthen bank the boss started by suggesting that they should think about a reunion after the war to which everyone to a man agreed. He then continued with an emotionally charged speech as he said, "Men, I am not a religious man and I don't know your feelings in this matter, but I am going to ask you to pray with me for the success of the mission before us. I would like you to get down on your knees and pray but don't look down, look up, with heads held high to the sky." The colonel then began his very special self-written prayer:

> God almighty! In a few short hours we will be in battle with the enemy. We do
> not join battle afraid. We do not ask favors or indulgence but ask that, if you

> will, use us as your instrument for the right and an aid in returning peace to the world. We do not know or seek what our fate will be. We only ask this, that if die we must, that we die as men would die, without complaining, without pleading and safe in the feeling that we have done our best for what we thought was right. Oh Lord! Protect our loved ones and be near us in the fire ahead, and with us now as we each pray to you.

The route to the airfield was lined with buildings and the men had to pass through several security checkpoints. The light fading, nearly 700 soldiers made their way down the road as airfield staff emerged and silently watched them pass by. Each squadron had its own location on the airfield and all planes for the mission were labelled with white chalk figures on the left-hand side just in front of the main cabin exit door. Every jumpmaster was given a manifest detailing each man who was in his stick. Wolverton's plane, flown by Colonel Krebs himself, was the lead aircraft and as such designated with a large number 1. Colonel Krebs taxied around the perimeter displaying his chalk number and allowing the other aircraft to fall numerically in line behind him. At 2350hrs the 45 aircraft were in line and ready for take-off. D-Day and destiny awaited.

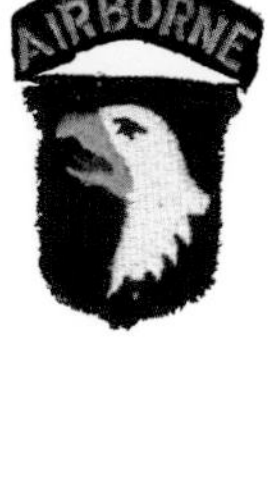
AIRBORNE

A stick from F/506 shortly before take-off – the jumpmaster can be seen distributing General Eisenhower's "Great Crusade" message to his men, in which "Ike" called for nothing short of complete and total victory for the sake of liberty-loving people everywhere. (NARA – colorized by Johnny Sirlande)

## Chapter 3
# RECLAIM THE NAME

## D-Day & Normandy

### D-Night and D-Day, June 5/6

Shortly before midnight on June 5, the 440th Troop Carrier Group began lifting off for France. Once fully assembled, the aircraft passed over Exeter and then headed out to sea. The moonlight shimmered on the English Channel some 1,500ft below. Conversation over the roar of the twin radials was not easy as the men, stern faces blackened and hands clammy from sweat, sat deep in thought. Buffeted by the wind and the other aircraft in the formation, each plane vied to keep its position in the great air armada. Wolverton's "bird" had an unexpected guest in the shape of Frank Ward Smith, a 40-year-old British war correspondent working for the BBC and a Sunday newspaper. The following weekend his poignant article entitled "I Saw Them Jump To Destiny" was published in the *News of the World* and also broadcast by the BBC. Everyone in the stick, including Wolverton, signed Ward Smith's notebook, and some like John Taormina and Jack Harrison wrote little messages under their names, such as "A plane, a jump and a God-damn chance to get even" and "The one jump I sure did sweat! We can lick em!" Immediately after landing

Taormina was captured and Harrison hit by machine-gun fire and mortally wounded. He died several weeks later in a German hospital at Rennes.

As the lead aircraft, Colonel Kreb's plane was fitted with GEE to help with navigation. In addition, every aircraft in the formation was carrying a "Rebecca" receiver/transmitter. This was part of a radar beacon and responder system. The idea was that Pathfinder Teams would precede the main airborne contingent and establish a "Eureka" beacon on the ground. The Normandy countryside below had already been dissected into a series of designated DZs by the military planners, with the Third Battalion allocated DZ "D" – an area of some 2 square miles situated a few hundred yards southeast of Angoville-au-Plain. Aircraft could then use their "Rebecca" to locate the "Eureka" beacon's signal and the main body of paratroopers would jump in the correct location.

But only squadron leaders (one in every nine aircraft) were actually allowed to switch their sets on, as it was wrongly presumed that too many in use at the same time would lead to saturation problems. This was to be a disastrous error and caused a number of sticks to be dropped in the wrong places.

As such, approximately two hours before the battalion's departure from Exeter, the first of the Pathfinder Teams had already left RAF North Witham. On board chalk no. 9 were ten Pathfinders and the 506th security detachment pulled from I Company at Hungerford station ten days earlier. They flew across the Channel with two other aircraft carrying the Pathfinder Teams from the 501st Parachute Infantry Regiment – all heading for DZ D. Two battalions from the 501st were also scheduled to drop onto DZ D with the task of capturing the locks at la Barquette. Ironically these sea locks had no real strategic importance or value to the outcome of the 101st Airborne Division's D-Day mission, and the 1,200 or so men from the 501st PIR who were tasked with taking and holding the objective could arguably have been better used elsewhere.

Upon reaching the Cherbourg Peninsula, the pilot of the chalk no. 9 aircraft had difficulty finding the DZ in the pitch black and made several passes over the area, each time attracting more and more ground fire. When the green light finally came on the plane was approaching the heavily garrisoned town of St-Côme-du-Mont from the north, following the main road. The stick was split in half when most of the Pathfinder guys came down north of the church where they decided to set up their "Eureka" beacon. Unfortunately, this was over a mile west of the area actually designated as DZ D. Meanwhile, the I Company security detachment was scattered and failed to rendezvous with the Pathfinders they were meant to protect. Ultimately, everyone on chalk no. 9 with just a couple of exceptions was killed, wounded and/or captured.

No one onboard the 440th Carrier Group had any idea how disastrously wrong things were going on the ground. But as the aircraft approached the Cotentin Peninsula in Normandy, a layer of clouds became visible to the pilots. The formation decreased altitude and flew under the clouds in order to maintain some sort of visual contact. During the straight run into the DZ heavy antiaircraft fire destroyed one plane and forced a number of others off course. The plane flown by 1st Lieutenant Ray Pullen and carrying troopers from I Company exploded in a brilliant flash of light. It veered off to the left and crashed in flames near the small village of Magneville, killing everyone on board.

Four minutes out from the DZ the planes slowed to 120mph and the red lights by the exit doors flicked on, signaling each jumpmaster to yell "Hook up" and begin his safety drills. After successfully checking each other's equipment, parachutes and fastenings, every man in the stick responded to "Sound off for equipment check" by shouting in sequence their individual positions – "Nineteen OK! Eighteen OK!" etc. Once satisfied all was in order, the jumpmaster beckoned everyone forward before returning to his own position in the stick. At 0140hrs, as the green light came on, the men moved down the fuselage and leapt into the black, tracer-tipped void. The 440th's drop was the most successful on D-Night, mainly due to Krebs' decision to fly underneath the cloud cover. Indeed, despite the fact that the only "Eureka" beacon marking DZ D was set up in the wrong place, the Third Battalion still had a high concentration of men drop on target. Out of a total of 45 sticks, eight landed on the actual DZ and 26 were less than a mile away in more heavily defended areas. However, the drop was still not as accurate as the planners had hoped, and the battalion was spread over a much wider area than had been expected.

However, two other aircraft from the group were terminally damaged on the run in before crashing into the English Channel. Although both aircrews were lost, one was able to drop its troopers from the MG Platoon, while the other, tragically carrying another group from I Company, went down in flames off Pointe du Hoc, leaving only four survivors. One of these was Private Leonard Goodgal of 1 Platoon:

Once over the French coast we hooked up and I could see water below – all was calm. Suddenly all hell broke loose. The plane was tossed around, and I thought we'd been hit in the tail – Pfc Niels Christensen then told me the right engine was on fire. Initially we went into a dive and then started to climb just as the green light came on. As we exited I was hanging onto Niels. My 'chute opened and I watched the burning plane crash into the sea. Looking down I realized that I was heading for open water. I jettisoned my leg bag, and as much other equipment as I could, and landed in shallow water just off the beach – I was completely lost. Then someone called out; it was Private Ray Crouch. We got together and tried to work out where we were. We later discovered that Niels and Lieutenant Johnston were the only others to get out of the aircraft alive. Moving west, we soon reached some cliffs but couldn't find a way up. As dawn broke a boat came into view – it was carrying US Rangers. I waved some white clothing at them hoping they'd pick us up, but the boat sailed on past. We walked further along the beach to a headland [Pointe du Hoc] that was being attacked by the Rangers and almost immediately came under fire!

Private William Galbraith later recalled the horrors facing I Company following their first ever combat jump: "On landing the first person I saw was 1st Sergeant Paul Garrison, who'd broken his ankle. I stayed with him and tried to help him along. He could barely walk and we couldn't keep up with the men around us. As the group moved ahead into an open field near La Basse Addeville, a flare went up and the enemy opened fire killing many of them."

This immediate loss of nearly 40 men killed and another 40 guys mistakenly dropped at Ste-Mère-Église, where they were faced with rising flood waters from the River Merderet as well as well entrenched German forces, virtually brought I Company to its knees as an effective fighting force.

Another stick from the 81mm Mortar Platoon was dropped in a large area of marshland near Isigny-sur-Mer. They were about 7.5 miles due east of the battalion's objective – the road and foot bridges across the Canal de Carentan. Some jettisoned their leg bags before landing, and everything they contained, including personal weapons and ammunition, was lost to the dark fetid waters.

Despite their rigorous training prior to D-Day the very real horrors of landing in occupied enemy territory quickly became obvious to the paratroopers. Many fell before exiting and held up their sticks with fatal consequences. The ground was ablaze with enemy fire. Tracers seemed to be coming in all directions and many pulled their legs up to make themselves smaller targets. Bullets pierced canopies, making a popping sound as they passed through.

There was a certain amount of luck involved; it was all too easy to be knocked unconscious or suffer a broken ankle or leg thanks to a bad landing, and this quickly made you a sitting duck for the waiting German troops unless you had your wits about you. In the words of 2nd Lieutenant Peter Madden of H Company: "My stick landed near Carentan, close to minefields protecting its northern edge. During my descent I was unable to release my leg bag and was knocked unconscious when I landed. When I came round the first thing I heard was Germans talking. I managed to untie the bag and crawled toward a hedgerow dragging the container behind me."

Corporal Hank DiCarlo, also of H Company, jumped as part of chalk no. 13 but it was a chaotic descent due to intense enemy fire, and as a result the stick was widely strung out but with the majority of the men landing in the northeastern corner of the designated DZ. After assembling his M1, Hank donned his homemade ammunition bandoliers and started out in search of friendly company. He made his way to a nearby road; however, he could find no features that were familiar to him and dropped into a ditch to take a compass bearing. Just as he was about to leave,

"I stumbled at the door and the crew chief had to steady me before shoving me out... I lost my leg bag on exit. I was looking at the machine-gun fire. It appeared to be moving in slow motion and I tucked my legs beneath me. A bullet grazed my hand and a few more went through the canopy making popping sounds."

Private Bobbie J. Rommel – Machine Gun Platoon, HQ Company

"I landed in the flooded area close to L'Amont and could see a fire burning furiously on the higher ground nearby. I had met up with three other men and led them towards the fire. I couldn't be sure what was burning at the time but thought it was an aircraft. We were shot at by figures running around the flames which forced us to dive under the water and swim away."

Captain Bernard J. Ryan – Assistant Battalion Surgeon

"When the red flicked to green nobody moved. I could hear people shouting, 'For Christ's sake let's go, let's get out, what's happening up there?' I was the 'push out man' and it was my role to clear the plane. I started pushing and shoving furiously from the back and suddenly the stick began to move (I think the delay may have actually saved our lives). When I got to the door Lieutenant Williams was still on board and was tucked into the left-hand side of the opening! On the way down I oscillated twice before slamming into the ground. Despite all our problems we had a good drop and landed close together."

Sergeant Ralph S. Bennett – 3 Platoon, H Company

"Our plane was flying fast and low. As my 'chute deployed, the machine gun fastened to my body was ripped away by the opening shock and the 31lb weapon broke my ankle as it fell. As I landed, I instinctively tried to protect my injured leg. Lying on the ground I felt sick and disorientated. As I came to my senses, I could see the glow from the barn burning at Tamerville. Hearing familiar voices, I realized Lieutenant Christianson and Sam Porter were moving toward me."

Pfc Kenneth G. Johnson – 2 Platoon, H Company

"We were told to wait in the door until we were back over land. Herb Spence, who couldn't swim, lost his nerve while we were over the water. He unhooked his static line and sat down. As we turned toward the French coast the crew chief told us he had no idea where we were. When the green light eventually came on everybody, except Spence, jumped."

Private Robert C. Dunning – 81mm Mortar Platoon, HQ Company

he heard men running toward him and a few moments later three German soldiers, silhouetted against the light of battle, came into view: "While the mental side of me was dealing with the shock of seeing real enemy soldiers, the physical side lifted my rifle and fired eight rounds – they all hit the ground. I reloaded and approached them from behind, I checked the bodies and discovered that all three were dead." Then DiCarlo cautiously made his way along the road. Sporadic small-arms fire was going on all around. Suddenly, over to his left, he heard the identification "click" of a "cricket" (a handheld identification device issued in the marshaling area) and could see someone hiding in the bushes. Nervously, DiCarlo gave the appropriate response. Pfc Otto Dworsky from H Company HQ stepped out of the bushes and was overjoyed to see DiCarlo. The pair moved off in a westerly direction and soon ran into a group of fellow US soldiers. The group was made up of men from different units, including a number from the 82nd Airborne Division, who had been dropped in the completely wrong DZ. DiCarlo and one of the 82nd men, whom he only ever knew as Roy, were detailed to work together, and the pair acted as scouts on the right-hand flank of the makeshift platoon.

When we were about half a mile from the footbridge we heard someone calling in a loud voice "Guzman! Guzman!" I later learned that this was a common German name. However, it was new to us and for some reason Roy found it hysterically funny and started laughing uncontrollably! I quickly put my hands over his mouth and tried to keep him quiet. We were hiding in a bush and could see a German soldier with a machine pistol slung over his shoulder, striding towards us. On reaching the bush he unbuttoned his fly and pissed all over us! I was amazed that he couldn't hear it splashing off our helmets and clothing.

Unbeknown to the men of the Third Battalion, they were now in fact leaderless. As the air formation had headed toward St-Côme-du-Mont, the Rebecca receiver in Colonel Kreb's lead aircraft had successfully detected the single "Eureka" signal. Suddenly an antiaircraft shell had burst adjacent to the plane, showering shrapnel against the fuselage. Nonetheless, when the green light came on Wolverton's stick had followed him out of the door. A stream of heavy tracer fire had seemed to be coming from all directions. In fact, the entire stick was about to land in an area containing a high concentration of enemy soldiers. Within 30 seconds of leaving the aircraft Wolverton himself was dead – he had become entangled in a tree and was shot hanging from his harness. Without exception the remainder of Wolverton's stick were all killed, wounded or captured. Following the lead ship was the number two aircraft whose troops landed in a line along the southern edge of the heavily defended St-Côme and also suffered many casualties, including Battalion Executive Officer Major George Grant.

View due south in 2003 along the old Route Nationale 13 through St-Côme-du-Mont. It is believed that Colonel Wolverton was killed at le Ferage – the area beyond the hedge seen here in left foreground. Allied prisoners including captains Bob Harwick and John McKnight would have been made to march this way en route to Carentan on D-Day.

St-Côme-du-Mont lies on the Route Nationale 13, the Cotentin Peninsula's main road that links the port of Cherbourg with the town of Carentan. At the time of the invasion, around 1,000 German troops from the 1058st Grenadier-Regiment were billeted in and around the town. The regiment formed part of the 91st Luftlande Infanteriedivision whose commander was General Wilhelm Falley. The 91st Luftlande had unexpectedly been sent to Normandy at the last minute to help reinforce the German military presence on the peninsula. Aware of this, Allied planners had shifted the DZ and objectives of the 82nd Airborne Division further east. General Falley and his adjutant were killed driving out of their Divisional Headquarters near Picauville near Ste-Mère-Église by an early morning patrol by men from the 82nd shortly after they had landed. It can be argued that this patrol, led by Lieutenant Malcom Brannen, had a far greater direct influence on everything the enemy did or rather did not do over the following 24 hours!

Among the units attached to the 91st Luftlande was the fearsome 6th Fallschirmjäger commanded by Colonel Friedrich von der Heydte, a legendary warrior, whose men were to become the nemesis of the 506th, and it too by chance was partially deployed in the small Normandy town of St-Côme-du-Mont. By unintentionally veering slightly away from the designated DZ, several of the aircraft had offloaded their paratroopers, including Colonel Wolverton, into a veritable viper's nest. These men had simply never stood a chance.

Protecting the entire eastern coastal sector of the peninsula was the 709th Infanteriedivision, which had previously arrived in Normandy during December 1943

# · "ROSIE" ROSENFIELD ·

On the eve of D-Day, over the flip of a coin, I became the jumpmaster of my G Company stick made up of two armorers, four demolition engineers [from C/326], one medic and a seven-man rifle squad. My mission was to jump and carry two inflatable rubber rafts to the footbridge. The engineers were to wire and then blow the bridge if it became no longer tenable to hold. Approaching the coast of France, the Air Force crew removed the door and I stood in the opening watching the waves below and the other planes around me. Just as we made landfall, tracers lit up the sky. We began to feel things hitting the aircraft, flak and stuff. Then a plane [carrying men from I Company] just burst into flames and crashed to the ground. I didn't see anyone get out!

When we got the green light, we pushed the bundles out of the door and jumped. That's the last time I saw anyone from that plane. My 'chute opened, I swung once and hit the ground. I heard firing, people running and hollering in German. I lay there alone and plenty scared in a small, hedgebound field.

Our orders going into the jump were not to load our weapons or dump our gas masks. I lay on the ground, got out a knife I had tucked in my boot, cut the straps of my 'chute and loaded my grease gun and pistol. Up until two weeks before D-Day, I'd always carried a carbine, but the M1A1, with which I was quite efficient, was taken away in the marshaling area and replaced by the submachine gun. Getting out of the 'chute I looked at my compass and found the direction of the assembly area. I followed the hedgerow to an opening and clambered through into a ditch on the other side. I climbed up the bank and found myself at a road and after a quick look either way ran across and jumped into the ditch on the other side. Laying there I heard some talking but couldn't make out whether it was German or English, so I got out my cricket and gave the signal and got an answer. The correct answer... what a relief that was!

The first person I met was one of our medics, S/Sgt Mike Weiden [Mike had broken a bone in his foot]. There were two or

Twenty-four-year-old S/Sgt Zolman "Rosie" Rosenfield from Woonsocket, Rhode Island, was a supply sergeant for G Company. (Barbara Bartel)

three other fellows with him. In a short time, our little group grew to 12 or 13 men, including Lieutenant Howard Littell who had previously been with G Company. Another guy was our company clerk at Battalion HQ, Ray Calandrella, whom I knew of, although we weren't buddies at the time, and a couple of other guys from H Company.

We started in the direction that Lieutenant Littell thought was appropriate and at one point we were on the edge of a German encampment. We didn't realize it until we got there and saw foxholes with tents behind and I can recall Calandrella going up to each trench in the row and thrusting his bayonet in but there was no one around. We got out of there quick and came to the edge of a town [La Basse Addeville] and Littell realized that we shouldn't be near any towns and then thought we had landed short of the DZ and were we going in the wrong direction?

Somewhere along the line, Weiden and three or four of the others split, leaving eight of us including Calandrella and myself. During the night we were fired on and returned the fire but never saw whom we were firing at. We found a little hill with over-hanging bushes and went up the side and hid all of the next day. Artillery shells screamed overhead making a sound like someone ripping a bed sheet in half. Others exploded overhead scattering fragments all around our position. At one point some Cossacks on horseback, I guess there were about four of them, stopped right at the bottom of the hill in a gully and were talking. We let them go because we simply didn't know who else might have been with them.

After nightfall we started out again hoping to meet up with our outfit. We hadn't gone far, maybe 500 yards, when we came across another raised road and Lieutenant Littell

and I crawled up the embankment to take a look around. Here down the road came some Germans, making a lot of noise and talking loudly. Littell motioned for us to keep quiet. Just as they got abreast of us one of our guys in the ditch coughed and a German began to run towards me. When this guy got within two feet, I almost cut him in two with the grease gun. The rest of the Germans scattered but didn't return fire. We waited a while before crossing the road and continuing on our way. Coming out of a field a little bit later we came across another dirt road but there was no opening in the opposite hedgerow, however, there was a little bit further down.

As the four of us got out onto the road we were challenged on both sides. Myself and the other fellow in front of me leapt into a ditch to our left. There must have been six feet separating the pair of us, but nobody moved and then I heard Littell holler from the field opposite, 'There's a load of them across the road – throw your grenades!' The Germans were shouting, 'Hunta Grenada, Hunta Grenada,' and screamed when the things went off.

Then the lieutenant ordered everyone forward into the field. Little did we know we were running towards an enemy gun position and a bunch of Germans came out and charged us with fixed bayonets! As one of the Germans came up on the kid in front of me I shot across his shoulder with my pistol but he must've been stabbed by the guy's bayonet and went down… then I heard an awful hissing noise from one of our own fragmentation grenades about two feet away. I'm not really sure what happened but can only assume that the kid must have had a live grenade in his hand and let it go after he fell!

But I can recall lying in the road a little while later and Littell coming across and turning me over. It was obvious that my left femur was broken, shattered because it was at such a crazy angle. I was bleeding from small grazing wounds to my forehead and stomach. Four teeth knocked out and a big chunk taken out of my left side. Fragments went into the back of my leg and came out in the groin area. Another half inch and I would have been a soprano! I got a couple of back wounds and another on the opposite side on my right thigh. Weeks later, I found out that there was a chunk of metal in my left femur that resembled a 9mm bullet which led me to believe that I could have been shot while lying on the ground. Anyhow, as I regained consciousness, Littell was dragging me into the ditch beside the road. He placed my musette bag under my head, gave me my canteen, and made me as comfortable as possible. I recall him saying that he couldn't stay, that he had to get out – he couldn't stay with me… so he shook my hand and took off. Now when Littell dragged me off that road he actually saved my life because later on as I was lying there a horse drawn vehicle with big iron wheel rims came by crushing everything in its path – including bodies. During the night I must have lapsed in and out of consciousness and the next time I came too, it was getting light and there were a bunch of Germans standing around pointing their rifles at me saying, 'Rouse, Rouse, Rouse!'

Well I couldn't 'Rouse,' I just could not get up and tried to make them understand. I guess one of them had grabbed me by the front of my jacket and tried to lift me and I probably fainted. A little while later they came back with a TSMG [Thompson submachine gun] and a clip from my own gun and wanted me to show them using sign language how to put the clip in and I finally convinced them that it was not designed to

fit. Then somebody saw my pistol and took that away. The Krauts were in a circle around the guy that took the pistol when it went off and some noncom came over and really ripped into him and snatched the gun away. That's when I realized just how green these troops actually were.

Later on, they came down and shoved a rifle under my behind and with a guy on either side, arms around their shoulders, they dragged me to the Aid Station at St-Côme-du-Mont. As they carried me in, I heard someone calling my name, telling me to take it easy. It was our battalion medical officer Stanley Morgan… Morgan patched up my leg and put a splint on it and I was placed outside opposite the school. As I was lying there, Mike Weiden came shuffling by and said they were going to take me to St-Lô. I asked him not to let them take me, my being Jewish, but he said there was nothing he could do, and I needed further treatment anyway.

Finally, the Germans came and loaded a bunch of us up on a truck and drove down to Carentan. From there we joined a convoy of six other vehicles and started out for St-Lô. I was on a stretcher directly behind the cab, up against cans of fuel. Next to me was a Canadian, also a stretcher case, and the rest of the truck was filled with wounded; American, English, Canadian and a few Germans.

The only visible sign of any medical markings was a small flag on the fender with a red cross – impossible for a plane going 400 miles an hour to see. All of a sudden, I realized that our truck was pulling over, stopping, and all the ambulatory patients jumping off and running into a field. Next thing I knew, four Allied aircraft came down the road from behind and strafed the column with 20mm cannon. The shells tore through our truck, right between the Canadian guy and myself!

After that we propelled ourselves to the tailgate with our elbows and hollered for help. Some guys came and carried us away just as the planes came back to finish off the truck which burst into flames. Afterwards a German doctor came over and personally blasted me in English saying our people were barbarians for firing on convoys of wounded people. Through gritted teeth I told him I would have been more than glad to see his Luftwaffe chase away our planes today!"

Rosie survived the rest of the journey to St-Lô. But it would be a far longer journey for full recovery. By the time the hospital was liberated on August 4, he and the rest of the patients were malnourished, and his wounds were infected. He was evacuated back to the United Kingdom for further treatment but it would be 14 months before he was fully fit. Rosie passed away at the age of 66 in 1983.

and comprised mainly older men. Ost-Bataillon 795 was attached to this division and was made up of Russian volunteers from the Soviet Republic of Georgia. These Cossack troops were immediately identifiable by their shoulder flashes designated "GEORGIEN" and quickly gained notoriety among the Allied soldiers. There were other nationalities serving in German uniform in Normandy, including Ukrainians, Mongolians and Muslim troops from Turkistan. The 701st Infanteriedivision covered the west bank of the Canal de Carentan while the 352nd Infanteriedivision had the eastern bank with the Second Battailon from the 914th Grenadier-Regiment tasked to hold the two bridges over the canal at the town of Brévands.

The German antiaircraft defenses and infantry of these various forces had begun firing as soon as the first Allied aircraft had appeared in the dark night skies above them. They had lit up the sky with thousands of rounds of tracer fire. To the people of St-Côme and nearby Angoville it looked like a massive firework display that had a bizarre beauty all of its own. As the parachutists began landing in gardens and orchards, the Germans had lowered their guns, bullets bouncing in all directions.

One such antiaircraft gun was based on high ground to the southeast of St-Côme on farmland near the village of L'Amont. A huge barn across the other side of the hill from this flak gun had been set ablaze, lighting up the night sky and giving the gun crew a clear view of any planes caught in its glow.

The marshland below L'Amont acts as a drain for the surrounding high ground, and during the winter months, an area of about 20,000 acres is often under water. The locks at la Barquette are on the seaward side of the marshes, and as the tide goes out the gates swing open, allowing fresh water to drain into the sea. When the tide comes in, they automatically shut, preventing salt water from contaminating the fertile plain. As an anti-invasion defense, the Germans had taken control of the locks and fixed them so that the marshland around St-Côme was always under water, no matter what the season. Dozens of guys from Third Battalion were

# An overview of the Drop Zone and events from June 6, 1944

RN13 (Main road to Cherbourg)
Utah Beach
la Rive
Vierville
Cauvin
Smaller areas of flooding
Houesville
18
Angoville-au-Plain
19
25
17
Railway to Cherbourg (57km)
16
20
DZ D
21
26
St-Côme-du-Mont
15
la Basse Addeville
22
23
Ferry
footbridge
le Moulin
Brévands
11
12
13
10
14
24
9
Pénême
7
Road bridge
5
6
8
River Douve
Canal de Carentan
Main area of flooding
3
4
2
MINEFIELDS
Bassin à Flot canal
River la Taute
RN13 (Main road to Paris)
Carentan
1
Railway to Carteret (43km)
Railway to Paris (314km)
RN803
27
1km

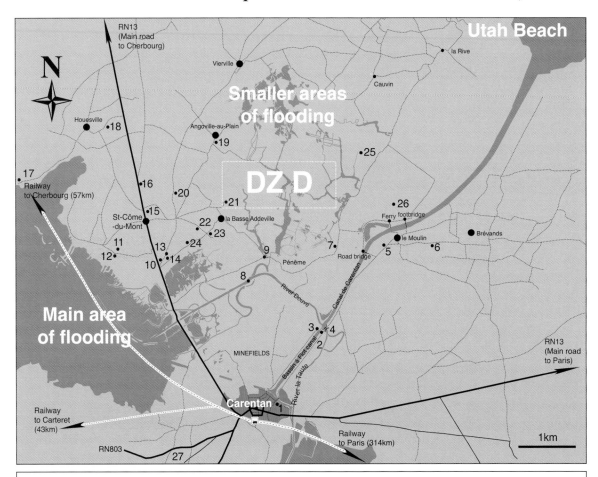

**MAP KEY**

1. Gloria milk factory
2. 3/506 area of operations June 15–22 (divisional security)
3. Lock keepers' houses (either side of canal)
4. Bailey Bridge built June 16–17
5. German Command Post (CP) in farmhouse
6. Phosphate factory
7. 3/506 aid station at Fortin Farm
8. la Barquette locks
9. 501st road block on D-Night (aka Hell's Corner)
10. 6th Fallschirmjäger CP and underground bunker
11. Oberstleutnant von der Heydte's temp HQ June 6–7
12. Rampan Manor
13. German antiaircraft gun position
14. Site of H/501 plane crash on D-Night
15. H Co CP at le Ferage, June 8–12
16. 3/506 HQ Co CP at Folleville Farm, June 9–12
17. G Co CP at le Boujamet Farm, June 10–12
18. I Co CP at le Vivier Château, June 10–12
19. Col Sink's CP, June 7–11 and G and I Co bivouac area, June 8–11
20. les Droueries Manor
21. Tamerville, where barn was set alight on D-Night
22. la Haute Maison
23. le Bel Esnault Château
24. Frigot Farm
25. les Rats farmhouse, site of Lancaster crash June 6
26. Site of P-51B Mustang crash June 7
27. 3/506 sector, June 13

Train Station
Metalled Road
Dirt Roads
Tracks

Pictured here on the left is the wartime home of the Jacquet family on Rue des Ecoles in St-Côme-du-Mont. From the outset of the German occupation, the left-hand side became the local area commander's headquarters and was known as the Kommandantur. In the days immediately following the invasion, the rooms on the right of the property became an aid station where Dr Stanley Morgan and his medical team worked to treat the Allied wounded taken prisoner. This amazing photograph was taken by Dr George Lage from the 502nd around 11/12 June after the aid station had been liberated and moved to Carentan. The church was targeted on the night of June 8, 1944, although it is still not entirely clear by whom, with the idea of denying the bell tower for use as an observation post. (George Lage Photo via Mark Bando Collection)

dropped in the floodwater, which in some places was more than 6 feet deep.

During the early hours of D-Day Colonel von der Heydte arrived by motorcycle in St-Côme and established a temporary command post in an old quarry opposite Rampan Manor, a historic manor house where the German forces stabled their horses and mules. From here von der Heydte had easy and uninterrupted access to the town's church – its ancient bell tower providing an excellent observation post – and could tap into the radio network previously established at Rampan to control, advise and direct his men. The spider web perimeter established by the German paratroopers trapped dozens from the Third Battalion who were desperately trying to find their way toward their DZ. An aid station for the American wounded was set up in the town and was run by Dr Stanley Morgan and several medics, who had already been captured by the Germans.

During the course of the morning more and more wounded were brought in, including several of the regiment's medics. All of the uninjured prisoners were taken to a field on the northern edge of St-Côme. Just across the road was an orchard, and hanging from one of the apple trees was a dead paratrooper, his body swollen and bloated. German reinforcements coming from the opposite direction were using the

Aerial view looking northeast from Carentan beyond the Bassin a Flot sea-lock, along the winding Canal de Carentan to le Grand Vey and Utah Beach in the distance. Third Battalion's main objective, the road bridge, was located just before the first bend in the canal near to the single line of trees on the right bank. The footbridge was situated further downstream beyond the large red-brick farm complex of le Moulin. With the edge of DZ D just visible in the upper left corner, this photo gives a real sense of perspective between the bridges and Utah Beach (upper left). The thick double row of trees in the foreground along the eastern (right) side of the Bassin a Flot was a German bivouac area and vehicle park on D-Night. The vacated enemy positions were subsequently re-used by 101st Divisional HQ. After the Battle of Bloody Gully, 2 Platoon, I Company were sent to the same area to provide security while a Bailey Bridge was being built over the nearby River Taute. The old Bailey Bridge is still there but slightly obscured by foliage in this photo. (Sylvain Corbin copyright MDPROD50)

dead man for target practice. With each burst of fire, the blood-caked body twisted and jolted in the tree. We believe that man was Bob Wolverton. After being pressured by the American prisoners, the Germans cut the colonel down and while doing so removed his dog tags and several other personal items before burying the body nearby. Afterwards, the same guards began selecting officers, senior NCOs and technical ranks including HQ Company commander Lieutenant Bill Reid, H Company commander Captain Bob Harwick and I Company commander Captain John McKnight along with his radio operator Sergeant Joe Beyrle, who were all taken to a command post at the opposite end of the village for interrogation.

A number of sticks had landed near Carentan itself about 2 miles away from DZ D and on the wrong side of the river so were now close to the minefields protecting the northern edge of the town. Every now and again the moon would appear from behind the clouds, casting an eerie light all around but occasionally also revealing a potential place to cross the swollen waters. Slipping into the dark, fast flowing tidal water was a terrifying business and even when some successfully managed it, usually by roping themselves together, some of the smaller groups were killed or captured before making it to their main objective of the road bridge.

Meanwhile, amidst the darkness of D-Night, several groups, including some who had swum the river, ended up converging at a road junction near Pénême, about a mile due west of the main objective. Third Battalion Operations Officer Captain Charles Shettle was the most senior man present, so it fell to him to take command. Now 30–40 men strong, Shettle decided to head east along the Pénême Road in the general direction of both bridges, avoiding one or two isolated farms along the way. At around 0445hrs Shettle's group reached a farm owned by Théophile Fortin. About

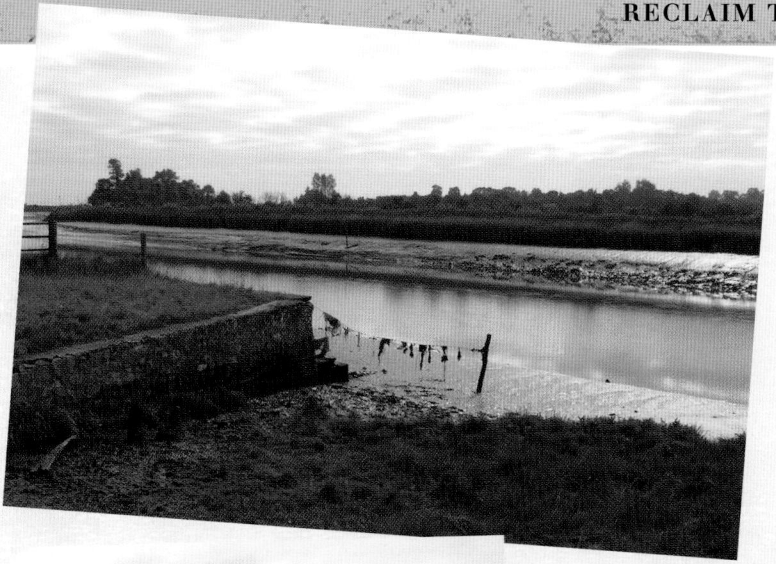

The remnants of the road bridge looking across the Canal de Carentan (called the Douve by US forces) toward the southern (German-held) bank where the initial five-man H Company assault took place at first light on D-Day. The photograph was taken shortly after dawn on June 6, 2004 – the 60th anniversary of D-Day and when the tide would have been at exactly the same level.

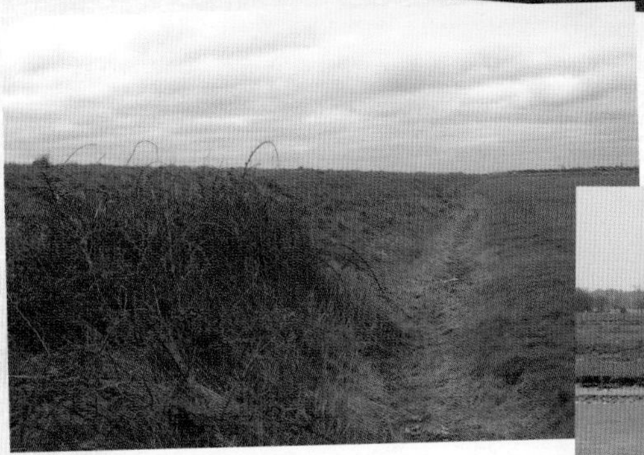

BELOW LEFT On D-Day members of H and HQ Companies from 3/506 dug in along this elevated roadway that led up to the main bridge.

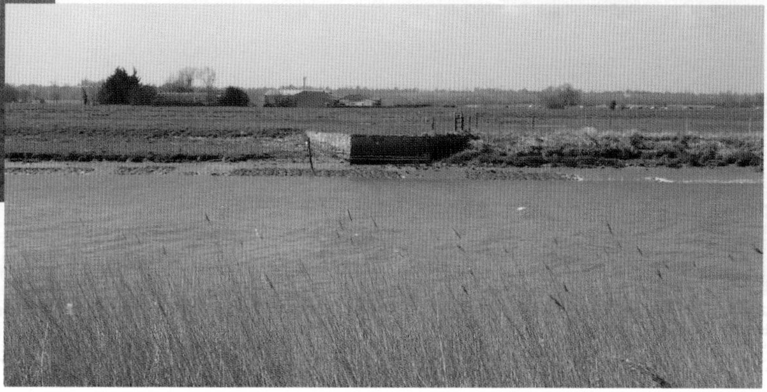

BELOW Panoramic view northwest as seen by the enemy across the canal toward the old road bridge, American positions and beyond. The roof of the old Fortin Farm can be seen in the middle distance on the left.

200 yards further on, branching off to the right, was a road that led directly to the battalion's key objective – the road bridge.

As dawn was breaking, Shettle's men were spotted by enemy troops dug in on the other side of the river. Under a wall of fire, the Americans leapt from the road and followed the low ground to its right before reaching the base of the dyke that afforded better cover. The dyke formed part of the canal's flood barrier and was about 10ft high and topped by a single-track road. His men continued for about 400 yards along the base of the dyke toward the road bridge where they found Lieutenant Ken Christianson and Pfc Sam Porter from H Company waiting for them.

At this point there should have been around 250 men at the position, but Shettle had only around 50 men at his disposal, including a handful of demolition specialists from 326th Airborne Engineer Battalion. The surrounding area was surprisingly quiet and Shettle wondered for a moment if the invasion could have been postponed. He was not alone in that thought. Everyone's attention focused briefly on a four-engined Avro Lancaster that came screeching overhead and crashed in flames about a mile or so due north at Les Rats Farm. Back to the job in hand, Christianson asked for volunteers to scout across the bridge and test the enemy's strength. At that very moment the northeastern horizon lit up, followed by a deep rumbling noise. The Allied naval bombardment of Utah Beach had begun, the invasion was officially underway, and everyone breathed a deep sigh of relief. Christianson sent five H Company men across led by Staff Sergeant Fred Bahlau. Upon reaching the other side of the river, the men split into two groups and headed in opposite directions using the opposing berm for cover. Progress was slow through the soft, exposed mud banks. Walking methodically downstream, in a half crouch, Corporal Hank DiCarlo noticed a sudden movement above him. Looking down from the berm was a German soldier, who was kneeling and pointing a Walther P38 pistol directly at him. The German fired and the bullet struck Hank in the upper right chest, knocking him to the ground. Flat on his back, he watched helplessly as the enemy grenadier peered over the embankment. Meanwhile Hank's colleague Pfc Don Zahn, who had heard the shot, was making his way back upstream. As soon as DiCarlo spotted him he pointed at the German. Only a couple of seconds had elapsed but to Hank it seemed like eternity. As soon as the German saw Zahn he panicked and took off running toward a line of trees. Zahn leapt up and dropped the German dead in his tracks with a flaming burst of fire from his Thompson submachine gun.

The rest of the group heard the commotion and made their way back downstream. There was a lot of German small-arms fire, but the men were protected by the berm and the rounds flew high above their heads. The immediate problem now facing them was how to get DiCarlo back across the bridge. Nearby was an 8ft wooden plank presumably left over from the recent bridge construction. The plank fitted perfectly between the ten prefabricated trusses supporting the bridge. Now under mortar fire, the scouting party quickly figured out that the only way Hank was going to get back was by going underneath the bridge using the plank as a kind of shuffleboard to crawl along.

Knowing that Bahlau's team could not hold off a larger-scale enemy attack, Christianson organized another party, this time led by Lieutenant Pete Madden, to cross over and assist so the bridge could be rigged for demolition by the small team from 326th Airborne Engineers. During the diversionary action that followed, on the friendly side of the bridge, Sergeant Stan Stockins was killed and Cpl Tom Bucher badly wounded in the throat.

Meantime, DiCarlo was beneath the bridge sliding along on the plank. It was a painful process as he slowly inched his way under the bridge's 130-yard span.

# The fighting at the Road Bridge

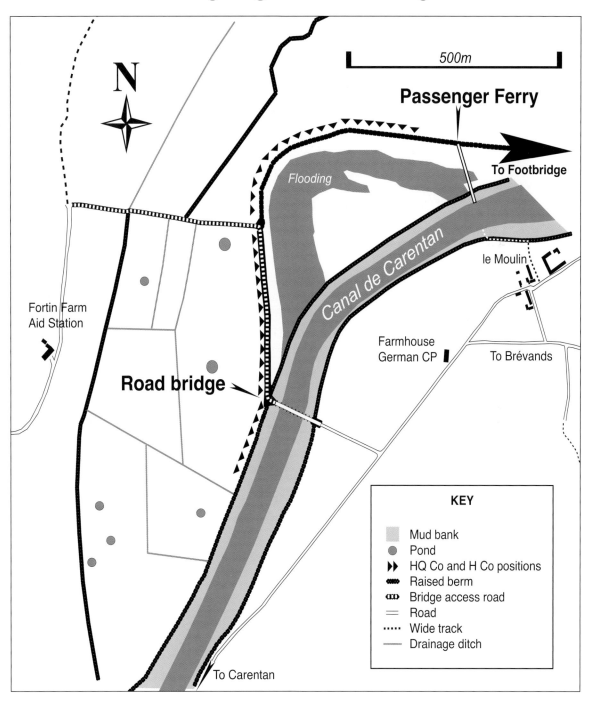

500m

**Passenger Ferry**

**To Footbridge**

*Flooding*

*Canal de Carentan*

le Moulin

Fortin Farm
Aid Station

Farmhouse
German CP

To Brévands

**Road bridge**

**KEY**

- Mud bank
- Pond
- HQ Co and H Co positions
- Raised berm
- Bridge access road
- Road
- Wide track
- Drainage ditch

To Carentan

# The fighting at the Footbridge

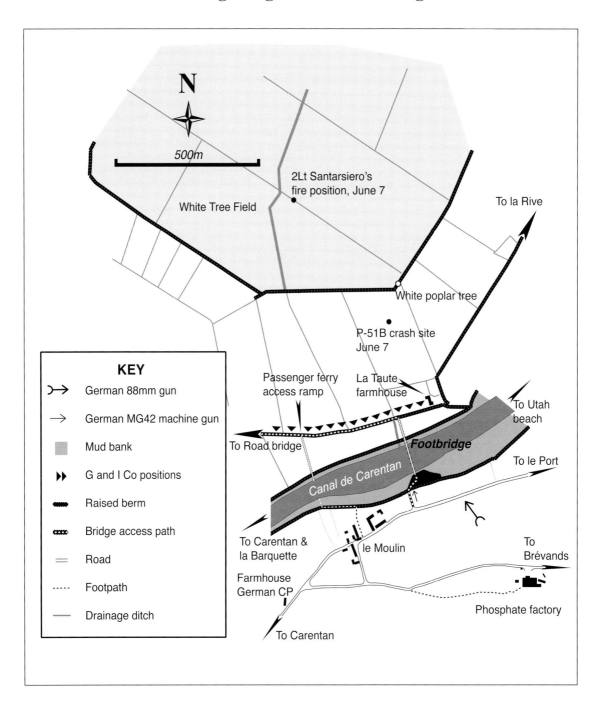

**N**

500m

2Lt Santarsiero's
fire position, June 7

To la Rive

White Tree Field

White poplar tree

P-51B crash site
June 7

**KEY**

>→ German 88mm gun

→ German MG42 machine gun

▓ Mud bank

▶▶ G and I Co positions

━ Raised berm

━ Bridge access path

= Road

..... Footpath

— Drainage ditch

Passenger ferry
access ramp

La Taute
farmhouse

To Utah
beach

To Road bridge

*Footbridge*

To le Port

*Canal de Carentan*

To Carentan &
la Barquette

le Moulin

To
Brévands

Farmhouse
German CP

Phosphate factory

To Carentan

Crawling forward, blood dripping into the murky water, he eventually reached the "friendly" bank and two colleagues hauled him to safety over the embankment using a jump rope.

As Madden's group reached the far side, they broke right and joined up with Bahlau and his men. The group, which was now about a dozen strong, formed a defensive line along the berm upstream of the bridge. But because of the overwhelming fire, the demolition team had to abort their mission (they eventually tried again later that day after dark when they successfully emplaced the explosive charges). Madden could see that there was no point in his group remaining any longer and during a brief lull withdrew under an umbrella of 60mm mortar fire provided from across the river by Sergeant Ralph Bennett. The only people who failed to make it back were Pfc Don Armenio and Staff Sergeant Harry Clawson who both disappeared while scouting upstream. Clawson eventually made it back to friendly lines but it was only much later that everyone discovered that Armenio had been captured.

After the initial flurry of activity, the situation at the bridge calmed down enough for everyone to start digging in. All of the battalion's radio kit had been lost on the jump and never recovered, so Shettle had absolutely no way of communicating with Colonel Sink and RHQ. As the day progressed, more troops arrived and were allocated positions along the berm but there was, of course, no sign of Colonel Wolverton nor many of the company commanders and platoon leaders. Shettle was forced to conclude, correctly, that by now they must be either dead or prisoners of war. During the afternoon he sent a small patrol to locate and recover equipment bundles and look for radio equipment in the DZ area. While patrolling the swampy ground behind Fortin Farm the paratroopers came across a dozen Ukrainian volunteers who promptly surrendered. When their weapons were removed they were found to be rusty and badly maintained.

A naval artillery observer who was attached to the 501st at la Barquette had begun calling in shells from one of the big battleships patrolling the invasion beaches. But it wasn't until late morning before the USS *Nevada* opened up. The first 14in round whooshed overhead, making a sound like an express train going through a tunnel. The men cheered as they watched the shells come down around L'Amont where the enemy antiaircraft gun was still active. This shelling, however, had devastating

Acting Cpl Mario "Hank" DiCarlo from 1 Platoon, H Company, pictured here in Germany during April 1945. Hank was part of S/Sgt Fred Bahlau's team on D-Day that made the initial crossing of the road bridge. In the moments following the crossing, DiCarlo was seriously wounded. Hank was taken to the battalion aid station at Fortin Farm and stuck in a tiny back room to die. Although by then the bleeding had stopped, he was short of breath and could feel a heavy bloated sensation in his right chest, signifying internal bleeding and a collapsed lung. Against the odds Hank survived his injuries and would find himself in many more dangerous situations while serving with the 506th but nothing else ever came close to the emotional rollercoaster he experienced on his first day in combat. (Hank DiCarlo)

Twenty-seven-year-old Sgt Stanley Stockins (HQ Company) pictured in 1943. Stockins was an exceptionally gifted amateur boxer and a member of the Regimental Boxing Team. He won most of his fights, including a brawl with Sgt Fred Bahlau in the supply room at Ramsbury! Fred had found Stan very difficult to work alongside initially but instantly regretted throwing the first punch as he was beaten into submission. Afterwards the two men buried the hatchet and became great friends. Mark Bando took Fred to Normandy for his first return visit in 2000. When they found Stan's grave at St Laurent, Fred was suddenly and quite unexpectedly overwhelmed by a wave of tearful emotion. (Stockins family via Richard McErlean)

Fred Bahlau accompanied by his trusted 1911A1 pistol dug in below the access road leading to the main bridge. The photo (taken after the bridge was bombed) was snapped using a camera liberated from one of the German coastal artillerymen captured on June 7 after the skirmish at the footbridge. (Chad Weisensel)

ABOVE RIGHT (Left to right): 2nd Lt Clark Heggeness (2 Platoon), Staff Sgt Fred Bahlau, Sergeants Phil Parker and Gordon Yates posing behind the access road with a variety of German pistols taken from the coastal artillerymen captured on June 7. (Mark Bando Collection)

consequences for the Allied prisoners who were in the process of being moved from St-Côme to Carentan. Luckily, Captain Bob Harwick managed to use the chaos of the attack to escape into a nearby swamp. After two days on the run, he would successfully link up with Colonel Sink and RHQ on the evening of June 8 at Angoville.

As late evening of D-Day approached, gliders carrying soldiers and equipment from the 327th Glider Infantry Regiment (GIR) started to land in the fields north of St-Côme.

## D-Day at the footbridge

The footbridge was slightly longer than the main bridge and just wide enough to get a horse and small cart across. Its southern end was laid onto a disused stone wharf. It was on the lower slopes of the hillside overlooking this footbridge that the Germans had positioned an 88mm gun. Near the northern end of the bridge was a large farmhouse called La Taute. One of the first men from Third Battalion to arrive was 1st Lieutenant Joe Doughty from G Company who, together with his assistant, reached the crossing at approximately 0500hrs on D-Day morning.

G and I Companies' original battle orders were to take control of both sides of the bridge as soon as possible, and in the half-light of early morning, Doughty took it upon himself to have a closer look at the crossing. As he made his way along the wooden beams below the bridge a German machine gun, hidden in the trees on the far bank, opened up. The bullets went high, hitting the woodwork above his head, forcing him to quickly retreat. Following his return, two more officers made a similar attempt to cross, but were beaten back by the same gun. Joe then ordered everyone to dig in and wait for his company commander, Captain Harold Van Antwerp. Of course, he did not know at the time, but the captain had been killed a couple of hours previously.

Now in daylight, anyone coming into the area behind the bridge had to run a gauntlet of enemy fire, including from the 88mm gun on the high ground opposite, which caused a number of casualties. Joe Doughty's colleague Lieutenant Turner Chambliss was waiting for his company supply sergeant, Zol Rosenfield, to turn up with a number of rubber rafts, and with that in mind decided to look along the river for a suitable launching point. The plan was to place all of the 60mm mortars and other heavy equipment on the rafts, then tow them manually across the river. From his position 30 yards from the bridge, Joe could see Turner repeatedly popping his head above the berm, when suddenly a bullet struck him in the mouth, leaving a gaping exit wound in the back of his neck. Turner died a few moments later in the arms of Sergeant Addison Marquardt from H Company who should have been at the other bridge.

All anyone could do now was dig in and hold on. Gunfire from the 88mm was sporadic but at this stage all it really damaged was the farmhouse (which G Company were trying to use as an observation post) and everyone's morale. Other than the

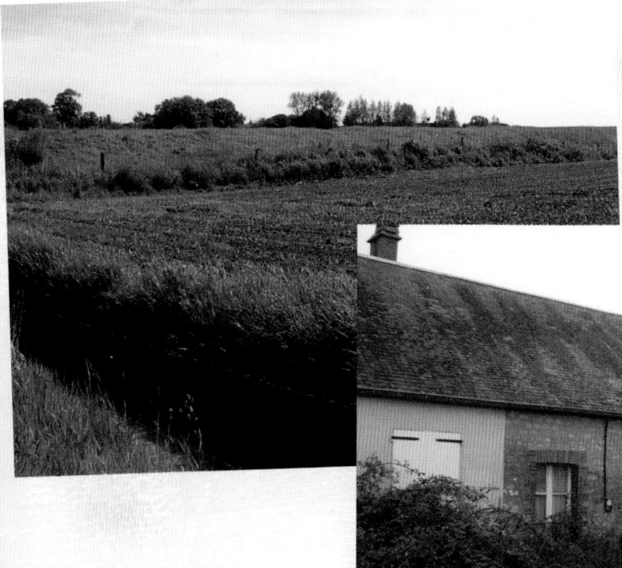

The G and (what remained of) I Company positions on D-Day and beyond were here at the base of the berm. The La Taute farmhouse was situated in the left corner of the field and the northern end of the footbridge ramp was located midway along the dike. The rooftops of le Moulin on the southern bank can just be seen above the berm on the right. Lt Turner Chambliss was killed here while searching for a safe place to launch rubber boats to ferry heavier equipment across.

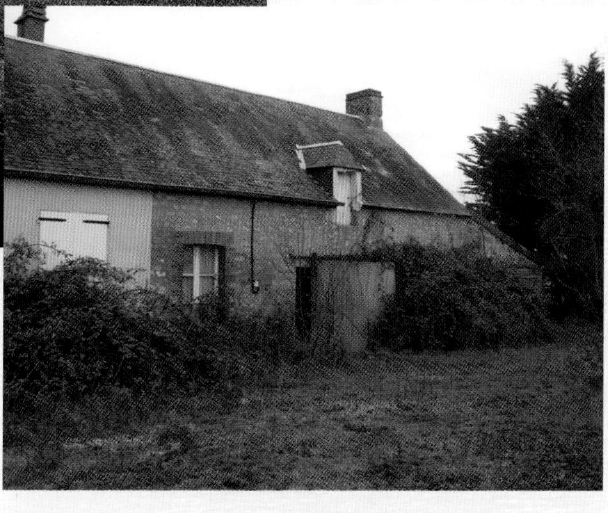

Fortin Farm became the Third Battalion Aid Station from June 6 to 8, 1944. Long abandoned and in poor repair, only everything to the right of the window is original.

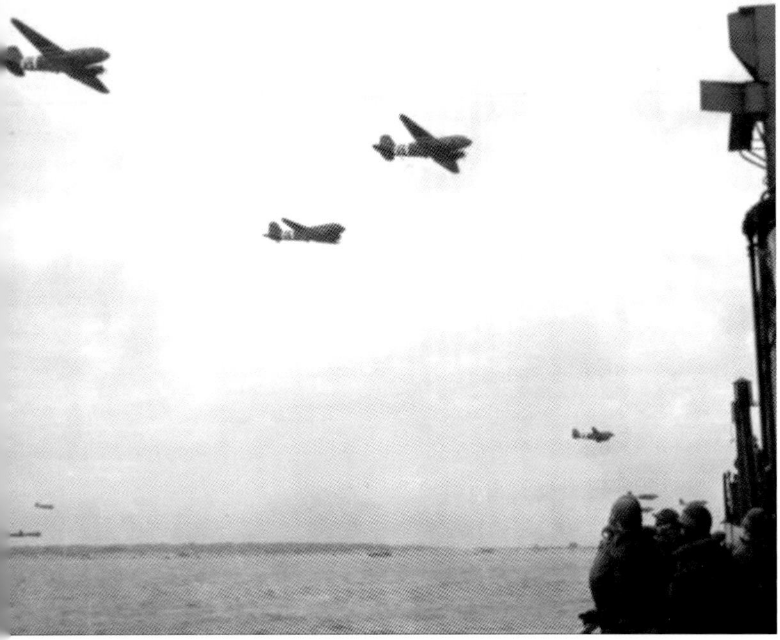

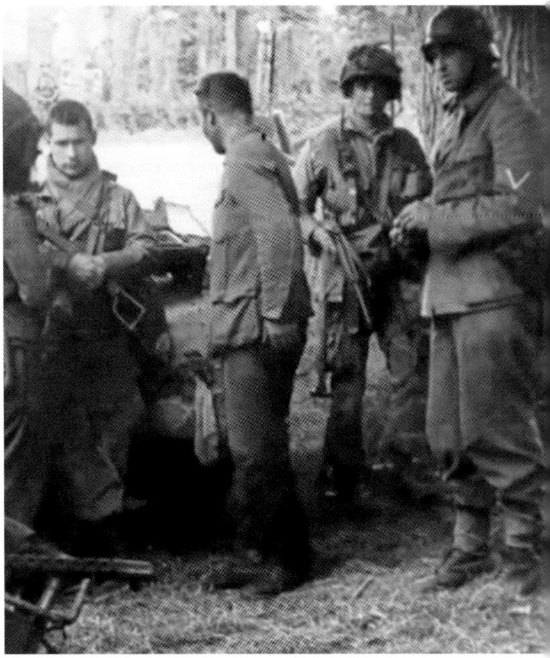

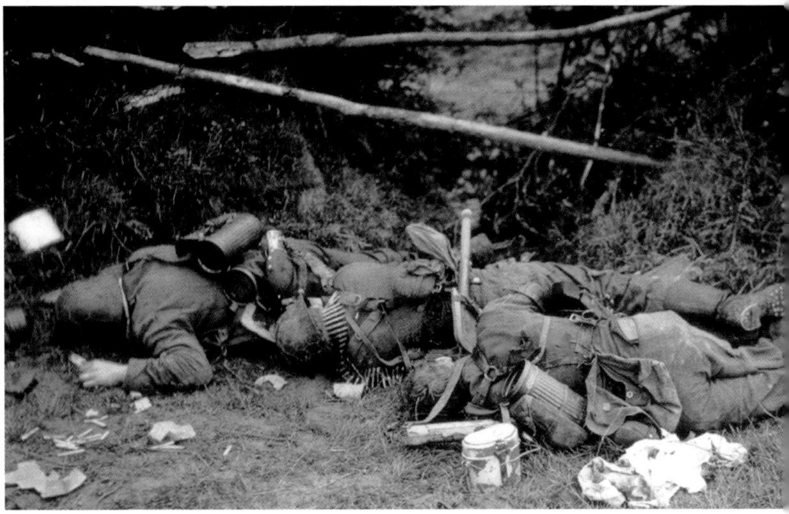

C-47s from Operation *Memphis* flying across Utah Beach on June 7 after dropping food, ammunition, and medical supplies between Hiesville and Ste-Marie-du-Mont. The early morning mission gave the entire 101st Airborne Division enough fresh equipment to support themselves for several more days. Up until that point, everyone had presumed that the German antiaircraft gun at L'Amont had been destroyed by naval artillery fire until several Skytrains strayed over DZ D. Flak burst all around as they dropped their loads, but they flew on undamaged. (NARA)

Paratroopers from the 502nd Parachute Infantry Regiment pictured here interrogating German prisoners during the first few days of the campaign. (NARA)

German dead somewhere on the peninsula. (NARA)

bridge there was not much else to hit! Just like Shettle, Doughty was also lacking a radio, but after noticing several Allied planes flying overhead, ordered one of his men, who had some signal panels, to lay out a message saying, "Bomb 1,000 yards" with an arrow pointing in the direction of the 88mm. Joe did not know that the Air Force had already been ordered by Divisional Headquarters to bomb both bridges and it was only a matter of time before the inevitable would happen.

# D-Day+1, June 7

As dawn broke on June 7, two companies of German coastal artillerymen were heading for the footbridge. From his in-depth position behind the bridge, 2nd Lieutenant Charles Santarsiero of I Company was watching through his binoculars and gave the order to open fire. All hell broke loose, and after a brief firefight the leading enemy company withdrew into the trees that bordered the western perimeter of a large enclosed meadow area known locally as White Tree Field. Santarsiero moved forward along a ditch and established a fire position around 80 yards away from the nearest Germans and thus prevented them from regrouping. Meanwhile paratroopers from the bridge headed out to assist. The gunfight raged for approximately two hours before the decimated Germans finally surrendered. The Third Battalion men returned to the footbridge with their prisoners, and the wounded were given first aid before being taken to Fortin Farm. At around 1300hrs, as Santarsiero was marching the prisoners along to Shettle, four P-51B Mustangs flew in low and fast behind him. Back at the footbridge, Joe Doughty presumed that at last somebody had seen his marker panels and the aircraft from the 353rd Fighter Bomber Squadron were going to attack the 88mm. But instead, the returning planes hit the bridge, dropping at least three bombs on target. Bridge timbers and large clods of thick mud were thrown 30–40ft into the air only to come crashing down over the G Company positions. Luckily Doughty and his men were well dug in behind the berm and nobody was injured. However, during the penultimate attack run, one of the pilots, Lieutenant Charles Huffman, lost control as he flew in low across the river from le Moulin. Rapidly losing altitude, Huffman managed to jettison two bombs before his plane rolled and clipped the ground with its right wing tip. The Mustang tumbled end over end and disintegrated in a huge fireball before coming to rest in White Tree Field. Lying on his back, eyes to the sky, Lieutenant Eugene Dance had watched as Huffman's aircraft was caught in the blast from a bomb dropped a split second earlier by his own wingman.

This was not to be the only Allied air attack of the day. A couple of hours later further along the berm at the road bridge, Santarsiero was preparing to move yet another group of prisoners to Fortin Farm when four P-47 Thunderbolts swept overhead from the direction of Brévands and disappeared from view. Aware of what had happened at the footbridge earlier in the day, everyone ran for cover. A few minutes later the planes returned and made two low passes from the direction of Fortin Farm, dropping ten mighty 500lb bombs and partly destroying the bridge. The planes then returned and began to strafe the paratroopers' position with cannon fire. Shettle's operations sergeant, Ed Shames, and Chaplain Tilden McGee took matters into their own hands, popping smoke while waiving air panels. Realizing their mistake, the pilots aborted their final attack and flew away. Incredibly, the

# PETE MADDEN

Moments after the road bridge was bombed by the US Air Force on June 7, Madden was badly injured by enemy mortar fire. A flight of P-47 Thunderbolts made two low passes from the direction of Fortin Farm, dropping their bombs. The ground shook and the explosions, possibly enhanced by the demolition charges placed the night before, sent water and bridge parts high into the air. Shortly after the bombing, just when everyone thought it could not get any worse, the Germans launched a mortar attack. Madden was blown out of his foxhole, receiving extensive shrapnel wounds to his back and right leg and taken to the aid station at Fortin Farm. Théophile and Odette Fortin, who had been sheltering in the garden with eight-year-old Georgette Revet, decided to enter the house to look for something to read. Pete asked Odette for fresh water and she returned to the garden to fetch some from the pump. At that exact moment a shell from the 88mm up by the footbridge exploded in the garden, killing Odette and little Georgette instantly. Powerless to help, Madden lay on the floor and watched the tragic scene unfold. Théophile was distraught and sobbing uncontrollably. Pete was torn apart by what he had seen and tearfully beckoned the Frenchman over to him. Grabbing Théophile's hand, he proceeded to give him everything he had in his pockets. "It was such a futile gesture but I felt I had to do something."

On June 8, during the afternoon when communications had been firmly established with Sink, most of the wounded, including Pete, were evacuated. "We were loaded onto jeeps two at a time and taken to Utah Beach. On the way we passed wagons piled high with dead Americans and eventually stopped to pick up a German officer. Our jeep driver and his buddy were both enlisted men and ordered the German to get in the back. He refused, bad move. The two enlisted guys were having none of this and without warning put a gun to the man's temple and blew half his head away. I never reported the incident, but it troubled me for years to come.

After being discharged from hospital, Pete was assigned to Division HQ at Greenham Lodge near Newbury where he worked throughout *Market Garden* as the UK Control Officer. After Holland, Madden returned to Third Battalion's HQ Company at Mourmelon, and took up his original post commanding the 81mm Mortar Platoon. During the final attacks on Foy, Pete was wounded again on January 14. "We came under heavy artillery fire and I sprinted to my CP. Ironically, as I entered the bunker, a piece of shrapnel came flying through the entrance and tore into my knee. The wound was serious enough for me to be evacuated to Paris. After the splinters of metal were removed from behind my patella I was shipped to a hospital in the UK." Even up to the day he died on August 20, 2008, Pete was still picking fragments of metal out of his body.

Formerly of the 81mm Mortar Platoon, 22-year-old, Lieutenant Pete Madden from Morgantown, West Virginia, was reassigned to lead 3 Platoon, H Company, into Normandy. Madden had been billeted with Dr Mills and his family at Kennet House in Ramsbury when this picture was taken in the back garden with their son Peter. (Peter Mills)

sandy soil that made up the berms had allowed the men to dig deep and these foxholes undoubtedly saved many lives. However, the pressure waves caused by the bombing resulted in dozens of perforated eardrums. To add insult to injury the American positions then came under a heavy mortar attack, from the Germans across the river, resulting in several injuries. Among the wounded was Lieutenant Pete Madden. Shortly afterwards Santarsiero was given permission by Shettle to try to find Colonel Sink, whose CP at the time was over 3 miles away at Caloville but was in the process of relocating to Angoville. Ultimately Santarsiero did not find Sink but along the way bumped into a group from Divisional Headquarters. By June 8, Colonel Sink had set up his new CP at Angoville and with General Taylor began to organize a plan whereby the 327th Glider Infantry Regiment would relieve Third Battalion as soon as possible.

Bob Sink pictured in the doorway of the Cousin family's farmhouse in Angoville. After leaving Caloville, the farm and its surrounding stables became Sink's CP between June 7 and 11. (John Reeder via D-Day Publishing Collection)

Since mid-morning of June 7, the 501st at la Barquette had been in combat with a contingent of Fallschirmjäger who had suffered heavy casualties. At around 1600hrs the Germans began to withdraw and were now heading toward the road bridge. Of course, they had no idea that it had been destroyed a few hours earlier. The Third Battalion rearguard dug in around Fortin Farm sent a runner to inform Shettle that they had seen the German paratroopers approaching. Captain Shettle immediately dispatched Lieutenant Ken Christianson back to Fortin Farm with a team of around a dozen men to block the advance. Standing on the edge of the Pénême road, Ken looked at the enemy through his binoculars and estimated the distance to be around 550 yards before he gave the order to open fire. The confused and shell-shocked Germans kept coming and Christianson's men simply kept firing. Eventually, after about two hours, the Germans began to surrender, and the Americans suddenly had approximately 190 prisoners to deal with. They began to march them down the road to a nearby barn in the grounds of Fortin Farm but the move was spotted by the 88mm crew over on the hill above the footbridge who immediately went into action. The exploding shells blew the prisoners into the air like rag dolls; one round fell short and came down on Fortin Farm, tragically killing two civilians who had been attempting to assist the wounded.

From here on in the German forces in the local area really began to crumble and under constant naval shelling were rolled back into St-Côme. By the morning of the 8th, with the 506th net closing around them, the enemy abandoned all their vehicles and heavy equipment and withdrew across the marshes to the railway line northwest of the town. The Germans then headed for Carentan, blowing bridges behind them along the way.

## D-Day+2, the German counteroffensive

Communications had been firmly established with Sink's new command post in Angoville. During the course of the afternoon the German POWs were removed from Fortin Farm and the medical team was able to evacuate most of the remaining wounded in jeeps supplied by the 326th Medical Company. Still vastly under strength, the battalion had done its job and was now placed in reserve, leaving what was left of the bridges under control of the 327th Glider Infantry Regiment. After dusk H Company, with Christianson in command, moved to an orchard in St-Côme, which had only just been liberated, called le Ferage, while G and I Companies were deployed into bivouac areas at le Boujamet Farm and le Vivier Château. Meanwhile Shettle had taken the bulk of HQ Company and marched them to the northern edge of St-Côme where he established Third Battalion's command post at Folleville Farm.

Colonel Wolverton was now officially listed as missing presumed dead. After being on the run and isolated since D-Day, Captain Bob Harwick had successfully rejoined the Third Battalion and was given command of the battalion on June 9, and immediately began replacing many of the missing company commanders. In the shake-up, Shettle took over command of HQ Company, Joe Doughty – G Company, Ken Christianson – H Company, and John Kiley – I Company.

During this period the remainder of the 506th PIR together with the 327th GIR (who had successfully crossed the Douve and fought their way along the Basin a Flot canal) enveloped Carentan and pushed the enemy away from the town. Far from being beaten, on June 11, the German 6th Fallschirmjäger made a tactical withdrawal and took up positions to the southwest. Colonel von der Heydte's now somewhat depleted force was bolstered by the arrival of the 17th SS Panzergrenadier-Division. The overall German plan was to break out through American lines and recapture St-Côme, drive a wedge between Carentan and Ste-Mère-Église, and force the 101st Airborne back to the beach. With artillery and self-propelled guns now in support, von der Heydte planned to advance his forces on the left flank along the undamaged Carteret–Paris railway line and then break through the American positions and head for Carentan itself.

A wounded American airman photographed here holding a souvenir respirator in the main square at St-Côme-du-Mont, 11/12 June 1944. The photograph clearly illustrates the wealth of equipment left behind by the German forces as they withdrew on June 8. (*Life* Magazine – Joe Scherschel)

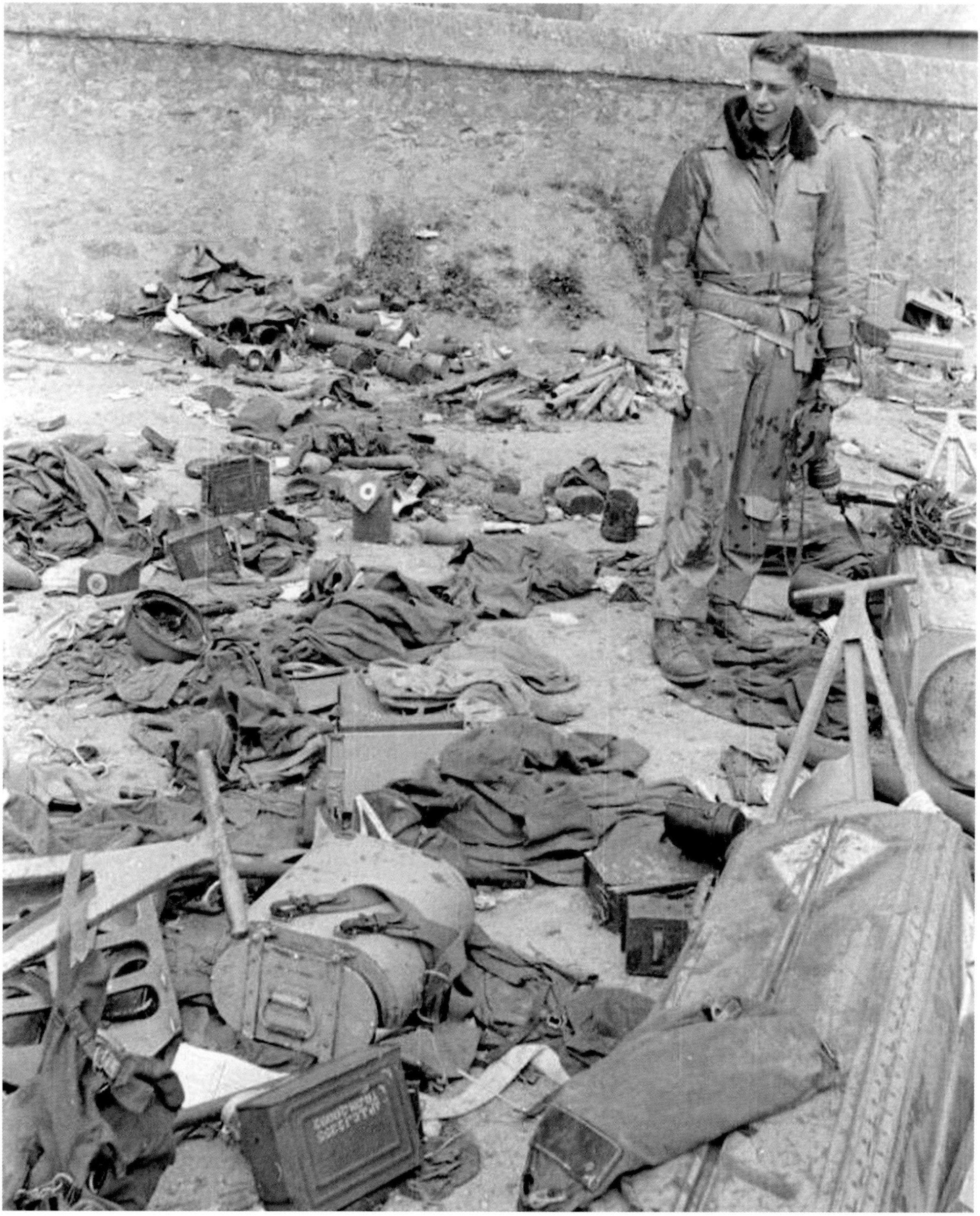

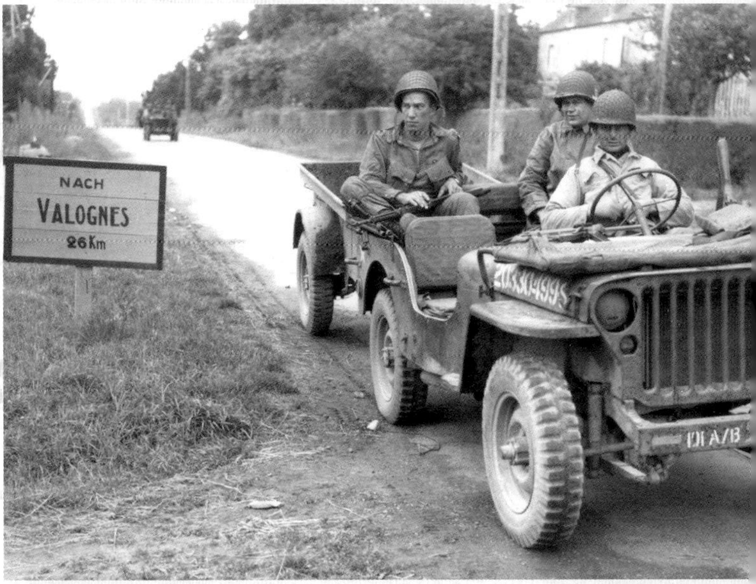
NACH
VALOGNES
26Km

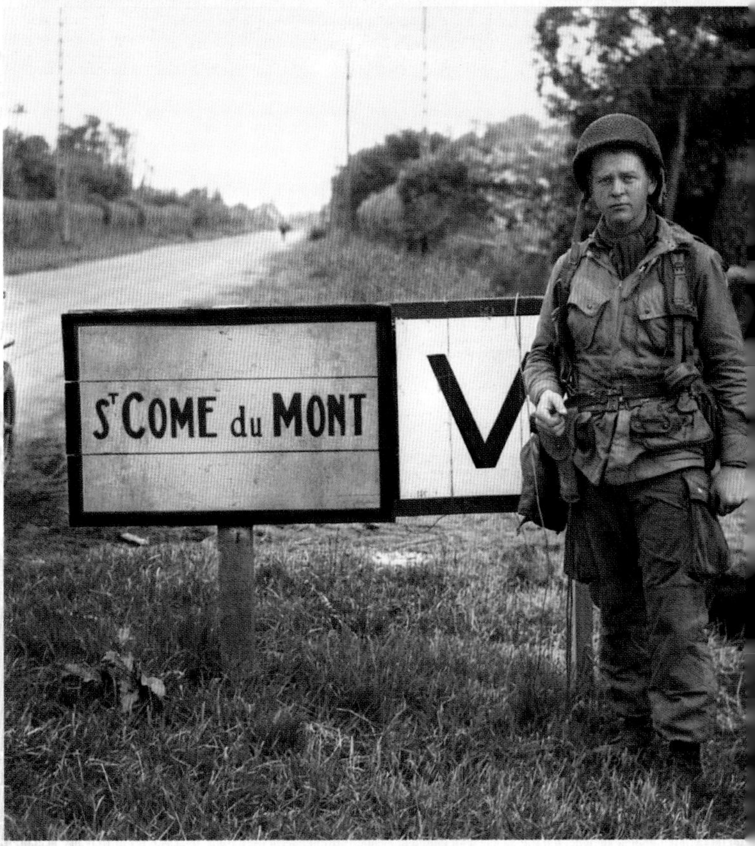
St COME du MONT

TOP Looking northwest along the RN13 toward Blosville. The men in the jeep are members of 1st Lt John Reeder's Regimental Communications Team and are en route from Angoville to Col Sink's newly established "third" CP in Carentan. The building in the background is Folleville Farm, Third Battalion's own CP.
(John Reeder via Mark Bando Collection)

BOTTOM Turning 180 degrees and now looking south along the RN13 into St-Côme, Reeder had this portrait snapped by one of his men.
(John Reeder via Mark Bando Collection – colorization by Johnny Sirlande)

OPPOSITE TOP On his journey to Carentan John Reeder had a picture taken next to the body of a German paratrooper killed by naval gunfire. The author believes that this could be somewhere northeast of St-Côme and the site was probably obliterated in 1994 when the new motorway junction was built.
(John Reeder via Mark Bando Collection)

OPPOSITE BOTTOM There were four bridges between St-Côme and Carentan along the RN13 (which became known as Purple Heart Lane). Reeder took this photo at the last crossing, "Bridge 4," over the River Madeleine looking northwest toward La Rue Mary and St-Côme. The Germans used Belgian Gates (like the one seen here) extensively in Normandy as mobile roadblocks.
(John Reeder via Mark Bando Collection)

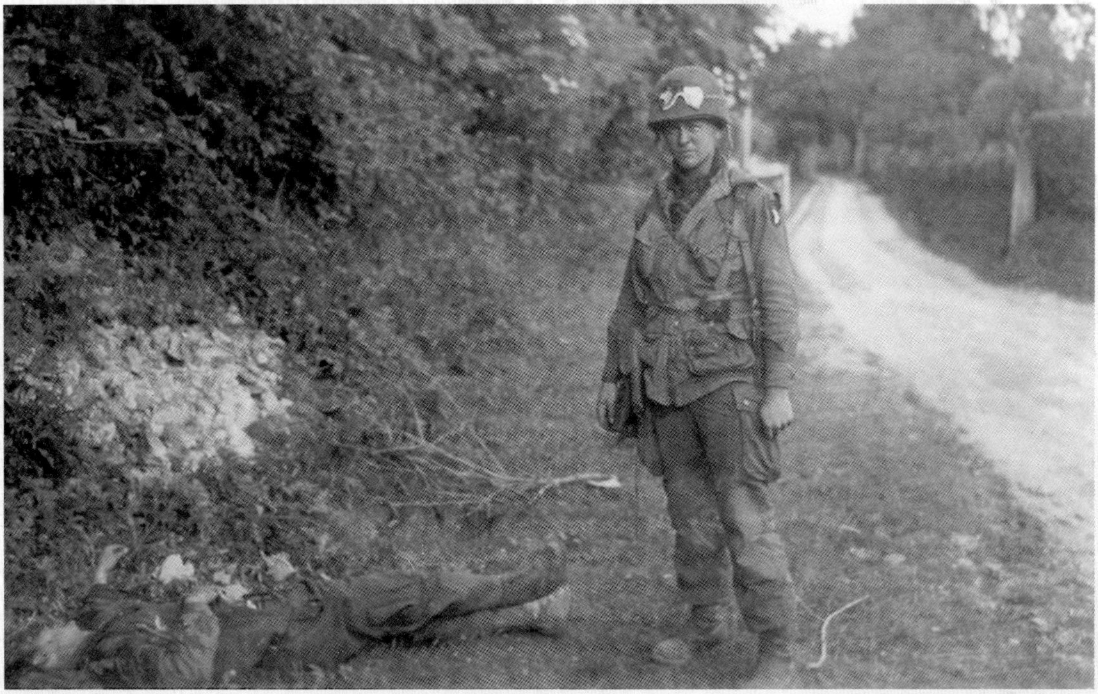

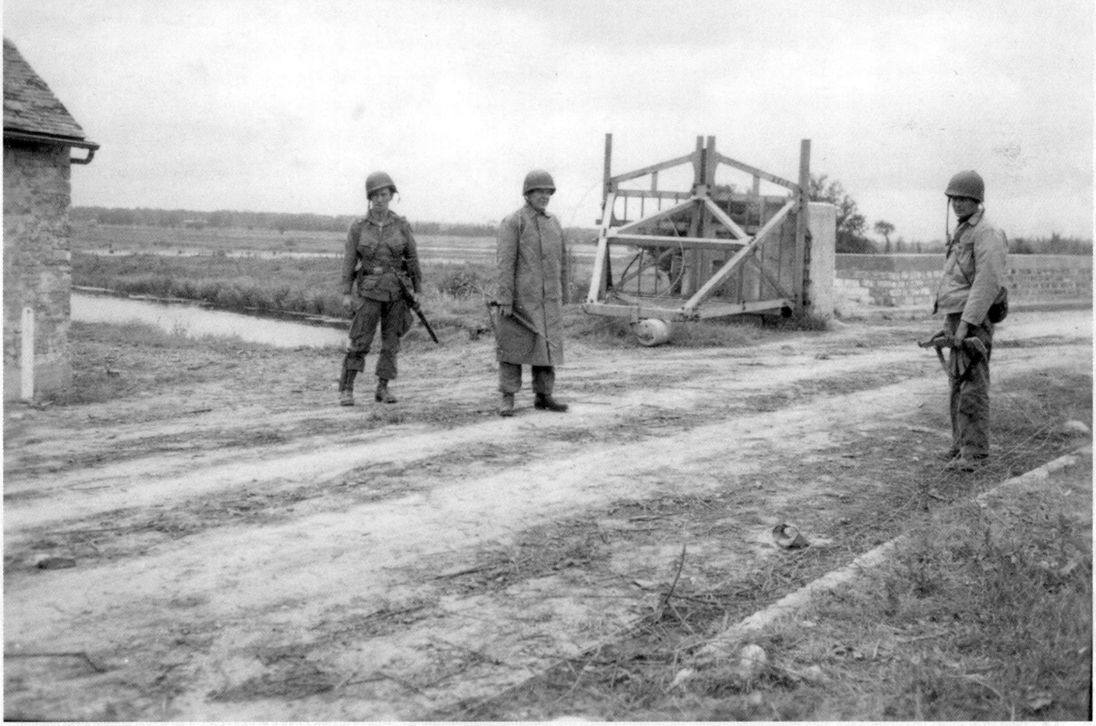

TOP During the first few days many wounded paratroopers were brought to Utah Beach and evacuated across the Channel back to hospitals in the UK. (NARA – colorization by Johnny Sirlande)

BOTTOM Adjutant Alex Bobuck and Lt Shrable Williams (Regimental HQ). Following his capture on D-Night, Alex (seen here on left), with a little help from Dr Morgan, convinced the Germans that he was a member of the Medical Detachment. He stayed to help the medics in St-Côme until the village was liberated on June 8. This photo was taken later that afternoon when Bobuck and Williams (who was also an escapee) reported for duty at the newly established Regimental CP in Angoville. Williams went on to lead the 506th Pathfinders and paved the way for the subsequent aerial resupply missions at Bastogne.
(John Reeder via D-Day Publishing Collection)

OPPOSITE TOP Le Boujamet Farm, Houesville – members of G Company relaxing in a bivouac area, June 10, 1944. (Harvey Jewett via Robin Vertenten)

OPPOSITE BOTTOM After Brévands and the Bassin a Flot were cleared by the 327th Glider Infantry Regiment, construction of a floating bridge over the Canal de Carentan commenced on June 10. Built by the 991st Engineering Treadway Bridge Company from First Army, the multiple pontoons re-cemented the crossing near le Moulin after both bridges had been knocked out on June 7. Together with the steel Bailey Bridge built over the River Taute on June 16, the floating crossing opened up a shorter and more efficient route into Carentan for the increasing number of trucks coming from Utah Beach.
(Mark Bando Collection)

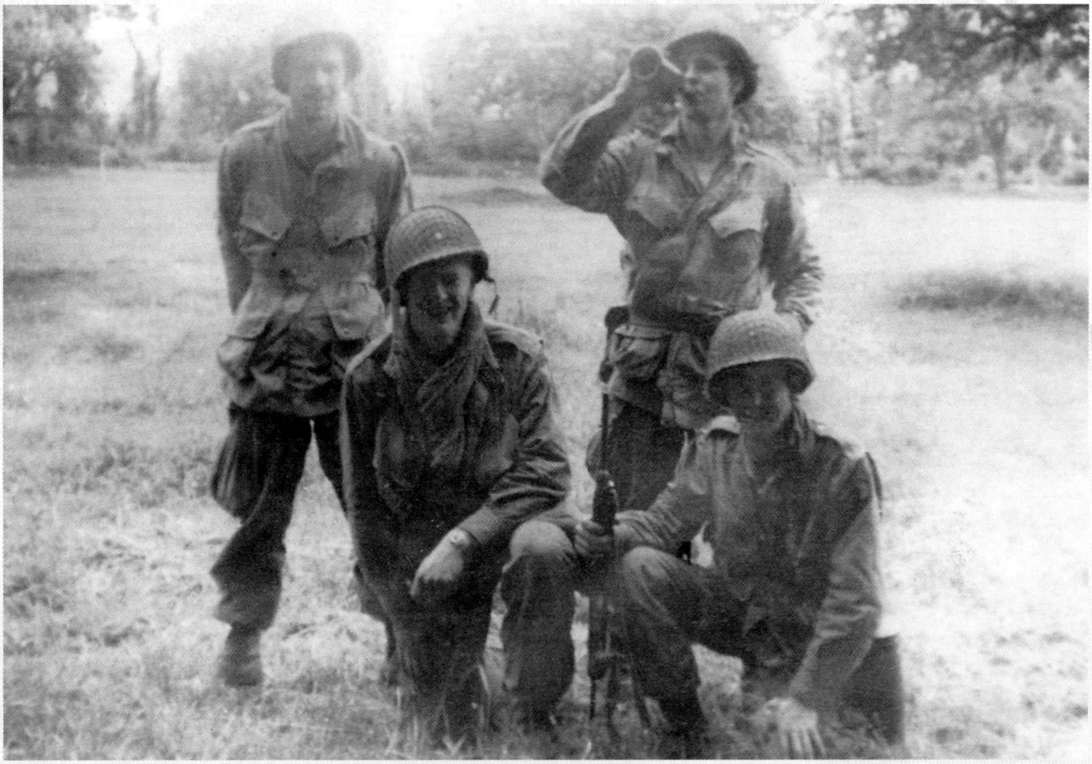

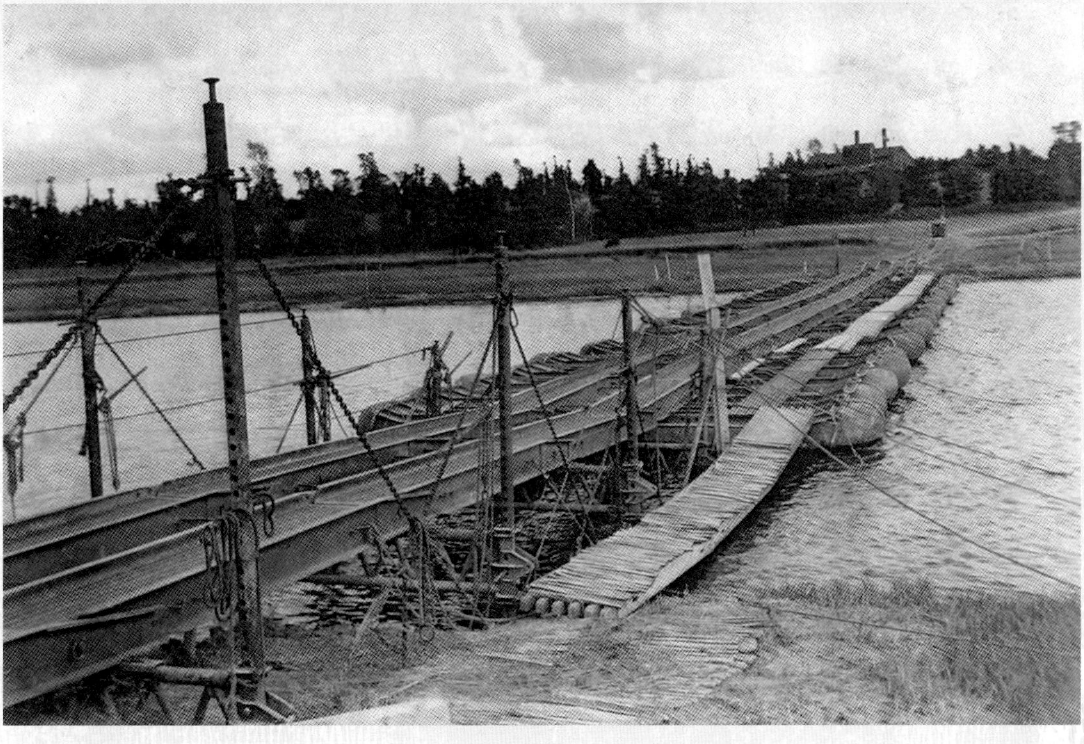

VINS ET SPIR TUEUX
R. LARSON
EPICERIE - COMESTIBLES

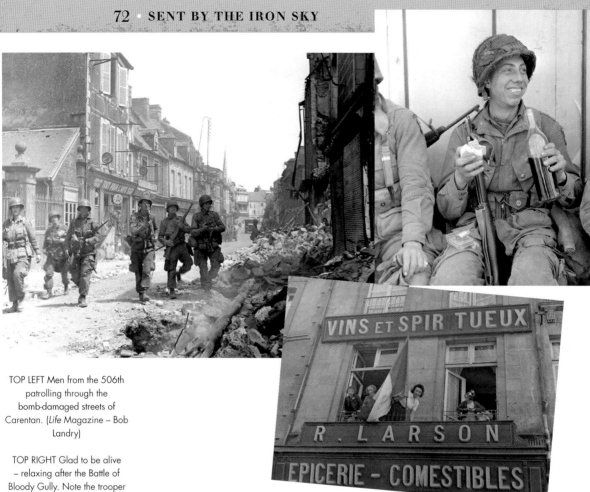

TOP LEFT Men from the 506th patrolling through the bomb-damaged streets of Carentan. (*Life* Magazine – Bob Landry)

TOP RIGHT Glad to be alive – relaxing after the Battle of Bloody Gully. Note the trooper on the right is wearing his gas detector brassard issued in the marshaling area. (*Life* Magazine – Bob Landry)

Mlle Roland Haugnard proudly raising her tricolore over Place de la République. Roland was instrumental in organizing the children, three of whom can be seen here, to present flowers during the three Silver Star Ceremonies that took place in Carentan between June 15 and 23. Sylviane LeFevre (right) presented posies to Bob Sink, Fred Bahlau and Harry Clawson. During the last ceremony on June 23, another child, four-year-old Danielle Laisney, was mortally wounded by enemy shellfire. (*Life* Magazine – Bob Landry)

The following day, June 12, Colonel Sink instructed his regiment to set up defensive positions west of Carentan and moved First and Second Battalions into the area. In the early afternoon, elements of the 17th SS and von der Heydte launched a disjointed and unsuccessful attack; as a result, Sink decided to go on the offensive and brought Third Battalion out of reserve in readiness for a full-scale regimental thrust that he had planned for 0500hrs on June 13. As such, on the evening of June 12, the 200 remaining soldiers from Third Battalion's original strength of around 600 gathered opposite the church in St-Côme waiting for their transport to arrive. The place was cluttered with abandoned German equipment. Despite being assured that they would be resupplied in Carentan itself, before they left the men scrounged as much ammunition as they could find.

At 0230hrs on June 13, the battalion was dropped off on the northern outskirts of Carentan, which was still burning following 24 hours of relentless aerial bombardment by the Germans. After a short march the outfit was ordered to wait in a field close to Sink's forward CP and was informed, much to everyone's surprise, that in fact there would be no ammunition resupply!

## The battle of Bloody Gully

As dawn broke the battalion was following a hedgerow above the feature that was to become known in airborne legend as "The Gully" (and "The Gulch" to the men of 2/506). A little over 1 mile long and lined on each side by high hedges, the gully was in fact the sunken drovers' road which stretched northeast from La Croix de Méautis in the south to the Carteret–Carentan railway line. West of the gully the land rises to a height of about 80ft, which gave the enemy a clear tactical advantage over the Americans. The Third Battalion area was divided into three fields, all bounded by dense hedgerows. For ease of reference I have numbered them 1 through 3, with the battalion's left or southern flank being field number 3. Owing to the acute convex slope, the use of handheld radios became virtually impossible. Most communicating had to be carried out by runner, meaning precious time and vital information was lost during the course of the battle.

By first light two machine gun teams from HQ Company were moving into position on the high ground above the gully. Their orders were to provide covering

An enlarged replica of a vintage World War II map recreated and annotated by the author.

FRANCE
CARENTAN (MANCHE)
GRID PROVISIONAL
FIRST EDITION
To CHERBOURG 57 km
To SAINT-CÔME-DU-MONT 3 km
To BLACTOT 800 m
To CARTERET 43 km
To BAUPTE 6 km
To PARIS 314 km
CARENTAN
St. Antoine
Sink CP
ROUTE NATIONALE N°803
ROUTE NATIONALE N°171
1
2
3
Gully
D443
To MÉAUTIS 2.3 km
To LA FOURCHETTE 1.5 km
Geographical Section, General Staff, No. 4234
Published by War Office 1944
10,000/3/44 S.P.C.
SCALE 1: 2,500
YARDS
METRES
Compiled and drawn by C.I.U. and War Office
Ground information supplied by T.I.S.
Photolithographed by War Office 1944

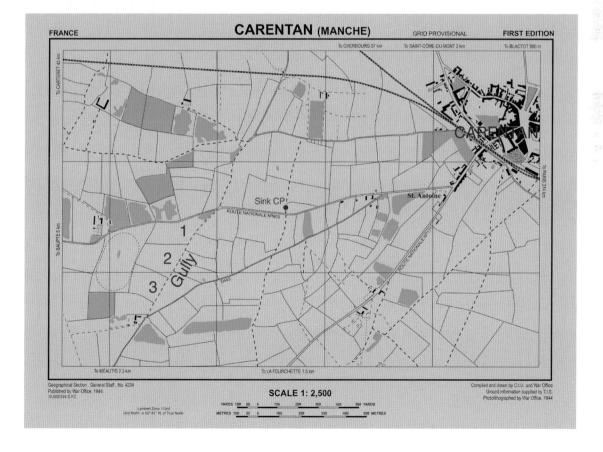

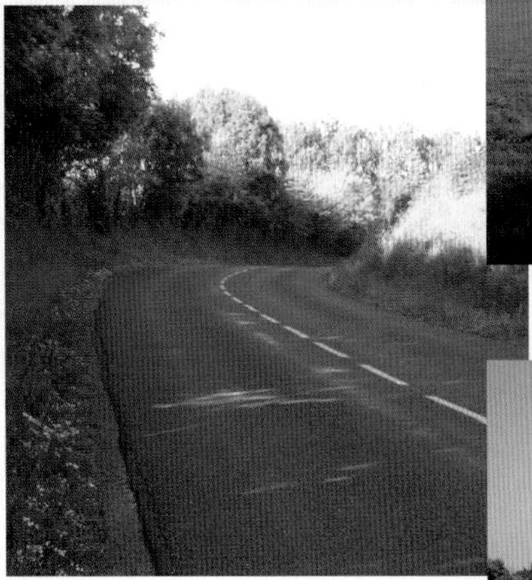

A photograph taken in 2005 showing the view east along the old RN803 (now D223) toward Carentan from the perspective of the German Stug to where the two American M5 tanks came around the bend. Field 1 is situated behind the hedge on the right.

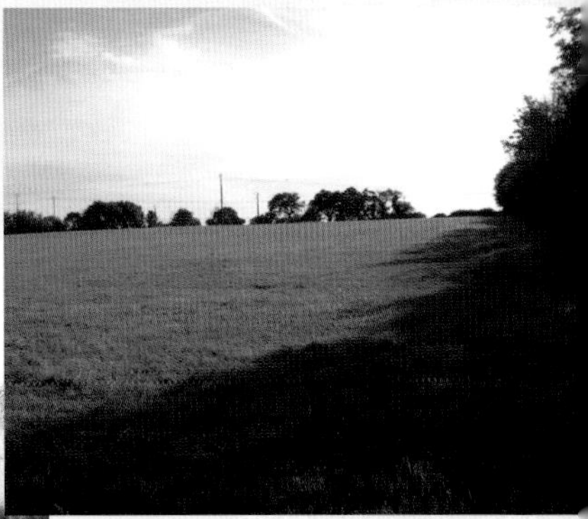

TOP This time the photograph shows Field 2 looking west from the gully. It is easy to see how the convex slope afforded protection from enemy fire emanating from the fields beyond. However, for G Company, there was no protection from the mortar or the machine-gun fire coming from the northern side of the RN803. The bullets cut through the hedgerow on the right with devastating consequences. G Company suffered almost 20 casualties in this field on June 13, 1944.

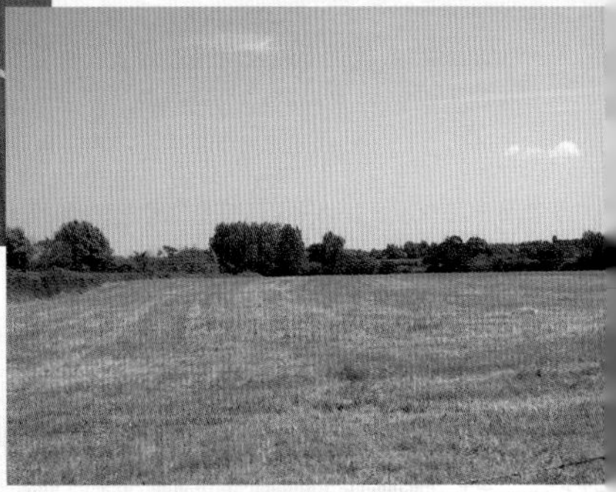

BOTTOM The view east in 2005 back toward the gully from the top of Field 1. The long hedgerow (left) parallels the old RN803 (now D223) and became the right flank for H Company on June 13. The photo was taken from the place where Ken Christianson was wounded. Further to the left would have been where the German Stug stopped and took out the two M5s. This field and section of the gully have changed significantly since the building of the new milk factory in the vicinity.

fire for the battalion from beside a hedge that bordered the RN803 road. After a brief exchange of fire with the Germans on the other side of the road, a squadron of M5 light reconnaissance tanks arrived and mistook the machine gunners for the enemy. As the lead tank moved along the main road toward the American gunners, it hosed the hedge with heavy fire, causing chaos. This, along with the pathetic opening artillery barrage, was not a good start for the Third Battalion.

By now G and I Companies had been deployed across the enclosed fields 2 and 3. Some members of I Company had been attached to H Company, whose orders were to attack alongside the RN803. After their earlier mistake, three of the M5s remained and moved along the road, to give H Company some direct fire support. Led by the great Ken Christianson, H Company moved out of the gully and started their way slowly along the hedge bordering the RN803. The open meadow to the left was the size of a football field. As the scouts reached the crest, the enemy opened up with a ferocious mortar and artillery barrage. The men split up and dropped to the ground. A German machine gun on the northern side of the road began pouring fire through a gate opening and immediately pinned everyone down. Private Bill Galbraith of 2 Platoon, I Company, later described the terrifying situation the outgunned and outnumbered American paratroopers found themselves in:

Private Jim Brown and myself were assigned to H Company, who had been ordered to attack along the right flank [Field 1]. As the scouts reached the crest of the slope the enemy opened up with a ferocious mortar and artillery barrage that continued, on and off, for the best part of two hours. Everyone split up and dropped to the ground. I got separated from Jim who had managed to drag our gun and tripod into the hedgerow up ahead. A Kraut machine gun was trained to fire through a gate opening just in front of me and had us all pinned down.

Meanwhile, Operations Sergeant Ed Shames was desperately trying to locate Second Battalion who were supposed to be advancing simultaneously across the other side of the road. But F Company of 2/506 had encountered a number of German Stug self-propelled guns (SPGs) and had been forced to withdraw, jeopardizing the entire Second Battalion's advance. Separated from the rest of H Company, Ken Christianson was at the top of the field with a small group of his men. Suddenly a Stug came lumbering along the road on a recon from Douville and stopped directly opposite. Completely unaware and heading directly toward the German SPG were the three M5s. Shames vividly describes the chaos of the rapidly deteriorating situation:

As the tanks came up beside me, I rose to my feet and trotted alongside, using them as a shield from the machine gun fire. I was trying to locate F Company and had been shadowing the tanks for a few seconds when suddenly a couple of 75mm rounds went through the lead tank and into the one directly behind it! The shots had been fired at point blank range and the lightly armored M5s didn't stand a chance. The explosions were terrific and a blast of searing heat threw me

The 17th SS-Panzergrenadier-Division used the Sturmgeschütz 40 armed with a powerful 75mm gun to try to force their way along the road and track from Douville (now called Donville) toward Carentan. This Stug was part of that German assault group and was knocked out probably by an AT round near Donville. The commander is still in the turret with what looks to be part of his brain on the track skirt. (George Lage Photo via Mark Bando Collection)

After Bloody Gully, Third Battalion's operations sergeant, Ed Shames, became one of the first enlisted men from the 506th to be awarded with a battlefield commission. Eddie is pictured here in London shortly after collecting his new lieutenant's uniform from Savile Row.

to the ground, scorching my face and eyebrows. The third tank started backing out and as it did I picked myself up and ran. My clothes were smoldering and my ears ringing but other than that I was OK.

I got straight on the radio to battalion [i.e Captain Harwick] and told them there was nobody on the right flank. The response was, "Are you sure? You'd better speak to regiment." After a nailbiting few moments I got through and [the Regimental Operations Officer] Major Harold "Hank" Hannah answered. "We've got a problem," I said, "There's no one on our right flank – repeat NO ONE." Hannah was astonished and replied, "Are you kidding me... who in the hell did you say you were?" Once I'd explained, Hannah told me to sit tight and wait for Colonel Sink to call. Within 10 seconds my "phone" rang, "Sink here... Shames, do you know what the hell you are talking about son?" "Yes, sir," I replied. He then said, "Get your ass back to my FCP [Forward Command Post] and give me a full situation report – NOW."

The Kraut machine gun started up again and the noise was overwhelming. I slapped my radio guy on the shoulder and shouted in his ear, "Don't go away – stay here." I forced my way through the hedge and dropped down onto the road. Smoke was pouring from the knocked-out tanks and I thought I was safe from the machine gun. I was wrong and stepped directly into its line of fire. The asphalt seemed to come alive as bullets peppered the surface. I started to run, zigzagging my way out of the killing zone and sprinted down the road to Colonel Sink's CP. I showed Sink my map. [Colonel, Regimental Executive Officer] Charlie Chase looked on as I began to point out the problem areas, doing my best to convince both men that the situation on Second Battalion's left flank was desperate. "We are wide open and taking extremely heavy fire from the northern side of the road, sir," I said. "Are you sure?" Sink responded. "Yes, sir," I replied again. Finally Sink said, "OK, Charlie [Chase], get up there with Shames and give me a full situation report." We set off and ran back along the main road. I told Chase how dangerous this was but he ignored me. June 13 was also my birthday and as we came under fire from the same machine gun I muttered to myself over and over, "born June 13 – died June 13." Chase kept saying, "Where's Harwick, where's Harwick?" Of course, I didn't know but it made me think that there was more to this than just a situation report. Much to my surprise we made it back to my radio operator who was still waiting in the same place that I'd left him. Colonel Chase got straight on the radio to Sink and confirmed everything that I'd said, before instructing him to find a unit, any unit, to fill the gap. He then went back down the hedge line and disappeared into the gully.

The knee-jerk action from the Stug crew of knocking out the two M5s in fact stopped any further German vehicle movement along the RN803. Private Galbraith recounted what happened after the Stug reversed away:

The Germans stopped firing and sent a couple of guys forward to where the tanks were burning in an attempt to outflank us. Through the hedge I could see another group of Germans gathering and fired my sniper rifle (that I had picked up in St-Côme) hitting one of them. I tried to squeeze off another shot but the trigger wouldn't work. In all the excitement I'd forgotten that the rifle was bolt action and I hadn't reloaded. Machine-gun fire started pouring across the road and I tried to throw a grenade over the hedge toward it. Unfortunately my arm got caught up in an equipment strap and it fell to the ground and rolled a few yards in front of me before exploding!

There was a lull in the firing and I broke cover and dashed forward to where Jim had set up our gun. As I slammed into the ground, I saw that Ken Christianson and another guy, Pfc Leo Lecuyer, had both been wounded. As Jim engaged with the enemy gun I moved along the hedge to see if I could help them. The lieutenant had been hit in the shoulder and Lecuyer was in very bad shape. I was applying a field dressing when a bullet hit Lecuyer's body, tearing him out of my arms and killing him. I then turned my attention to Christianson and doctored him up. As he crawled away, I prayed that he'd make it back to our medics in one piece. Before he left, I took his .45cal automatic pistol, as I knew he wouldn't be needing it where he was going.

This photo was taken in 2016 of the author in the I Company sector of Bloody Gully with Dave Rothmund (right) from Chicago. The recent heavy rain had washed this US 60mm mortar shell out from the earth bank where it had lain buried for over 70 years – could the round have possibly been left behind in 1944 by Jimmy Shuler or Harold Stedman? We will never know but they were the only two mortarmen working in this vicinity during the battle.

The struggle to advance had been just as difficult for G Company in Field 2 and they sustained almost 20 casualties, as Pfc Jimmy Martin recalls: "Due to a lack of ammunition we couldn't deploy our 60mm mortars. Before moving forward, we were ordered to fix bayonets and had just started to bridge the slope of the field when the intense shelling started. Most of 2 Platoon was in the center of the field but quickly dispersed to the hedges on either side. Shrapnel was flying everywhere and I was next to Pfc Owen Magie when he was killed. Sergeant Austin was caught in the face and Pvt Mull was badly wounded and died the following day." Machine-gun fire from an enemy gun was causing problems in Field 1 and was passing through the hedgerow on G Company's right flank. Its bullets were slowed by the hedge's dense earth bank, thus saving many from more severe injury.

But thanks to Shames' quick-thinking, Sink had already ordered in antitank guns and air support along with Second Battalion of the 502nd to plug the gap left by F Company. Earlier in the morning Brigadier General Maurice Rose, the 2nd Armored Division's commander, and General Taylor had worked out a plan of attack using Rose's tanks and airborne infantry reserves. This new force, which had only just cleared the beach, was sent, with supporting artillery, to relieve the beleaguered 506th at Bloody Gully. Some of the enemy fire was coming from an apple orchard on the left flank just beyond Field 3. Earlier Harwick and Shettle had sent an artillery observer up onto the high ground behind the gully to direct fire onto the enemy positions. But when the barrages failed to materialize, I Company had to deploy its two 60mm mortar teams. Although the gunners did not have enough ammunition to support a full counterattack, they were successfully able to silence the enemy machine guns in both the G and H Company areas as Private Harold Stedman, 3 Platoon, I Company, recalled:

> We did not have enough ammunition to support the counterattack. In the gully, Frank Lujan and I scrounged as many 60mm shells as we could from the people around us, and stuffed them in our cargo pockets, but still it wasn't enough. Staff Sergeant Jerry Beam pointed out our target on the map. Jimmy Shuler and Jerry O'Christie had the other tube and were ordered to take out the machine gun in the H Company area. We were deployed a short distance behind the gully where the ground was higher and devoid of overhanging branches. We set up roughly in line with our respective targets. I used the tube without its base plate and managed to put ten rounds into the orchard over to our front left. I guess we came close enough to keep them quiet for a while…

Although the short mortar barrage from I Company seemed to do the trick, Shettle and newly appointed I Company commander John Kiley both felt that the German positions in the orchard and field over on the left flank beyond the front line still posed a significant danger. Shettle ordered what remained of G Company to attempt a counterattack by joining forces with I Company and by 0745hrs they were ready to go.

The counterattack, comprising some 50 men, started around 0900hrs. Immediately I Company entered the orchard, they came under heavy fire from a concealed enemy position. The men had not gone more than 20 yards when German mortar shells began to rain down onto the tops of the densely planted trees. Showered with branches and leaves, Kiley was desperately trying to find a way to neutralize the enemy fire, but the overwhelming barrage forced him to withdraw.

At 1030hrs several Sherman tanks from 2nd Armored arrived via a dirt road east of the gully. I Company was extremely relieved to see them and watched in awe as the Shermans' 75mm rounds slammed into the western side of the orchard, temporarily breaking the enemy's grip. This was the opportunity that Kiley needed to extract his men, leaving the tanks to finish the job.

Back in Field 1, Third Battalion's right flank was in danger of crumbling and the attack had turned into defense. Later Colonel Chase would "sack" Bob Harwick from his role as battalion commander for his part in these events, clearly believing

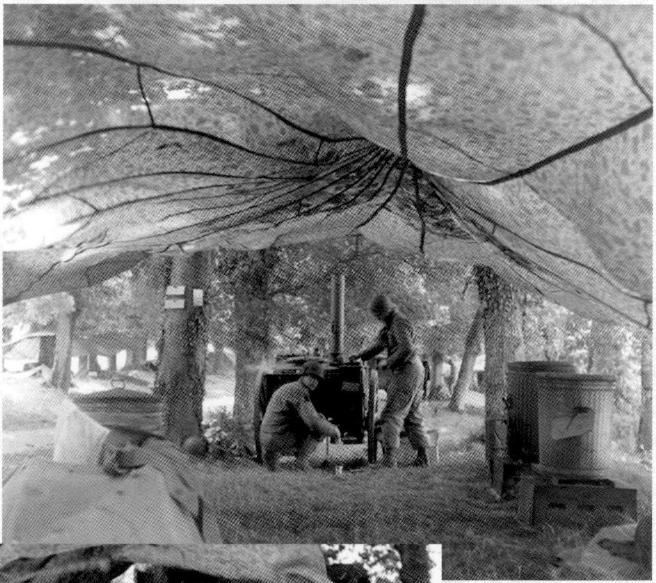

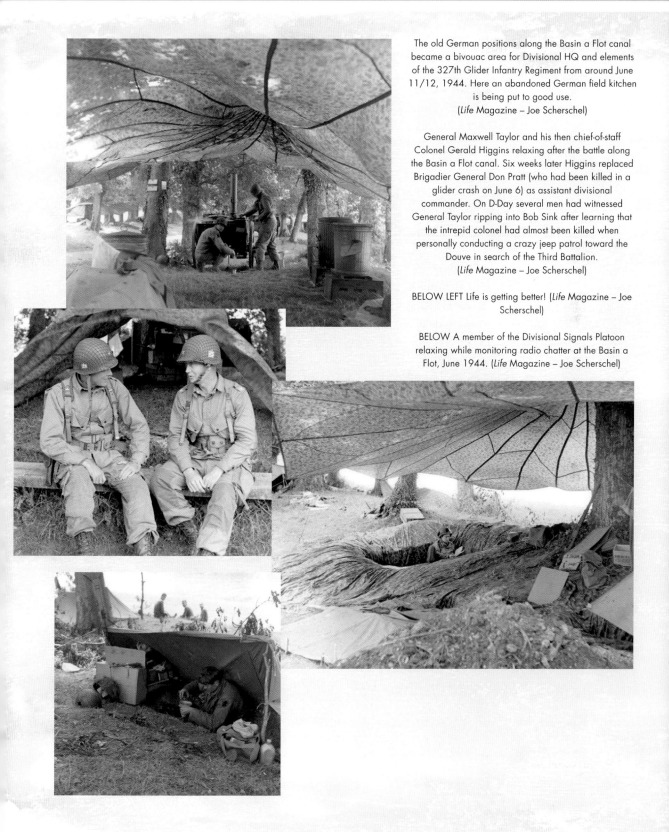

The old German positions along the Basin a Flot canal became a bivouac area for Divisional HQ and elements of the 327th Glider Infantry Regiment from around June 11/12, 1944. Here an abandoned German field kitchen is being put to good use. (*Life* Magazine – Joe Scherschel)

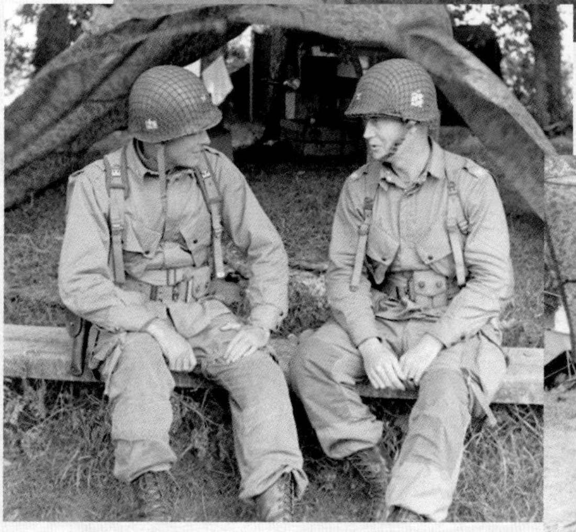

General Maxwell Taylor and his then chief-of-staff Colonel Gerald Higgins relaxing after the battle along the Basin a Flot canal. Six weeks later Higgins replaced Brigadier General Don Pratt (who had been killed in a glider crash on June 6) as assistant divisional commander. On D-Day several men had witnessed General Taylor ripping into Bob Sink after learning that the intrepid colonel had almost been killed when personally conducting a crazy jeep patrol toward the Douve in search of the Third Battalion. (*Life* Magazine – Joe Scherschel)

BELOW LEFT Life is getting better! (*Life* Magazine – Joe Scherschel)

BELOW A member of the Divisional Signals Platoon relaxing while monitoring radio chatter at the Basin a Flot, June 1944. (*Life* Magazine – Joe Scherschel)

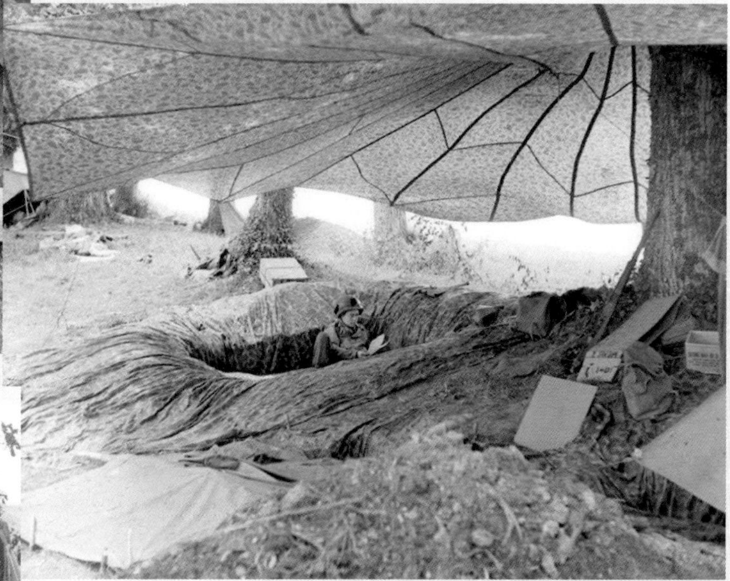

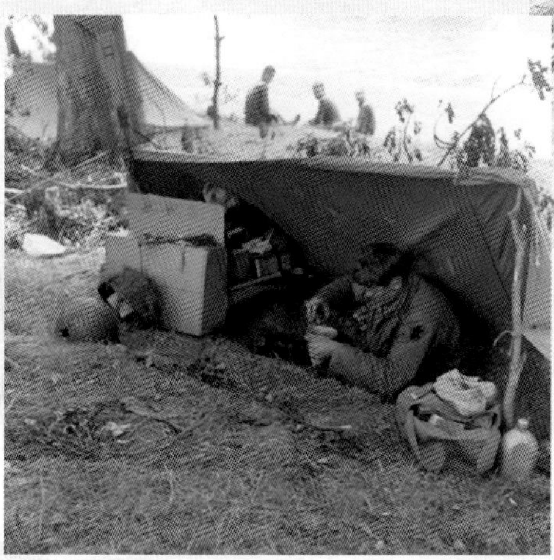

RIGHT Bob Sink and Charlie Chase (rear right) look on as tanks from 2nd Armored Division roll through Carentan, circa June 16, 1944. (NARA)

FAR RIGHT Carentan, June 20, 1944. S/Sgt Harry Clawson and S/Sgt Fred Bahlau, both from H Company, proudly wait beside S/Sgt Bruno Schroeder (Regimental HQ) to be called forward by General Taylor to receive their Silver Stars. Eight others were also honored that day, including Divisional Artillery Commander Tony McAuliffe. (NARA)

The first Silver Star Ceremony hosted by General Taylor took place in the town square in Carentan on June 15, 1944 to honor the 101st Airborne colonels Sink, Michaelis, Johnson and Harper. (NARA)

S/Sgt Bahlau pictured afterwards with a local lass admiring his Silver Star. (NARA)

A young Mongolian POW and a German child soldier being processed somewhere behind Utah Beach. The Mongolian forces were all but abandoned by the Germans during the evacuation of St-Côme-du-Mont. (NARA)

OPPOSITE PAGE Elements from 1 and 3 Platoons, H Company, were sent to Cherbourg along with 1/506 around June 22/23 to guard German prisoners. This photograph shows the garrison at Fort Roule surrendering to US forces on June 26. (NARA).

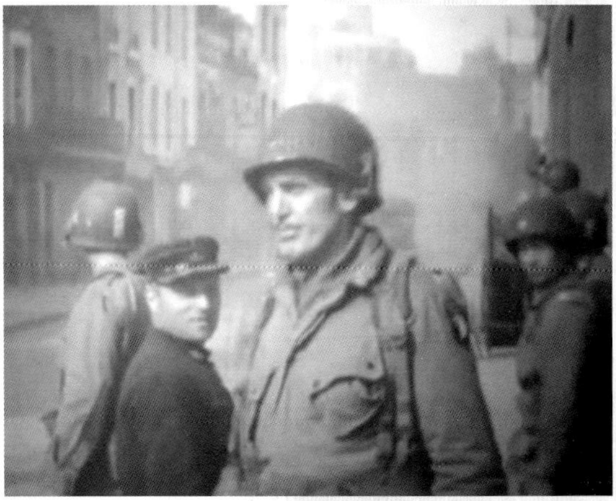

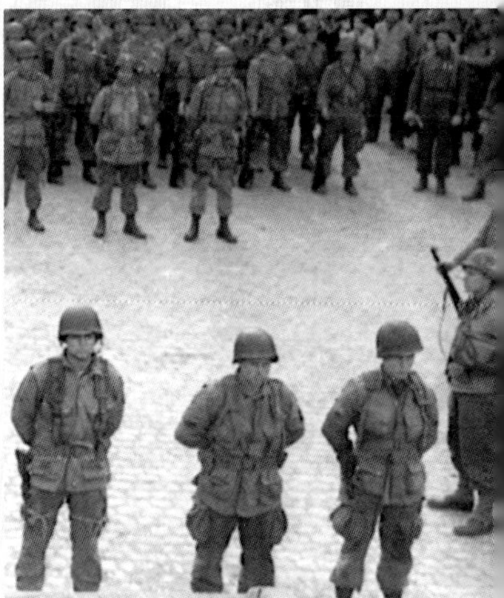

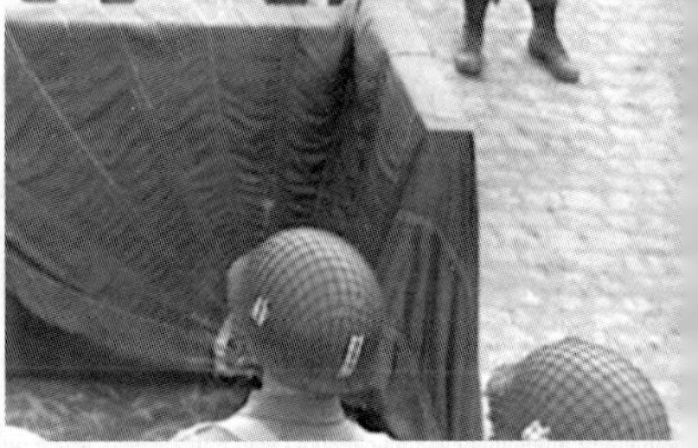

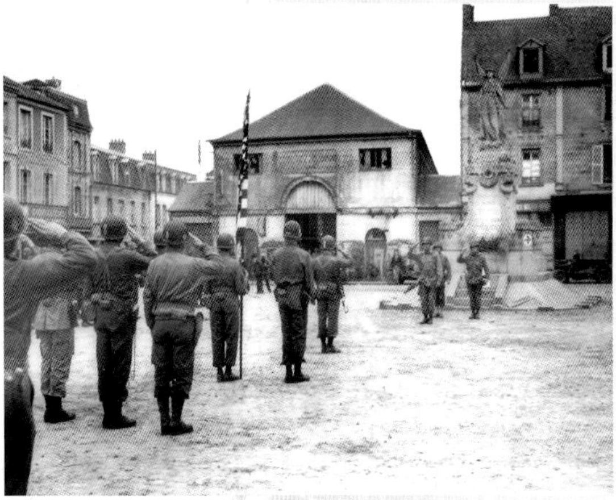

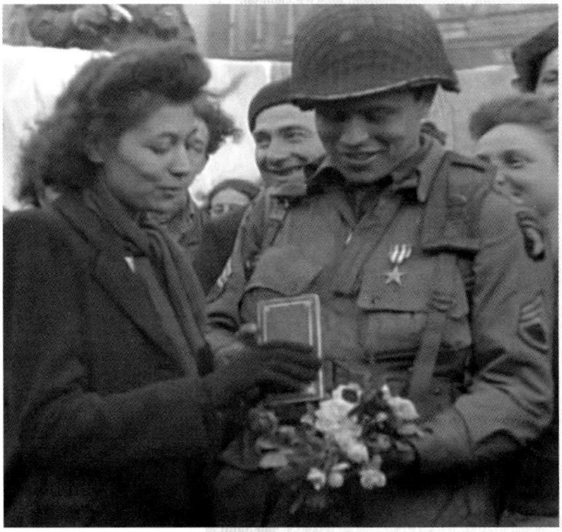

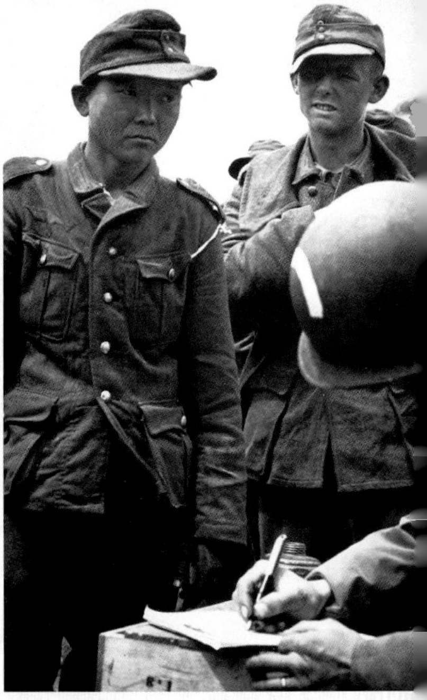

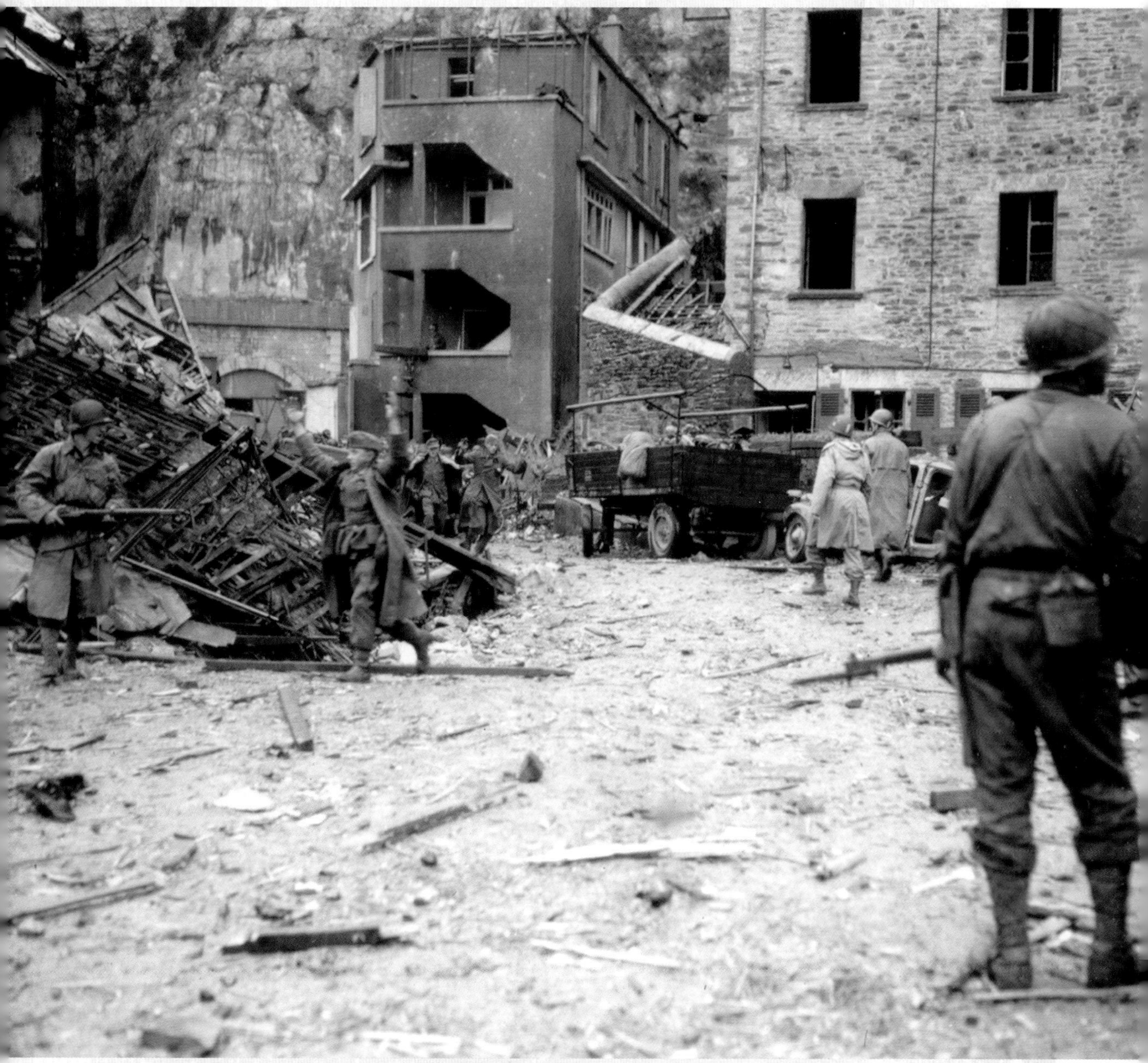

These Germans captured near Cherbourg seem more than happy to be prisoners of war. (NARA)

that he had been negligent. However, many considered his decision was far too harsh. Although the Germans were now also on the back foot there was still an enormous amount of activity to H Company's right as they headed back to the gully with German artillery exploding behind them. The gully was chaotic, and with radio communications still poor there were no clear orders coming through to tell the retreating soldiers what to do. Many just sat it out and waited for instructions that finally came via I Company, who transmitted the news that the battalion was pulling out under cover of the Shermans. It transpired that the Germans had commenced their attack simultaneously with the Americans. By mid-afternoon, the First Battalion of the 502nd had arrived with more tank support enabling Third Battalion to withdraw. In truth, the battle could have gone either way that day but thankfully the German units did not effectively communicate with each other either and as a result did not have the confidence to fully press home their attack. Luck had a lot to do with the final outcome, especially with guys like Ed Shames who just happened to be in the right place at the right time.

Third Battalion now formed part of the divisional reserve and began digging in on the western edge of Carentan. While in the canal's port area, Bob Sink and Maxwell Taylor made good their respective CPs in the town's courthouse, which had previously been a German HQ. From the perspective of the 506th, the Battle of Bloody Gully turned out to be the last serious engagement of its Normandy campaign. The following morning, June 14, the 502nd together with elements of the 327th Glider Regiment pushed south-westward from Carentan, mopping up German resistance as they went. By 1600hrs the 502nd had successfully linked up with the 82nd Airborne, 3 miles away at Baupte, removing any possible enemy threat to the 506th's western flank. Meanwhile, back in Carentan soldiers from the regiment were lining up for haircuts in the town's reopened barbershops! During the respite Major Oliver Horton was also appointed commander of 3/506, relieving the exhausted Captain Harwick who was returned to his old job with H Company.

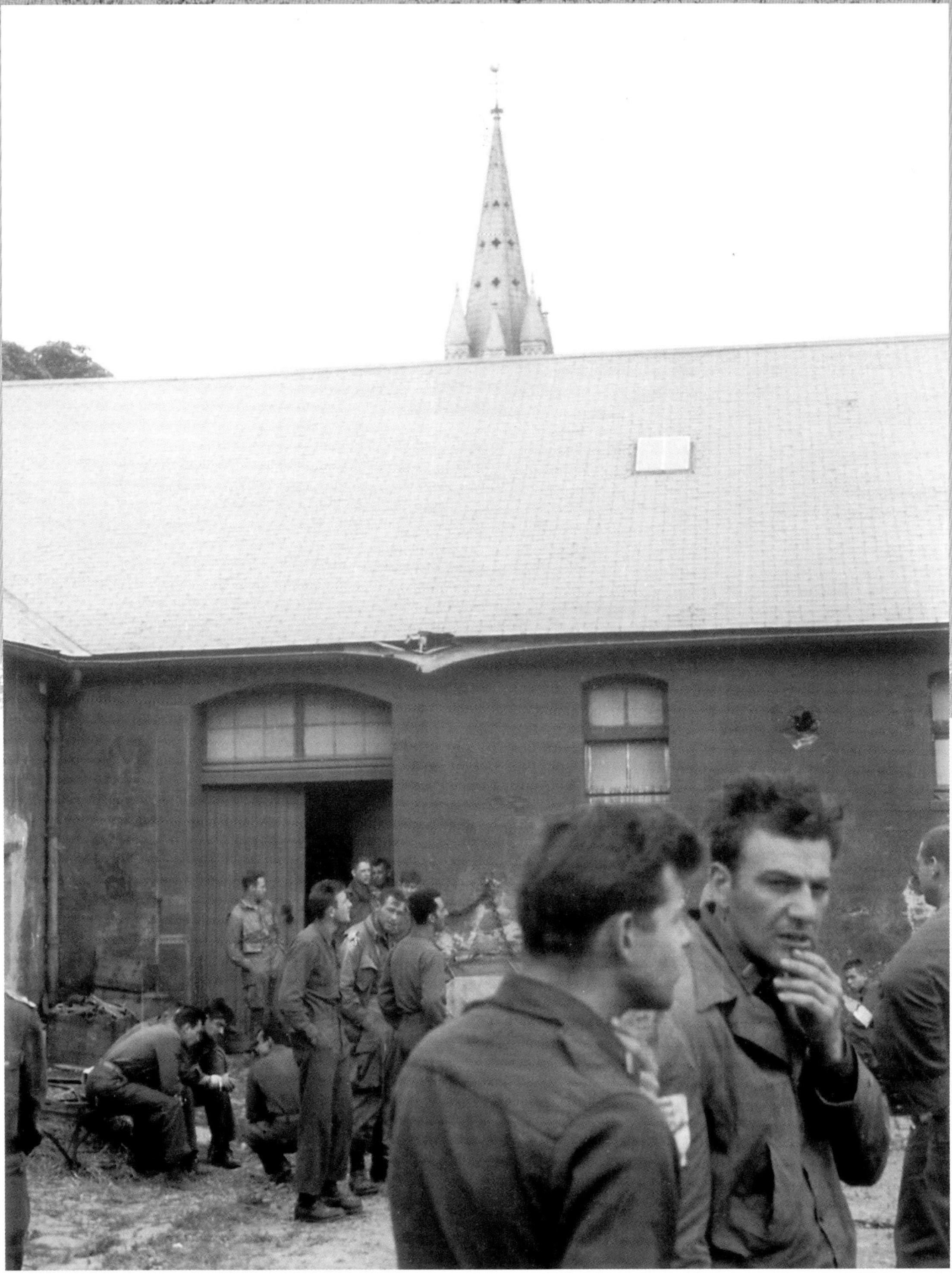

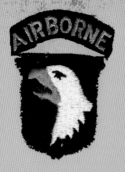

Chapter 4

# SEARCHING SOULS

## POWs 1944–45

At noon on D-Day, around 80 prisoners, mainly from the Third Battalion, were marched from le Ferage along the RN13 toward Carentan. As the group passed through St-Côme the men were alarmed by the number of German reinforcements entering the town. They had been on the road for about 15 minutes when the first naval bombardment came crashing in, scattering everyone into the marshes on both sides of the causeway. On arrival in Carentan, the POWs were joined by about 120 other captured soldiers, including a number of British and Canadians prisoners. There the men were packed into trucks and driven south to St-Lô. Shortly after leaving Carentan the convoy was attacked by a pair of Spitfires, leaving several dead and dozens wounded. The battered trucks finally arrived in St-Lô during the early afternoon and the prisoners were marched to a temporary compound on the northern side of the city.

June 6, 1944. Cpl Marty Clark from the Third Battalion's Machine Gun Platoon (looking at camera) and Communications Sgt John Taormina (seen here in background) are among the first Allied prisoners to arrive at Dépôt de Remonte, St-Lô. (ECPAD)

The walled complex at Dépôt de Remonte in St-Lô was made up of a number of huge stable blocks and was therefore perfect for containment. Later that day, June 6, the Allies began bombing the city, and although much of the center was badly

damaged the stables remained untouched. However, the large civilian hospital was hit and its 700 patients evacuated to the nearby German underground hospital. The German hospital was overwhelmed and the following day most of the wounded prisoners from Third Battalion were moved to Mortain, where the Germans had established a military hospital in a historic abbey. By late July, with the front line moving closer to Mortain, the hospital was evacuated to Rennes, where the Germans had converted an old French garrison into a prison, Frontstalag 221, complete with its own hospital.

By July 27, the Allies had broken out of Normandy. By then the prison hospital at Rennes was in a terrible state as the Germans had been unable to supply food or medicine to the wounded POWs for some time. As the Allies closed in on Rennes, the hospital came under heavy shellfire. After that it did not take long for the last remaining Germans to beat a hasty retreat, and on August 4 General Patton's Third Army rolled in. Next began the task of liberating the hospital's 574 American, British and Canadian patients back to the UK.

Meanwhile, the POWs who had been left behind at St-Lô at Dépôt de Remonte were sent on June 7 to a makeshift camp – Hôtellerie Notre-Dame – in the village of Troisgots, a few miles south of St-Lô. Due to the lack of food, the place soon became known as "Starvation Hill." Here the men were split into three distinct groups. The main body, numbering around 700, was then sent southwest by road to the military base at Rennes where they too would be housed in Frontstalag 221. This group included those whose footwear had been stolen by the Germans. Two smaller groups were also mobilized for movement in a southeastly direction to transit camps at Alençon and Chartres. The first departed by truck around June 10, and the other followed on foot two weeks later.

On the afternoon of June 7, 1944, the Hôtellerie Notre-Dame at Troisgots became a temporary prison for the POWs evacuated from St-Lô. Named "Starvation Hill" by the prisoners, their short stay was marred by the desperate lack of food. The building was ideally suited to being a prison as it was partly surrounded by a high wall.

# THE BROWN BROTHERS

Shortly before D-Day, Jack Brown's squad from I Company was "volunteered" for a special mission. Transferred by truck to North Witham Airfield, they were informed that they were to act as security for the Third Battalion Pathfinder detachment.

The I Company detachment landed south of St-Côme on the other side of the church; unable to assemble, they went to ground and waited for daybreak. Jack ended up in an enclosed field at the back of the town with his squad leader, Sergeant Sid McCallum, in a small group led by an arrogant officer from the 501st. Two members of the Third Battalion's junior staff were also present, Sergeant Joe Gorenc (whom Jack and Sid knew well) and Corporal Bill Atlee. Shortly after dawn, Atlee was killed in an ambush and the group split in all directions, leaving Jack alone.

On June 8, just as German forces were withdrawing from St-Côme, fearing he'd been compromised, Jack shot an enemy soldier. His "victim" was very young and as the boy's life ebbed away they struck up a whispered conversation. The last words the German kid uttered stayed with Jack for the rest of his life. Shortly afterwards Jack was captured and eventually ended up at a work camp in Kleinweiler, Bavaria. Over the following seven months Jack did a variety of jobs, from tree felling to railway and canal repairs, plus snow clearance during the exceptionally harsh winter of 1944/45. After being accidentally hit on the knee with an axe by one of the German guards, Jack was hospitalized and underwent surgery, but the wound became infected. With a sky-high temperature, fearing the worst, one of the doctors simply shut Jack in a freezing empty barrack block. Luckily the low temperatures broke the fever, but he was left with a permanent limp. When the camp was liberated by French Moroccan troops on April 29, 1945, Jack's weight had plummeted to a mere 89 pounds.

He eventually boarded a ship on May 26 and sailed for the United States. It was only after arriving home that Jack learned that his brother had been killed in Belgium.

Twins Jim and Jack (right) Brown pictured in 1943 outside their parents' house at Oakland, California. (Byron & Robby Moore)

# Dépôt de Remonte, St-Lô – June 6, 1944

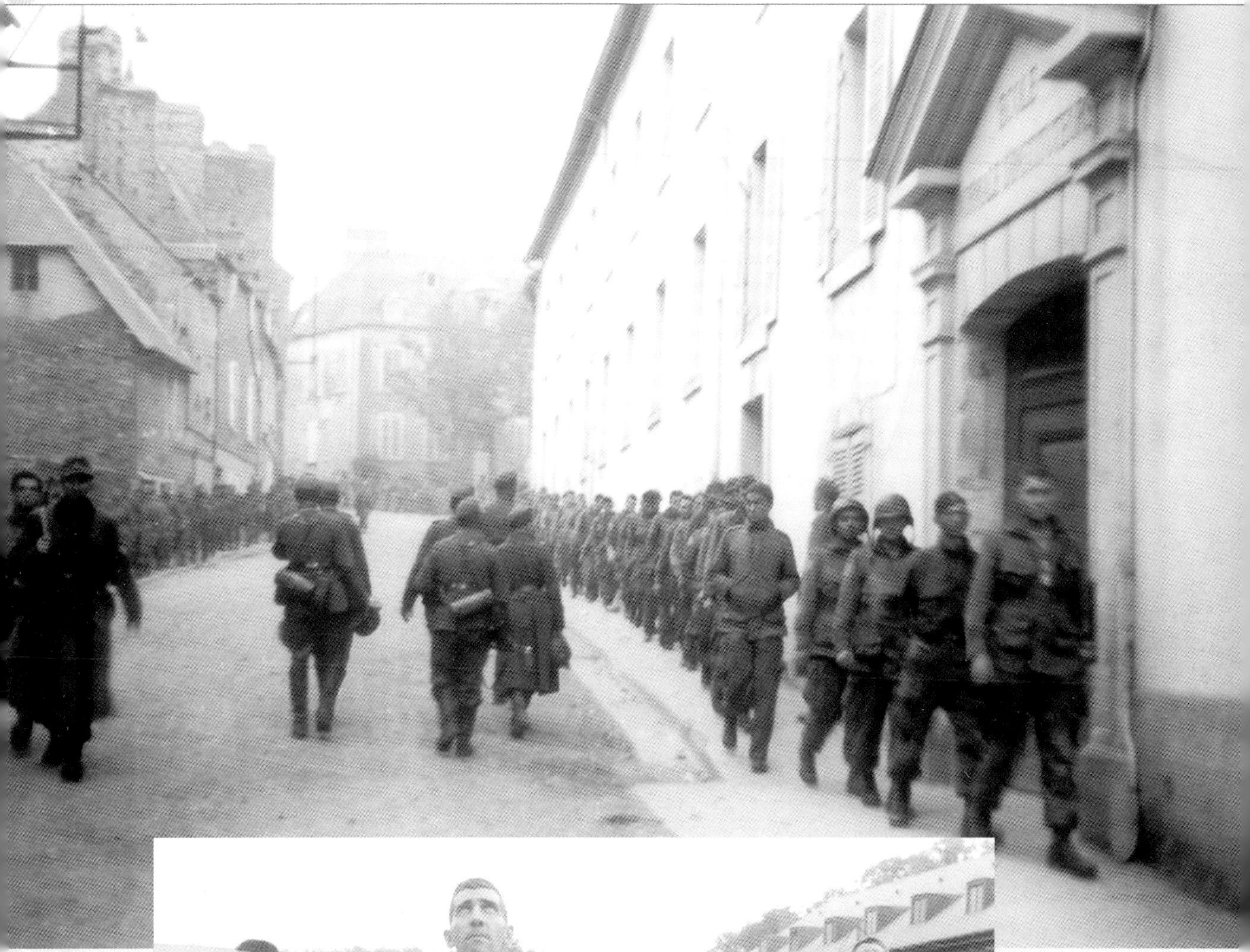

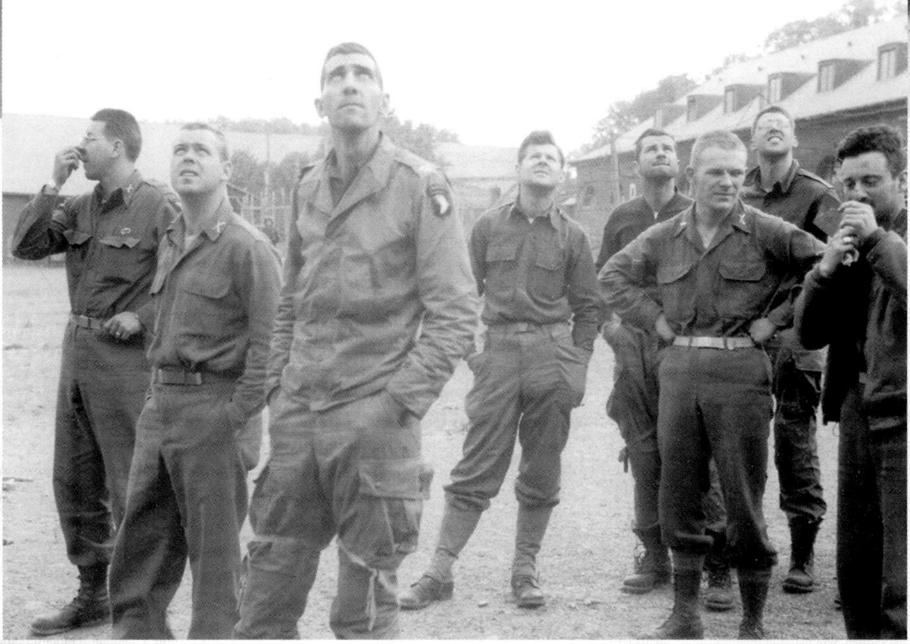

OPPOSITE TOP 1300hrs June 6, near the northern edge of St-Lô. The first prisoners to arrive were de-trucked and marched to the cavalry barracks which was only a few hundred yards away from where this picture was taken. (ECPAD)

OPPOSITE BOTTOM I Company commander John McKnight (third from left) watching Allied bombers approaching the town of St-Lô. John was held captive for 13 months and by the time he was liberated his weight had dropped to 67lbs. (ECPAD)

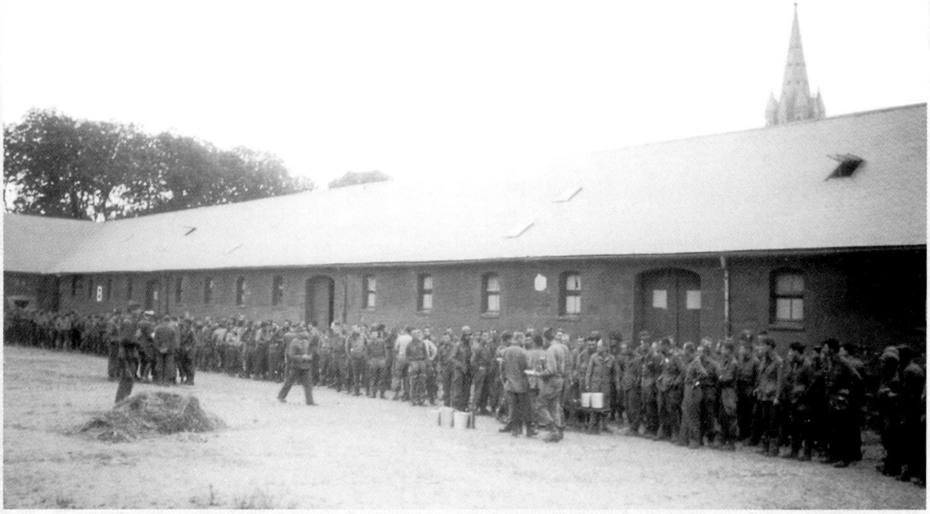

As the afternoon wore on the men were told to stand in line and were fed their first meal of the day – a very thin, watery soup. On the left a German officer and his team are interrogating a number of prisoners. In the background is the church of Ste-Croix. (ECPAD)

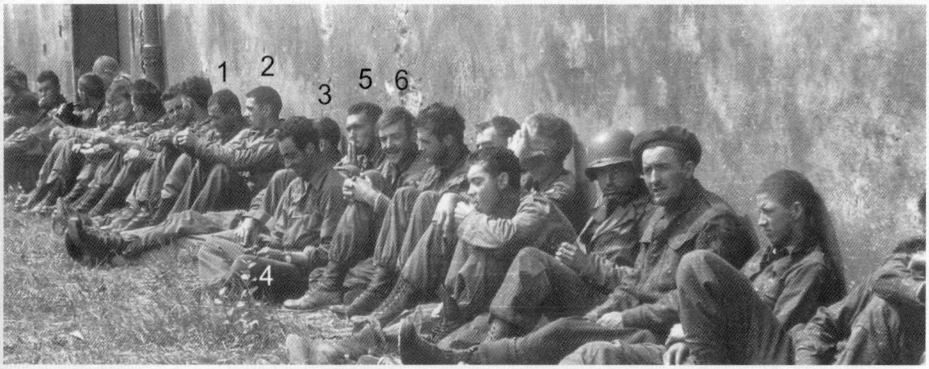
1
2
3
5
6
4

Sitting amongst this group of prisoners are six men from HQ Company from Third Battalion: (1) Cpl Clarence Kelley, (2) Pvt Joe Mielcarek, (3) Cpl Marty Clark (partially hidden), (4) S/Sgt John Taormina, (5) Pfc Don Ross and (6) T/5 Charles Riley. Taormina, Ross and Riley all jumped with Colonel Wolverton over St-Côme. (ECPAD)

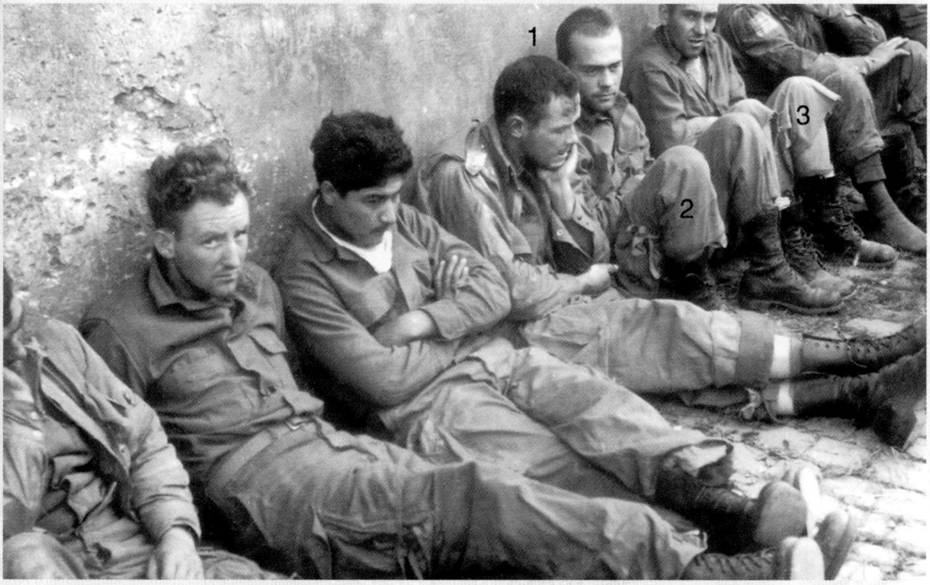
1
3
2

More of the same group: (1) Cpl Marty Clark, (2) Cpl Clarence Kelley and (3) Pvt Joe Mielcarek – all members of the Machine Gun Platoon. Marty and Joe were among those who escaped while en route to Châlons and made it back to England. On October 6, outside the battalion CP at Boelenham Farm near Opheusden, Marty was badly wounded by a mortar burst and a fragment of shrapnel pierced his right lung, almost killing him. (ECPAD)

# JOHNNY GIBSON

On June 9, after a three-day journey covering nearly 56 miles, Johnny arrived at the evacuation hospital in Mortain:

"I was told I'd be working with another airborne medic and Mike Weiden appeared in the doorway. I couldn't believe my eyes and ran over, throwing my arms around him, crying in disbelief. After we had both calmed down, Mike told me he'd been there for a couple of days and had arrived with the wounded from St-Lô. A room on the second floor had been set-aside for wounded prisoners and we were working under a German medical officer who Mike called "the Commandant." This guy was about 50 years old and handled workloads that would have pushed younger men to their limits. He treated all patients from both sides equally – hell, after a week or so he even put me on his payroll – which turned a few heads especially at my first pay parade!

A Spanish family lived and worked at the hospital assisted by two local girls. The husband seemed to be a decent man but his family would have nothing to do with me even though I spoke good Spanish. On the 10th two men were brought in with severe gunshot wounds. One was an airborne engineer called Henry Loebe. Both were in a critical condition and needed specialist care. An ambulance arrived the following day and moved a number of patients including Zol Rosenfield, Jack Harrison, Richie Johnn (whose leg was in bad shape and had to be amputated) and the two new arrivals. I stayed behind but Mike Weiden and one of our orderlies traveled with the guys to Stalag 221. Richie was lying on a stretcher in the hallway and the French girls wished him luck and kissed him on the cheek. As he was leaving Henry Loebe grabbed my arm and said, 'If I ever get out of this alive, I'll owe my life to you buddy… see you later,' and waved goodbye.

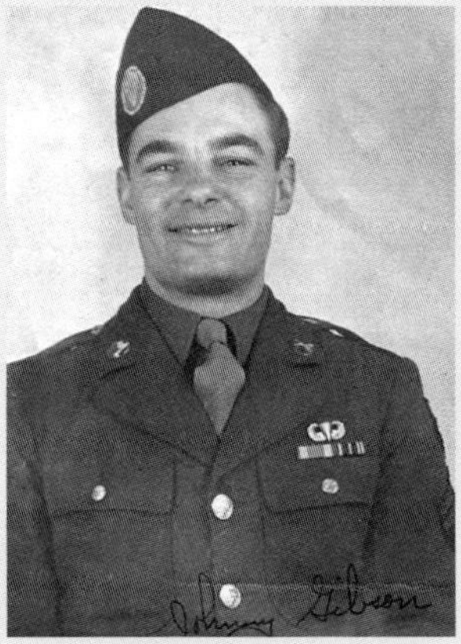
Johnny Gibson
Corporal John Gibson from Tucson, Arizona. (Johnny Gibson)

Two weeks after Weiden's departure for Rennes, the number of patients under my care had risen to over forty. They varied in rank from colonel to private and came from various Allied divisions. Although I was a prisoner it did not alter the fact that I was still an American paratrooper. I cherished my role and was always neat and presentable. Once a week one of the French girls would take my uniform home to wash and iron. One person who objected to this was the heavily built German head chef who ran the kitchen. Sly and disagreeable, he hated all Americans and went out of his way to make life difficult for me. However, his English speaking-assistant, who had worked as a butler in New York before the war, was the total opposite, but could not protect me from the daily harassment dished out by his boss.

Summer arrived with a vengeance and the heat encouraged flies. Bandages and medicines were in short supply, but the resulting maggots did us a favor by helping to clean the festering wounds. By the beginning of July, the Allies had total air superiority. Most of the French rail network had been damaged or destroyed, and the Germans were only able to move safely by night. Ambulances were continually arriving at Mortain but, despite the fact they were all clearly marked with red crosses, some had been strafed and I was often dragged outside to look at damaged vehicles. As the tide of war turned in our favor, attitudes began to harden and I felt more vulnerable especially when German soldiers, en route to the front, would stop for food at the hospital kitchen. The head chef would often encourage soldiers up to the second floor to stare at the wounded and verbally abuse me. By late July the front line moved closer to Mortain and it was decided to evacuate the hospital. Under cover of darkness, we were driven to Stalag 221 where I was reunited with Mike Weiden.

The prison hospital at Rennes was heavily guarded and ringed with barbed wire. Weiden was at his wits' end trying to cope with all the problems facing him. The conditions within the hospital were deplorable. The Germans were no longer able to supply the hospital and food was scarce. The only medical supplies left were crepe bandages and an antiseptic tincture called Mercurochrome. There was no gauze, tape, aspirin, sulfa powder, or proper sanitation – it was a total "hell hole." I thought Mortain was bad, but this was far worse.

I asked Mike Weiden how Henry Loebe was doing and was saddened to learn that he'd died soon after arriving at Rennes. Mike gave me the job of looking after 14 seriously wounded in a room on the main floor. One of the first men I recognized was Zol Rosenfield who looked like a skeleton, as did most of the

wounded. As the Allies closed in, so the hospital came under heavy shellfire. Someone got permission to go outside with a white sheet and managed to stop the shelling. It wasn't long before the few remaining Germans took off, leaving two Polish soldiers to guard us. I had been at Rennes for precisely one week but it seemed much longer. As soon as the Krauts left, the Polish unloaded their rifles and handed them over to us. On August 4 General Patton's Third Army liberated Rennes, which was an incredible day full of joy and happiness.

Next began the task of evacuating the hospital's 574 patients to Britain. The process took three days and Third Army threw every resource it had at the problem. We were going to be reassigned to another outfit in France as our request to return to 3/506 had been denied. A couple of days later Mike and I were sent to a marshaling area in Cherbourg and split up. Finally, two weeks later after a heck of a lot of messing around I was flown back to London in a Piper Cub and after a few nights on the town headed back to Ramsbury."

Johnny Gibson returned to Abbaye Blanche circa 2005 and is seen here on the main steps with one of the resident Catholic nuns, Sister Sarah.

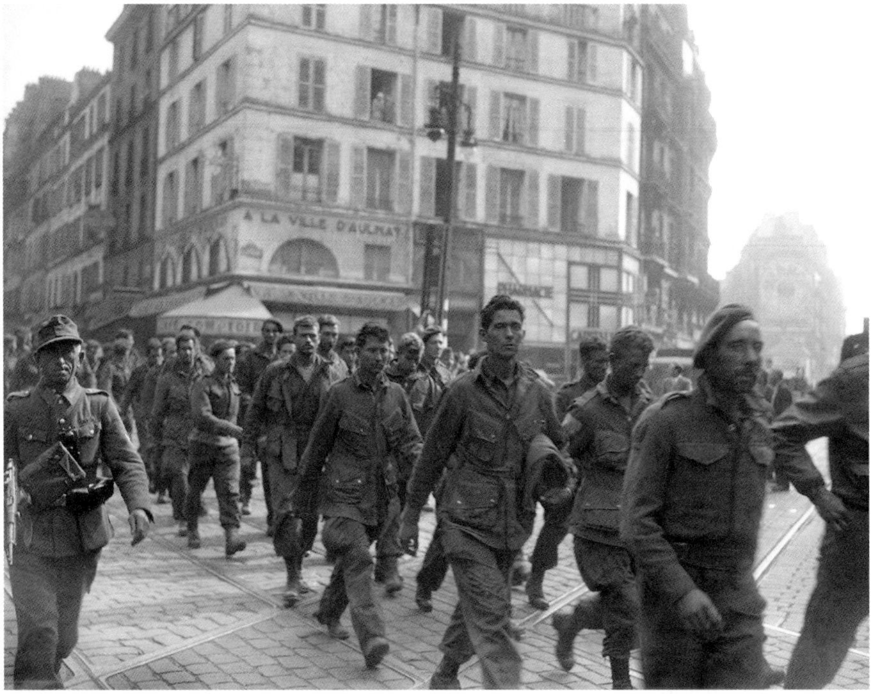
A LA VILLE D'AULNAY

Allied prisoners captured on and shortly after D-Day being marched through Paris, circa June 20, 1944. American and British paratroopers are clearly visible in both photographs. (Photo by Keystone-France/ Gamma-Keystone via Getty Images)

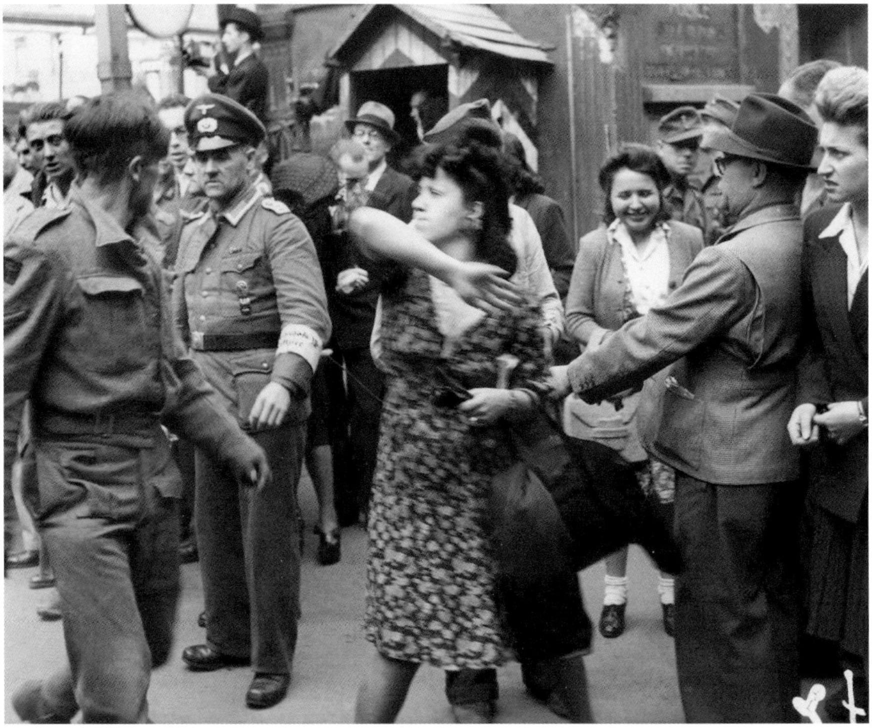

Finally, the column reached Gare de l'Est station where some civilians, like this woman, took great pleasure in abusing the unfortunate captives. (Photo by Keystone-France/ Gamma-Keystone via Getty Images)

Shortly after their arrival at Alençon, a number of men from the first group were selected for a march through Paris. In total, some 2,000 Allied prisoners converged on Paris for the "Walk of Shame" that took place around June 20. Flanked by armed guards, the prisoners were formed into three enormous columns and marched through the city to Gare de l'Est railway station. At the head of the column were dozens of cameramen, all eager to photograph every aspect of the "humiliated" servicemen. Loudspeakers were dotted along the route, spewing propaganda along the lines of "all paratroopers are convicted criminals and rapists!"

From Gare de l'Est, the POWs, including men from Third Battalion, were loaded aboard dozens of boxcars and sent via Château Thierry to Reims and then onto Frontstalag 194, a former French Army cavalry barracks, at Châlons-sur-Marne. Although every available rail network was utilized, the journey to Châlons still took 23 days as the tracks were in constant need of repair due to Allied bombing. Many POWs saw these "hold ups" as a chance to escape, but when SS guards were brought in to carry out spot checks and head counts the escapes stopped due to a genuine fear of reprisals.

The sanitation and water supplies at Frontstalag 194 were poor but at least the men received one Red Cross food parcel each week. Some of the enlisted guys were only held at Châlons for a few days before being sent southeast across Germany to Memmingen VII-B in Bavaria. Here, like many other private soldiers, they were put to work felling trees, repairing railways and canals and clearing snow and ice during the harsh winter of 1944/45. This camp was finally liberated by French Moroccans on April 29, 1945 and the POWs eventually returned by ship to the United States.

Meanwhile, approximately 1,000 POWs were moved from Châlons to Limburg Stalag XII-A in Germany in mid to late August when it became clear that Paris would soon be liberated. This POW camp was situated south of the Ruhr valley a few miles east of Koblenz and close to the border with Belgium and France. As a transit camp the primary function was to process all newly captured POWs before sending them on to other camps deeper inside Germany. Traditionally the new arrivals would be interviewed, documented, and issued prison numbers. Due to the transient nature of the camp, no letters or Red Cross parcels were possible. However, the men were allowed to fill in one postcard containing the most basic information, which was then sent via the Red Cross to the next of kin. In total, the Stalag held around 20,000 soldiers who came from all corners of the globe. The men from Normandy were assigned to three large marquees with straw scattered across the floor, but conditions were still tolerable with the prisoners receiving three small meals a day. By November it had begun to turn cold and by December around 7,500 more Americans arrived from Belgium after the Battle of the Bulge, which coincided with the worst winter in 50 years.

Joe Beyrle was Capt John McKnight's radio operator for Normandy and was captured in St-Côme by von der Heydte's men on June 6, although, thanks to the loss of his dog tags, he was presumed killed. In January 1945, after several disastrous attempts, Joe successfully escaped from Stalag III-C Altdrewitz, near the Polish border at Küstren. "Two days later, after walking toward the sound of advancing artillery fire, I ran into a Soviet tank squadron who, much to my amazement, were using 'Lend-Lease' Shermans. The only Russian words I knew were Amerikanskii Tovarisch (American Comrade), which at least kept them from shooting me. The Russian troops quickly found an officer who spoke a little English and I was able to explain my situation. Somewhat reluctantly the Russians handed me a submachine gun and a brief lesson on how to look after it. I was assigned to one of the tanks, whose commander was a woman, and became one of her supporting infantrymen." Ironically Stalag III-C was liberated a few days later, after a 48-hour tank battle, and around 25,000 Allied POWs were set free.

One month later Joe was wounded in the groin. Years later Beyrle learned that his tank commander, the legendary Aleksandra Samusenko, who at 23 was only a year older than him, had been killed just one month after he was wounded. He was eventually repatriated back to the United States on the HMTS Samaria, the same passenger liner that had brought the 506th to the UK on September 15, 1943. Here Joe is pictured reunited with his parents, who in his long absence had held a funeral mass for their son. One of Joe's sons, John Beyrle, would eventually return to Russia as the US ambassador, while another, Joe Beyrle II, served in the Vietnam War as part of the 101st Airborne Division. (Joe Beyrle II)

By early January 1945, the camp was dangerously overcrowded, so approximately 400 men originally captured in Normandy were sent by rail to the American NCO prison camp at Fürstenburg III-B, southeast of Berlin. Three weeks later thousands more POWs were forced-marched east by the Germans along three routes. The northern route emanated from East Prussia and followed a course through Pomerania to Fallingbostel. The southern began at Teschen near Auschwitz and continued through Czechoslovakia to Moosburg in Bavaria. The central route started in Silesia and finished at Luckenwalde III-A near Berlin. The event became known as "The Long" or "The Hunger March," and thousands died on the much longer northern and southern routes, with many POWs, like John McKnight of Third Battalion, forced to cover a distance of 500 miles or more.

Pfc Don Ross (right) having fun with a fellow ex-POW buddy and two US Army girls in Paris, June 1945. Ross had survived incarceration in an offshoot of the infamous Flossenbürg concentration camp near Sokolov in Czechoslovakia. In early March, with the Allies virtually on the doorstep, the POWs had risen up and disarmed their captors. Ross subsequently served alongside Czech guerrillas as well as the Red Army before eventually linking up with US forces, by which time he had long hair, a beard and weighed around 115lbs.

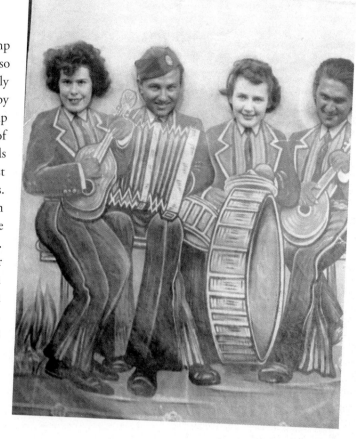

There were already 7,000 men at Luckenwalde III-A, and the huge influx of starving POWs who had survived the forced march made living conditions there extremely difficult. The POWs were herded into an area containing seven enormous circus tents. All through March the weather was horrendous, with high winds and heavy rain ripping into the "big tops." Luckenwalde was finally liberated on April 23, 1945, and all of the POWs from the 101st Division were flown to Mourmelon in France, where the division still had a rear-echelon presence, before being returned to the United States.

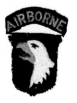

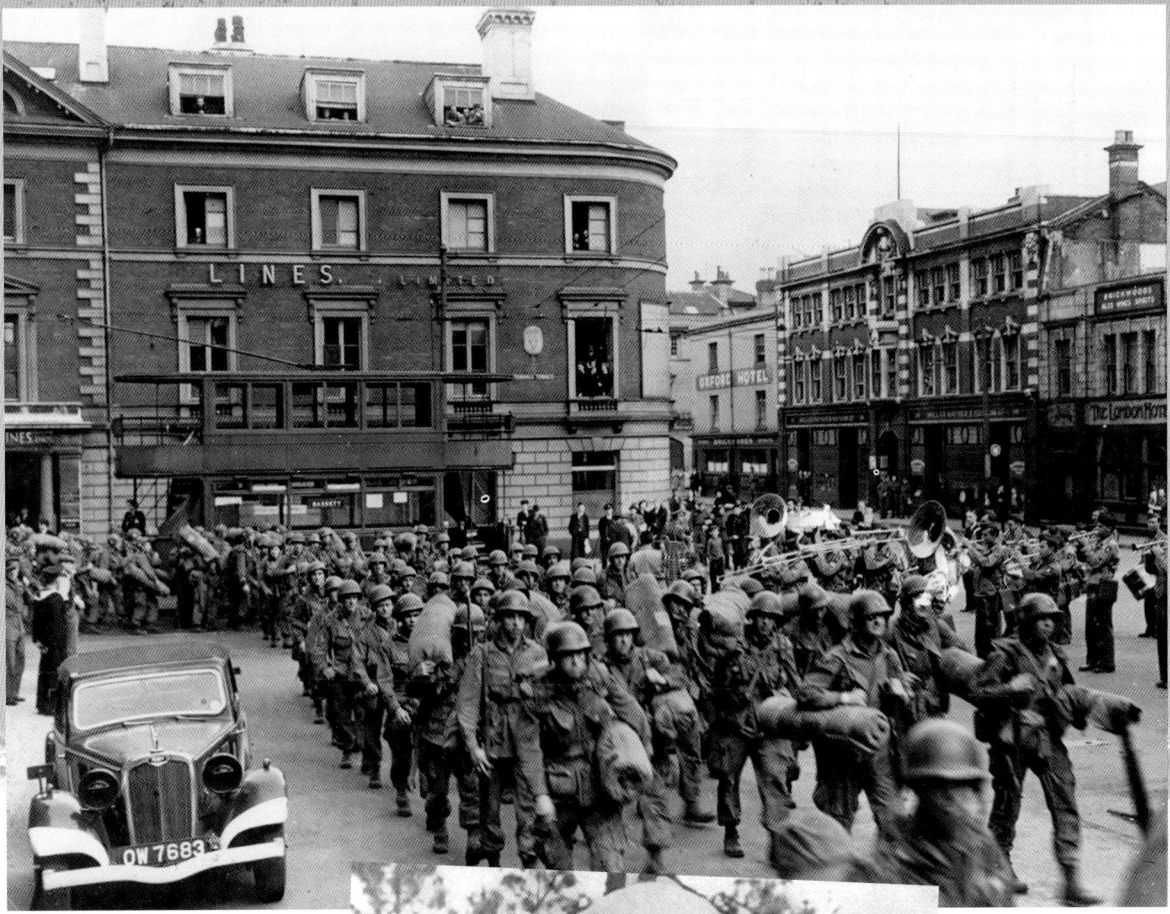
LINES.
OXFORD HOTEL
OW 7683

A band plays as elements of the 101st Airborne Division march through Southampton toward the town's railway station. (Johnny Gibson)

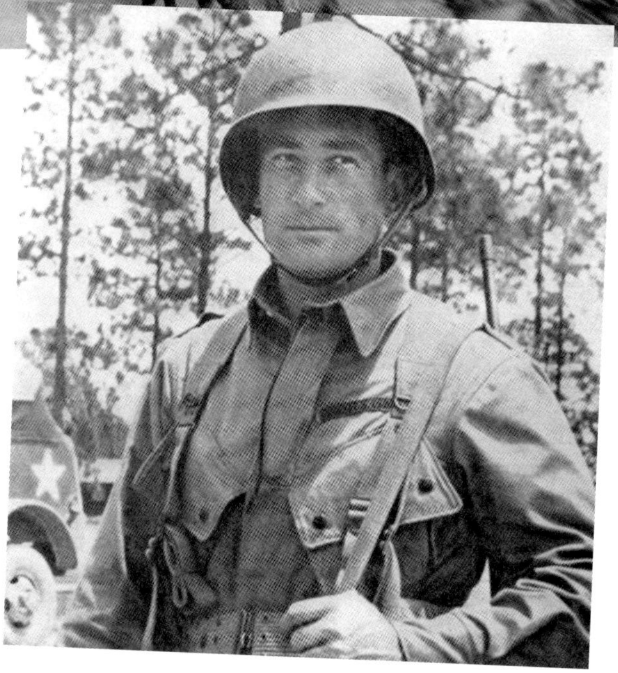

Maj Oliver Horton was formally given command of 3/506 on June 19, approximately two weeks after Bob Wolverton's death. Horton was a southerner from North Carolina, who had previously worked for Col Robert Strayer in 2/506 as his Executive Officer. Horton did not quite possess the same tactical ability as Wolverton, but nevertheless he was a more than capable leader.

## Chapter 5

# TIME IS SHORT

## Return to England and False Alarms

For those members of the battalion who had returned from Normandy in July 1944 physically unscathed, it seemed that they had moved from one life into another. While in France, the 101st Division had forged a formidable reputation among the Germans, earning the nickname "butchers with big pockets." There can be no doubt that the contribution made by the 506th had only served to enhance the reputation for brutal efficiency.

"Home" for Third Battalion was still Ramsbury, which, despite all that the men had gone through, remained just as tranquil as it had seemed before. The only sign that there was still a war on was the sound of transport aircraft coming and going from the airfield up on the hill.

Once again, Parliament Piece was utilized as a home away from home for the junior officers. Most of the seniors were relocated to other locations around the village and there were a number of other changes to the battalion's table of organization. The most serious change affected H Company, where Captain Jim Walker was given command after Bob Harwick joined the battalion staff as Executive Officer.

To celebrate the battalion's return from Normandy, two parties were hastily organized and took place on consecutive evenings in Marlborough Town Hall. The first, for all the 506th officers, was held on Friday, July 14, with the following evening reserved exclusively for the enlisted men from Third Battalion. It is fair to say that a good night was had by all! After receiving a sizeable amount of back pay, the regiment was given seven days' leave and set off to places all around the United Kingdom for fun and frolics.

As the weeks passed, more and more escapees began to drift in. These soldiers were classified as Zone of the Interior, which meant that they could return to the USA to recover and/or take up training posts. Even though it was well within their rights to do so, every single Third Battalion man refused the "ZI" option and instead opted to return to the unit. The more seriously wounded were still recovering in medical facilities up and down the country.

On August 10, a parade took place on Hungerford Common, led by General Eisenhower himself. The review was followed by an awards ceremony, where it was announced that the 101st Airborne Division would now be part of the First Allied Airborne Army, under command of US Lieutenant General Lewis Brereton. The "First Triple A," as it was known, was an amalgamation of British, American and Polish airborne forces and in total now comprised nearly 30,000 men.

Hardened by battle, 3/506 had learned a lot about each other, but the new training program was going to be as tough as anything that had gone before. It was a question of trying to bring each new replacement to the same level and experience of the combat veterans, although this time around, not necessarily by the book. The

LEFT This picture was taken in the graveyard of St Peter's church, Marlborough, probably at the time of the enlisted men's party. Slightly worse for wear are, from left, Pvt Earl Widmen, Pvt Harold Stedman, and Pfc Walter "Luke" Lukasavage, all 3 Platoon, I Company. Harold would go on to save Luke's life on September 22, near Veghel. Luke was horrifically wounded when a German tank opened fire as he was taking aim with a bazooka. "Luke was hit in the face and neck before he had a chance to fire," recalled Harold. "For a moment, I thought he wasn't going to make it, as his head was a mess with blood pouring everywhere. I had a T-shirt that Jim Brown's sister Juanita (whom we all knew as Johnny) had sent me a week or two before Holland. Taking the clean white shirt, I stuffed it into the gaping hole in Luke's jaw before dragging him down a dirt ditch to our medic, Bill Kidder." Lukasavage spent the next two years recuperating. (Harold Stedman)

RIGHT 1st Sgt Fred Bahlau (HQ Company) sitting on the bridge over the River Kennet near the old watermill at Ramsbury during August 1944. Fred subsequently won a second Silver Star at Opheusden. After Bastogne, "Fast Freddie" was awarded a battlefield commission and posted to C Company. (Fred Bahlau via Mark Bando Collection)

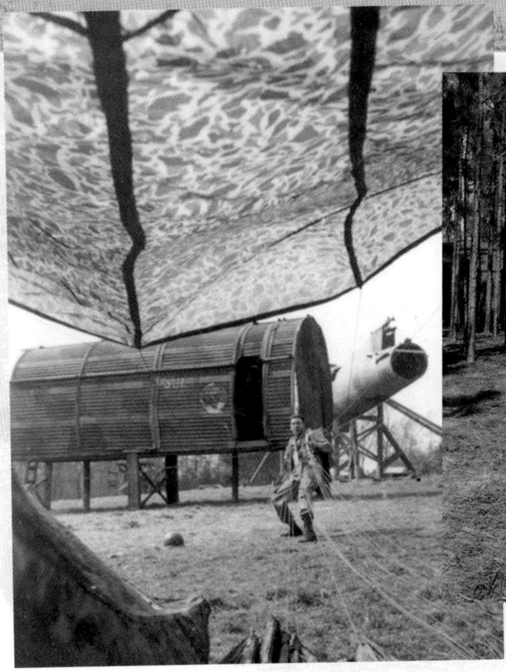

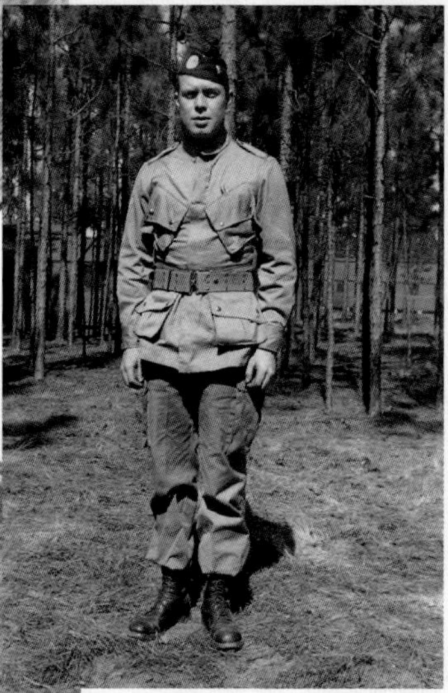

FAR LEFT The para-school at Chilton Foliat went into overdrive in the aftermath of the Normandy Campaign trying to train and qualify the new blood now flowing into the regiment. (NARA)

LEFT The original leader of 1 Platoon, I Company, was Gerry Howard Jr from Ohio. Gerry was killed along with everyone from "Chalk 15" when his plane went down in Normandy. The enormous loss of men from I Company in the Normandy campaign meant that the new replacements had no time to get to properly know each other or their senior NCOs before Holland. On September 18, the company suffered heavy casualties north of Vlokhoven, including Howard's own replacement, Mickey Panovich. (Bill Galbraith)

battalion wanted the new men to fit in and did their level best to treat them accordingly. But green replacements still had to be drilled and instilled with the same esprit de corps. The lessons learned in Normandy were enormous, key among them not to underestimate the ability of the enemy. Range work and field problems on Salisbury Plain began in earnest, including combat training against armored vehicles. Several daylight parachute exercises took place, with emphasis being placed on efficient assembly drills.

At 1100hrs on Sunday, August 27, a memorial service took place in the grounds of Littlecote Park to honor the 414 men of the 506th killed or still missing in Normandy. An organ prelude and a hymn were followed by an address by Chaplain Tildon McGee, with the title "Our Heroic Dead." Bob Harwick wrote of the ceremony:

> It doesn't take long for the less pleasant phases of combat to be forgotten; most likely because you don't want to remember. Sunday afternoon formations are never popular and after having worked five straight weekends, the griping was wonderful to behold. But there was something in the beat of the drum and the doleful, slow music of the funeral march as we stepped to our places that brought the hedgerows of Normandy very close. There were no more comments. The entire regiment seemed to revolve around the thump of the drum. There was some tenseness in the ranks as when we marched to Carentan and I'm sure the flood of memories, which swept over the men, were the same as mine. The sudden crash of mortars and shells in the drum, the musical background of

sharp, singing bullets, and deeper distant fire. In the organ solo were the forms on the roadside, wrapped in green camouflaged parachutes and tied with their own silk lines.

The hopeful list of missing slowly dwindled as one by one the troopers were brought in. The brief words of the chaplain, "these men died for their country, for its fields, for its…" That's one way, but then more simply and in a manner the men understood, "… they died because they wanted to go home, their deaths have brought that home a little closer for those that still live." The list of dead rolled across the parade ground. Each name hitting as the drum beat hit before. Rolling through the alphabet, passing a hundred and not yet to "J." Names we did not know, names so familiar it was a shock to hear them. They were now something more than a statistic.

A little girl in a printed dress walked across the review field and placed a small bouquet on the ground – one tiny bunch of flowers alone on acres of green lawn. The rolling rang out. Three crashes rolled across the drums and from their dissolving thunder came the call of taps. As the last plaintive order note faded, the order, "Pass in Review" rang out, the land seemed to roar into "Onward Christian Soldiers" and the battalions swung into line and moved out. For the first time the men realized they were veterans. The regiment had said, "so long" to its first dead.

By September the strength of Third Battalion totaled around 650 officers and men. Forty percent of the battalion was made up of new personnel direct from the United States, while others came via the parachute school at nearby Chilton Foliat. During this time, against much protest, the American paratroops were also issued a "new style" olive-green regular uniform and high-buckled boots, intended to replace the tan jumpsuits and brown lace-up high-leg boots. However, by far the greatest improvement was made to the parachutes that were now fitted with a British model quick-release attachment, making the standard American T5 parachute much easier to get out of after landing.

In mid-August, the regiment was ordered to prepare for a jump at Rambouillet, 20 miles southwest of Paris. Luckily the operation (codenamed Transfigure) was canceled, as it was later discovered that a German panzer division had been waiting in the forest directly opposite the intended DZ. In early September, the 506th was alerted to two further operations in Belgium, the first at Tournai and another in the vicinity of Liège. However, George Patton's Third Army captured both objectives before the airborne missions could even get off the ground. Instead an entirely different destination and destiny awaited them.

# The Reckoning, Littlecote, Sunday, August 27, 1944.

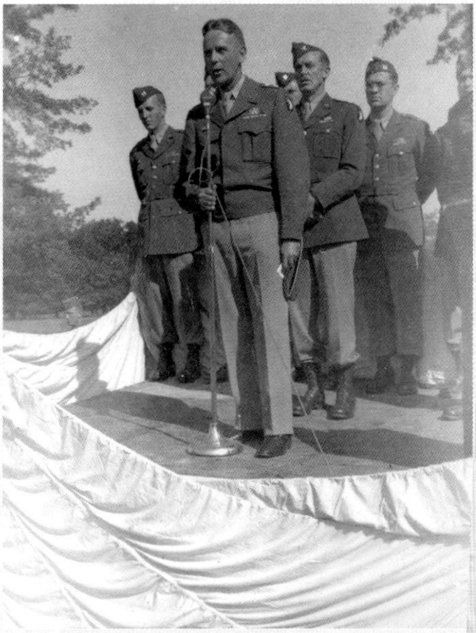

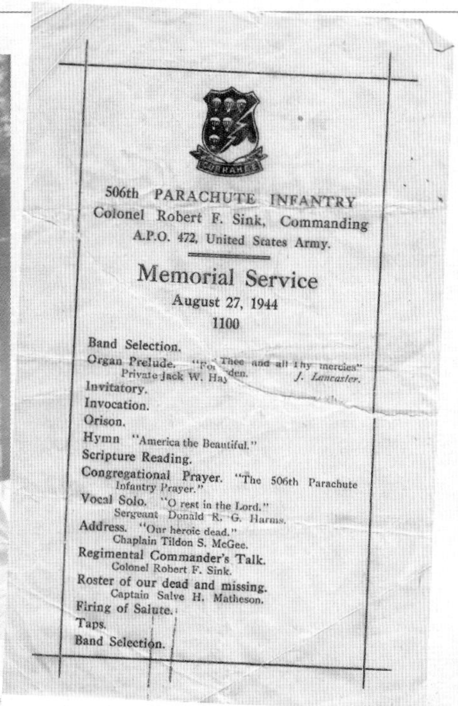

506th PARACHUTE INFANTRY
Colonel Robert F. Sink, Commanding
A.P.O. 472, United States Army.

## Memorial Service

August 27, 1944
1100

Band Selection.
Organ Prelude. "For Thee and all Thy mercies"
Private Jack W. Hayden. J. Lancaster.
Invitatory.
Invocation.
Orison.
Hymn "America the Beautiful."
Scripture Reading.
Congregational Prayer. "The 506th Parachute Infantry Prayer."
Vocal Solo. "O rest in the Lord."
Sergeant Donald R. G. Harms.
Address. "Our heroic dead."
Chaplain Tildon S. McGee.
Regimental Commander's Talk.
Colonel Robert F. Sink.
Roster of our dead and missing.
Captain Salve H. Matheson.
Firing of Salute.
Taps.
Band Selection.

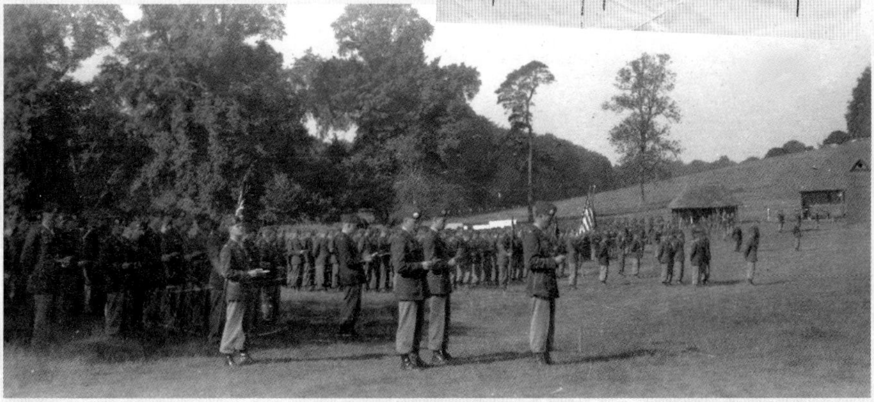

Gen Taylor at Littlecote on August 27, 1944, addressing the regiment at the beginning of the Memorial Service, flanked from left to right by Capt Salvatore Matheson, who had the unenviable task of reading out the names of the 414 dead and missing, Colonel Bob Sink and Capt Max Petroff, the 506th Adjutant.

The order of service.

The regiment assembled in the deer park and are pictured here reading the regimental prayer written by Capt Jim Morton, which was partially inspired by Bob Wolverton's D-Day missive.

BELOW LEFT Chaplain Tilden McGee making his empowered sermon entitled "Our Heroic Dead."

BELOW RIGHT Sgt Bill Meyers (subsequently killed during the fighting in Holland) leads the Honor Guard as nine-year-old Patricia Owen places the wreath. (All photos John Reeder via D-Day Publishing Collection)

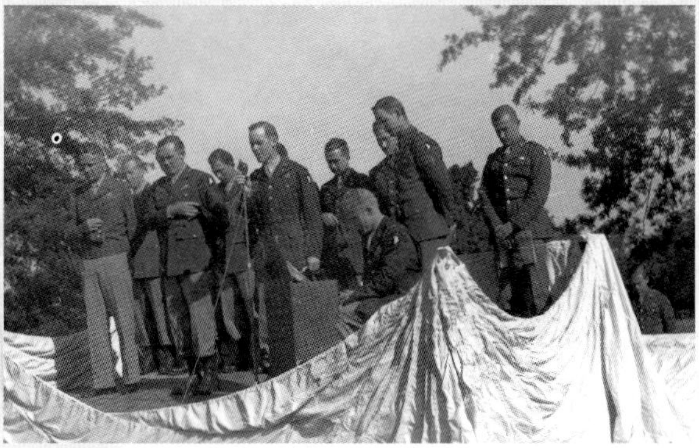

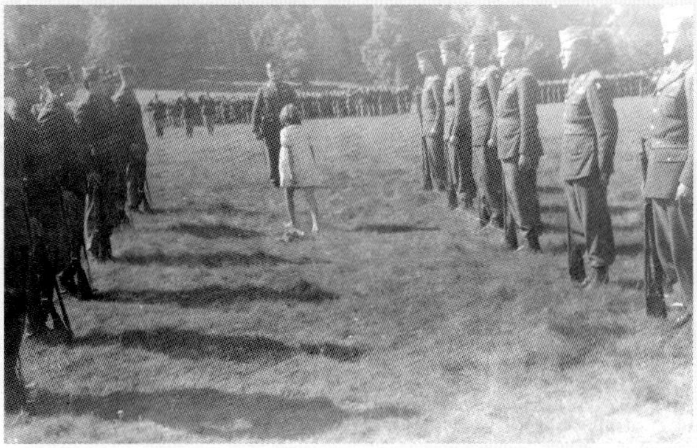

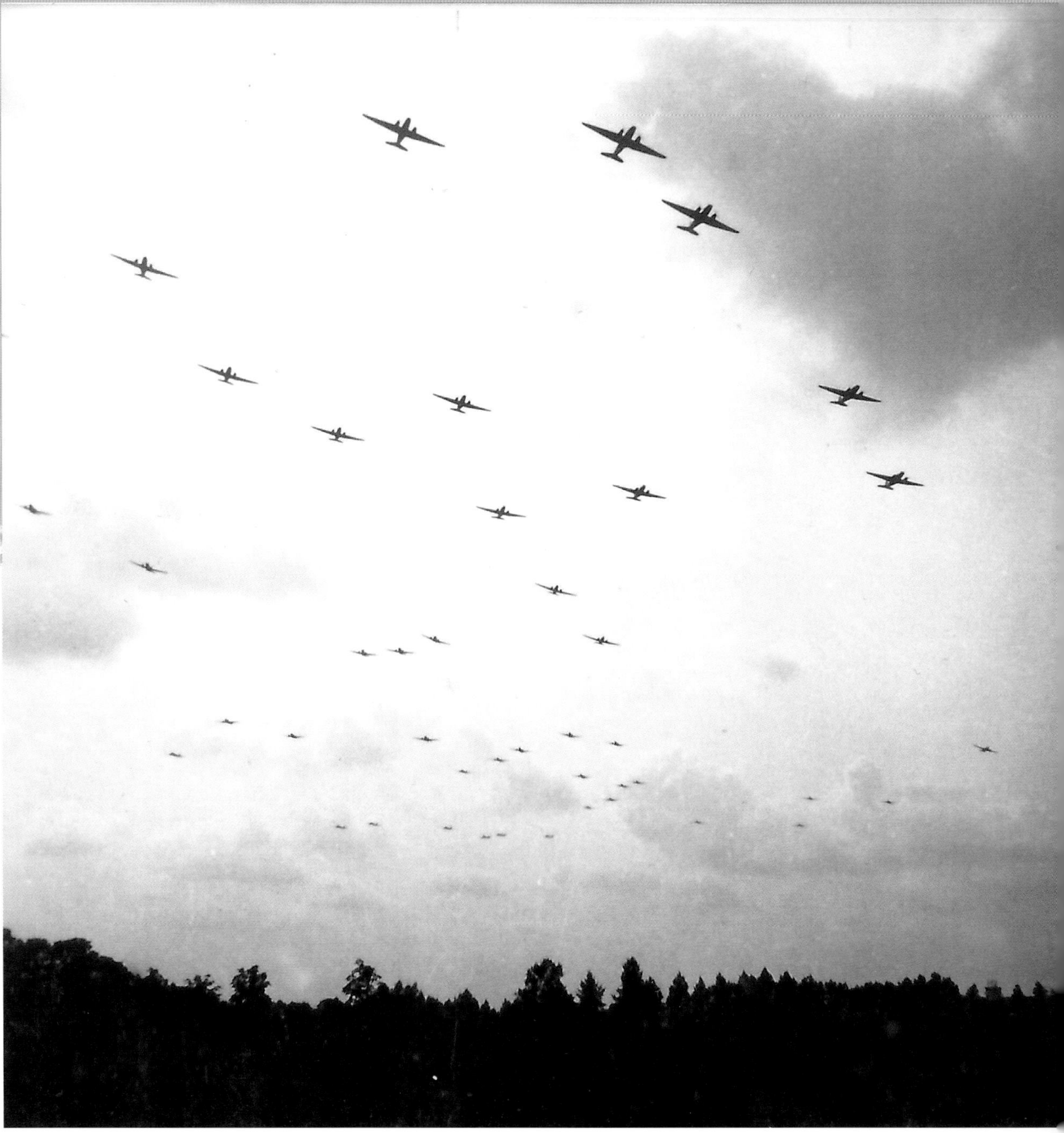

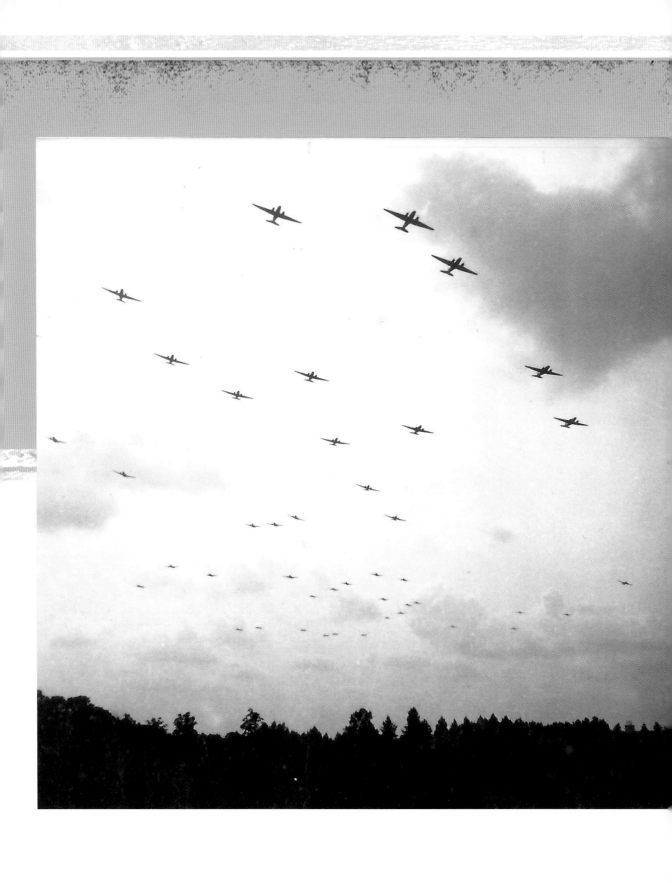

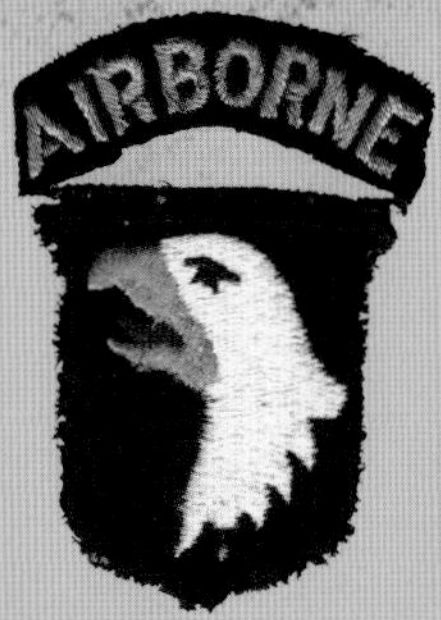
AIRBORNE

Chapter 6

# FIRE LIKE A RIVER

## Operation *Market Garden*

### The battle for Eindhoven, September 17–18, 1944

Late on the morning of September 14, Colonel Sink gathered Major Horton and the other battalion commanders for an emergency staff meeting at Littlecote House. Once gathered the colonel revealed he had received an assignment from SHAEF (Supreme Headquarters Allied Expeditionary Force). Horton returned to Ramsbury and quietly asked Bob Harwick, who was now Third Battalion's Executive Officer, to gather the platoon commanders. A few minutes later, clutching notebooks, the officers casually strolled in for what they believed would be another routine meeting. The atmosphere soon changed when Oliver revealed, in his heavy southern drawl, that they had been placed on standby for a mission, codenamed *Market Garden*, and had to be prepared to leave early the following morning for Chilbolton Airfield near Andover in Hampshire. *Market* was to be the airborne phase and *Garden* would be the ground assault led by the British XXX Corps and Second Army.

September 17, 1944, 82nd Airborne, Grave. (Netty van Kooijk)

The operation had already gone through several incarnations at the planning stage before finally evolving into *Market Garden*. In brief, the original idea,

codenamed *Comet*, had been for the British 1st Airborne Division and the 1st Polish Parachute Brigade to capture bridges at Grave, Nijmegen and Arnhem before linking up with British ground forces from XXX Corps. The intense political wrangling, constantly changing weather and rapidly deteriorating tactical situation bogged everything and everyone down. Eventually the operation was postponed to Sunday September 17 and was modified to include a much larger airborne force. In total, some 30,000 men would take part in the operation, including the American 101st and 82nd Airborne Divisions. Lieutenant General Frederick "Boy" Browning, commander of the British Airborne Corps, was appointed deputy commander of the First Allied Airborne Army, to assist Lieutenant General Lewis Brereton in combining all three forces. If all went well, over 16,500 paratroopers and 3,500 glider men would be on the ground in less than 90 minutes. All British and Polish elements were ordered to remain at their departure airfields where they were already assembled, while the Americans were hastily mobilized. As well as Chilbolton, the 101st would be deployed to airfields throughout the Newbury area, such as Membury, Ramsbury and Greenham Common.

The main route for XXX Corps was now going to be Eindhoven, Grave, Nijmegen, and Arnhem. As soon as the drop began the Guards Armoured Division was to lead the advance. The 101st Airborne was to seize bridges along the main axis of advance, ensuring that the British had expedient passage northeast to Grave and into the 82nd Airborne's area of operations. In the meantime, XXX Corps was to provide artillery support wherever and whenever the situation permitted.

The 442nd Troop Carrier Group returned to Chilbolton Airfield, from where they were to fly 3/506 and 3/501 to Holland. The 442nd was split into two groups, referred to as serials, with each serial consisting of 45 aircraft responsible for delivering one battalion of paratroopers onto separate DZs, designated by letter, with DZ "B" at Son, the 506th's designated DZ.

The Third Battalion advance party arrived at Chilbolton on Thursday afternoon. The following morning, September 15, the main body arrived from Ramsbury and was split across several ring-fenced compounds. Rapidly the walls of the briefing area became covered with a plethora of notes and maps, while the sand tables were transformed into rolling flat countryside studded with the green fields, canals, roads, bridges, and small villages so typical of the Netherlands.

At about 0700hrs on the morning of the 16th, the officers gathered in the briefing room. There was no loud talking or cheerful banter but a deep willingness to absorb every single detail of the operational plan. Major Horton orientated the group with the high-level plans and then discussed the wider regimental mission to capture Eindhoven and its four bridges over the River Dommel by 2000hrs on Sunday, the 17th. Third Battalion's specific job was to secure one of the four target bridges – the Elzentbrug adjacent to the Van Abbe Museum of Art. The area was dissected by deep drainage ditches and canals and straddled one of the principal routes converging on Nijmegen. At the time little was known about enemy dispositions, but it was believed that the bulk of the defenders would be from the parachute school operated by the Wehrmacht 25 miles away at Den Bosch. The briefing room bustled through the night with activity, but despite this many still went away with only a vague idea of what they would be doing post drop. Equally significantly, because so little was known about the Dutch resistance, few were unable to identify or even distinguish between bona fide underground workers and opportunistic time wasters.

Before leaving England, Lewis Brereton sent this message to the troops:

> You are taking part in one of the greatest airborne operations in history. The success of your mission today relies not only on navigation and flying skill and courage of the aircrews but also the courage and speed of the landing force – here rests the difference between a quick decision in the west and a long, drawn-out battle. I know I can depend on you.

The layer of fog that had enveloped the airfields finally began to lift and by early morning the paratroopers were out by their individual C-47 aircraft and anxious to get going. After the aircraft had been cleared, the men clambered aboard and waited for what seemed like hours for take-off. Finally, shortly after 1030hrs the 45 planes

The great air armada turning over Geel in Belgium shortly before lining up for the drop zones. (Chris van Kerchhoven via Ronald Ooms)

Soldiers from 2/506 jumping at Son. (Tom Peeters)

from the 442nd carrying 3/506 joined the southern stream with around 400 other "ships" and headed for Ghent. At the same time around 1,000 planes carrying the 82nd and British Airborne Corps were flying the longer northern route toward targets at Nijmegen and Arnhem.

On the ground, thousands looked on in amazement as the greatest air armada of all time passed overhead. Hundreds of ships and barges moored in Kentish ports blew their sirens as the planes headed out over the North Sea toward Belgium. Jumpmasters looked out of open cargo doors and marveled at the numbers of aircraft involved. Crossing the Belgian coast, the "Skytrain stream" was joined by a fighter escort, whose job was to provide both high and low air cover.

Shortly before the battalion took off from Chilbolton, four Pathfinder Teams ripped skywards from an airfield at Chalgrove in Oxfordshire. Two of those planes were carrying the 506th and 502nd Pathfinder Teams destined for DZs "B" and "C" respectively. Flying in close formation, the pilots successfully delivered both teams. Four minutes later all the beacons and marker panels were deployed and operational, ready for the main drop to come in.

The journey across Belgium to Ghent was quiet until the southern route planes crossed the enemy line at Rothy and antiaircraft fire began erupting through the formation. Come what may, after flying over Geel in Belgium the planes were locked into their final run toward Son. The red lights flicked on, signaling the troops to stand, hook up and check equipment. The closer the planes got to the DZ, the greater the flak. The little black puffs of smoke looked harmless from a distance, but they delivered a deadly cargo of ragged steel. These antiaircraft positions should have been neutralized two hours earlier by the US 8th Air Force, but many of the American bombs had failed to hit their targets.

"A burst of 20mm antiaircraft fire came through the seats and out through the top of the fuselage! Lieutenant David Forney panicked and jumped moments before the green light came on. By then the rest of us were so damn worked up that when the light did change to green, we emptied the plane in a matter of seconds. I was amazed by the size of the landing area, with almost no trees and very few obstacles. My head was too far down and snapped backwards as my 'chute opened. Somehow my kit bag tore loose and I lost everything including my TSMG [Thompson Submachine Gun]. Later, as I was heading towards the assembly area, I spotted my pack. Everything was fine except for my ammo, as all of the clips had burst open like a jack-in-a-box. I was not happy, but we were all safely on the ground as the second wave came in."

Corporal Mario "Hank" DiCarlo – 2 Platoon, H Company

"Although it seems difficult to believe, this was the first time that I'd ever parachuted with a machine gun. To make matters worse the gun was also loaded and made ready with a belt of 50 rounds. The aircraft was undulating so violently on the flight over that I became airsick. Being stuck at the back of the stick, I threw up all over the floor right beside the crew compartment. The stench was miserable, and the soles of my boots got soaked with vomit. When the green light came on, I slipped in the doorway and because of the weight of the gun, I had to crawl out the door on all fours like a donkey."

Private James A. Melhus – MG Platoon, HQ Company

"The base plate from my 60mm mortar got forced up into my groin, damaging my spine and hip. Despite having difficulty walking I refused medical aid and asked my ammo carrier Wayman Womack for assistance. Womack ran over to a nearby farm and returned with a wheelbarrow. With Womack at the helm that old wheelbarrow became my primary method of transportation for the next three days!"

Private Harold T. Stedman – 3 Platoon, I Company

"A plane crashed and burst into flames and it was so close that I had to crawl behind a water-filled cattle trough to protect myself from the intense heat."

Corporal John W. Gibson – Medical Detachment

"I was almost killed getting out of my parachute when a couple of steel helmets smashed into the ground beside me. I looked up and saw a C-47 beginning to break up and one of its wings came away and floated to the ground like it was made from tissue paper."

Corporal Bobbie J. Rommel – HQ Company, MG Platoon

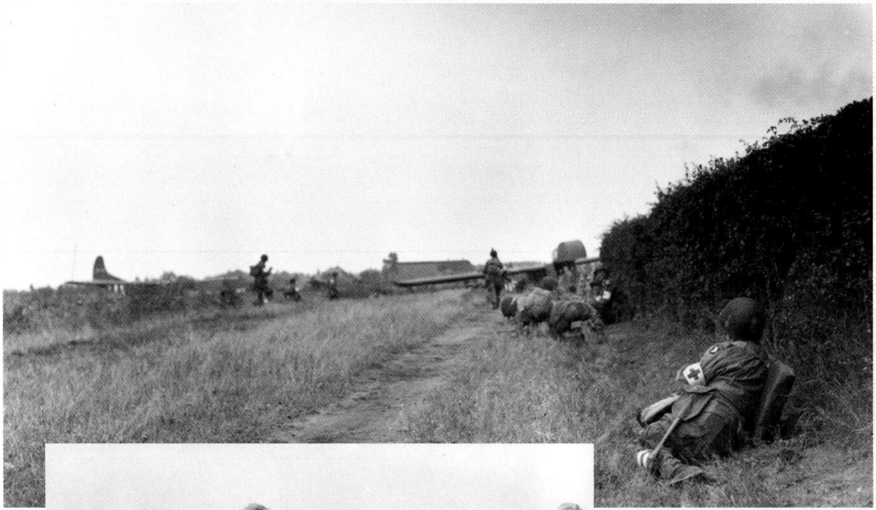

Dr Louis Kent and some of the regimental medics preparing to move off the drop zone. Note the smoke from a burning aircraft drifting across hedge on the right. (NARA)

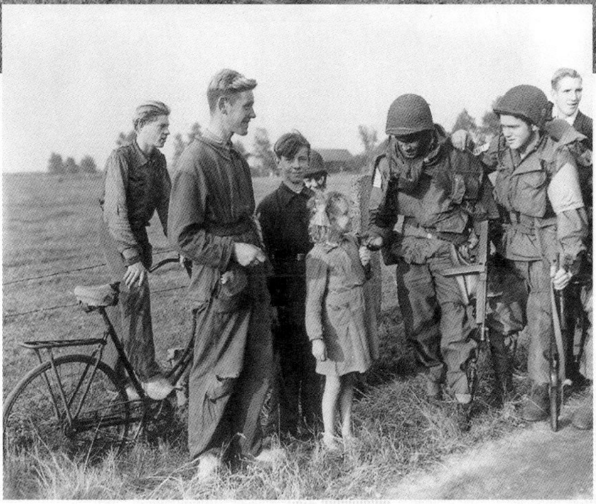

Soldiers from 506th Regimental Headquarters giving chewing gum to local children along the main track to Sonniuswijk that ran west across the drop zone. (NARA)

The pulsating drone of the armada drew ever closer to Son. From the air the crew chiefs and jumpmasters could now clearly see the red smoke and white identification panels stenciled with the letter "B" which had been set up earlier by the Pathfinders. Ten seconds after crossing the Wilhelmina Canal that signified the edge of the drop zone, the red light switched to green and the jump began. For the sky soldiers, the vast 400-acre site seemed to reach out to infinity. Being the first to jump, Third Battalion was given the job of securing the DZ. In total nearly 2,200 personnel from the 506th dropped from 131 planes onto DZ "B" and were expected to be assembled and cleared within one hour of landing. Oliver Horton was impressed by the way the 442nd Tactical Carrier Group flew his men into battle. Every aspect of the jump was superior to Normandy, and due to the lack of any crosswind most experienced easy and safe landings. The jump even had its humorous moments as recalled by First Sergeant Gordon Bolles of H Company: "When we got on the road after the jump, I spotted a wounded man near one of the farmhouses

# Third Battalion's Line of Advance into Eindhoven, September 18, 1944

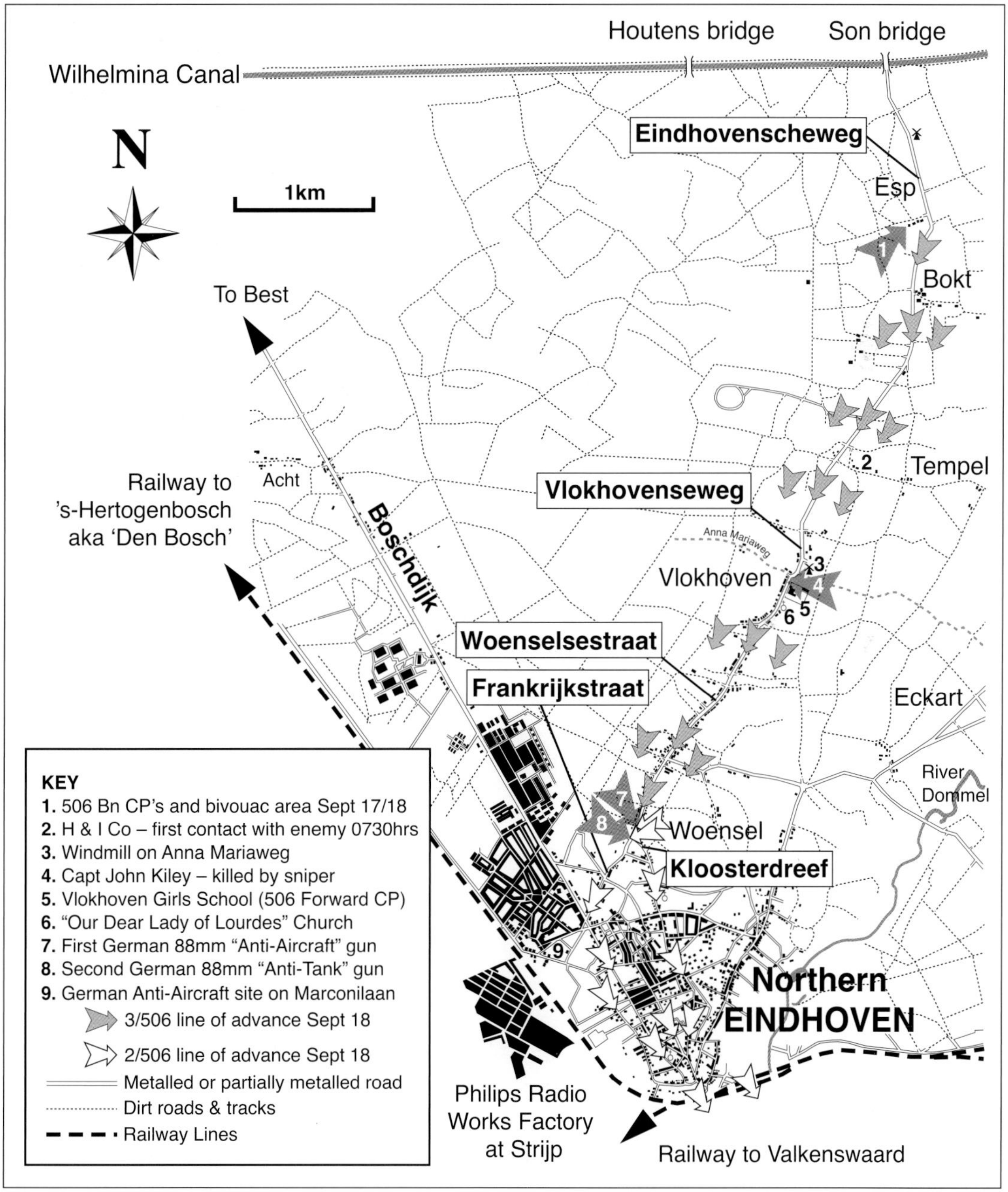
Houtens bridge
Son bridge
Wilhelmina Canal
N
1km
Eindhovenscheweg
Esp
Bokt
To Best
Tempel
Vlokhovenseweg
Railway to
's-Hertogenbosch
aka 'Den Bosch'
Acht
Boschdijk
Anna Mariaweg
Vlokhoven
Woenselsestraat
Frankrijkstraat
Eckart
River Dommel
Woensel
Kloosterdreef
Northern EINDHOVEN
Philips Radio Works Factory at Strijp
Railway to Valkenswaard
KEY
1. 506 Bn CP's and bivouac area Sept 17/18
2. H & I Co – first contact with enemy 0730hrs
3. Windmill on Anna Mariaweg
4. Capt John Kiley – killed by sniper
5. Vlokhoven Girls School (506 Forward CP)
6. "Our Dear Lady of Lourdes" Church
7. First German 88mm "Anti-Aircraft" gun
8. Second German 88mm "Anti-Tank" gun
9. German Anti-Aircraft site on Marconilaan
3/506 line of advance Sept 18
2/506 line of advance Sept 18
Metalled or partially metalled road
Dirt roads & tracks
Railway Lines

View toward the Aloysius Boys' School, showing the 88mm gun knocked out by D/506. (NARA)

and called out for a medic – 'milk' sounds almost identical to 'medic' in Dutch – a farmer misunderstood what I was saying and came over and tried to hand me a pitcher full of milk!"

Still aircraft were lost and the men already safely on the ground watched as several planes went down in flames. In total, four of the C-47s assigned to the 506th PIR (all from the 436th Troop Carrier Group based at Membury) crashed or made crash landings on or near the DZ. But during this operation no aircraft transporting men from the Third Battalion were shot down.

Just after 1330hrs, the 502nd PIR flew in from Greenham Common and Welford airfields to begin their drop on the far side of the jump field. It had not taken long for the battalion to secure the DZ whereupon they waited to be relieved by the 502nd. Afterwards Horton's men reverted to regimental reserve. The reorganization of the regiment was completed with virtually no enemy resistance except for occasional incoming mortar and sniper fire. Collection points for ammunition and supplies were located in woods on the southern edge of the DZ. Twenty-five minutes after the main drop, the first of around 70 gliders arrived bringing the 506th PIR's command, reconnaissance, signal, and medical personnel, along with the first batch of jeeps. Two collided as they were landing, causing a number of casualties.

Following on behind Regimental Headquarters, Third Battalion now moved south along the main road toward Son and its vitally important bridge crossing, which was only 2 miles away. The local inhabitants came out to cheer them along and were merrily handing out beer when the shooting started. Up ahead, First

Battalion had been forced into a flanking maneuver around the western side of the town, while Second Battalion attempted a direct assault on the bridge. Unbeknown to the regiment, the small German garrison in the town had been recently enhanced to about 90 men. To protect the Wilhelmina canal from air attack there were also two 88mm antiaircraft guns. The first was located in a field a couple hundred yards northwest of the bridge, and it was this gun that seriously delayed First Battalion's advance, causing several casualties, including Lieutenant George Retan formerly with I Company of Third Battalion and a close friend of Ed Shames. The other 88mm, fully mobile, was sighted in front of the Aloysius Boys' School about 300 yards away from the bridge and was successfully taken out by a bazooka team from Second Battalion.

In the late afternoon the German defense force was forced to pull back to the far bank of the canal but not before they blew the bridge. The huge explosion threw debris and planks hundreds of feet into the air. Beside himself with surprise and anger, Bob Sink took the cigarette from his mouth and threw it on the ground, calling the Germans all the cuss words under the sun. Some of the Third Battalion men including Sergeant Ralph Bennett joined a mixed group from the 506th who bravely swam across and managed to push back the enemy, while engineers attempted to fashion a floating walkway. With the work complete, 3/506 were last to cross the ramshackle pontoon and safely made it to the other side of the canal around midnight.

Clearly the original idea to take Eindhoven on the first day was now totally out of the question. With the sole exception of 2nd Platoon from G Company (who were selected for divisional security back in Son), the regiment spent a cold, damp

After the bridge was blown at Son, a Bailey Bridge was constructed allowing British armor to continue north to Arnhem. Here we see a Sherman tank heading in the direction of Sint Oedenrode and Veghel. (Tom Peeters)

and misty night in a nearby hamlet. To the west vivid green tracer fire arched into the blackness and loud explosions were heard coming from the direction of Eindhoven. The enemy were already withdrawing to the southwest, trying desperately to stem the British advance. During the early hours Major Horton was informed that he was going to be leading the attack the next morning. At 0600hrs on Monday, September 18, Third Battalion kicked off the regimental assault. Forming an extended line straddling the highway, H and I Companies led, with G and HQ Companies following on behind in reserve.

First to leave were Captains John Kiley (who had recently taken on a new role as Operations Officer) and Derwood Cann, who along with their respective operations and intelligence departments started south in the direction of Eindhoven. The initial advance had been split into four phase lines, with the fourth being Vlokhoven, a suburb of Woensel situated on the outskirts of the city. The men were spread out about 15 minutes ahead of the battalion and it was their job to locate enemy threats and maintain cohesion between H and I Companies by radio. As the advance party moved out, the two rifle companies deployed into the fields on either side of the main road known as Eindhovenscheweg. Along the route at regular intervals were public air-raid trenches and trees and streetlights painted with thick white "blackout" stripes. At 0730hrs, Kiley's patrol had their first contact a few hundred yards north of Vlokhoven. At the same moment both assault companies came under fire, with 1 Platoon from H Company led by Lieutenant Rudie Bolte bearing the brunt of the fighting east of the highway. 1 Platoon had worked their way south through the fields before arriving at a dense hedge near a place called Tempel. The barrier was almost impenetrable except for a hole about the width of a man at its center. First to go through was the lead scout, who was immediately shot in the chest. Taking a deep breath, Corporal Hank DiCarlo followed and dived through the gap and landed heavily in a deep drainage ditch.

One after another, amid sporadic bursts of enemy machine-gun fire, about a dozen guys dived through the hedge. Meanwhile, Lieutenant Bolte had noticed a small section of exposed wire fence further along the hedgerow, and decided it was an ideal spot to gain entry into the field beyond. The NCOs told him it was foolhardy but, perhaps anxious to prove himself, Rudie took no notice. Grabbing hold of the wire with both hands, he bravely swung forward into the field, whereupon a single bullet pierced the front of his helmet, killing him instantly.

Back in the field, the rest of the men were fighting for their lives. Immediately to the front was a building, and directly behind that an open-ended barn and two enormous haystacks. Lieutenant Dave Forney, Hank DiCarlo and several others were attempting to outflank the machine gun when they came under fire from behind the haystacks. The house was empty, but as the men moved closer the shooting intensified. Lieutenant Forney was out in front when he was shot and collapsed. After seeing Forney go down, Private James "Sharkey" Tarquini displayed incredible courage and sprinted into the house. Thinking on his feet, Sharkey pushed a packing crate against a wall in a back room. Holding his M1 like a battering ram, the diminutive Bostonian leapt onto the crate and smashed through a window. Once outside, he ran into an alleyway and killed the German soldiers who had been shooting at his comrades.

Meanwhile, while all this was happening, 2 Platoon was also taking casualties. Anxious to keep up momentum, Executive Officer, Lieutenant Roy Kessler (then acting H Company commander) came forward with Gordon Bolles to where Bolte had been trying to slide under the fence. Realizing the spot was still zeroed, Bolles tried to stop Kessler from doing the same thing but he didn't listen. As Roy reached out and grabbed the wire he was shot. The bullet went in just above the collarbone.

With Rudie and Dave both out of action, the company called in the assistant commander of 3 Platoon, Lieutenant Bob Stroud, to take charge. When he arrived, most of the guys were still pinned down in the ditch but there was another channel running to the right, along which Staff Sergeant Frank Padisak had managed to crawl. Stroud told Sergeant Don Zahn to lay down a base of 60mm mortar fire to cover Padisak. They were just getting ready to attack when Stroud was informed that Padisak (known as the "Slovak") had silenced the enemy gun. The Slovak had clearly won the morning, but the platoon had paid a high price with Rudie killed and Dave so badly injured that it would take him several years to recover.

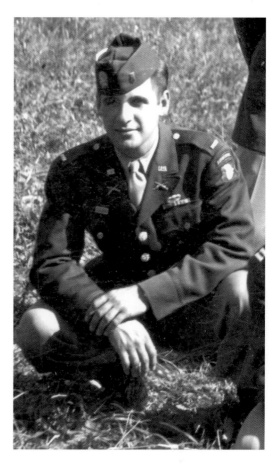

Lt Robert Stroud took over command of 1 Platoon, H Company, on September 18, 1944 during the advance to capture Eindhoven. Bob was an aggressive and capable leader in his role as platoon commander. (Lou Vecchi)

It seemed to Kiley that the battalion's advance was fragmenting into chaos. Several accidents happened when the soldiers misunderstood what they were being told by Dutch civilians attempting to help. To make matters worse, all radio contact had been lost with Major Horton, whose last known position was with G Company at the rear. Horton did eventually turn up in his jeep and immediately sent Derwood Cann back to H Company, still reorganizing after the fight at Tempel, for a situation report. Two hundred yards beyond a burnt-out German halftrack was a large Catholic church. Kiley decided to take a better look, walked across the street and stood obstinately in full view, carefully studying the church and road up ahead. Moments later there was a sharp crack and the captain fell to the ground in a welter of blood after being struck in the neck by a single bullet – he was dead within seconds.

# BILL GALBRAITH

"During the attack on Eindhoven… my boss, operations officer, Captain Kiley sent me back with a message for Major Horton – which was to order H Company to get back on line or the entire battalion would be flanked! I nodded and ran back along the sidewalk for about 100 yards and bumped into Jim Brown, who was carrying a radio for 2 Platoon. I figured it would be quicker for Jim to make the call… Jim had just finished speaking when a bullet smashed into the handset only inches from his face. It scared the hell out of me, but Jim seemed completely unshaken as he unslung his rifle, said 'See ya later' and walked away." Shortly after John Kiley had been killed, Galbraith was scouting ahead with I Company and took cover in the entrance of the nearest house when a shell from an 88mm positioned further along the street hit the building across the road, scattering debris everywhere. Seconds later, another high-velocity projectile hit the same building but this time the explosion sent Galbraith tumbling into the street. The force of the blast crushed his left leg, shredding everything below the knee. Fearful of enemy machine-gun fire, Galbraith desperately tried to drag himself back to safety when a third shell impacted: "I was hit in the shoulder by shrapnel, which completely paralyzed my right arm. Ploughing through the broken glass and debris, I painstakingly pushed myself backwards along the sidewalk with one hand and managed to get into the doorway of the next house."

The owner of the property grabbed Galbraith and hauled him inside. "Medic, Bill Kidder, came rushing through the open door closely followed by Jim Brown and Joe Madona. Kidder injected me with morphine and as he was bandaging my leg commented 'my war was now over.' I thanked the Dutch guy, Peter Klompmaker, for rescuing me. As Jim and Joe left the house, I handed my cherished Colt.45 (that I had taken from Ken

Bill Galbraith, Jim Brown Sr and Jack Brown on June 30, 1945. Originally from Long Beach, California, Bill would have been 21 years old when this photograph was taken. (Bill Galbraith)

Christianson at Bloody Gully) to Joe and wished them luck; ironically both were killed on January 13, 1945."

Bill was eventually sent to a British field hospital in Brussels to have his leg plastered before being returned to the UK. Several weeks later in November, Galbraith found himself on a US Army Hospital Ship bound for home. "After a lengthy period of rehabilitation I was discharged in June 1947. However, on a brighter note, Anna Nertney, whom I had met while on leave in Scotland after Normandy, wrote me the whole time and eventually I plucked up the courage and proposed. The following Christmas in 1948, Anna came to the States and one week later we were married."

Bill, Anna and the family pooch back in the USA, circa 1950. (Bill Galbraith)

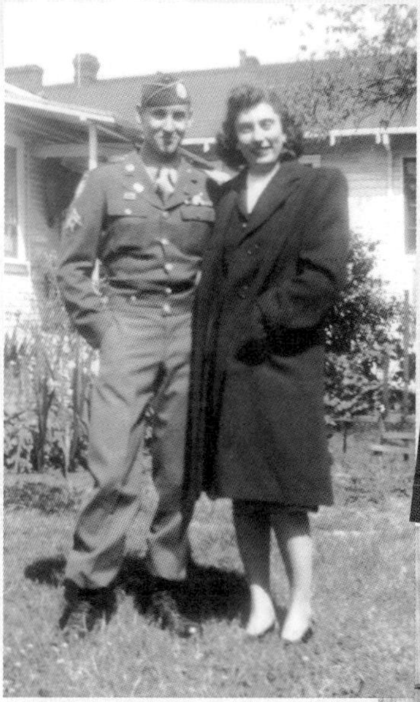

I Company Medic Cpl Alvin William "Bill" Kidder was actually classed as British when he joined the US Army on December 7, 1942. The 21-year-old came from Alberta in Canada and he did not file for American citizenship until September 1945. Bill undoubtedly helped to save many lives during his time in combat, including Bill Galbraith's. He is seen here with wife Marion at home in Alameda, California, after winning a lottery place home from Europe in February 1945. (Scott Kidder)

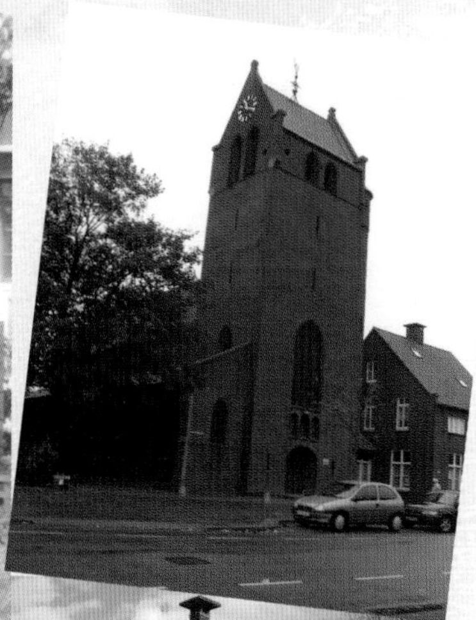

Onze Lieve Vrouw van Lourdes (Our Dear Lady of Lourdes) Catholic church, known locally as the Vlokhoven Tower. On Sunday September 18, most of the local population were attending mass. During the service they began to hear small-arms fire coming from the street. Luckily the building had a back door, which allowed most of the congregation who lived on the same side of the street to escape. However, those like the Klerks family, who lived on the other side of the square, had no choice but to remain with their priest, Father Odemaere. When it was safe everyone emerged and began shaking hands with the soldiers. The Klerks' son Jos later recalled the delight at their liberation: "Mum placed a chair outside our house and Captain Robert Harwick came over and sat down. I asked him about the insignia on his collar and he unclipped one of the silver bars and gave it to me. All these years later I still have them, a treasured souvenir from an amazing day."

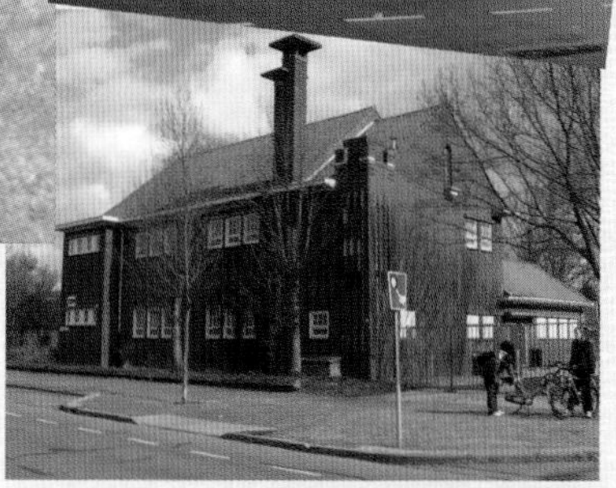

Vlokhoven School today. By midday on September 18, Colonel Chase had established a Forward Command Post at the school. During the clean-up of the town Third Battalion captured some 50 German soldiers, some of whom were wearing civilian clothing.

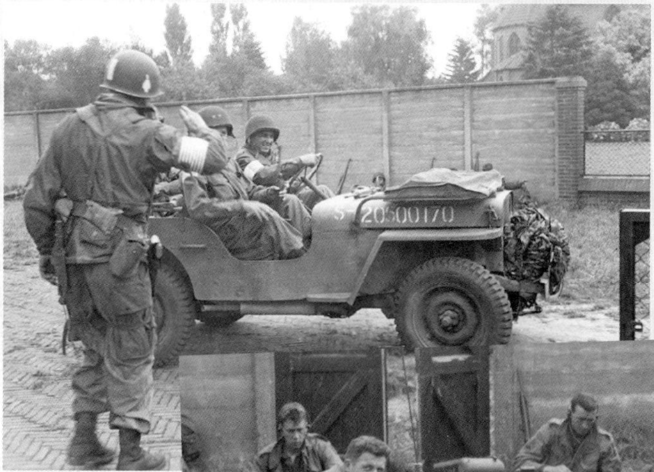

Bob Sink salutes General Taylor from a side entrance as he departs the 506th Command Post at Vlokhoven School around 1400hrs on September 18. In the background is the church. (John Reeder via D-Day Publishing Collection)

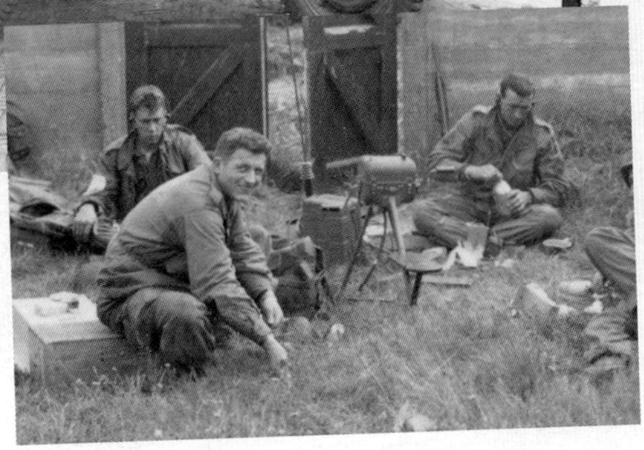

(Left to right): Louis Tuttle, Charles Bolte and Richard Roderick from RHQ Communication Team relaxing around their radio set and hand-generator in the walled play area behind the school. (John Reeder via D-Day Publishing Collection)

LEFT The second 88mm antitank gun positioned along Woenselsestraat, opposite the junction with Kloosterdreef, after it was neutralized. (Tom Peeters)

MIDDLE Damage to a house in Kloosterdreef caused by the antitank gun in Woenselsestraat. Elements of D and F Companies of Second Battalion probably used the upper floors of this building to pour direct fire onto the crew during the final stages of their assault. (Tom Peeters)

RIGHT This photo, believed to be the commander of the two 88s, was taken shortly after he was captured at Woensel. The guns most probably arrived in the town during Dolle Dinsdag (Mad Tuesday) and belonged to Flak-Brigade 18, part of Kampfgruppe Köppel. In the Netherlands, September 5, 1944 became known as Mad Tuesday, when German troops rapidly withdrew across the southern borders desperately trying to escape the Allied advance. (Tom Peeters)

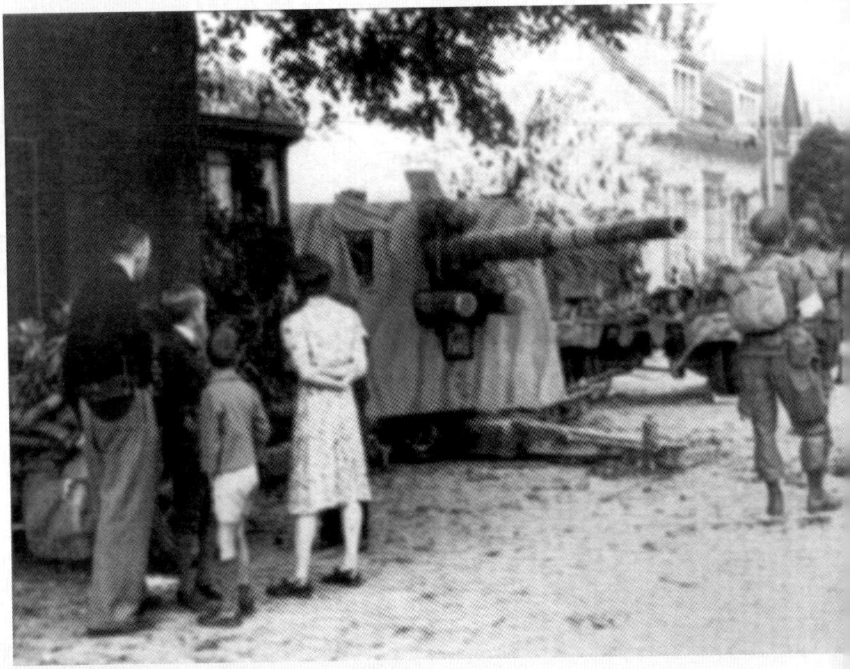

Despite Kiley's loss, the forward elements of Third Battalion pushed on before running into the two 88mm guns. The first, a Flak 18 antiaircraft gun, was located on the eastern side of the street outside a grocery store. The second gun – a static Flak 18 antitank variant complete with armored shield – was located 150 yards behind the first, in an open area between two houses. Harassment from enemy machine-gun fire forced many to seek shelter in the recessed doorways along the Woenselsestraat – the street leading directly toward the guns. I Company began to return fire as the first shell came screaming in, scattering debris everywhere. Seconds later, more high-velocity projectiles exploded into nearby buildings, causing several serious casualties. The guns were soon silenced by patrols from D and F Companies from 2/506, who then made a wide sweep around them, punching through the German right flank into the city and putting an end to any further organized resistance. The link-up with the British now seemed imminent when Colonel Sink and the assistant divisional commander, Brigadier General Gerald Higgins, rendezvoused with a recon patrol from the Household Cavalry northwest of Vlokhoven. But, in reality, the main body of XXX Corps were still several hours away from their official rally point at the Sint Joris church in southern Eindhoven.

At the same time the leader of the local Dutch resistance, John van Kooijk, explained to regimental intelligence that there was a telephone service network, operated by the Philips Corporation, which his group used to exchange sensitive

information. Colonel Sink wasted no time and set up a "liaison" team that included Ed Shames, to exploit this golden opportunity.

The enemy were using most of the churches in Eindhoven as valuable observation posts, but ironically the Americans were forbidden to fire on any of them with anything other than rifles. More civilians joined forces with the US troops as the 506th moved deeper into the city. Some were wearing official Partisan Action Netherlands (PAN) resistance armbands, while others simply wanted to be involved in the fight. Many were destined to become scouts or translators. Capturing buildings intact, such as post offices and telephone exchanges, was vitally important although of course some had already been destroyed. Shortly after midday, Second Battalion sent a message to Sink confirming that they were now in control of the Dommel bridges.

Third Battalion soon took over the Elzentbrug sluice, while First Battalion were handed temporary control of the crossings at Stratumseind, which had also been secured. Colonel Sink and Major Horton occupied a large imposing property diagonally across the street from Elzentbrug and the art museum. The large three-story townhouse, known as Den Elzent, had previously been the German military HQ. Sink called a battalion commanders' meeting and began drawing up more in-depth defensive plans for the area. Major Horton did his best to keep his troops in line, but formations were almost impossible as the men were being dragged away

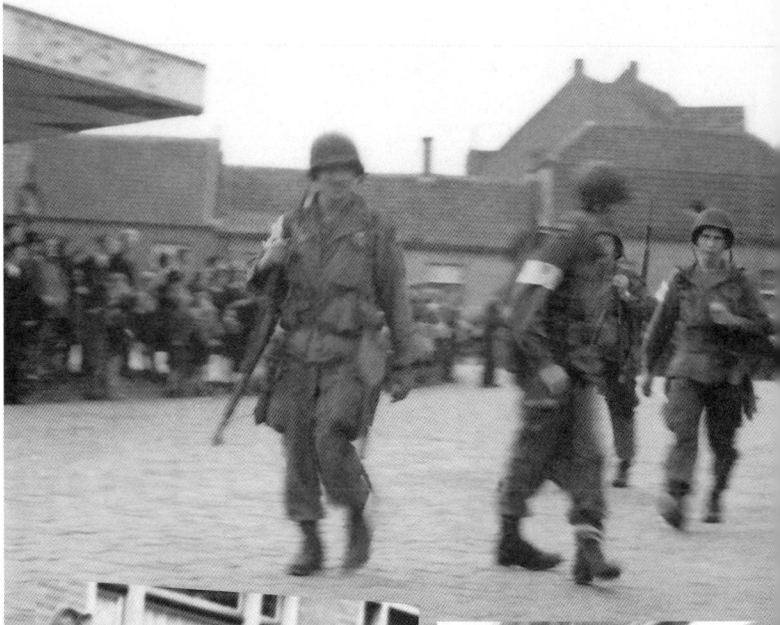

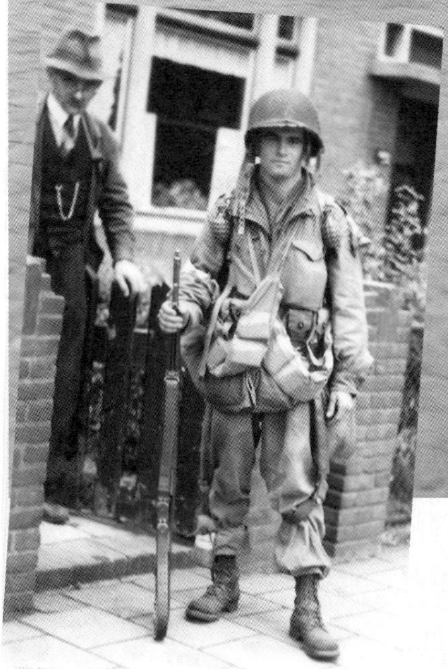

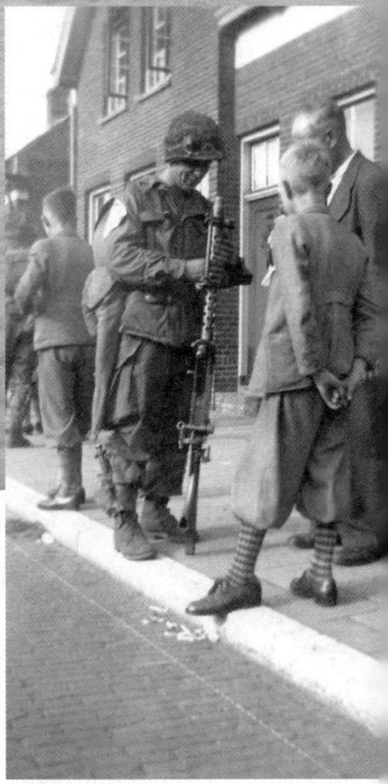

The crowds begin to gather as members of 3/506 reach the Texaco Groot Tourisme Service Station at the junction between the Boschdijk and Marconilaan roads. (J.J.M. van Kruijsdijk via Tom Peeters)

Tech Sergeant Alcide Leveille from RHQ Communications Platoon, posing with Mr Kluijtmans in front of his house on Frankrijkstraat. (John Reeder via Tom Timmermans)

A gunner from 3/506 shows local boy Tini van de Voort the workings of a .30cal MG during a brief lull in the advance along the Boschdijk. (Tom Timmermans)

OPPOSITE PAGE

Paratroopers from the 506th searching German prisoners near the Philips Company electricity substation on Lijmbeekstraat just off Boschdijk. (Tom Timmermans)

This picture of a Third Battalion trooper posing with locals at Stratumsiend, close to St Catharina church, was taken shortly after the 506th arrived in Eindhoven. A few hours later, when the British turned up, the streets were packed to breaking point. (Tom Peeters)

Luftwaffe personnel at de Wal on September 18, captured by the local PAN resistance, wait patiently on Elzentbrug to be searched by troops from 2/506. The Elzentbrug sluice was a main objective for 3/506; however, due to the enemy rearguard action at Tempel and Vlokhoven, Second Battalion were first to arrive. (Tom Timmermans)

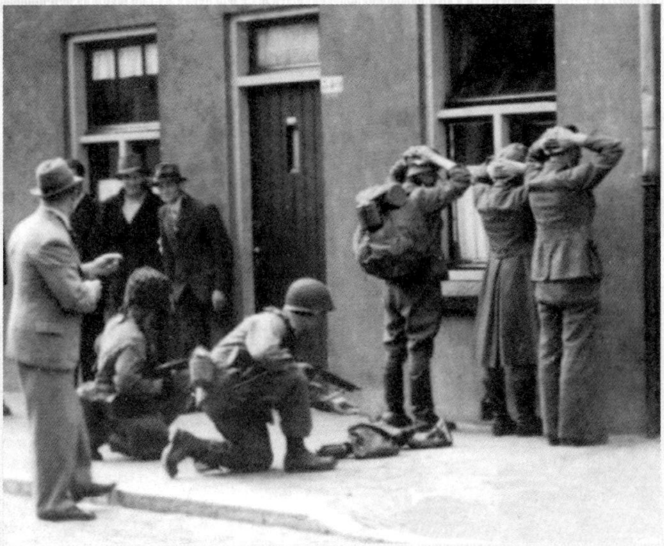

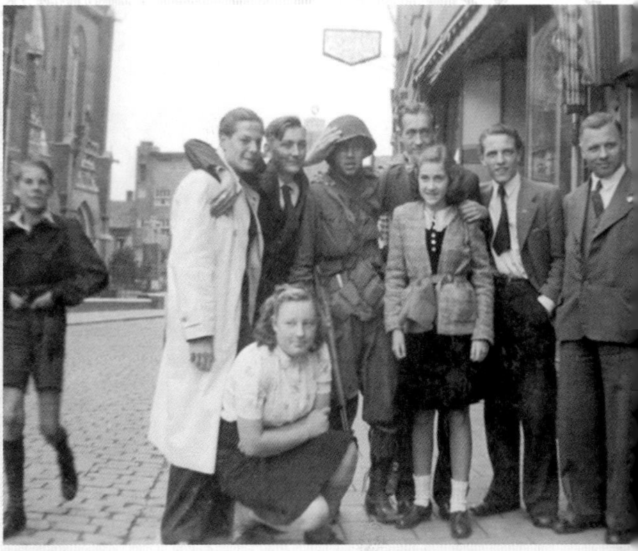

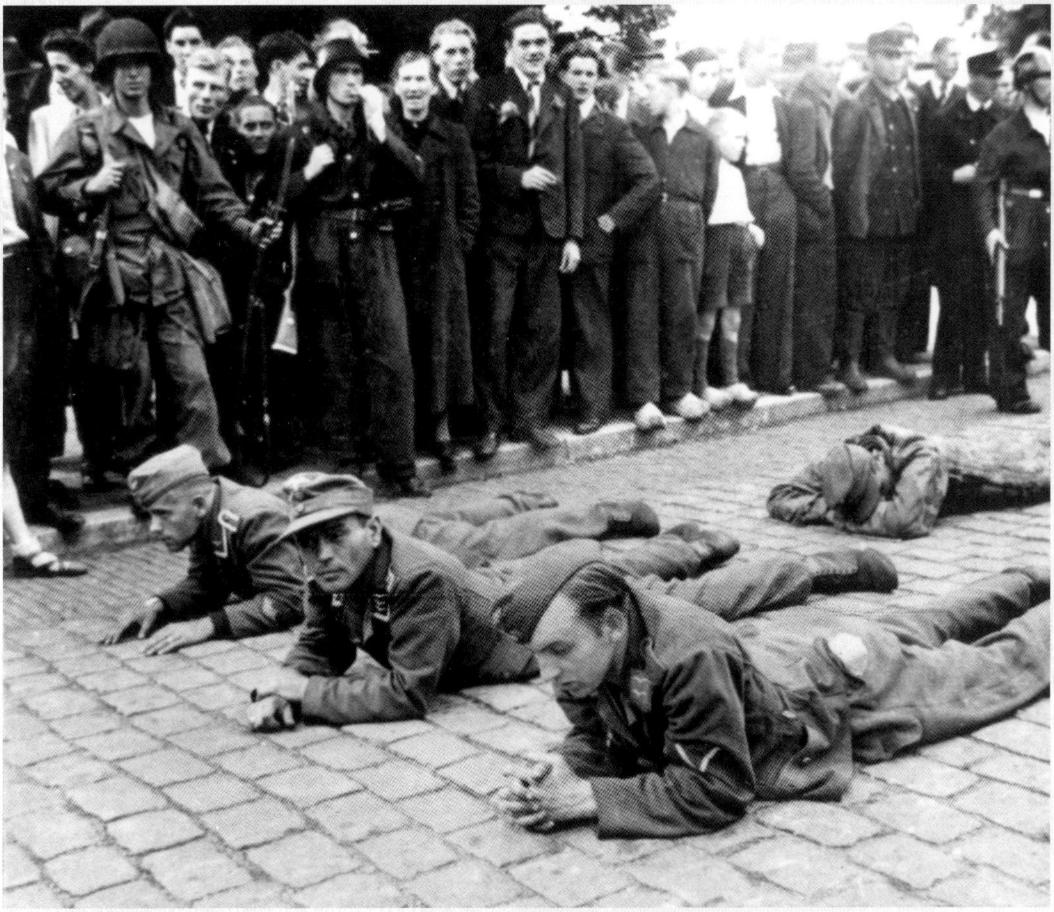

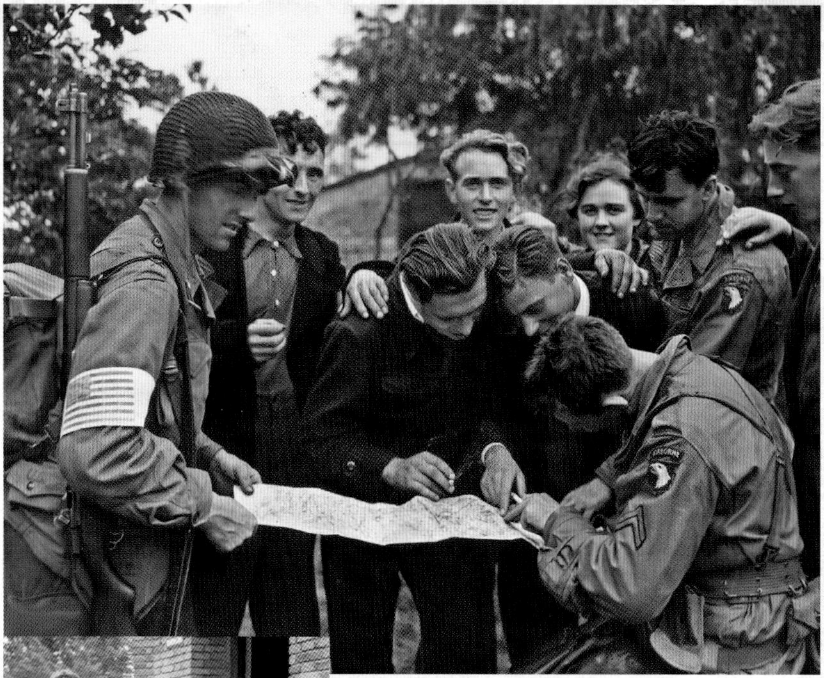

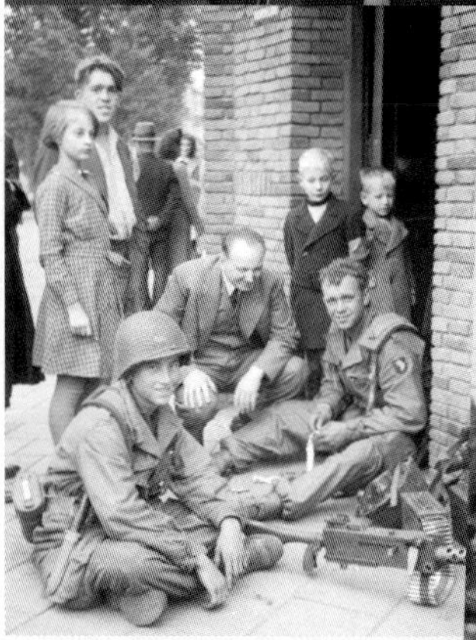

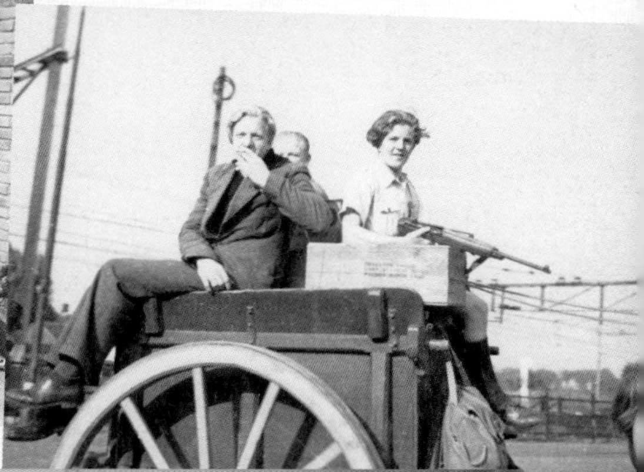

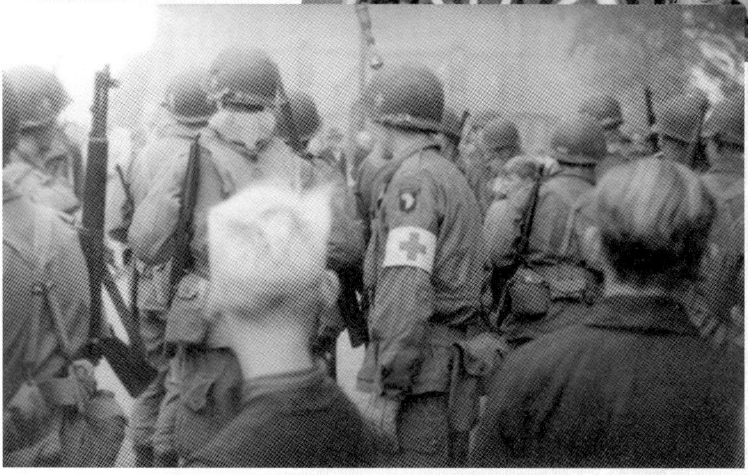

Men from RHQ in Eindhoven working closely with locals to locate and capture the enemy. (Left to right): Pfc Bob Watts (KIA April 13, 1945), Pvt Lehman Gunn and Cpl Alfred Tucker. (NARA – colorized by Johnny Sirlande)

This machine-gun crew from the 506th take a moment to smile while covering the corner of Stratumsdijk and Geldropseweg with their A-6. (Tom Timmermans)

This civilian, pictured on the Overweg into Eindhoven, was one of many farmers who volunteered to carry supplies from the DZ to the regimental collection point at the Sint Josef Milk Factory situated on the banks of the Dommel between de Wal and Paradijslaan. (Tom Peeters)

3/506 gathered before being sent to Paradijslaan, Elzent and Villa Park. (Hendrik Beens via Tom Peeters)

OPPOSITE PAGE

Bob Harwick, Oliver Horton and Sgt Don Embody touring the Demer area shortly after the liberation of Eindhoven. Note the .38 Smith & Wesson revolver on Horton's belt and German belt and ammo pouches around Don's waist. (Tom Timmermans)

Cpl Nathan Bullock, admiring a pair of souvenir clogs. Bullock is also sporting a lapel brooch, which like the shoes was most probably a gift from an adoring member of the local population. (Tom Timmermans)

Bazooka across chest, this Third Battalion trooper snatches a moment to reflect while outside the Van Abbe Museum of Art in the center of Eindhoven. (Tom Timmermans)

The two soldiers looking directly at the camera are Cpl Fayez Handy (front) and Sgt Garland "Tex" Collier from the Machine Gun Platoon. Twenty-five-year-old Tex had taken over from "Doc" Dwyer as section leader and was in command of four guns. Tex was killed by mortar fire on October 5, while working with H Company a few hundred yards west of Opheusden. At the time of writing (2019) Collier's body has yet to be recovered or identified, but perhaps one day he will be found and returned to his family. (Tom Timmermans)

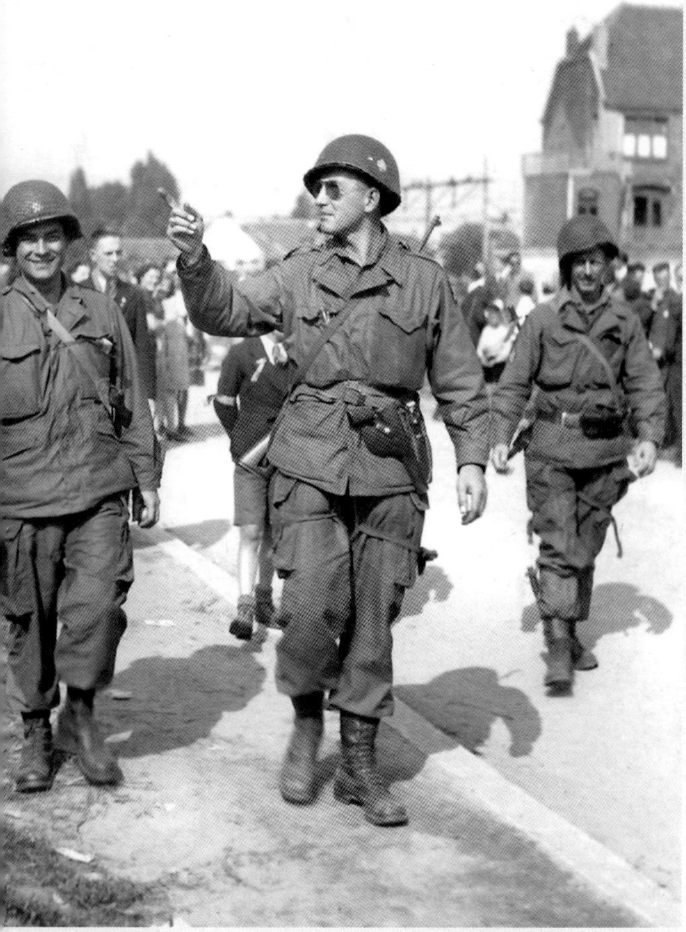

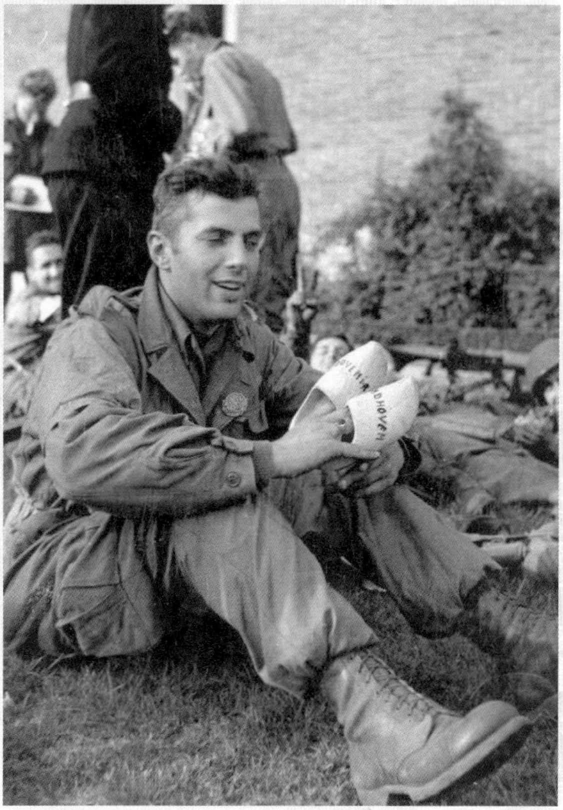

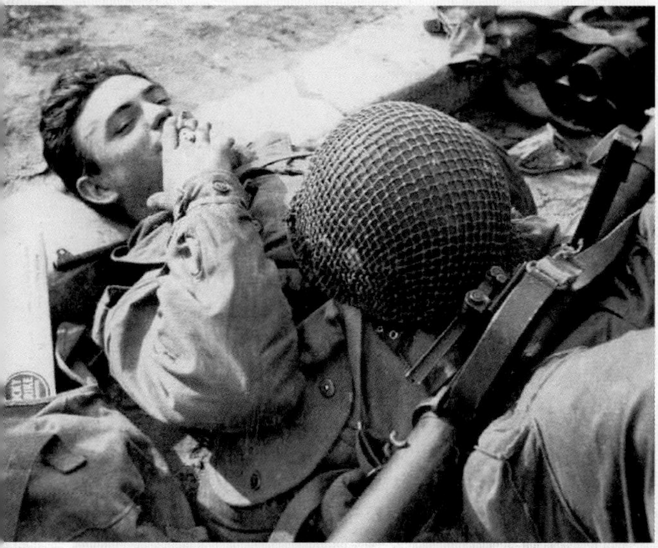

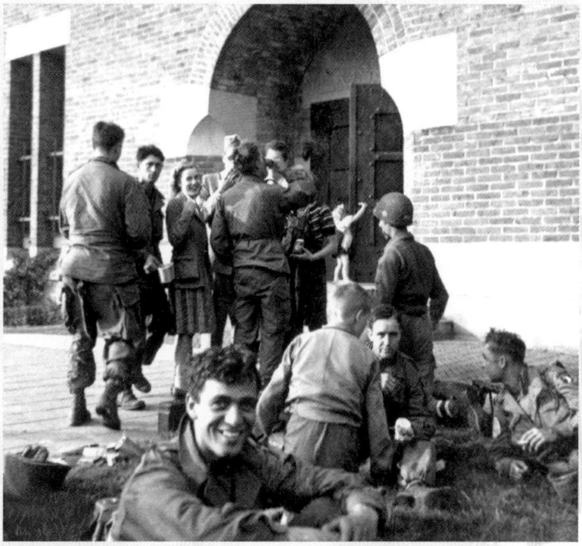

1st Sgt Fred Bahlau at the Sint Josef Milk Factory, Eindhoven. The factory became the main collection and distribution point for the 506th's equipment and supplies. (Fred Bahlau via Mark Bando Collection)

into homes and bars by locals desperate to celebrate their liberation. By early evening each company had been assigned a sector within the battalion area. But even after the battalion had dug in, the civilians still kept arriving to say hello and party. Thankfully this only lasted as long as the arrival in Eindhoven of the British armor. A single column of over 11,000 vehicles and tanks met with such an overwhelming welcome that the streets became gridlocked and nothing could move. At 1530hrs on D+1, over 400 gliders landed on the LZ at Son, bringing with them more troops and heavy support.

A steady stream of vehicles was now moving northward, bringing everything and anything from bridging equipment to bulldozers. Although the enemy had been pushed from Eindhoven, they were by no means beaten, especially when forward elements of the German SS 107th Panzer-Brigade began to threaten the city. Supported by a ferocious armory of Mark V Panther tanks and self-propelled guns, the brigade had recently been rerouted by train from Aachen. Unbeknown to the Americans, the immediate threat was not aimed at Eindhoven itself but a newly built Bailey Bridge at Son.

Meanwhile the British attached a squadron of tanks and a recon troop to the 506th to form a mobile task force to patrol the surrounding countryside. After receiving fresh orders to widen the regiment's defenses, Third Battalion was sent to the small town of Winterle, 6 miles west of Eindhoven. As it was getting dark, enemy Pathfinder aircraft flew in overhead and ominously dropped yellow flares across Eindhoven. The streets were still jammed with vehicles and civilians as the bombers came in and dropped their loads. Before long the southern part of the city

The old Philips Lamp & Valve Factory (left) and the Radio Works Eindhoven (right) in the industrial area known as the Strijp. At the outbreak of the war, 113,000 people lived in Eindhoven, with 25,000 working here at Strijp. The industrial area was instantly recognizable across the city by the Philips Lichttoren (Light Tower). Constructed in 1929, the Lichttoren was part of the Lamp & Valve Factory and was topped by a huge illuminated Philips sign. In the early thirties, Philips had purchased several large power stations and manufacturing companies. Each factory had its own independent power plant for generating electricity, with its own direct, secure telephone service link back to Eindhoven. During the occupation, at considerable risk, Frederick "Frits" Philips shared these service lines with the resistance groups across the region and used the subsequent intelligence to guard against factory inspections and searches.

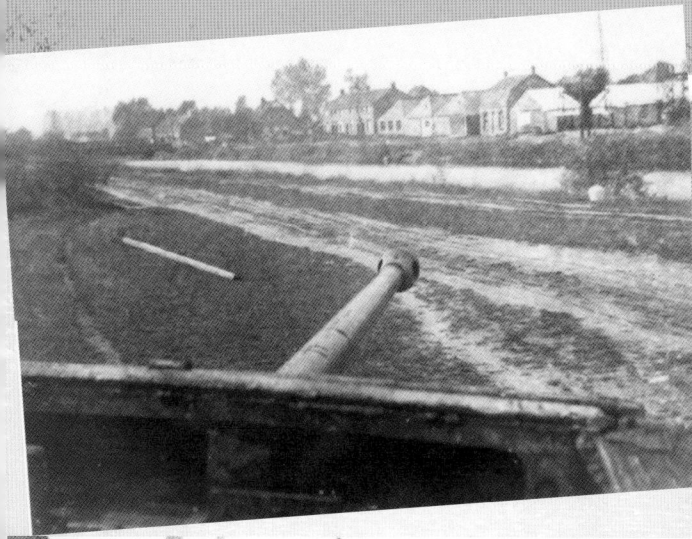

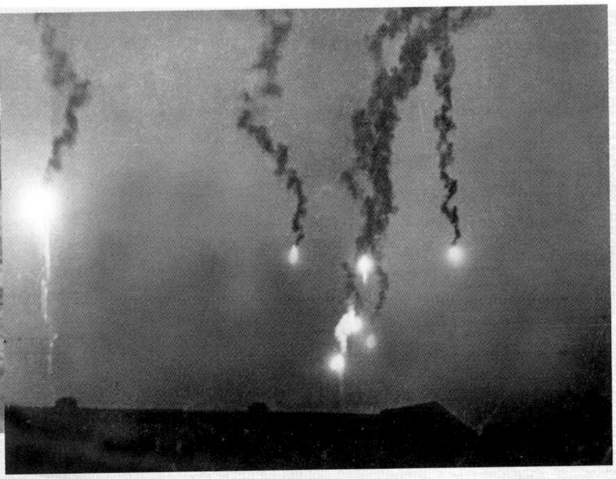

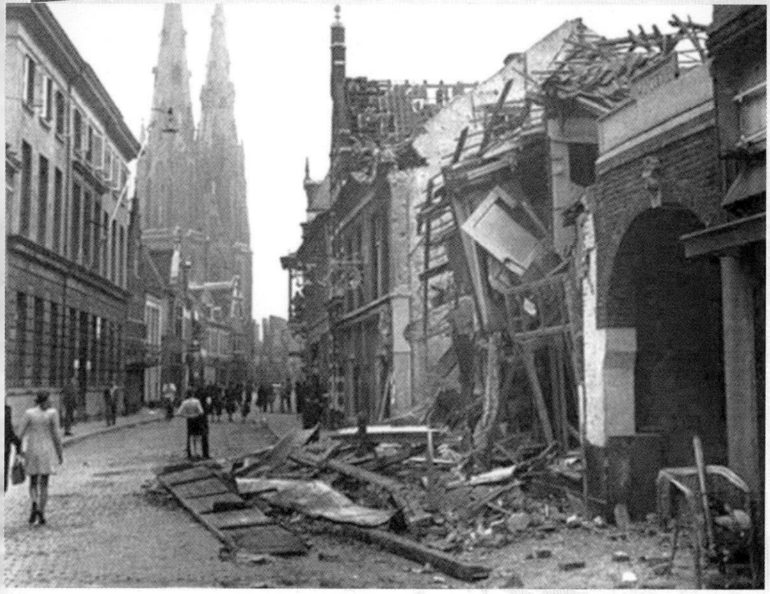

ABOVE LEFT On September 19, four German Mark V tanks, supported by infantry, attacked the Bailey Bridge (seen here on left) from the east. One of the tanks was knocked out and this picture, taken from the turret, shows just how close the enemy came to succeeding. (Tom Peeters)

ABOVE RIGHT Before the German air raid the northeastern edge of Eindhoven was clogged with tanks and vehicles. The first flares appeared overhead at about 2030hrs, followed a few minutes later by the bombers. Before long the southern part of the city was in flames, telephone lines were down and the mains water pressure had failed. Streets close to Col Sink's CP at Den Elzent were badly hit. A British ammunition truck exploded and it was virtually impossible to evacuate the residents of the affected areas. (Peter Hendrikx)

In total 800 people were wounded and 227 killed during the bombing, including Sgt Bill Myers, who three weeks earlier had led the Honor Guard at Littlecote. (Peter Hendrikx)

was in flames. Over the next 20 minutes two more raids struck home, blocking vital roads. In total, 227 civilians were killed and 800 wounded. It was a disaster of biblical proportions and one that Eindhoven would take years to recover from.

The following morning, Third Battalion returned to Eindhoven and quickly realized how lucky they had been. Moving through ruined streets strewn with glass and smoldering embers was a sobering thought for all concerned. During the night most of 1/506 had been sent to Son to help defend the Bailey Bridge, while elements of 2/506 were recalled to Nuenen. This was well timed, because shortly after dawn on September 20, the German 107th Panzer-Brigade launched another attack. Thankfully the vital bridge at Son remained in Allied hands, but even with the extra British tank support the various task forces were ultimately unsuccessful in stopping the enemy advance, and as darkness fell, everyone returned to Eindhoven.

By now British armor and troop strength had grown sufficiently to allow the 506th to be re-tasked. At least the people of Eindhoven were now free, but for them life would not get any easier for some considerable time to come. When the Allied battle lines were drawn along the corridor to Arnhem, nearly 300,000 German troops became "trapped" in the Netherlands. However, at their disposal was an almost unlimited supply of tanks, self-propelled guns, and 88s.

Over the next few confusing days, the 506th was constantly on the move, plugging gaps, fighting off attacks and counterattacks along the highway. By September 21 the German 107th Panzer-Brigade had joined forces with two other fighting groups. The newly amalgamated force turned away from Son and began launching a series of ferocious attacks along the "supply corridor" transport hubs of Sint Oedenrode, Veghel, and Uden. The town of Veghel was particularly crucial due to its position on the road networks, railway system, and its close proximity to the Zuid-Willems-Vaart Canal. Due to the constant German attacks the 40-mile stretch of road between Eindhoven and Arnhem became almost impossible to keep open. Fighting became so fierce along the route that the 101st Airborne Division nicknamed the road "Hell's Highway." Fortunately, the division now had a limited number of rocket-firing RAF Typhoons at its disposal, but there were still other operational issues to be overcome.

Major Horton and his men were moving toward Uden on September 21, behind Charlie Chase, who was leading a small advance party from Second Battalion. After marching 10 miles, Horton's force went into reserve as backup for the 502nd and spent what was left of a cold, wet night, shivering in a wood on the outskirts of town. No sooner had they dug in that they were ordered to march back to Veghel, where about 40 enemy tanks were attempting to seize the town and destroy the bridges over the canal and the River Aa. Arriving around midday, Third Battalion were thrown into a confused and drawn-out fight that was raging through the town. Luckily nobody was killed, but Lt Alex Andros from H Company remembers the utter frustration of the day:

> 3 Platoon were instructed to attack along a road, where the Germans had a machine gun position with superb fields of fire. Because of the low ground we could only move forward through deep drainage ditches. It took us all day to get to a point where we could actually do some good. During a flanking attack later in the afternoon, Sgt Richards and my assistant Willie Miller were ahead of me, about 50 yards from the enemy positions. I was deeply concerned by the accurate grazing fire coming in our direction especially after several bullets ripped through the top of my backpack! Moving forward, I had just reached Richards as he screamed out, "To hell with this, I can't take it anymore, let's get up and just go for it." The entire squad charged ahead only to find that the Germans had pulled

out, leaving two young paratroopers behind manning a machine gun. These two kids had kept us at arms' length all that time. After pulling back we were too damn tired to dig foxholes so we used the ditches for cover instead. It rained all night and the following morning, I woke to find that I'd been sleeping the sleep of the dead in about five inches of water. It was miserable.

Eventually the enemy were outflanked by the British tanks and withdrew to fight another day.

Over the next three days the intermittent poor weather described by Alex Andros severely hampered air support. Luckily, due to the intelligence provided by the Dutch resistance, the division, sustained by British armor, was able to block several more German tank assaults along the 4-mile stretch of highway, except for Uden, where Colonel Chase and his small advance force had established themselves but were now completely isolated. In fact, the situation became so critical that the commander of XXX Corps, Lieutenant General Brian Horrocks, turned many of his artillery units around to assist. By the afternoon of September 22, the battalion were back in semi-reserve when the enemy launched another set of attacks against Veghel. This time the thrust was directed against the 501st PIR who were defending the main railway bridge over the canal. A lucky break in the weather meant that division was able to coordinate air strikes on the large enemy force. H Company of the 506th sent men to the bridge, while its G Company deployed into defensive positions nearby. But after G Company had dug in the company came under a heavy barrage that left two dead and several injured.

Charged with holding Veghel at all costs, the Divisional Artillery Commander, General Anthony McAuliffe, threw together a task force comprised of the 506th and several other American units, as well as a squadron of British tanks. In the meantime, to relieve pressure, 1/501 pushed several miles to the west and occupied the town of Schijndel, capturing nearly 400 prisoners, while McAuliffe's makeshift force deployed around Eerde to shield Veghel.

H Company's 2nd Platoon found themselves deeply involved in the fighting on what became known as "Black Friday." It was crucial to hold the line near the railroad bridge west of Veghel, and the platoon commander, Lieutenant Clark Heggeness, had been designated to defend a small bridge at Dorshout which spans the River Aa. That morning Clark had about 20 men at his disposal as they quietly moved into position around the bridge and joined a machine-gun team from the 501st. By a stroke of "luck" the 107th Panzer-Brigade had broken through after crossing a bridge over the River Aa a few miles further north. The bridge had previously been rigged for demolition but had failed to detonate. It seemed obvious to Heggeness that the crossing he was defending could be used to either support an attack on the highway or recapture the main canal crossing that was less than a mile away. With the bridge at Dorshout now on 2 Platoon's right flank, the position held commanding views across the river, railway embankment and into the open fields beyond. The young lieutenant split his small force into two groups and waited. During the afternoon two tanks appeared supported by around 250 infantry and began firing wildly at the bridge. Along the northern side of the embankment there was a 15ft-wide drainage ditch, with unusually steep banks about 9ft deep and full of water that the tanks stood absolutely zero chance of crossing. However, about 50 enemy soldiers clambered over the embankment and moved cautiously into the open ground behind a nearby farm. Heggeness told his troopers to hold fire until the enemy force was perfectly bracketed. Everyone was on edge as the Germans began to fan out, and were no more than 50 yards away, when Clark gave the signal to open fire. All hell broke loose. It was slaughter as the Germans, completely exposed, were mown down.

Eventually, after several failed attempts to regroup, the enemy abandoned their assault and withdrew in total disarray. At this point the lieutenant led one section over the bridge. Keeping at a safe distance, they followed the retreating enemy from behind the embankment. Moving to the west, Heggeness and his men came to a small farmhouse about 400 yards away from the bridge where they spotted a Sherman tank. Thinking the Sherman was attacking the enemy flank, the troopers waved their orange recognition panels. Much to everyone's surprise, the infantry accompanying the tank opened up, killing one of Heggeness' men. Realizing that the tank had been captured, the paratroopers took cover behind the farmhouse as the tank turret turned toward them and fired a couple of rounds. Blanketing the area with smoke, Clark and his men lobbed just about every grenade they possessed and were relieved when the tank and infantry withdrew into a nearby wood.

Veghel itself was heavily shelled during the late afternoon and early evening as the 327th Glider Infantry Regiment arrived to take up defensive positions either

LEFT View west across the bridge over the River Aa from where 2 Platoon, H Company, held the line on September 22, 1944. The enemy force came in from the right.

RIGHT Looking east from the ditch back along the railway embankment toward the Aa and the bridge. Back in 1944 the ditch proved to be a natural obstacle for enemy tanks. September 22, 1944 was a day the men from H Company would not forget in a hurry, when 2 Platoon earned a Regimental Citation for its defense of the line near the railroad bridge west of Veghel.

side of the main bridge, allowing Major Horton's men to take a short break and begin preparing for the next day's battle. There was no clearer sign of the ferocity of these numerous small battles than the fact that Horton's men were forced to get used to the smell of roasting flesh coming from the myriad of British and German tanks burning all around them.

Soon after dawn on September 23, the Germans launched several small-scale attacks and throughout the day their artillery rained down across Veghel, forcing everyone, soldiers and civilians alike, to desperately seek shelter in basements and cellars. Later in the afternoon Second and Third Battalions reorganized and pushed north to attempt to link up with a forward patrol from the Guards Armoured Division. When the British were unable to connect, both battalions were redirected to the nearby village of Heuvel to establish a temporary defensive line facing east.

Over the next 48 hours, the enemy were able to deploy a much larger force, including 6th Fallschirmjäger-Regiment, who had tenaciously fought against the 506th in Normandy. The German task force launched a series of probing attacks and managed to cut the highway near Koevering. The 506th were moved to Uden, where they rejoined Chase's small beleaguered force, and the Third Battalion were tasked to defend an open area northwest of the town overlooking the Leigraaf Canal. By late afternoon of the 24th, enemy tanks and artillery were spotted moving toward Koevering. Under cover of darkness, the enemy strengthened its stranglehold on Hell's Highway and the following morning Third Battalion was sent into action.

Leading south down the highway, the battalion moved on Koevering, flanked to the right by 1/506. As Major Horton entered the village, the leading elements came under well-directed artillery, tank and small-arms fire. I Company maneuvered around the enemy front line to the right, as the men from H Company's 1 Platoon pushed forward, hugging the ditches. Heavy bursts of machine-gun fire were coming from a large red-brick farmhouse, located directly alongside the main road, several hundred yards ahead. The platoon split into two assault groups. The first continued forward, while the second team, led by Staff Sergeant Frank Padisak, attempted to encircle the building from the west.

Padisak's team left the highway opposite a neatly planted orchard and proceeded along a dirt road partially lined by a row of tall poplar trees. The team headed west for nearly 400 yards, until reaching a minor intersection. Approaching the junction, the men came under a hail of bullets, coming from the red-brick house, which was now only some 300 yards away across an open field. John Purdie was in the lead, closely followed by Lloyd Carpenter, Johnny Hahn and Hank DiCarlo. Just ahead, the ditch turned left through 90 degrees toward the main highway. Purdie and Carpenter made the turn when a Sherman, flying a Jolly Roger pennant, came out from behind the house and slowly began to move toward them. Purdie and his men were momentarily confused but hesitantly displayed their orange flags to show that

TOP Koevering looking south along Wolvensteeg toward the red-brick farmhouse and Hell's Highway from the ditch (left) where Cpls John Purdie, Johnny Hahn and Pfc Lloyd Carpenter were killed on September 25, 1944.

BOTTOM H Company group photo taken at Camp Mackall, 1943. (Standing, left to right): Frank "The Slovak" Padisak (wounded at Foy), Bruce Paxton, John Purdie (KIA Koevering), the infamous thief and deserter Howard "Sonny" Sundquist, Nick Snyder (wounded at Foy). (Front kneeling, left to right): Alex Spurr (wounded at Foy), Stan Stasica, Bob Martin, Johnny Hahn (white T-Shirt and braces, KIA Koevering), Bob "Whitey" Hoffman, and Godfrey "Jon" Hansen (KIA Eindhoven). According to Lou Vecchi and Hank DiCarlo, Sundquist was in prison for theft and rape during Normandy and Holland and was posted back to 1 Platoon at Mourmelon. Captain Walker and Frank Padisak unanimously blocked the move and apparently "side swiped" him to First Battalion. Not long afterwards Sundquist went AWOL and vanished without a trace. Months later he was arrested and given a substantial prison sentence for desertion. (Mark Bando Collection)

they were friendly. Seconds later the tank began pumping HE rounds into the line of poplar trees behind the Americans. The first round blew Hank DiCarlo out of the ditch and onto the gravel road. With no better place to go, but luckily completely uninjured, he immediately dived back and crawled up to Hahn to check if he was OK. When he did not answer, Hank turned Johnny over and found that he was dead, most likely killed by concussion, as there were no visible wounds on his body. Crawling around the corner of the ditch, DiCarlo did his best to render first aid to Purdie and Carpenter, who were both mortally wounded by shrapnel. Hank looked at his watch, 1720hrs, and mentally noted the time that his chums had died. Everything had happened in the blink of an eye, but as Hank switched his attention back to the tank he wondered why it was now reversing. At that moment Second Battalion came bowling in with British tank support and managed to dislodge the enemy troops occupying the red-brick farm. By nightfall, the enemy had been cleared from all but a very small area to the south and Hell's Highway was never cut again. It is interesting to note that one week after the main highway was captured by the 506th, two more routes had to be opened due to lack of momentum from XXX Corps.

After the two main battles at Veghel were over, the 506th successfully drove the enemy from Koevering and connected with the 501st. The 506th seaborne echelon, bringing in much needed transport, supplies and replacements for all three battalions, had also arrived at Veghel. British forces continued to attack toward the north, relieving the 506th and the 502nd. Third Battalion returned to their original foxholes in Uden only to be sent back to Veghel on the 27th, to stem one of the last German counterattacks. Although the division had taken over 3,000 prisoners, the enemy were by no means neutralized. The Battle of Hell's Highway ended quietly for the 506th at Uden, with the men believing their job in the Netherlands was well and truly finished.

## An Overview of the Island Campaign

Arnhem
Wageningen
Nol in 't Bosch
Heelsum
Heveadorp
Westerbouwing
Oosterbeek
The Neder Rijn
Renkum
3
2
Elden
Driel
Heteren
Randwijk
1
Indoornik
Kesteren
Opheusden
The Linge River
Hemmen
Zetten
9
8
6
7
10
4
Lienden
Elst
Dodewaard
Hien
11
Andelst
Valburg
Wely
Herveld
Slijk-Ewijk
5
Oosterhout
N
The Waal
Lent
1km
Nijmegen

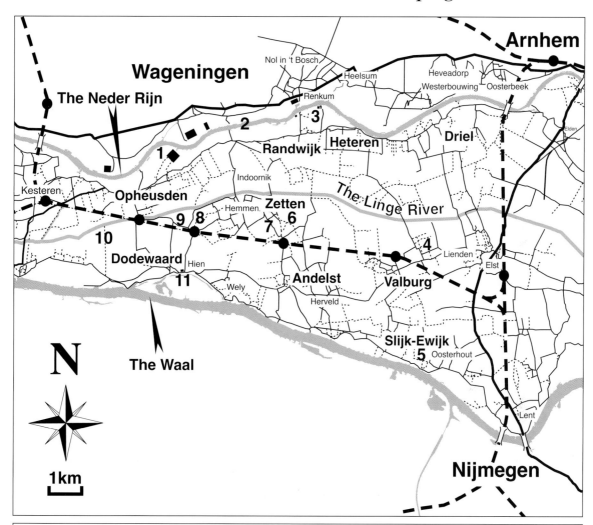

**KEY**

**1.** Wolfswaard Brick Factory
**2.** Crossing Point for Operation "Pegasus 1"
**3.** Renkum Brick Factory
**4.** Schoonderlogt – 506 CP Oct 28–Nov 25
**5.** 101st Airborne Divisional CP – duration
**6.** De Fliert – 3/506 CP Oct 9–28
**7.** Dutch Reformed Church – 506th CP Oct 5–19
**8.** Boelenham Farm – 3/506 & 506th CP Oct 3–5
**9.** Site of Captain Harwick's jeep crash Oct 6
**10**. Eldijk – 2 Ptn H Co defensive area Oct 5
**11.** The Christian School – 3/506 CP Oct 5–8

Brick Factories & Industrial sites
Metalled or partially metalled road
Dirt road/track
Railway Line & Station

But at the beginning of October, the 101st was both surprised and disappointed to learn that it would not be going to a rest camp in France. The announcement stated that they would now be moving 30 miles further north to "the Island" near Arnhem to take over from the British. Ultimately, General Taylor came to regard the assistance given to the 101st by the Dutch underground as crucial in the liberation of Eindhoven, Son, Sint Oedenrode and Veghel. Before the battalion moved out, many were given time to visit the temporary cemetery opposite the DZ at Wolfswinkel and pay their respects to those who had been killed during the last ten days.

## "The Island" campaign October 3–November 27

In 1944, the civilian population of the Betuwe, "the Island," numbered around 40,000 people and many of the towns and villages within it – such as Kesteren, Opheusden, Zetten and Valburg – were made up of deeply religious farming communities, while others, like Echteld, Randwijk, Dodewaard, Heteren and Driel, depended on shipbuilding, tobacco, and jam-making industries. Brick manufacture was another important employer, with at least a dozen factories situated along the Rijn and the Waal. Dissected by three main railway networks and the Linge Canal, the Island had superb transportation links to Arnhem, Nijmegen and also larger industrial cities to the west.

On September 17, Allied fighter planes had attacked German antiaircraft sites in the Betuwe, as the first gliders passed overhead to begin the landings at Renkum and Wolfheze along with thousands of British paratroopers. The 82nd Airborne Division had successfully completed their original mission to capture and keep open the Waal

Major Horton moved his HQ into Boelenham Farm that had only just been vacated by the British. The spacious new CP and message center was shared with Col Sink and RHQ and situated close to the Hemmen-Dodewaard railway station. Almost every room on the ground floor was utilized by the Americans, except for the kitchen, which the owners, the Tap family, retained as their living area. Executive Officer Bob Harwick found a comfortable bed upstairs in what had previously been a nursery. Attached as a mobile reserve were the Fifth Battalion, Duke of Cornwall's Light Infantry, commanded by LtCol George Taylor who set up his HQ in one of the large barns next to the house (just visible on the right).

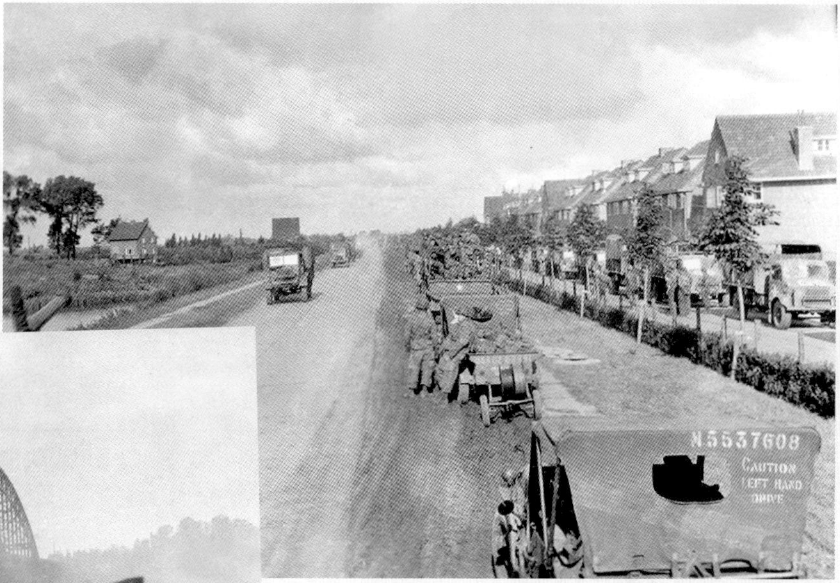
N5537608
CAUTION
LEFT HAND
DRIVE

ABOVE October 2, 1944 – this picture taken by John Reeder shows the 506th PIR moving north through Grave while en route to the Island. (John Reeder via D-Day Publishing Collection)

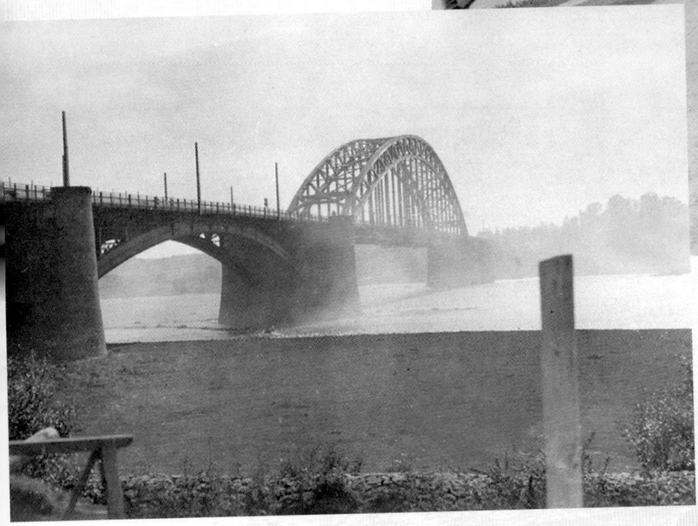

Another photo taken by John Reeder as the 506th reached the road bridge at Nijmegen. Note the smoke being released to screen the crossing from enemy artillery. (John Reeder via D-Day Publishing Collection)

River bridge at Nijmegen. During the early afternoon of October 1, the 506th PIR were alerted for a possible move to the city. Meanwhile, in the area known as the Veluwe over on the southern bank of the Rijn, the Germans began evacuating most of the civilian population. This event should have rung alarm bells but the event seemingly went unnoticed by the British. The following morning, the 506th were moved by road from Uden to Nijmegen to support the 82nd for what was to become perhaps the toughest phase of the entire campaign. The regiment was replacing a part of the 43rd Wessex Division at Opheusden. The land around the small town was made up of reclaimed floodplains consisting of open pasture and numerous apple and cherry orchards enclosed by deep drainage ditches and dijks. The Island campaign would all too soon become a succession of brief defensive stands, fierce fighting, and continuous outflanking movements for the depleted and fatigued paratroopers and ultimately would prove to be some of the darkest days for Third Battalion.

When Second and Third Battalion took over the main line of defense, both sectors had been peaceful for well over a week. When the Third Battalion moved into Opheusden the Machine Gun Platoon were ordered to occupy the railroad

## Opheusden, October 5, 1944

Neder Rijn
N
2
Opheusden
3
Dalwagenseweg
4
Smatchkamp
Tolsestraat
1
Parallelweg
10
Biezenwei
Dalwagen
Parallelweg
Linge Canal
9
5
8
7
6
Opheusden Station
Dalwagenseweg
1km

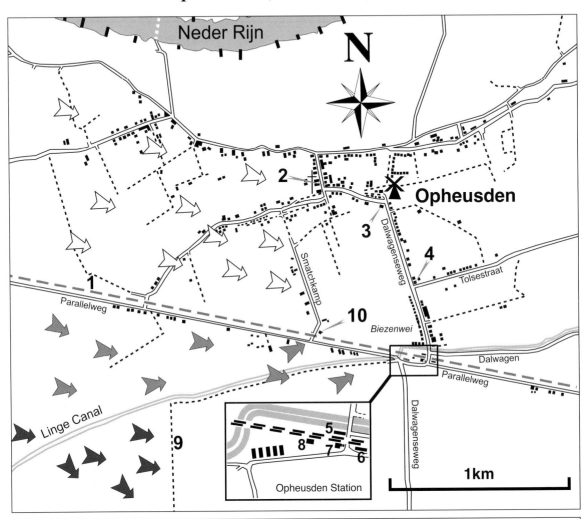

KEY

1. S/Sgt Harry Clawson & Pfc Morris Thomas – field graves discovered Dec 1971
2. G Co CP Hervormde School
3. 3/506 Aid Station at the doctor's house
4. H Co CP
5. Waiting Rooms at Railway Station
6. Waiting Rooms at Railway Station
7. Opheusden Station, MG Ptn CP
8. Barn used by HQ Co to store equipment
9. 2 Ptn H Co
10. 3 Ptn H Co CP

IR 957 line of attack – Oct 5,1944
IR 958 line of attack – Oct 5,1944
IR 959 line of attack – Oct 5,1944
Metalled or partially metalled road
Dirt roads & tracks
Railway
Windmill
Church

station. Lieutenant Bill Wedeking, commanding officer of the platoon, was immediately concerned by his limited fields of fire but tried to make things work. Major Horton then decided at the last minute to send two of Bill's most experienced sergeants, Chuck Easter and Tex Collier, along with four gun teams, across to H Company. As the Germans were known to be holding the high ground on the Veluwe, Second Battalion moved forward to the Neder Rijn to defend a wide front along the dijk north of Opheusden to Heteren. Third Battalion took over a sector 2,000 yards long, facing west from the northern edge of Opheusden, extending south through the railway station toward Dodewaard.

With G Company covering the northern flank, two platoons from H Company dug in around the level crossing on the southern edge of town. First Lieutenant Alex Andros and his 3 Platoon were positioned along a dirt road that meandered from the northern edge of Opheusden down to a small railroad crossing, where Andros established his CP in the abandoned signalman's house. North of the Waal, I Company was holding a small pocket of land where company commander Lieutenant Fred "Andy" Anderson made the nearby jam factory at Dodewaard his CP. Of course, the soldiers made complete and full use of the extra "sugar rations" that the factory provided.

At 0300hrs on October 5, the enemy began probing the main Third Battalion front line, between 1 Platoon and 3 Platoon of H Company. Two hours later the 957th, 958th and 959th Infanterie-Regiments from the 363rd Volksgrenadier-Division launched the first in a series of fanatical and costly attacks that would last for nearly three days. The main aim for the Germans was to punch through, gain some momentum, and ultimately seize the bridge at Nijmegen. Elements of the MG Platoon were in vulnerable outpost positions way ahead of the main line of defense with very little or indeed no infantry support. When the German artillery and mortars opened up, followed by wave after wave of infantry, the four machine gun teams were forced to withdraw, leaving most of their casualties and equipment behind in no man's land.

Meanwhile, Lieutenant Bob Stroud and 1 Platoon were positioned several hundred yards away, straddling the tracks at the railway station. Stroud had established his CP in a heavily fortified concrete pillbox that had previously formed part of the Dutch defense line in 1940. As it was getting light, the area around the station began to erupt with explosions. The noise was overwhelming. Moments later, through the slit in his pillbox, Hank DiCarlo spotted movement along the tracks and opened fire with his light machine gun (LMG). Several enemy soldiers were hit and the rest spread out into the shrubs and bushes either side of the railway lines.

Lieutenant Alex Andros (foreground) and his assistant 2nd Lt Willie Miller from 3 Platoon, H Company, pictured here at Saalbach, Austria, in 1945. Miller was wounded in the neck during the attack on October 5. (Lou Vecchi)

"The railway crossing soon became cluttered with enemy casualties and since we were in such close proximity, we began exchanging grenades back and forth across the embankment. I sent my runner Elmer Swanson to look for stretcher-bearers, and he returned some 20 minutes later with Dr Morgan and several other guys from the medical detachment. At roughly the same time, Bob Sink arrived and wanted to know what the hell was going on. I told him frankly that we were getting our butts kicked, and he asked if we could hold on for another couple of hours while First Battalion was being deployed! With the enemy pushing forward on both flanks he realized that it was virtually impossible for 3 Platoon to remain any longer. After Sink's visit, I sent my radio operator Gene Johnson over to Chuck Richards with orders for him to pull out. Johnson returned almost immediately saying that Richards was being overrun and the Germans were now breaking through on the right."

First Lieutenant Alexander Andros – 3 Platoon, H Company

"We dug in along a 7ft-high flood barrier to the west of Dodewaard that ran due south from the Linge Canal. The artillery we experienced that morning was unbelievable. Bert Bailey was near the top of the dike when a shell exploded and blew his head clean off his shoulders. Still complete with helmet, Bailey's head rolled down the embankment and stopped at my feet. It was a horrifying experience staring down into his expressionless face, knowing that only minutes before we had been talking to each other."

Sergeant Kenneth G. Johnson, 2 Platoon, H Company

"At about 0600hrs, Cpl Fay Handy reported to my CP and gave me a few sketchy details of what had just happened to the four guns attached to H Company. As Handy was briefing me, I noticed that one of his hands was pouring with blood and he said, 'Look, Lieutenant, no finger!' One of our guys sprinkled some sulfa powder on the stump and bandaged the injured hand before sending him off to the aid station at the other end of town. Roughly 30 minutes later, Chuck Easter arrived and told me that all four machine guns had been destroyed and their crews including a young Dutch volunteer had been annihilated. I was shocked by what he said and sent him back to the battalion CP with a runner to inform Major Horton of the situation and grab a hot meal. I later learned that after filing his report, Chuck was in one of the barns next to the CP when an artillery shell exploded through the roof, mortally wounding him."

First Lieutenant William "Bill" P. Wedeking – Machine Gun Platoon

"I was helping three other medics carry a dead soldier out the back door of the aid station in Opheusden when a shell struck the front of the building. The terrific blast knocked all four of us to the floor... The shelling forced Doc Ryan to relocate our operation to the Regimental Aid Station in Zetten. One of our younger medics, Tom Call, was conveying wounded by jeep to the school there when he slumped forward absolutely stone dead! We checked his body from head to toe but failed to find any obvious wounds. On further examination, Dr Ryan pulled down on an eyelid and found a tiny penetrating wound hidden in the skin. Incredibly a sliver of shrapnel had come over the windshield and under the rim of Tom's helmet, penetrating deep into his brain. There was no blood, nothing – we were all totally stunned."

Corporal John W. Gibson – Medical Detachment

View west along the tracks from Opheusden station toward the enemy threat as seen by Bob Stroud and Bill Wedeking on October 5, 1944.

All that morning the CP at Boelenham was under constant harassment from across the river. General Browning arrived to discuss the situation and immediately advised Sink to evacuate to the Dutch Reformed Church at Zetten, where the tall steeple made a superb observation post from which to monitor the battle. Just before 1000hrs, after a meeting with Sink, Major Horton went to see Bob Stroud at the station for an update and was killed by enemy machine-gun fire. Corporal Hank DiCarlo later recalled the rapidly deteriorating situation and Horton's death:

Suddenly the area erupted with explosions and as the majority of our equipment and ammunition was still in the shed at the station, we ran a relay race back and

# RALPH BENNETT

"I was in a large tool shed on the northern side of the railway junction, peering across the tracks through my field glasses. It looked like the entire German Army was coming my way in what seemed like one black solid mass. I took two men and moved forward along the edge of the embankment. We'd only gone about 25 yards when we heard German voices coming from the other side of the tracks. I threw a grenade and scrambled across the railway lines and found myself looking down on a dozen or so enemy soldiers, who were standing in a wide waterlogged ditch on the other side. Simultaneously, they lifted their heads and looked up toward me. They were so close I could see the horror and panic in their eyes. I emptied an entire clip from my TSMG into their faces and ran like hell back to the CP. Although I did not realize it at the time, that shooting became a defining moment that haunted me for the rest of my life. When I got back to warn the platoon, Lieutenant Andros told me that Harry Clawson had been hit and I was now the new platoon sergeant."

While Bennett had been away, Andros and Clawson had been desperately trying to contact the battalion by handheld radio when a shell had exploded, killing Andros' signaler and wounding Clawson. Andros himself was incredibly lucky to escape with nothing but a flesh wound and a dent in his steel helmet. Three or four men from the platoon started firing from the corner of the signal house as the enemy tried to advance across the junction. During the exchange of fire Second Lieutenant Willie Miller was seriously wounded in the neck. The crossing soon became cluttered with enemy casualties as grenades were exchanged back and forth. But with the enemy pushing forward on both flanks and overrunning vital positions, it was impossible to remain.

Meanwhile due to lack of stretchers, Dr Morgan and his medics, who had come forward with Sink, were unable to remove all the wounded from the house. Morgan decided to stay and look after the remaining casualties until the rest of medics could return. It soon became apparent that they would not be coming back, so when Andros and his men pulled out, the "Doc" opted to stay behind with the remaining wounded, including Clawson and a young machine gunner called Morris Thomas. As Bennett later recalled:

Ralph Bennett seen here on November 12, 1944, receiving his much deserved Silver Star from LtGen Lewis Brereton. The 60mm mortar sergeant won the award while covering the withdrawal of H Company from Opheusden on October 5. (Ralph Bennett)

"With enemy troops about to envelop our position from both the north and south, I decided to cover the withdrawal with my 60mm mortar and two men. There was a wooden hay cart behind the house and Alex climbed on top to spot for me. I held the tube almost vertically and let the first bomb go. Open-mouthed we all watched as the shell launched directly above our heads and came down no more than 10 yards away! At least it gave me a starting point from where I was able to adjust and drop the other shells more accurately behind the embankment. We could hear screaming coming from the other side of the tracks. I think our shells temporarily fooled the Germans into thinking that the spot had been zeroed by artillery, which at least kept them from trying to cross the railway line again. At this rate I only had enough mortar ammo to last me for about ten more minutes but it bought enough time for Andros and the others to get out. When I ran out of ammunition I threw the tube into a waterlogged ditch. Dr Morgan did not want to leave when I told him it was time to go. Pulling myself smartly to attention, I saluted and told the Doc that I would do my best to get back."

Bennett had only been gone a few minutes when the signal house was overrun, and despite his protests, Doctor Morgan was marched to the nearby town of Ommeren. Although their injuries were by no means life-threatening, Clawson and Thomas were left behind. Morgan glanced back and saw a column of dense smoke rising from the building and thought of the two men now trapped inside. At some point afterwards the Germans moved the bodies of Clawson and Thomas to a forward aid station on the southern side of the railway embankment, where they had established a temporary cemetery. The corpses of the two Americans were then buried on the northern side of the tracks, presumably to keep them separate. Over the weeks that followed, the shallow graves were covered by floodwater and any external sign of their existence washed away.

forth trying to collect it. Moments later, we saw movement along the tracks and poked our LMG through the slit in the pillbox and opened fire. I saw several enemy soldiers fall before the rest spread out into the bushes on either side of the railway lines.

A little while later as we were preparing to pull back from the pillbox, Major Horton arrived and asked where we thought we were going. I respectfully replied that heavy machine-gun fire was coming down the tracks and that at any moment we would all be surrounded and killed. I could not believe it when he stepped out from behind the bunker to take a look for himself! Horton was struck in the midsection by one of the very guns I'd just warned him about and died a few minutes later. Despite applying immediate first aid, there was nothing more we could have done for him. A few minutes later, Doc Morgan who was just passing by stopped for a second and said, "Hey, DiCarlo, what in the hell are you doing here… I thought I took you off jump status?" I could only respond with a shrug and a sheepish smile. Shaking his head before continuing, the doctor added, "Right now we have a bit of a situation to deal with, but rest assured I will take care of you later."

The Dutch Reformed Church on Kerkstraat, Zetten, became the 506th Regimental Command Post from October 5–9, 1944.

ABOVE RIGHT 81mm Mortar Team in action somewhere on the Island.

Following Horton's death, Bob Harwick stepped up to take command. Bob was highly respected and despite the terrible circumstances his appointment was warmly received by the men. The battalion was now about to plunge into the toughest period of fighting it had ever encountered. As just one example of the intensity of the rapidly developing battle, back in Zetten, Staff Sergeant Roy Burger had already burned out three 81mm mortar barrels before completely running out of ammunition.

Earlier that afternoon in the southwestern sector near Dodewaard, the left flank of I Company came under heavy infantry and tank attack, forcing Andy Anderson to call for support. Luckily the 321st Glider Field Artillery Battalion and British gunners from the 79th Field Artillery Regiment managed to thwart the advance. But that evening the enemy began to regroup and concentrate its attention on I Company's weaker southern flank, along the River Waal. After the "murder mile" had begun to stabilize, First Battalion moved forward and recovered some of the ground that had been lost. That night the entire Third Battalion was ordered south of the railway, to form a defensive line 400 yards wide, continuing north into Opheusden, and linking up with First Battalion. Throughout the chaos of October 5, Second Battalion's positions remained unchanged. However, the new order of battle followed a line from north to south, beginning with I Company along the Waal at Dodewaard.

A vigorous and aggressive patrolling policy was maintained throughout the night of October 5/6 by all frontline units, under a protective shield of harassing artillery fire. In the lull that preceded first light on October 6, a heavy mist descended over the area. G Company's 3rd Platoon, led by Lieutenant Linton Barling, were

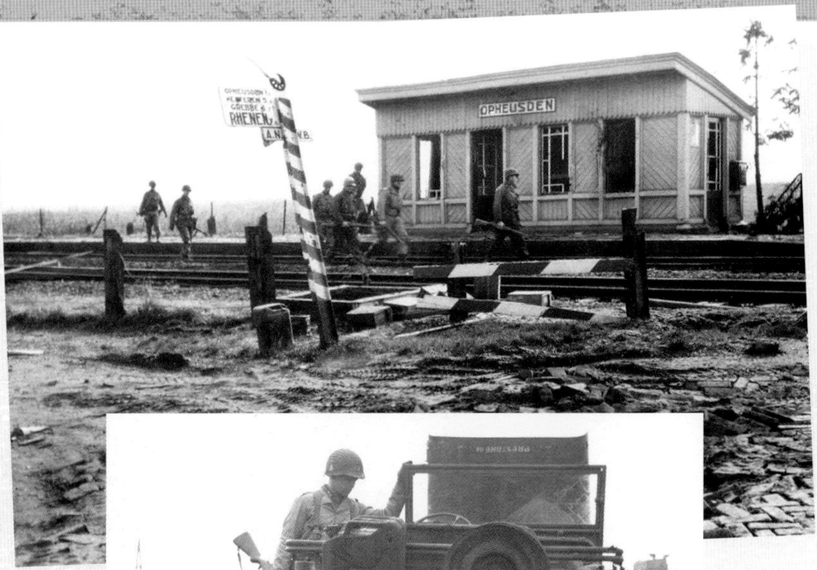
OPHEUSDEN

Lt Linton Barling was killed here at first light on October 6, 1944 in the railway station at Opheusden. Linton's 3 Platoon were working with 5th Duke of Cornwall's Light Infantry, who were expected to be joining them via a flanking movement. Barling heard voices up ahead and, thinking they were British, moved forward in the fog to make contact. The voices turned out to be German and after a brief exchange of fire, the enemy displayed a white flag. As Barling passed the waiting room on the western side of the station, the door flew open and he was killed instantly by a burst of machine-gun fire. (Al Krotchka, D-Day Publishing Collection)

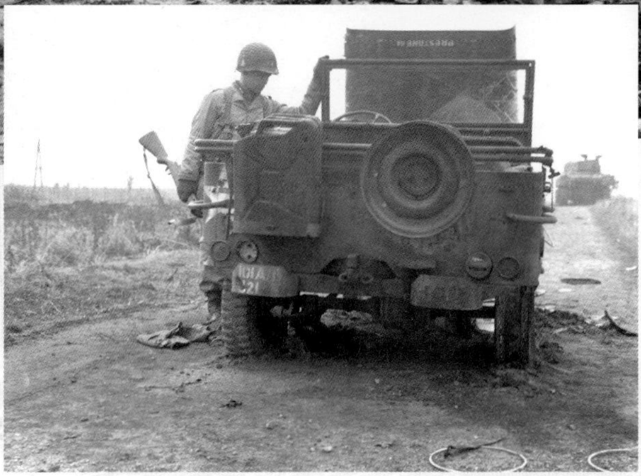

The roads around Opheusden quickly became littered with wrecked vehicles like this 101st Division jeep along the Linge Canal. (Peter Hendrikx)

moving westwards along the railtracks when they clashed with the Germans, who had moved into the station and were now threatening the Main Line of Resistance (MLR) at the level crossing. Simultaneously, the 957th Infanterie-Regiment attacked along the northern side of the station, pushing First Battalion back 500 yards and pinning down H Company. The remainder of G Company were immediately released from reserve and sent to defend the tracks in an attempt to recapture the station.

Nearby, Battalion Supply Sergeant Ben Hiner was in a house on the southern side of the station, peering through the mist from a second-floor window, when he saw a number of soldiers eerily emerging from an orchard about 300 yards away. An enemy advance party had found a gap in the lines and were now moving in extended file – about 10 feet apart – in an attempt to outflank the town. At first, he presumed they were Americans, but then noticed that the men were wearing long woolen overcoats. The silence was shattered the moment Hiner opened fire on the gray-clad figures. Staff Sergeant Fred Bahlau and Lieutenant John Weisenberger had been resting in a large railway building that was nearby and immediately ran over to

# LEO JEUCKEN

Seventeen-year-old Leonardus "Leo" Jeucken joined Third Battalion as an irregular in Eindhoven and fought with HQ Company up until his death at Opheusden on October 5, 1944. Captain Jim Morton was so impressed by Leo's actions that he even wrote him up for a posthumous citation on his eventual return to the United States:

"At daylight a German infantry regiment with supporting elements launched a heavy assault on our defense line extending from Opheusden to Dodewaard, held at that time by Third Battalion. The Machine Gun Platoon was deployed in the village of Opheusden and to the immediate south with the railroad as limiting point. The section of two .30 cal. MGs to which Jeucken had attached himself was deployed forward of the north-south road leading into Opheusden, the gun positions about 50 yards apart. Sergeants Charles Easter and Garland Collier were killed in action in this identical sector. The guns were commanded by Cpl Nathan Bullock of Kennet Square, PA, on the right and Sgt Fayez Handy of Bakersfield, CA, on the left. Company commander was Captain James G. Morton of Garden City, NY. Subject, Jeucken, was serving with the right gun under command of Cpl Bullock. He functioned as an ammunition bearer and provided rifle protection to the flank of the depleted crew. In the German attack, our left gun was knocked out leaving Bullock's gun in an exposed untenable position surrounded on three sides by German infantrymen. The enemy closed to within 30 to 50 yards of the machine-gun position.

Pvt Clyde Benton, the gunner, was seriously wounded by grenade or shell fragments and dragged to a sheltered position by Cpl Bullock while Pfc Morris Thomas took over the gun, firing point blank at the enemy. Exposing himself with complete disregard for his personal safety, young Jeucken crawled forward to his side to help keep the gun in action.

Pfc Thomas then was severely wounded, falling back from the gun. Although he had seen two soldiers shot down while trying to keep the gun firing, Jeucken unhesitatingly went forward to become the gunner. He fired the gun and prevented the enemy from advancing until he himself was shot dead. Since the position was captured by German troops, it was not possible to evacuate Jeucken's body, and it is believed he is buried in a common grave. Pfc Thomas was left in the overrun position, and is now presumed dead.

Jeucken, who participated in every combat engagement of the 506 PIR in Holland up to the time of his death, served with outstanding gallantry. He is recommended for the highest military award that the United States can bestow on a friendly civilian who aids our armed forces in combat with the enemy."

James G. Morton
0-366352
Captain, USAR-Ret

Leo Jeucken was just one of many irregulars and official Dutch resistance who joined the Allies in the desperate battles throughout the Island.

support Hiner. However, the overwhelming weight of return fire forced them back to the ground floor. The Germans made no attempt to clear the house but instead circled around to an adjacent building and crossed over the road. The three Americans then moved forward, managing to get behind the enemy troops, and close enough to lob a few grenades into the rear of the column. A brief firefight followed, during which Bahlau and Hiner captured 11 prisoners. For the most part the Germans were just boys wearing brand new uniforms. When the group returned to their original location, they were glad to see that the long-awaited vehicles from HQ Company had finally arrived. After several trips through furious enemy fire, almost all the battalion supplies, including the 11 prisoners, were successfully delivered to a new CP, established further south at Hien during the night after Boelenham was abandoned.

A couple of hours earlier, Colonel Sink had called Captain Harwick, who was now safely in Hien, to report that a German raiding party had broken through the G and H Company front lines, ahead of another possible heavy attack, and asked him to investigate. Sink wanted Harwick to send out a patrol to assess the situation and capture an enemy soldier for interrogation. But on the spur of the moment Harwick decided to do this himself. The captain called for a jeep, then tried to drive north, but enemy artillery prevented him from reaching Opheusden. Somewhere north of Dodewaard, Bob spotted Lieutenant Clark Heggeness, who by pure chance happened to be in the vicinity. Realizing that the Germans were now pushing down the railway tracks toward Boelenham Farm, Bob decided it might be better to head toward Hemmen and asked Clark to go with him. The driver turned around and took a more circular route to the farm, where Harwick intended to get an update from 5th Duke of Cornwall's Light Infantry (DCLI), who were hanging on by their fingertips to the old 506th CP.

Shortly after arriving Harwick went into the kitchen, and as he moved through the scullery toward the back door, a burst of automatic gunfire shattered a window to his left. However, the British seemed quite unconcerned that the Germans were now right on their doorstep. This was all Bob and Clark needed to know as they turned and ran back to the waiting jeep. Thinking he could outflank the enemy, the anxious driver sped down the straight narrow driveway and turned right onto the road leading to Opheusden. Following the line of the railway, the men had driven no more than 500 yards when they ran straight into a German patrol. Bob yelled at the driver to "step on it" and ducked down. Initially the Germans seemed surprised but then opened fire. They sped past at 50 miles an hour on the bumpy country road, and although the jeep was hit, Bob thought they had got away with it, until the driver did not make the slight bend up ahead!

The jeep plunged into a drainage channel on the left-hand side of the road, catapulting Bob and Clark head first into the freezing water, losing their weapons and helmets. Gagging on a mouthful of mud, as he struggled to stand, Bob was acutely aware of a sharp pain over his left eye. Clark was already dragging the driver from the water. The unconscious and unknown trooper had been shot in the head, and what little life remained ebbed away as he lay in Clark's arms. The men were sitting ducks.

Initially the two officers moved along the channel that eventually fed into the Linge Canal. Upon hearing German voices, the two men remained motionless amongst the rushes. It seemed that the Germans were laughing at what had just happened. Clark and Bob could now see rifle barrels probing back and forth through the reeds as if trying to locate them. Thankfully a patrol from 5th Duke of Cornwall came up from Boelenham and attacked the Germans, allowing Bob and Clark to make good their escape. Following the channel, the men crawled under a small bridge to the northern side of the road and virtually waded all the way back to Opheusden. By the time they reached the Third Battalion outpost, they looked like a pair of Halloween ghouls, uniforms shredded and faces caked with blood. Naturally, of course, the first question anyone asked was "Where's the damn jeep?"

Bob thought there might be a slim chance that driver was still alive. He also wanted the maps and reports that were tucked into the doors of the abandoned vehicle. After being told the rough whereabouts, Fred Bahlau and Ben Hiner volunteered to take their jeep and mount a rescue mission. Fred drove like hell along the canal and eventually found the captain's jeep on its side. Jumping into the murky water, the two men managed to salvage Harwick's papers. But floating face down, the driver was obviously dead. They recovered his body and headed back to Opheusden. Bob was in tears when he saw the lifeless driver and blamed himself for the young soldier's death. Afterwards Bahlau and Hiner were able to return to Hien, where their boss Jim Morton was anxiously awaiting news. Perhaps slightly tongue in cheek, the two men apologized for their absence. Morton knew that they had both gone beyond what was expected and put them up for the Silver Star – the second such award for the intrepid Bahlau.

Later that afternoon the Germans forced First Battalion back to the eastern edge of Opheusden, where they were ordered to form a skirmish line with 5th Duke of Cornwall's Light Infantry. Colonel Sink and the British commander, Lieutenant Colonel Taylor, decided that a combined attack was the best course of action. However, due to a series of mishaps there would be virtually no British and American artillery support available for the assault. As a result, the entire mission was doomed to failure and both units came under heavy 88mm cannon fire as soon as they moved out. At one point the German commander even allowed the casualties to be removed to the windmill. At 1600hrs the Cornishmen from B Company led another brave attack, only to be thwarted again by enemy mortar and machine-gun fire. Meanwhile, elements of First Battalion, supported by a troop of tanks from the

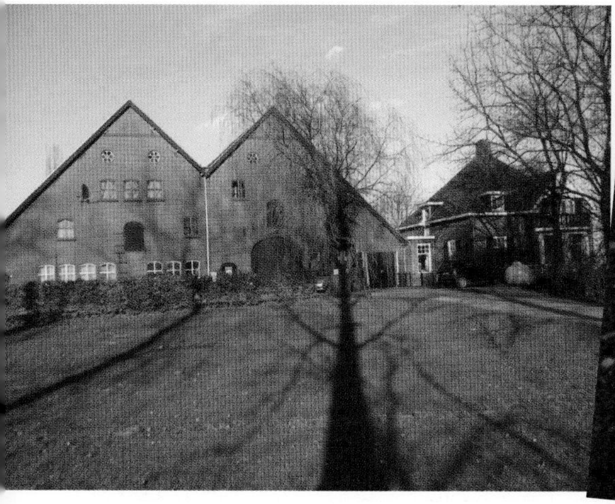

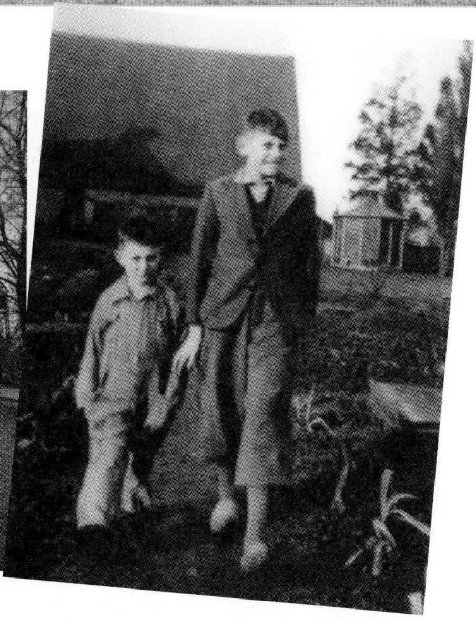

De Fliert was a large fruit farm owned by the Den Hartog family and became Third Battalion's CP on the night of October 7, 1944. The huge four-story barn (seen here on the left) was a useful storage and sleeping area for the troops.

The farm was also home to six-year-old Max Nathans, a Jewish child, who the Den Hartog family housed throughout the war. Out of the 22 members of Max's mother's family, 16 were murdered in the concentration camps. (Max Nathans)

Royal Scots Greys, were fighting for control of the railway station where the Germans had sited an antitank gun close to the canal bridge.

The overall situation on October 6 had not been helped by the superb observation afforded from the enemy positions across the river. The fact that the Germans were still advancing when the Anglo-American attack began only added to the confusion. Luckily a squadron of RAF rocket-firing Typhoons happened to be overhead on a separate mission. Orders were received that if any potential targets could be marked with red smoke then they would be neutralized by the fighter-bombers. The ensuing air strikes proved so successful that the Germans were forced away from the western edges of Opheusden. Not long after the air strikes, it was decided to replace 5th DCLI and 1/506 with Third Battalion of the 327th Glider Infantry Regiment. Before returning to his own HQ at Slijk-Ewijk, General Taylor visited 5th DCLI to personally thank them for their efforts. Colonel Sink later went on to say: "These troops attacked on schedule with vigor and determination in the face of withering enemy fire. Their courage and ability was an inspiration. Their gallantry was outstanding and instilled in my men the highest regard for the fighting ability of the British Infantry."

At around 0100hrs on Monday, October 7, a battalion of enemy soldiers launched yet another attack along the railway lines between 3/506 and 3/327 GIR, who were now defending the area to their north. The German force overran the positions along the tracks, forcing Third Battalion to tactically withdraw to shorten the line and contain the assault. However, around 350 enemy soldiers broke through and advanced north of the Linge Canal toward Hemmen. At first light First Battalion were resting in an assembly area near Boelenham Farm, when they spotted the force moving toward them. Over the next 30 minutes the advancing Volksgrenadiers were quite literally torn to shreds in an intense artillery and mortar bombardment.

Seven hours later, another German assault was stopped south of the tracks by Third Battalion and the Glider Infantry, who on this occasion had full mortar and artillery support. By nightfall Third Battalion were relieved and the 506th's involvement at Opheusden came to an abrupt end. The battalion moved to an assembly area southeast of Zetten located around a large farm called De Fliert. Although German Infanterie-Regiments 957, 958 and 959 had suffered devastating losses during the three-day battle for Opheusden, they were not going to relinquish their foothold on the Island without further bloodshed.

After the hell of the previous few days, Third Battalion was placed in regimental reserve around Zetten, along with First Battalion. Over the following week, both units were debriefed and reorganized, given showers, and issued new clothing before catching up on some very much needed rest. Bob Harwick and the battalion staff moved into their new CP at De Fliert.

Many were now showing signs of battle fatigue, and the constant random enemy shelling made already shattered nerves worse. During one barrage, Private Jose Tellez went completely mad and began screaming uncontrollably while loosing off his submachine gun. Luckily Tellez was wrestled to the ground before he could do any real harm either to himself or other members of his platoon.

When Second Battalion was finally pulled out from its positions along the Rijn, Third Battalion were assigned to replace them. On October 14, the battalion occupied the dijk between Opheusden and Heteren. The battalion soon discovered that its new home was behind the main dijk, overlooking a brick factory at Wolfswaard. The higher ground across the river on the Veluwe was still providing the enemy with commanding views, allowing them to target any daylight movement with devastating efficiency. Subsequently the area between factory and dijk became a "no man's land" that could only be patrolled at night.

Previously the Germans had dug a tunnel through the wall of the dijk and the battalion used it to gain access to the factory, where an OP had been established to monitor movement across the river. Each OP team would spend three days at the factory observing the road between Rhenen and Wageningen. Many local families had chosen to take refuge here from the shelling and were now living inside the large ovens built into the factory walls. Often the soldiers on OP duty and the Dutch would share evening meals together. Despite being right on top of the Germans, all the factories along this stretch of the river were important to the enemy and spared from direct artillery fire. The German

The commanding view offered to the Germans from the high ground at Westerbouwing south across the Neder Rijn onto the Island. Note the rail bridge at Driel seen here on the far left.

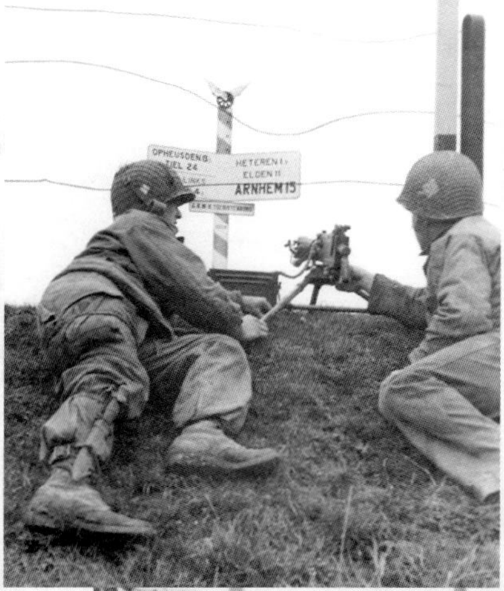
ARNHEM 15

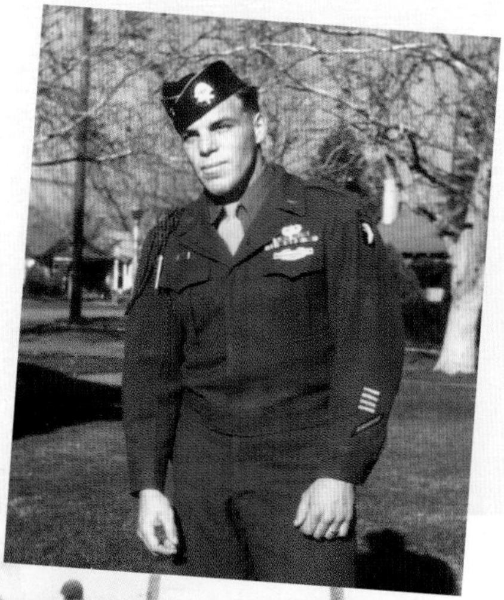

FAR LEFT This gun team are seen here behind the dijk road overlooking the brick factory at Renkum. (Mark Bando)

LEFT Harold Stedman, pictured here on December 22, 1945 after returning home to Modesto, California. (Tom Stedman)

BELOW Tunnel previously dug by the Germans through the main dijk wall near Wolfswaard, now occupied by troopers from I Company.

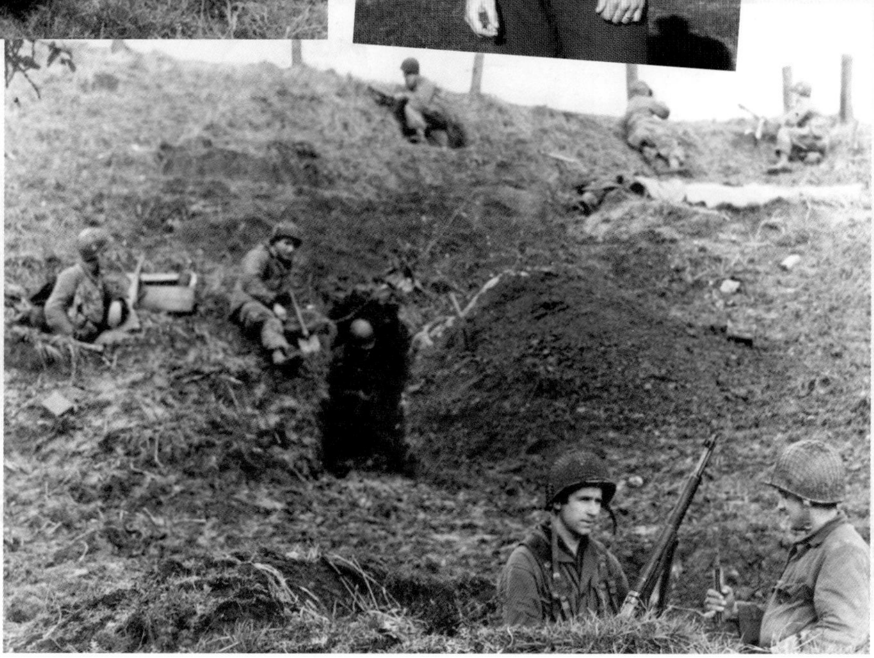

commanders believed that one day they would recapture the Island and resume brick production to help rebuild some of the more heavily bombed German cities.

As the weather worsened and winter rain began to set in, the men made small "tactical" fires from sand, lightly soaked with gasoline, in a desperate attempt to keep warm. Soon faces became coated with a thin layer of soot, making everyone's teeth look pearly white. Because rations were so poor, many began to exhibit signs of scurvy and locally sourced fresh meat was soon added to the diet to combat this. From time to time the British directed a battery of low-intensity spotlights across the river. The heavy cloud base common at this time of year allowed the ambient light to reflect downwards onto the enemy-held ground. But this did not deter the enemy from crossing the river for exploratory patrols. One evening in the I Company sector, Harold Stedman (from 3 Platoon) was just finishing a stint on OP duty in an old building close to the river. At around midnight, the mortarman cycled back to the RV where his colleague Frank Lujan was waiting to take over. Handing Frank the bike, Harold told him that everything was quiet and headed off to his foxhole. Lujan never returned from his shift and a couple of days later the German propaganda radio station "Arnhem Annie" announced that his best friend had been captured.

Between October 19 and 21, the Allies ordered the evacuation of thousands of the women and children from the Island. Most families were put on boats at Slijk-Ewijk and sent across the Waal. Many of the men remained behind because the authorities needed help to round up the abandoned livestock. Zetten was the last town to be evacuated, and the civilians were driven 50 miles southwest to Tilburg. Third Battalion were preparing to hand over control of their sector to the First Battalion. But H Company's 1 and 3 Platoons were asked to remain and help support the forthcoming mission, Operation *Pegasus 1*, being run by 2/506 to rescue a group of British paratroopers from the Veluwe. Three separate five-man advance patrols were sent across the Neder Rijn River to Wageningen, one of which was led by Lieutenant Alex Andros and Regimental Intelligence Officer Captain Bill Leach. Leach needed information on enemy troop strength and movements, and the location of a Nebelwerfer rocket launcher which had been causing problems for some time. The team would be crossing the river in small rubber rafts underneath an intermittent barrage from a pair of 40mm Bofors guns. After safely crossing, the patrol headed across a wide flood plain toward the nearest tree line. Despite a couple of close calls, Andros made it into Wageningen and was able to carry out a very valuable reconnaissance. Immediately after returning, Leach and Andros reported their findings to Bob Sink.

The evening of the 21st was the day *Pegasus 1* became a reality. Along the southern bank, members of H Company were assigned three outpost positions across a 2-mile front currently maintained by First Battalion. The first was next to the brick factory at Wolfswaard. The second was centrally located by the ferry opposite Wageningen, and the third was situated 900 yards further east on the dijk near Randwijk. Two or three nights before the operation, the two Bofors guns, about half a mile apart, fired tracer shells across the river for several minutes every hour. The tracer was marking the left and right parameters of the designated rescue area, and as long as the British paratroopers kept within these arcs, they were heading in the right direction. By Saturday night, all the boats to be used by 2/506 had been placed under apple trees in the H Company area adjacent to the river. Night routes were laid out using tape and additional artillery placed on alert, in case anything went wrong.

Looking east across the final operational area for 3/506 toward the Arnhem/Elst railway embankment at Driel. The Germans had blown up the bridge on September 17, 1944.

Before being deployed, Ralph Bennett reported to the H Company CP in Zetten for a final briefing. Throughout the evening, constant enemy mortar and artillery was landing immediately behind the operational area. Shortly after midnight, a red flashlight, blinking the "V" sign, was spotted across the river. The men from 2/506, who included Ed Shames, quietly carried their boats into the water and proceeded to paddle into the darkness. Once inside the bridgehead, it took about 30 minutes and several trips to evacuate all 149 paratroopers. Ralph Bennett was behind the dijk, near the ferry, and watched the returning boats. After everyone was safely ashore, H Company pulled back to create a protective shield behind them.

A few days later the regiment handed over to the 501st PIR and moved away to defend the northeastern sector of the Island at Driel. By the beginning of November, the battalion was being held in reserve at the tiny hamlet of Lienden. Scattered all around were burned out British tanks and trucks, a testament to the heavy fighting that had taken place in late September. Despite the fact that most of the machine guns lost at Opheusden had now been replaced, the MG Platoon only had ten men left out of an original strength of 40. Bill Wedeking's CP was located in a small abandoned farmhouse near the demolished railway bridge. Despite having fresh water from a hand pump, everyone still used purification tablets and supplemented their meagre rations with vegetables and partly frozen fruit. Wednesday, November 1, 1944, was "All Saints' Day" and the locals made their way along the mud-covered main road to give thanks at the church. Newly promoted to major, Bob Harwick and his men attended the service. Bob sent his prayers out to his parents, which was something he had done since Normandy. As the congregation was leaving, Bob's men collected their weapons, put on their helmets and returned to the war.

For some time, the enemy had been sending propaganda leaflets across the Rijn, packed into specially modified artillery shells. In response, the regiment made a broadcast in German across the Arnhem-Elst railway embankment at Driel with limited success (one or two made it across). The embankment was over 50ft high and marked the boundary at that time between the 506th and the Germans. All three battalions were deployed around Driel, where the First Polish Parachute Brigade had originally landed on September 21. The first rotation for Third Battalion began shortly before midnight on November 3. The troops were deployed into a wide area of damp farmland west of the railroad embankment, including a jam

A New Englander from Massachusetts, Major Lloyd Patch was a short but muscular leader who had been responsible for destroying a gun battery on D-Day for which he was awarded the Distinguished Service Cross. Lloyd took over command of 3/506 from Bob Harwick on November 21, 1944. Despite Lloyd's impressive track record with First Battalion, the veterans from Third Battalion truly believed that Harwick was cut from the same cloth as Bob Wolverton and, therefore, the only true candidate for command of them. This photograph was taken in Austria after Patch had been promoted. (Bob Webb Jr)

Andelst, December 1944. A jeep is photographed being driven through floodwater along Tielsestraat near to the Leigraaf Canal. (NARA)

This picture shows men from the 1/506 preparing to leave Lienden en route for Mourmelon-le-Grand, France, at 0600hrs on November 26, 1944. (NARA)

factory that became very popular with the guys. During the cold, wet nights, regular patrols were sent out to maintain contact with elements of the British 50th Infantry Division, situated a couple of miles away to the south.

Before the 152nd Infantry Brigade officially took over, Bob Harwick's men were sent to Nijmegen, where they joined the 82nd Airborne Division for much needed showers and recreation. Everyone was happy to scrub away the dirt and grime of the last few weeks in preparation for an awards parade headed by Major Generals Brereton and Ridgway. During the ceremony Fred Bahlau, Ralph Bennett and Ben Hiner received their Silver Stars. A few days later the battalion returned to the line for its last four-day rotation with a new commanding officer, Major Lloyd Patch. Surprisingly, Harwick had been reassigned to First Battalion, where he became Lieutenant Colonel James LaPrade's Executive Officer.

The men knew they were being relieved in a few short days and did not wish to be pushed into taking any unnecessary risks. Night patrols became extremely unpopular, and the bad weather only increased everyone's desire to be somewhere else. Even the Germans seemed to be cutting back on their patrol activity, which although it made everyone a little uneasy, they reassured themselves that soon it would no longer be their problem. Over the last two weeks, the excessive rainfall had caused water levels along the Rijn to rise alarmingly, and the subsequent flooding forced the MLR at Driel to be withdrawn by almost 500 yards. There was a rumor circulating that the enemy might take advantage of the flooding by demolishing part of the dijk wall in their sector, and as a precautionary measure, around Thanksgiving the men were briefed on Operation *Deluge*, the army's default plan to evacuate all Allied troops to the higher ground.

As the flooding grew more widespread so did the cases of trench foot. Finally, during the early hours of November 25, Third Battalion officially handed over control of the 506th sector to the Second Battalion Seaforth Highlanders. At long last, after 71 days of hell, the regiment was being sent to a rest camp in northeastern France – Mourmelon-le-Grand, near Reims. The battalion formed the rear echelon with RHQ and followed the main body 24 hours later, crossing the Waal in motorboats, before being loaded onto British trucks and driven to Mourmelon. It was typically overcast and still drizzling with rain when the guys arrived, and first impressions were not good, but at least they had dry billets and proper beds where they slept and slept and slept.

***

In total, during *Market Garden*, the 101st Airborne Division lost over 900 men killed, 4,000 wounded, and 1,000 captured or missing. Between 1945 and 1966, the bodies of 27 American servicemen MIA at Opheusden were discovered and given proper burials. To this day *Market Garden* remains a controversial operation, hotly debated by historians and veterans alike. But what cannot be disputed is the unquestionable courage and determination of the Third Battalion and the 506th Parachute Infantry Regiment.

On December 3, 1944 the enemy demolished a section of the main dijk about a mile behind the railway embankment at Driel. The massive explosion ripped a 150ft-wide gap and flooded the land east of the railway between Elden and Elst. Seeping through culverts and drainage ditches, the floodwater soon found its way across the Island, forcing the British and Canadian forces, the few remaining civilians, and thousands of livestock to migrate along the River Waal toward Zetten and Dodewaard. However, the Germans had an unexpected surprise when the territory held by their own forces near Opheusden also sank into the deluge. In January 1945, Zetten was virtually destroyed when the Germans counterattacked against the British. A vicious tank and infantry battle raged in the snow for several weeks until the Germans finally gave up and withdrew. The Germans finally capitulated on May 5, eight months after the 506th first went into action on the Island.

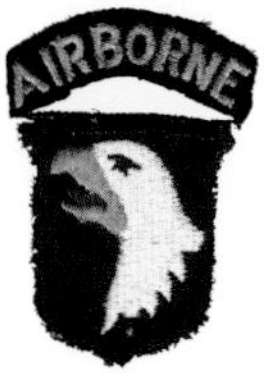
AIRBORNE

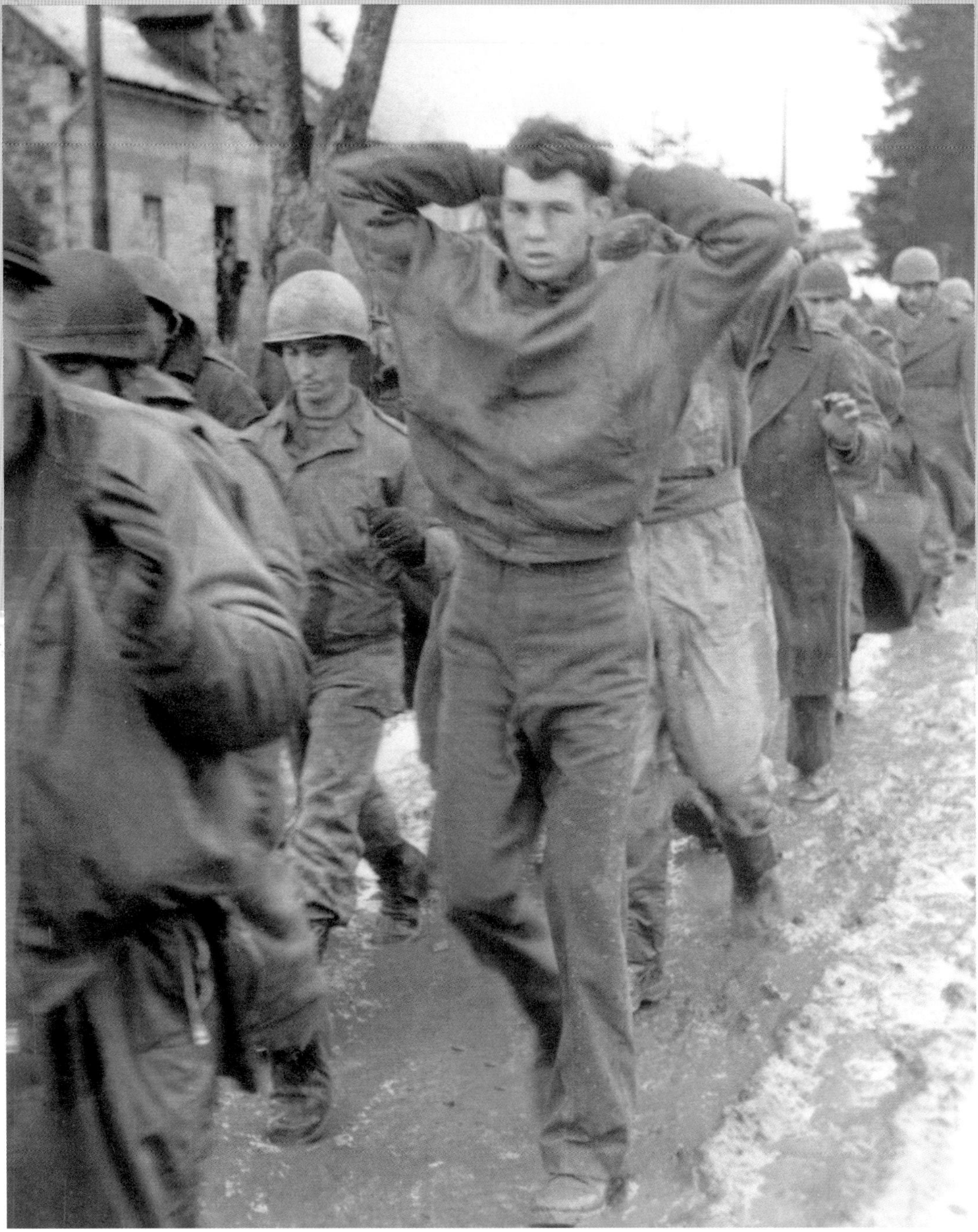

# Chapter 7

# WORDS LIKE STONE

## Bastogne

Situated outside the dreary, long-suffering garrison town of Mourmelon-le-Grand, Camp Chalons had been used by the French Army as a barracks and training area for decades, and the surrounding countryside still clearly showed the scars from World War I. Adjoined to an airfield, the camp ironically had been used by the Germans as a parachute school and tank depot. Despite its grandiose name, Mourmelon was really no more than one long street dotted with a few shops and cafés. Shortly after a belated Thanksgiving dinner, the troops received their barracks bags and mail. Everyone thought, at least for now, that the war might be over, so getting weapons repaired and re-equipping seemed fairly low on the list of priorities. In most cases the battalions set up training companies to give replacements a week or ten days of instruction and orientation. Around 600 replacement officers and men were flown in from the United Kingdom to make up the huge losses the 506th had suffered in Holland. The squalid conditions on the line during the last three weeks in Holland had seen hundreds hospitalized with non-combat related injuries, such as infections, yellow jaundice and emersion foot. Despite the enormous influx of new soldiers,

American soldiers captured during the opening German attack. (NARA)

the most radical changes to the battalion were felt among the leadership, with every company receiving at least two or even three new officers.

The camp became synonymous with reconstruction and cleanliness as the powers that be were expecting at least three months' rest in their new winter quarters. Ironically, again the weather took a turn for the worse and heavy rain reduced everything to a 6in-deep sea of mud. Once the sludge had been overcome with tons of imported gravel, things started to get back to normality. Accommodation was basic but clean, with the junior ranks sleeping 32 men to a room. Locally a bar of soap could buy you almost anything – liquor, laundry, even a woman if you tried hard enough. On the walls of their barracks each platoon painted a scroll bearing the names of comrades who had died in Normandy and Holland. By the end of November, acting company commanders Joe Doughty (G Company), Jim "Skunk" Walker (H Company) and Fred "Andy" Anderson (I Company) finally received their captain's bars. Immediately the three officers began the painful process of writing letters of condolence to the families of their men who had been killed and wounded over the last few months.

The only real topic of conversation on everyone's lips was Paris and it was planned to send the regiment to the queen of European cities one company at a time. Back-dated leave passes from Holland slowly began to filter through, and despite the fact that there had been several reports of a sniper taking potshots at

BELOW Twenty-two-year-old Sgt Harley Dingman of 3 Platoon, I Company. Dingman was later awarded the Silver Star for his courage, leadership, and initiative during the withdrawal from Foy on January 14, 1945.

Mourmelon, December 1944. Sgt Bob Martin (right) and senior NCOs from 1 Platoon, H Company, joking with newly commissioned Don Zahn. (Left to right): Zahn, Lou Vecchi, Hank DiCarlo and Frank Padisak. (Hank DiCarlo)

Regimental bar at Camp Chalons. Cpl Bob "Whitey" Hoffman (H Company) poses while dishing out drinks.

The American Red Cross Club, Gare de l'Est, Paris, December 1944. (Left to right): Lou Vecchi, Ralph Bennett, Bruce Paxton, Helen Briggs, Spencer Phillips and Hank DiCarlo. (Mark Bando Collection)

Allied troops in Reims, the city was still popular, but ultimately everyone dreamed of Paris. After what the men had been through, the three- or seven-day passes could not come fast enough, and inevitably many took matters into their own hands and went AWOL.

Those lucky enough to make it to Paris dined out on fine wine and expensive champagne and stayed in beautiful hotels, such as the prestigious George Cinque along the Champs-Élysées. Many began their leave at the Café de la Paix or "Caffay De La PX" to meet old friends and decide which places to visit. Helen Briggs, from the American Red Cross, was now stationed at Gare de l'Est and arranged tea dances and sightseeing trips for the boys. Although not exactly on Helen's tour list, many guys could not resist the famous red-light district at Place de Pigalle. Four years of German occupation had not seemingly changed Paris in any way except for the fact that it now cost a small fortune to buy anything. Barroom banter changed back and forth between "women" to "when the war was going to end," as by now most soldiers just wanted to get it over with and go home.

When the surprise German offensive began, the MPs hastily collected and contained everyone they could find at the American Red Cross until they could get transportation back to Mourmelon. Meanwhile, at Camp Chalons the troops woke to find that the nearby airfield was unusually active. The guys soon learned that the Germans had attacked along the border with Belgium and the 101st were being sent in behind the 82nd Airborne, who were the pre-designated combat reserve. Shortly after 2200hrs on December 17, the division began to mobilize and prepare for movement. The 506th had less than one day to get organized, and frustratingly most of their weapons were still in with the 801st Airborne Ordnance Company being assessed for repair. When the order came to mobilize, the 801st went into overdrive, took on more armorers and, over the next 48 hours, overhauled around 5,000 firearms. Those unlucky enough to go to the front unarmed were told that

The 501st PIR were among the first to leave Mourmelon for Bastogne and members of Second Battalion can be seen here waiting to board their transportation. (NARA)

their personal weapons would follow within a few hours. Unsurprisingly, when that did not happen, many joked that they had been equipped with nothing more than a hangover and a pair of silk stockings!

As the battalion was preparing to leave, two soldiers from a quartermaster unit arrived and began distributing ammunition. The allocation was pitiful and those who had rifles walked away with fewer than a dozen rounds each. The following afternoon, un-briefed and under-gunned, the regiment clambered aboard 40 8-wheeler semi-tractor units and set off for Werbomont in the freezing hills of the Ardennes. As the vehicle lights went on, some people tried to sleep, some talked quietly, while others stared into the night lost in their own thoughts.

At the time, the divisional artillery commander Brigadier General Tony McAuliffe was in charge of the 101st, after Max Taylor had been recalled to Washington for a conference. McAuliffe had already left Mourmelon ahead of the divisional advance party. Fortuitously, during an impromptu meeting with VIII Corps Commander Lieutenant General Troy Middleton at the barracks in Bastogne, the 82nd's deputy commander, Lieutenant General Jim Gavin, appeared with a vitally important update. Gavin had just traveled 30 miles from Werbomont, to inform Middleton that elements of First Army were in very serious trouble. After some quick thinking, the generals decided it would be better to send the 82nd, who were already "in-country," north to Werbomont and informed the MPs to redirect all 101st traffic to Bastogne.

Lacking any form of "snow chains," the heavy rear-wheel-drive vehicles were ill suited to the icy road conditions and the 107-mile journey was fraught with delays. Finally, during the early hours of Tuesday, December 19, the 506th along with the 321st Glider Field Artillery de-trucked at a crossroad in the village of Champs, 3 miles northwest of Bastogne. Half-jokingly, the drivers were told by the guys to keep the engines running, as they would be back sooner rather than later. It was an unusual way to begin a large-scale combat operation, but this mission would mark the most courageous chapter in the history of the 506th.

* * *

Nicknamed "Hitler's Fireman," Feldmarschall Walter Model's unexpected thrust northwest across the German border into the Belgian Ardennes on December 16 jeopardized the entire American First and Ninth Army front. The Allied footprint across this part of Europe was maintained by three big US Army groups: First, Third and Ninth. Forming part of the First Army battle group in the central Ardennes and on its first deployment was the 9th Armored Division. Two others (the 4th and 28th) of First Army had been seriously reduced in strength due to continuous battles around the Hürtgen Forest, where the fighting had raged since September 19.

Deceptively referred to as Operation *Die Wacht am Rhein* ("Watch on the Rhine"), this "Last Hope" offensive was the brainchild of Feldmarschall Gerd von Runstedt. The ambitious plan was to drive a wedge between the British in Holland and the Americans in France, and to capture the Belgian seaport of Antwerp by making a breakthrough in the Ardennes thanks to largescale tank and self-propelled gun (SPG) support. Before the launch of the operation the 88-mile front ran from western Germany along the Belgian border to eastern Luxembourg and encompassed an astonishing 250,000 German troops. Heeresgruppe B, together with 5th Panzer-Armee, led by General der Panzertruppen Hasso von Manteuffel, formed the central part of the attack; 6th Panzer-Armee, commanded by the infamous SS-Oberstgruppenführer Josef "Sepp" Dietrich, and General der Panzertruppen Erich Brandenberger's 7th Armee were tasked with the northern and southern areas.

The Germans achieved total surprise when the operation was launched on December 16 and penetrated a remarkable 50 miles in just three days. Major General Norman Cota's 28th Infantry Division fought a gallant rearguard action to the north, which allowed the 10th Armored Division vital time to occupy and deploy its tanks around Bastogne in an attempt to stem the tide. Despite the overwhelming situation, First Army did an incredible job, and their actions made for a valuable contribution to the safe and efficient deployment of the 101st Airborne. This was exactly what Hitler and his senior commanders had been hoping to avoid; their explicit intention had been to achieve their tactical aims before any of the Allied parachute divisions could be deployed.

First to arrive, 1/501 went straight to the village of Neffe, 2 miles east of Bastogne, where a number of German tanks were massing. Luckily for the Americans, this Panzer-Lehr were an inexperienced training outfit. However, they provided essential backup for the 26th Volksgrenadier-Division and the 2nd Panzer-Division. Collectively these three main assault groups made up the 47th Panzerkorps and had been tasked to capture the city of Bastogne itself. Many of the personnel who made up these Volksgrenadier, or "People's Army," units were conscripted teenage boys and older men. There could be no clearer illustration of just how desperate this attempt was to turn the Allied tide than that the 26th Volksgrenadier-Division would be at the very forefront of the battle.

Several makeshift American tank forces had been formed by the 10th Armored Division to defend the eastern approaches of Bastogne. The 10th, known as the "Tigers," was commanded by Major General William Morris, who had dispatched two groups, codenamed Combat Command A and B, to the battlefront. Each command was made up of around 50 tanks, supported by infantry, engineers and antiaircraft units. Led by Colonel William Roberts, Combat Command B (CCB) was divided into three Task Forces: "Desobry" which was sent north to Noville, "Cherry" which headed northeast to Longvilly, and "O'Hara" which moved southeast to Wardin. The three groups worked hard to establish roadblocks and stem the advance of the 47th Panzerkorps.

The presence of Team Cherry at Longvilly actually influenced the CO of Panzer-Division-Lehr, Generalleutnant Fritz Bayerlein, into delaying his attack on Bastogne. This was a disastrous miscalculation on his part, because at that exact moment, the city was his for the taking. Back in Bastogne at the barracks known to the Belgian Army as "Caserne Heintz," McAuliffe decided to take over Middleton's basement CP when the VIII Corps commander moved southwest to Neufchâteau. The bunker system in the basement of the barracks was accessed by a single flight of stairs. Although softly spoken, 46-year-old McAuliffe was a brilliant tactician and felt that the 101st Airborne could realistically hold Bastogne for 48 hours before needing full backup from George Patton's Third Army, who at that moment were 100 miles away, fighting through the "West Wall" beyond Saarbrücken. Patton's staff had trained for such a scenario and when General Eisenhower asked him to counterattack from the south, Patton was confident he could

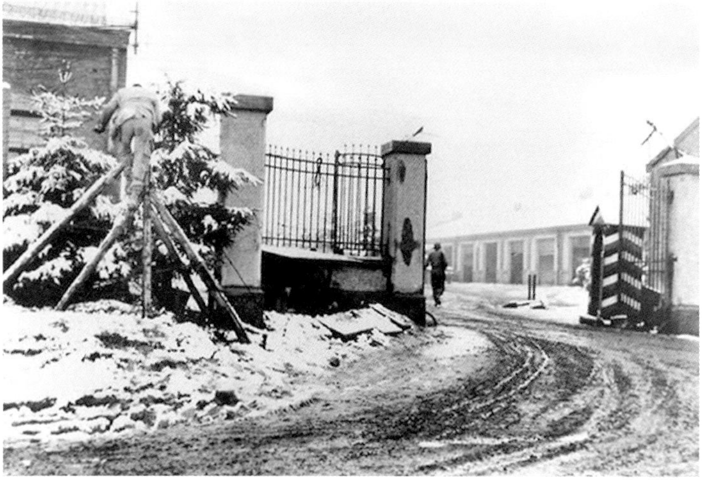

The main gate at Caserne Heintz situated on Rue de la Roche in late December, 1944. The twisted fixings that can just be seen on top of each post originally supported a cast iron eagle and swastika motif that arched over the entrance. (Reg Jans)

# Bastogne Overview, 1944

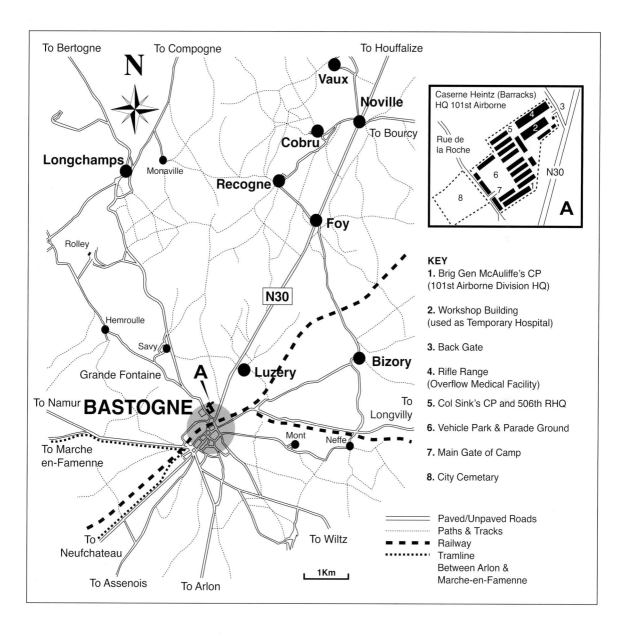

To Bertogne

To Compogne

To Houffalize

N

Vaux

Noville

Longchamps

Monaville

Cobru

To Bourcy

Recogne

Foy

Rolley

N30

Hemroulle

Savy

Bizory

Grande Fontaine

Luzery

A

To Namur  **BASTOGNE**

To Longvilly

Mont  Neffe

To Marche
en-Famenne

To Wiltz

To
Neufchateau

To Assenois  To Arlon

1Km

Caserne Heintz (Barracks)
HQ 101st Airborne

Rue de
la Roche

N30

A

**KEY**

**1.** Brig Gen McAuliffe's CP
(101st Airborne Division HQ)

**2.** Workshop Building
(used as Temporary Hospital)

**3.** Back Gate

**4.** Rifle Range
(Overflow Medical Facility)

**5.** Col Sink's CP and 506th RHQ

**6.** Vehicle Park & Parade Ground

**7.** Main Gate of Camp

**8.** City Cemetary

—————  Paved/Unpaved Roads
·············  Paths & Tracks
▬ ▬ ▬  Railway
··········  Tramline
Between Arlon &
Marche-en-Famenne

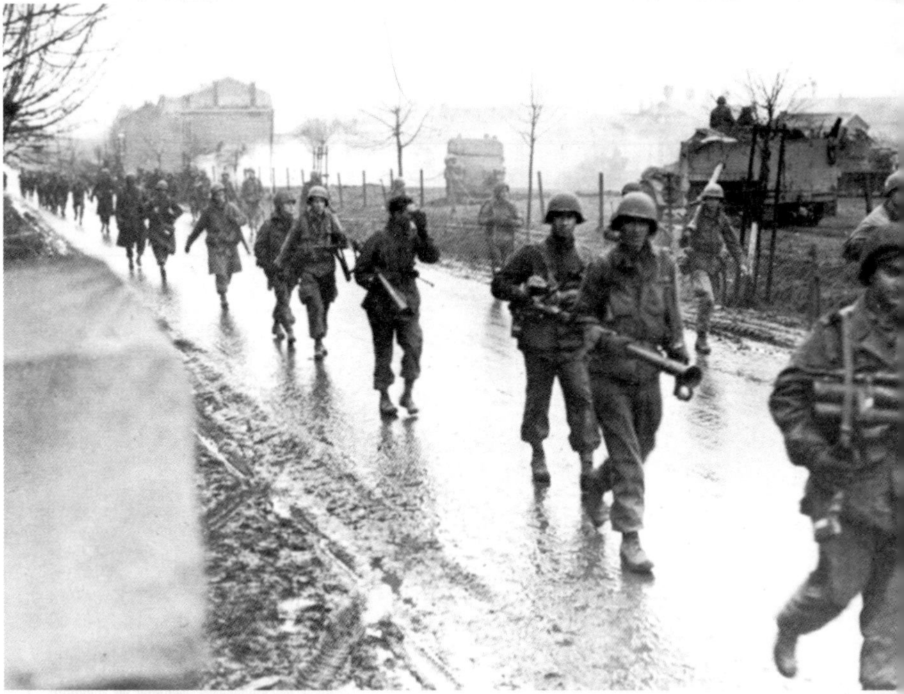

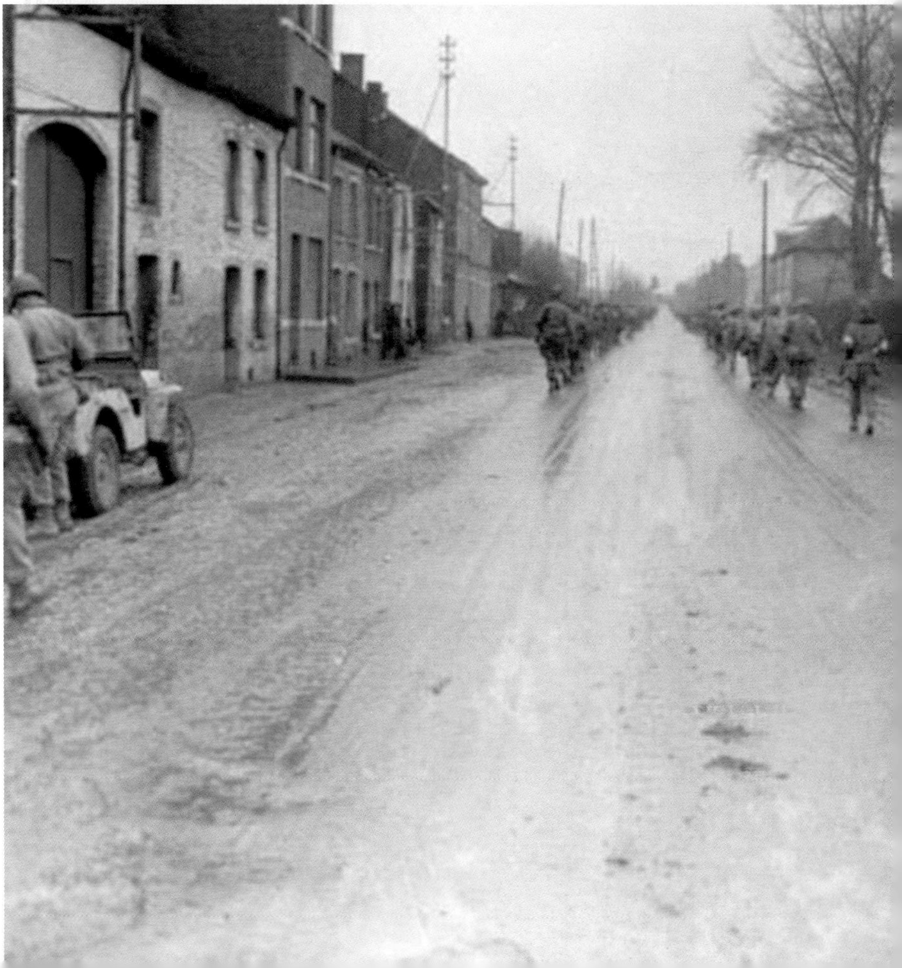

TOP Paratroopers from the 506th advancing past armored vehicles parked behind Caserne Heintz along Route de Houffalize (N30) to Noville. (NARA)

BOTTOM 2/506 turning onto the N30 bound for reserve positions behind Bois Jacques and the Main Line of Resistance. (NARA)

OPPOSITE TOP Moving north out of Bastogne along the N30 toward Foy and Noville. (NARA)

OPPOSITE BOTTOM Many of those civilians who left Bastogne on December 18 to escape the encirclement found themselves far worse off. Hundreds were forced to the front lines at Champs and other places to dig trenches for the Germans, who did not care if they lived or died. Eventually liberation came on January 12/13 when troops from the 17th Airborne Division broke through and dislodged the enemy. Around 800 people trapped within the city found shelter in the spacious underground cellars and vaults of the Notre-Dame Catholic boarding school and French Franciscan Monastery. Bastogne's mayor, Leon Jacqmin, took control of the civilian crisis and appointed a team of volunteers, including two local doctors, to assist. Because of its facilities the boarding school became a bakery and food distribution point. Animals were collected from nearby stables and butchered before being delivered to the school. As the siege continued, the cellars of Notre-Dame also became an overflow aid station for casualties. (Photo by Keystone/Getty Images)

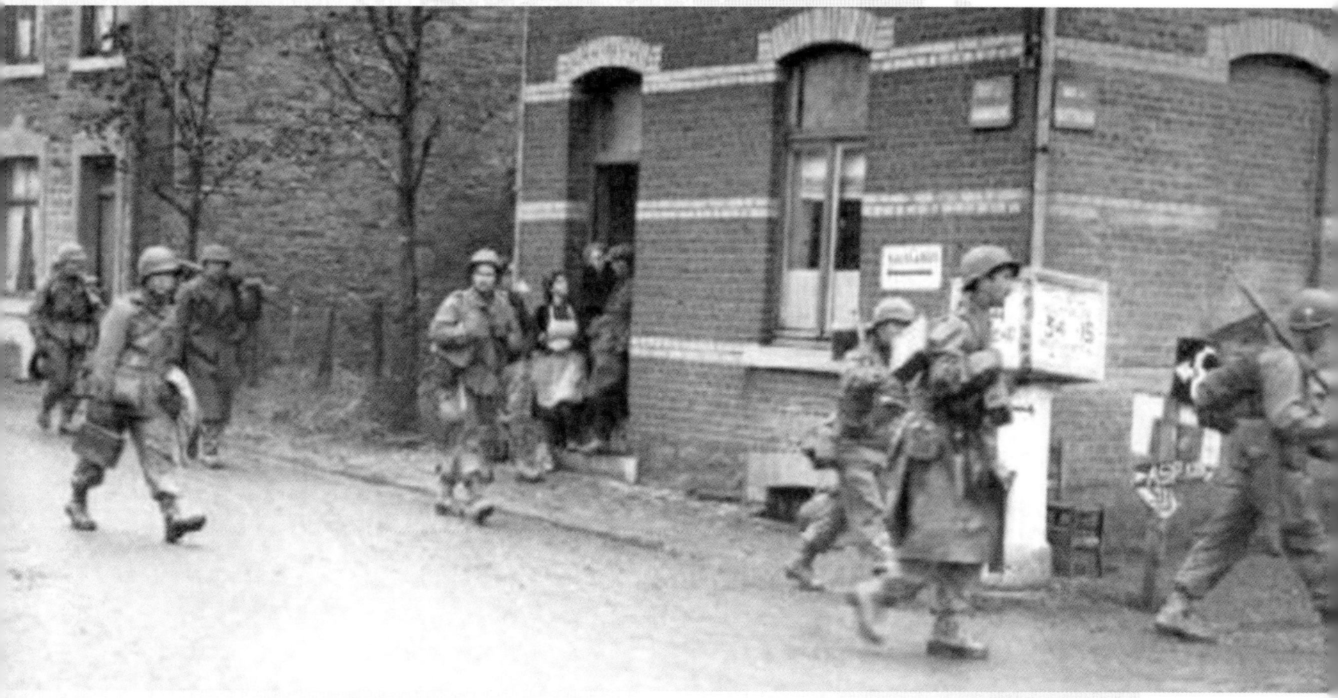

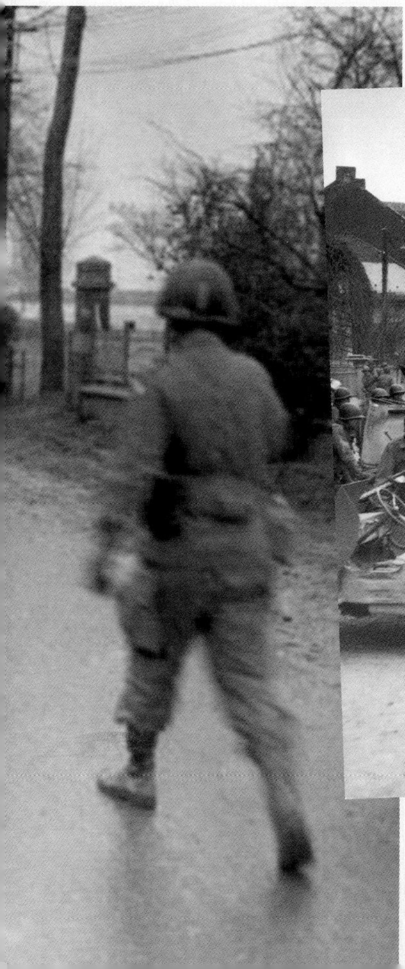

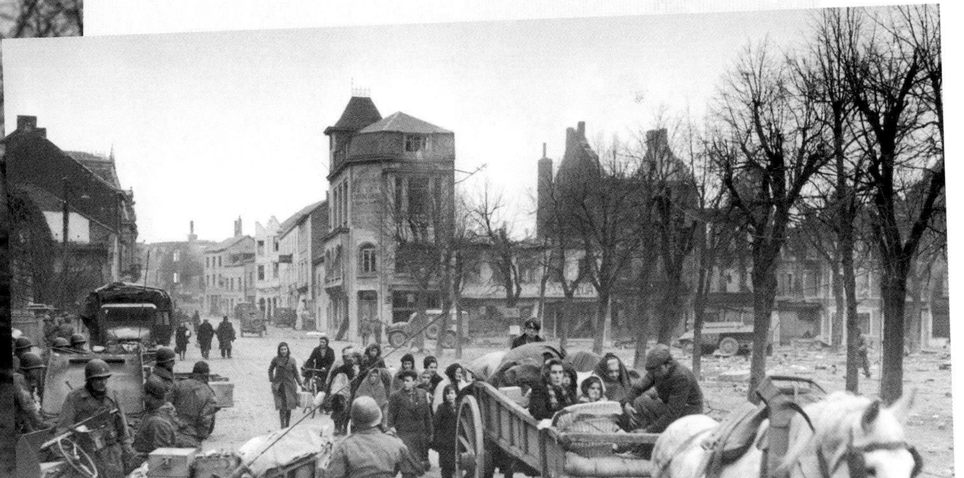

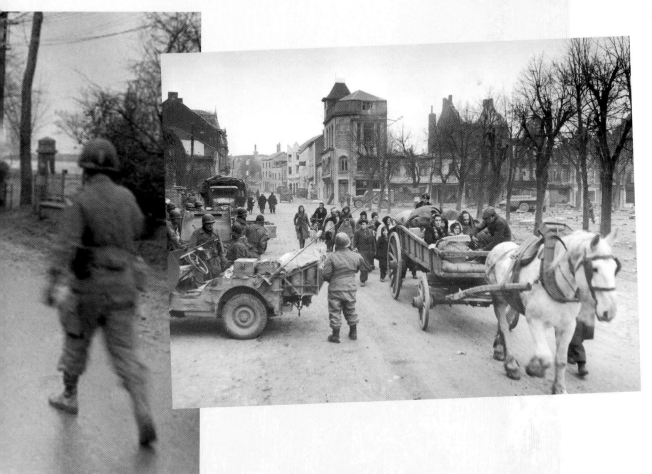

deliver. While Third Army was being redirected, Patton mobilized his 4th Armored Division, who were being held in reserve near Fénétrange, 20 miles further south across the border with Alsace Lorraine.

As Troy Middleton was leaving for Neufchâteau he smiled and wished McAuliffe good luck, adding, "Now Tony, don't let 'yerself get surrounded." Although Middleton would be instrumental in organizing the splendid Allied tank tactics during the next few weeks, luckily McAuliffe chose to ignore his advice. Instead McAuliffe decided to gamble everything on an 18,000-man defensive ring around Bastogne, 14 miles in length, believing that it might be easier to command, defend and maintain. In contrast, the enemy forces directed against the 101st at that time numbered around 38,000. Ultimately, von Manteuffel and his 5th Panzer-Armee would need total control of the roads around Bastogne to stay on course for Antwerp. As McAuliffe was settling in to his new basement home, Captain Willis McKee from the 326th Airborne Medical Company arrived, seeking permission to relocate the field hospital for the 101st closer to Bastogne from where it was currently situated at Herbaimont. Believing the hospital was safer where it was, Tony refused and this "off the cuff" decision turned out to be a disastrous and costly mistake when the entire hospital was overrun and captured by the Germans. This, coupled with the enemy encirclement that followed, meant that from December 19 to 26 none of the wounded or dead could be evacuated from Bastogne or the immediate surrounding area.

When Third Battalion arrived at Champs during the early hours of December 18, nobody seemed to know what was happening, which was symptomatic of the chaotic situation the Allies now found themselves in. The troops quickly set about digging temporary defensive positions on the edge of the village. Barely audible in the distance, the men could hear explosions coming from Neffe and Noville. A few hours later, the men joined 1/506 and a few others, including the 321st Glider Field Artillery, and marched to a large holding area not far from the barracks. From here the 321st with their 75mm pack howitzers were detached and sent to Grande Fontaine and Savy. Colonel Sink established a CP in one of the accommodation blocks overlooking the holding area on the northern side of the barracks. The previous occupants had departed in such a hurry that the remnants of their supper, along with several half-written letters, were still spread across tables in one of the rooms. Painted in large letters on the wall were the words "We'll be back – The Yanks" which solicited a number of sarcastic responses from the American paratroopers.

The battalion waited five hours in the bitter cold before any further orders arrived. A fortunate few had heavy overcoats, but most were simply clad in the basic combat uniform. The platoon commanders briefed their men as best they could on the uncertain tactical situation ahead but knew only one thing for sure and that was

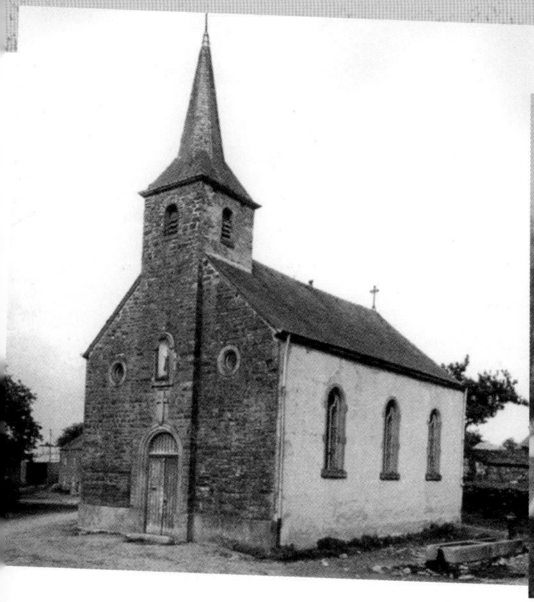

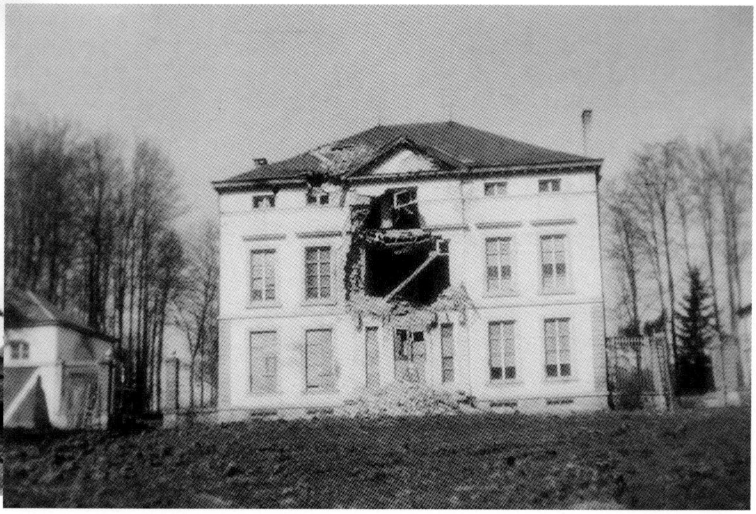

ABOVE LEFT Pre-war photograph of Chapelle Sainte Barbe situated in the center of Foy. The farm that became 1 Platoon, H Company's OP before the battle can just be seen here on the left. Badly damaged during the fighting, the 16th-century chapel was rebuilt in 1950. (Joël Robert)

The White House, Recogne, circa 1946 – the photo shows the damage inflicted during the battle. Note the diagonal stripe painted on the small building to the left of the main house denoting the d'Hoffschmidt family connection. (Reg Jans)

that the boys were heading north. Leaving the holding area, 3/506 made its way to the main road, Route de Houffalize (also referred to as N30), and began their march into history.

The city seemed quiet, and those civilians brave enough to remain handed out hot coffee as the paratroopers passed by. A few moments later the men came across the first elements of the 10th Armored Division, who had by now been fighting a rearguard action in Bastogne for the last eight hours. Before Third Battalion moved out of the city, First Battalion, commanded by Lieutenant Colonel James LaPrade, was sent ahead to penetrate beyond Foy into Noville in support of Task Force Desobry.

Situated in a geographic bowl, Noville was virtually surrounded by rolling hills, making the town difficult to protect from the 2nd Panzer-Division. It was vital for First Battalion to help stabilize Noville in order to give Third Battalion more time to establish and strengthen its defensive positions at Foy.

As Third Battalion trudged north during the early afternoon along the main N30 road, they were perplexed to see increasing numbers of troops from the 28th Infantry Division and remnants of the 9th Armored Division heading toward them. Many of the beleaguered troops were horrified when they saw the paratroopers advancing. Most of the retreating soldiers had cold weather clothing and seemed quite well prepared for a winter war. The only extra kit Patch's men had at their disposal was either discarded by these soldiers or liberated later. Wisely, the paratroopers would not let any of these soldiers pass by without taking every single round they possessed. Luckily, further along the road there was a pile of assorted ammunition, thoughtfully deposited by the guys from 10th Armored.

The battalion was now leaving open ground and entering a region covered by dense spruce and evergreen woodland. Straddling the main road, overlooked by

# Third Battalion's Line of Resistance, Foy, December 19, 1944

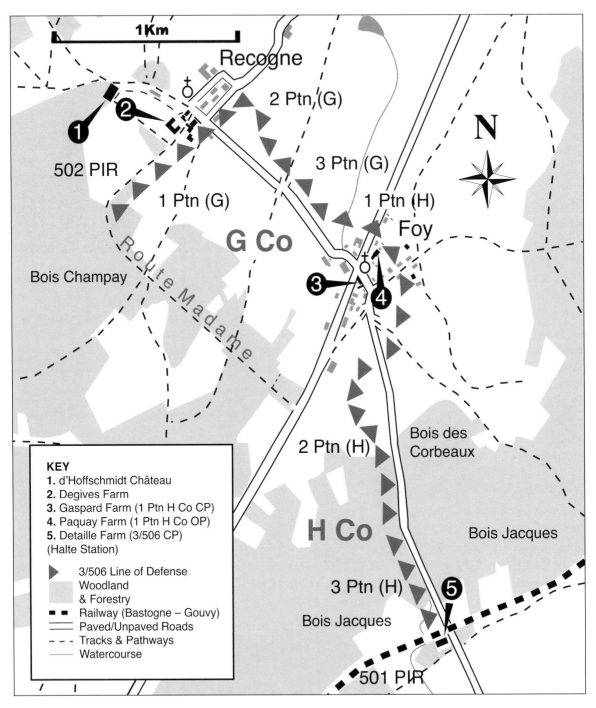

**1Km**

Recogne

2 Ptn (G)

3 Ptn (G)

1 Ptn (H)

**N**

1 Ptn (G)

Foy

**G Co**

Bois Champay

502 PIR

Route Madame

2 Ptn (H)

Bois des
Corbeaux

**H Co**

Bois Jacques

3 Ptn (H)

Bois Jacques

501 PIR

**KEY**
1. d'Hoffschmidt Château
2. Degives Farm
3. Gaspard Farm (1 Ptn H Co CP)
4. Paquay Farm (1 Ptn H Co OP)
5. Detaille Farm (3/506 CP)
(Halte Station)

▶ 3/506 Line of Defense
    Woodland
    & Forestry
■■■ Railway (Bastogne – Gouvy)
═══ Paved/Unpaved Roads
- - - Tracks & Pathways
──── Watercourse

undulating hills, the tiny farming community of Foy was built around a crossroads in a natural hollow and the perfect staging area for the enemy to launch an attack against Bastogne. At the crossroads central to the village on the eastern side of the N30 was a dour 16th-century gray stone chapel. In 1944, the village consisted of 26 farms and dozens of barns and outbuildings, with a total population of around 130.

Third Battalion Surgeon, Capt Bernard "Barney" Ryan (left) pictured here with Regimental Dentist, Capt Samuel "Shifty" Feiler, celebrating midnight mass for the walking wounded at Caserne Heintz on Christmas Eve. The markings on the wall behind Feiler (who was a Jew) suggest that it could be part of a candlestick drawn to symbolize the Jewish festival of Hanukkah. Known to his colleagues as the "walking aid station," Shifty was a brave and effusive New Yorker, who spoke excellent German. (Mark Bando)

## Defending Foy, December 19–20, 1945

When Third Battalion reached Foy during the late afternoon of December 19, the men were deployed along a 2-mile front stretching from the railway line at Bizory to Recogne, a small hamlet about 1 mile to the northwest of Foy. Overlooking Recogne is the Château d'Hoffschmidt, locally known as the White House. The d'Hoffschmidt family owned most of the surrounding farm and dense woodland along the ridge overlooking Foy called Bois Champay. Before the war, Baron François d'Hoffschmidt employed dozens of local people as domestic staff, forestry, and farm workers. Close to the château was a large tenant farm run by Nestor Degives, from where there was direct road access to the ridge and Bois Champay. This logging track, called Route Madame, would later become a vital patrol conduit for the Americans. Bob Sink was waiting at Foy to personally direct each company toward their final locations.

G Company moved west and took up positions next to 3/502 facing toward Recogne. The MLR for Joe Doughty's men ran down Route Madame past Degives Farm along the northeastern edge of Recogne, before paralleling the road back into Foy. Colonel Patch established his CP on the extreme right flank of the MLR at Detaille Farm (also known as Halte Station). The sector allocated to H Company followed a secondary road that ran perpendicular to the N30 for about 1,500 yards to the railway embankment and the battalion CP. After a bit of initial confusion, Bob Stroud decided to deploy 1 Platoon in a line across the N30 on the extreme northern edge of Foy. Because of the wide frontal area H Company was expected to cover, Major Patch brought elements of I Company out of reserve and deployed them around the battalion CP.

This house at the crossroads in Foy is still owned by the Koeune family. Back in 1944 Jules Koeune opened up the cellar as a shelter to the women and children from the village. The house was reduced to an empty shell during the fighting.

Bob Stroud gathered his NCOs and explained that the battalion was going to create a north-facing defensive bubble around the village. Immediately afterwards, Hank DiCarlo and Lou Vecchi set off to look for a decent elevated observation post. Behind Hank's position, adjacent

"Foy was so quiet when we arrived it seemed almost like a ghost town. The only sound being made was by us as we dug in. I didn't see any civilians but noticed dozens of animals still in their pens and stalls. As they appeared to be hungry, especially the pigs, we thought it best to release all the livestock we consequently came across. I deployed my squad on the western side of the road across the open ground with the church behind us over to the right."

Sergeant Louis J. Vecchi – 1 Platoon, H Company

"3 Platoon took up positions in Bois Jacques and my assistant, Willie Miller, dug in on our far-right flank. I believed in the buddy system of two men to a foxhole and placed each trench about 100 yards apart. However, the forest was so dense that a single enemy soldier could have marched between any of our positions without ever being seen."

First Lieutenant Alexander Andros – 3 Platoon, H Company

"When the Germans launched their attack, most of the men in Foy over the age of 17 headed west. Along with many others my dad went to Recogne leaving mom behind to look after my brother, two sisters, and me. The idea was for them to return after the Germans had passed by but of course that never happened. On December 18, we watched the first American convoys moving through the village en route to Noville. In the evening as the sound of battle began to draw nearer, we went across the street to Mr Koeune's house on the corner. The Koeunes (who were related to my mother) ran a successful fruit and vegetable business and allowed us to shelter in their substantial cellar. By the time the Americans began to dig in around us there were about 45 people, predominantly women and children, sheltering in the basement."

Maguy Marenne – schoolgirl, Foy

"During first contact, I dropped three enemy soldiers while one of our replacements, Frank Kneller, sank to the bottom of our trench and curled up in the fetal position. Between shots I shouted for Kneller to pull himself together and he quickly gathered his wits, stood back up, and faced the enemy. I was glad that he did because moments later my machine gunner, Don Hegeness was hit and began calling for help. Handing Kneller my M1, I sprinted about 70 yards through the fog and smoke to save Don. The tank shells were landing ahead of us and I could feel the pressure wave from explosions against my chest. Bullets were whizzing above our heads and twice on the way back I was physically blown off my feet. At one point we were sent sprawling to the ground when a shell glanced off the side of my helmet, leaving a groove in the steel! An inch lower and it would've taken my head off!"

Sergeant Kenneth G. Johnson – 2 Platoon, H Company

to the church, was a three-story farmhouse, whose upper floors afforded them perfect views across the area to the northeast. The house had two improvised concrete grain shafts built into the back wall descending to a storage area underneath the building. Once they had created their nest of liberated blankets, Hank and Lou took it in turns to "stag on" through the night. The H Company line now blended nicely with G Company to create a semi-circular pocket around Foy, which ran southwest across the Bizory road and meandered through Bois Jacques to Detaille Farm.

At dusk an enemy recon patrol appeared through the mist, walking along the main road straight into the H Company front line. As one of the Germans cautiously moved forward he was challenged and shot at close range. After a brief exchange of gunfire, the patrol slipped away, leaving their colleague lying dead in the road.

Lieutenant Len Smith, who was Bob Stroud's new assistant, was quite badly shaken after several of his men were wounded by random shellfire during the night of December 19. This did not go down well with Stroud, who despite having his hands full, was forced to arrange the evacuation of the injured men himself. Earlier that same evening, just as it was getting dark, Clark Heggeness of 2 Platoon, H Company, handed a basic sketch map to Second Lieutenant Harry Begle, one of the new intake following Holland, and sent him across to the railway to make contact with the 501st who were supposed to be holding the ground on the other side of the tracks. Begle did not even have a password at this point and was seriously worried that he might get "accidentally" shot. Unable to find anyone from the 501st, Harry eventually reported back to Clark with the "good news" before bedding down with some of his men in a large haystack directly opposite 2 Platoon's positions.

Pfc Joe Harris, 1 Platoon, H Company. On the first night, Sgt DiCarlo, wrapped in a blanket for extra warmth, was doing his rounds and stopped to spend a few moments with Harris. Carefully shielding a cigarette, Joe nervously remarked, "Whatta you think Hank? Is this where the crap finally hits the fan?"

While Begle was on patrol, one of his squad leaders, Sergeant Ken Johnson, was making sure his replacements understood exactly what was expected of them. The open ground now occupied by 2 Platoon had previously been used as a quarry, leaving the area littered with dozens of holes that the troopers put to very good use. Closest to the railway and the Third Battalion CP, Alex Andros and 3 Platoon were also none the wiser concerning the actual whereabouts of the 501st.

During the night the Germans also made many attempts to penetrate the perimeter around First Battalion at Noville. Heavy artillery and tank fire could be heard throughout the early hours, and shortly after 0700hrs on December 20, the reserve Tank Destroyer (TD) platoon moved forward to Noville. The MLR at Foy was covered in a dense fog that only served to amplify the sound of 2nd Panzer-Division now advancing on Noville from the east. The German commander, von Manteuffel, had opted for a three-point envelopment that in the event turned out to be a poor decision. In a further attempt to close the net,

Members of 2 Platoon, H Company, pictured in the early days at Camp Mackall in 1943. (Left to right): Ken Johnson, Alex Spurr, Charles Stenbom, Lloyd McGee, Gil Hunteman, and Frank Malik (front kneeling). Cpl Stenbom lost both legs in Holland and was invalided back to the US while Sgts Spurr and Johnson were both seriously injured during the fighting around Foy.

On December 19, 1944, Heggeness and Begle established 2 Platoon, H Company, here along the Bizory road that ran south to the railway line and Detaille Farm (Third Battalion CP). Bois Jacques can be seen up ahead where Alex Andros and 3 Platoon dug in. The German attack came through Bois des Corbeaux across the open fields seen here on the left.

78th Volksgrenadier-Regiment sent several companies supported by tanks to flank Foy and encircle Recogne.

Around 0700hrs, one of Hank DiCarlo's men quietly alerted him to the arrival of the tanks, one of which was now idling directly below his OP. Another tank came clattering around the corner through the mist. At that moment all hell broke loose as the tank began firing randomly from left to right. With tank shells exploding all around, Stroud decided to abandon his CP. But before withdrawing, Stroud moved forward to double check the situation with DiCarlo and was horrified to see the German tank still parked outside the OP. A number of enemy soldiers were nonchalantly standing around so he ran back downstairs and grabbed a bazooka. Poking the barrel through a hole in the roof, Bob fired one rocket into the Panther's tracks, which rapidly backed away into the fog. Realizing the OP was compromised, Stroud issued orders to DiCarlo to abandon the building.

Ignoring Stroud's instructions, Hank, who was on the other side of the property, began to shout fire control orders to his men dug in below. At that precise moment he was more concerned about the enemy troops now advancing in front of him than any lost tank. Hank's men continued to fire until a tank entered the perimeter with its gun aimed directly at him. This was probably the same tank targeted a few minutes earlier by Stroud. Without hesitating, Hank – still in the OP – turned and jumped down the grain shaft as the first round tore the top off the silo. Fortunately, there was still enough hay in the basement to break his fall. After destroying the OP, the enemy tank crew focused their attention on the tracer rounds emanating from 2 Squad's machine gun. Previously, Lou Vecchi had told his gunners to remove

View southeast along the edge of the modern-day Bois Champay looking toward Foy and the N30 which became Third Battalion's MLR from December 20, 1944. Back in the day the open fields (on the left) were covered by several protrusions of dense woodland. The animals feeding in the foreground are North American bison, currently bred for export by the d'Hoffschmidt family.

every tracer round from their ammunition belts, but they had not bothered. As he moved forward to chew them out, the same tank then turned toward him and fired. The shell exploded into one of the trees behind, severely damaging Lou's hearing. Just when he thought they were all done for, a Sherman Tank Destroyer hidden in a nearby house took out the tank at extremely close range.

Hank managed to rejoin his squad, who were then handed another unexpected stroke of luck when the mist returned and descended across the battlefield. All small-arms fire stopped for around ten minutes. The fog slowly lifted and once again the Americans and Germans were in full view of each other. Then the fog descended again. A few minutes later, as it was lifting, the men could see more enemy troops coming in, and word came down the line that they had to pull back to the high ground above Foy.

Initially the sector protected by 3 Platoon, H Company, remained relatively untouched by the German attack; however, the other two platoons were not quite as fortunate. Harry Begle was still dozing in the haystack opposite the MLR when a burst of machine-gun fire ripped through the straw. A few moments later the clatter of enemy tanks grew louder through the fog, followed by a heavy barrage of mortars. Heggeness ran over and shouted in Begle's ear that Platoon Sergeant Alex Spurr had been shot in the left knee and he needed help to evacuate him back to Battalion HQ. The two men had only carried Spurr a short distance when Clark ordered Harry back to the MLR with instructions to hold out for as long as possible. The platoon was still dug in along the road but could not see the enemy due to the heavy mist and smoke. Suddenly three SPGs supported by infantry appeared directly opposite Ken Johnson's position. A nearby 75mm gun attached to H Company burst into action and took on the enemy armor.

Unaware of the encirclement, back on the LOD, Second Battalion were in fact moving in to take over the H Company sector and Detaille Farm. 2/506 had been in reserve and turned up around mid-morning to allow H Company to join the rest of the battalion and make its way back to the high ground in Bois Champay above Foy.

After regrouping on the high ground, Captain Walker informed Bob Stroud that the battalion was now on a warning order to mount a diversionary attack into

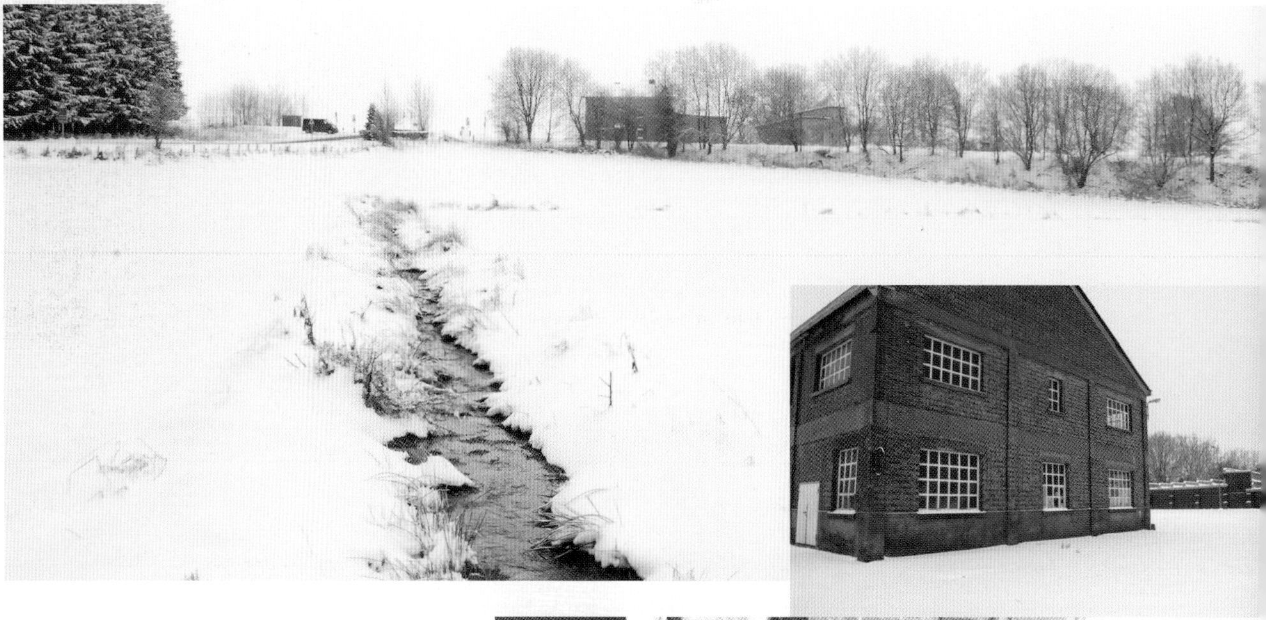

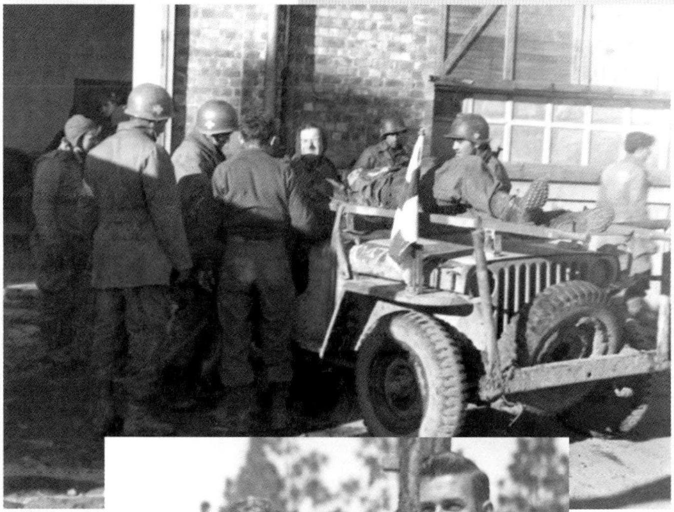

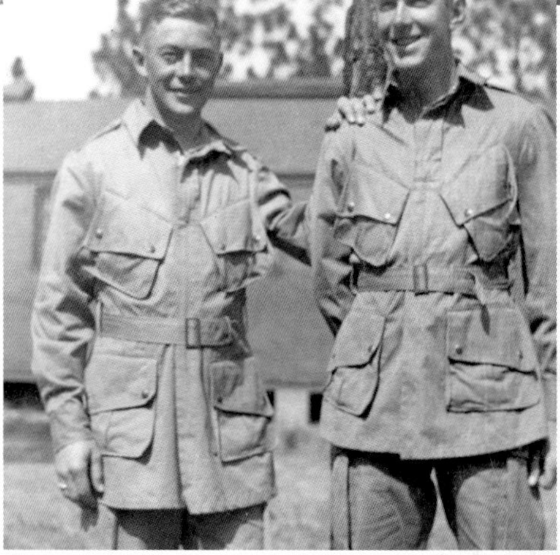

ABOVE Lieutenant Harry Begle from H Company led his men along this very stream on December 20. In the distance can be seen the railway embankment and Detaille Farm (Major Lloyd Patch's CP). Back in 1944, everything right of the watercourse was woods and the area (left) open fields. Although the heavy snow didn't arrive until Christmas Eve you can see just how much it changes the landscape.

ABOVE RIGHT "Shifty" Feiler established a secondary aid station directly behind Colonel Sink's CP in the indoor 100m rifle range (seen here in the background) at Caserne Heintz. Originally the range acted as an overflow facility for those with non life-threatening injuries, although this changed as the siege progressed. The accommodation and workshop building (seen in the foreground) became the main divisional hospital from December 20 to 26. Luckily penicillin, sulfadiazine and blood plasma were in plentiful supply thanks to VIII Corps, who had left behind most of their medical depot. During the siege almost 1,000 casualties were dealt with by the various medical facilities in the city.

Wounded arriving at the divisional hospital opposite the indoor range. The soldier on the stretcher appears to be German. (NARA)

Don Zahn and Bob Martin from 1 Platoon, H Company, pictured here at Camp Mackall, North Carolina. Don would later be awarded the Distinguished Service Cross for his fearless actions across Normandy, Holland and Belgium. (Lou Vecchi)

Lou Vecchi (1 Platoon, H Company) pictured in Austria 1945. "With my hearing now completely gone, I was in agony and went over to ask Bob Stroud if I could be evacuated for treatment. Stroud agreed but as I was preparing to leave our supply guy came over and demanded I hand back my Army issue wristwatch! I couldn't believe it and promptly told him where to go. Moments later a jeep arrived and took me along with a few others to the rifle range at the barracks. The freezing cold sand-covered concrete floor was horrendous and after 24 hours I decided to hell with it – the front line has gotta be better than this place – so I picked up my gear and headed back to Foy, blood still trickling from my ears." (Lou Vecchi)

Foy to facilitate First Battalion's escape from Noville. Stroud had only just finished digging in with his runner and Lieutenant Len Smith. Although the ridge was mostly concealed by woodland, the open field in front of the tree line dropped away in a short convex incline. While trying to catch up on some personal admin a shell exploded in the trees, wounding both Stroud and Smith, the latter losing the use of one arm. After saying goodbye to the platoon, both men were evacuated to the range. At that moment Stroud did not know that the divisional hospital had been overrun and his chances of evacuation were now impossible.

Earlier in Noville, Bob Harwick had been anxiously waiting and hoping that the fog would not lift. Moments later the first of many enemy barrages screamed in, creating yet more smoke and dust and bringing visibility down to less than 20 yards. Within a few minutes the countryside became a confusion of clanking treads, dark shadows, and dirty yellow flashes as the tanks fired blindly into the town. American casualties began to mount, leaving countless gaps in the line, and communications with Bastogne had for all intents and purposes broken down. After four hours the situation had become so acute that Harwick called in his company commanders for a final briefing. Another couple of attacks, he explained, would finish First Battalion as a fighting force and he put forward a plan for withdrawal. One of Bob's men volunteered to run the gauntlet and drive a jeep carrying wounded down the main road with a note for Brigadier General McAuliffe.

At about 1230hrs a radio operator in one of the tanks attached to 1/506 picked up a message telling all available armored units to assist the infantry in fighting out of the burning town. Forty-five minutes later the order came through via one of the forward observers to withdraw as soon as possible. First to depart was Moose Mehosky (who had been reassigned in Holland) and C Company, with orders to push forward at all costs with a ramshackle convoy and four Shermans. The tank destroyers who had been assigned to support A Company formed the rearguard to prevent the Germans from following. The continuing heavy fog provided much needed cover and Harwick set off as soon as the remainder of the wounded were loaded. The lead tank was hit going in to Foy and the crew forced to scramble for their lives through the flames.

After Stroud and Smith were evacuated, it was down to Frank Padisak to gather the remaining members of H Company and assign them to their respective lanes of attack alongside I Company. With the help of two tank destroyers they drove the Germans back a couple of hundred yards into the fields north of Foy, clearing the road in front of First Battalion, who were now approaching from the north. Padisak's luck finally ran out when he was wounded and he was sent back to Bastogne.

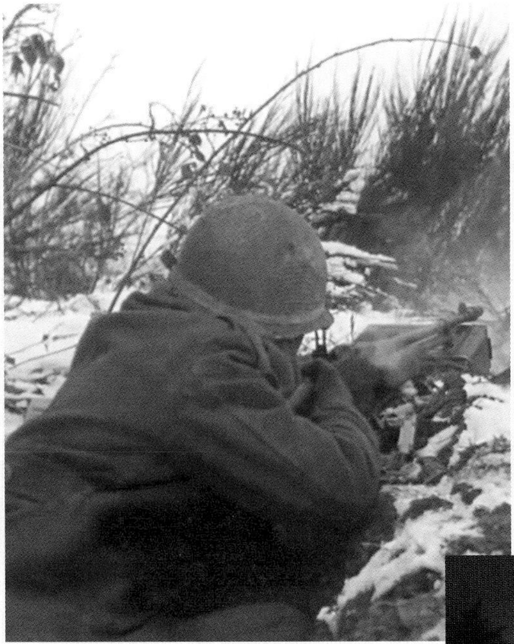

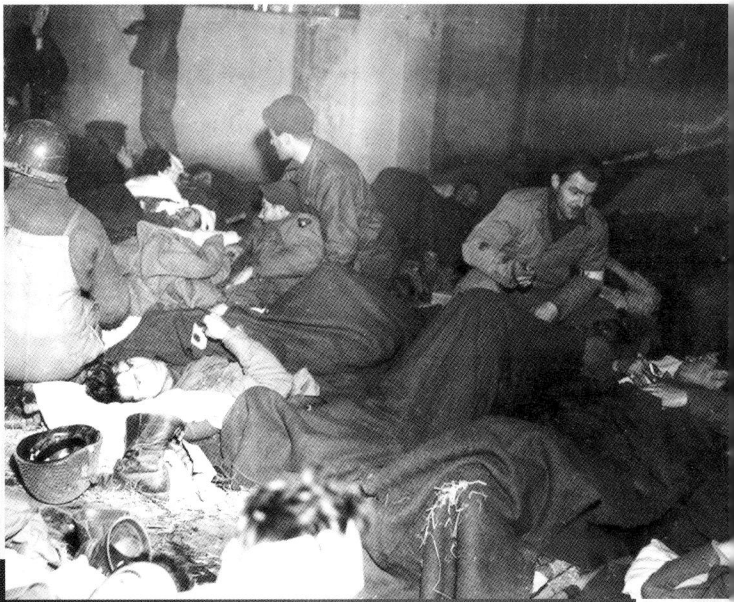

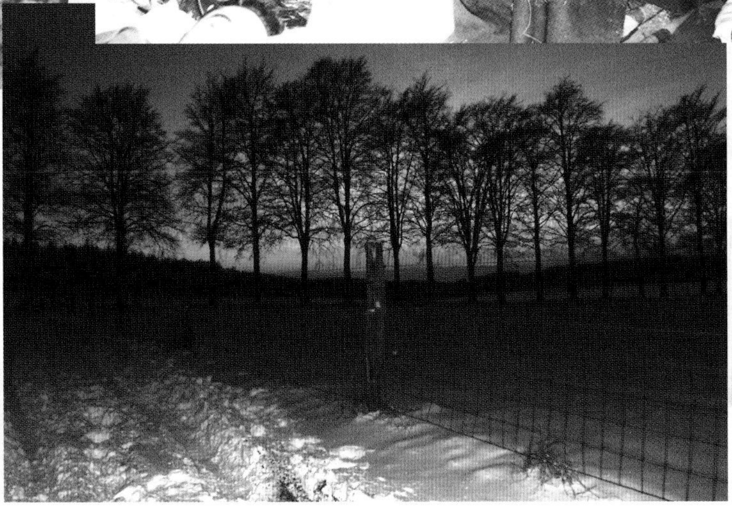

American paratrooper opens up with a Browning Automatic Rifle somewhere along the perimeter. (NARA)

A mixture of American casualties gathered somewhere inside the encirclement possibly from the chapel at Bizory. (Johnny Gibson)

A thick blanket of snow covers the view south at dusk from Foy and Recogne toward the Third Battalion MLR in Bois Champay. During the Battle of the Bulge heavy snow like this did not arrive until midday on Christmas Eve.

Meanwhile, one of the Shermans attached to 3/506 was now actively engaging enemy targets behind 1/506. Bob Harwick ordered his men to dismount and push forward on both sides of the road into Foy, killing and capturing a number of enemy soldiers along the way. During the chaos several of Bob's men were hit by friendly fire. Luckily, the enveloping Germans were forced back, leaving the road ahead clear for Bob's convoy to proceed to safety. Disheveled and torn, the First Battalion task force had been through a tough couple of days, but the troops knew they had done everything in their power to hold Noville.

"Our platoon was told to move forward with two squads down into Foy, with mine nearest to the road," remembers Sgt Hank DiCarlo. "Sergeant Patterson and his 60mm mortar squad were to stay in the woods along with a couple of machine-gun teams to provide fire support. The attack started around 1100hrs and advancing down the hill we came under immediate fire. We reached the first outbuilding and began to push the enemy back. Breaking into smaller groups we systematically cleared each house, barn, and shed, leapfrogging between positions. Corporal Bill Gordon became the first casualty. I stopped to check but he was dead. As First Battalion passed through our lines, I saw my old platoon leader, Moose Mehosky, for the first time since Normandy. 'Moose' was his old self, totally composed and in full control of his situation."

"We found ourselves out front of our own riflemen and came under fire from one of the buildings," recalled Harold Stedman from I Company.

> We took cover behind a wall and launched most of our 60mm rounds at the house. Just as Womack went back for more ammunition our lieutenant [Don Replogle] arrived with the rest of the platoon. For a few minutes, sniper fire from the house held everything up until Womack returned with another ten shells. Within a minute or two we were down to our last three mortar rounds and it was my turn to get some more. As I crossed a small opening between two barns a bullet clipped my ear. Instinctively I threw myself on the ground and played dead for a few moments before attempting to move again. When I got back to Womack, the platoon had taken the house, killing three enemy soldiers. Two others were taken prisoner, one of whom was an officer. This guy was tall and looked mean and for some reason the guys thought he was the sniper who had just been shooting at us. The Kraut was refusing to put his hands in the air so I ran over and kicked him hard in the backside but still he refused to comply. One of the boys roughed him up and then asked our lieutenant if he could 'take him to the coast' and was told under no circumstances was anyone going to 'shoot' this man for just being arrogant.

That day the joint US forces destroyed over 20 enemy tanks and captured over 100 prisoners. Of the gallant 600 who had originally gone into Noville, fewer than 400 remained to tell the tale. By late afternoon Harwick's men were moved back to the outskirts of Bastogne and placed in regimental reserve. After consolidating, Third Battalion dug in a few yards north of the road to Recogne and waited for further orders. Hourly patrols were sent out through the night to the 502nd who by now were comfortably holding the adjacent sector above the château.

## Holding the line, December 21–24, 1945

The MLR at this time was no more than one man deep, and at 0330hrs the following morning Third Battalion again came under attack. Enemy armor advancing down the

# Third Battalion's Main Line of Resistance, December 21, 1944

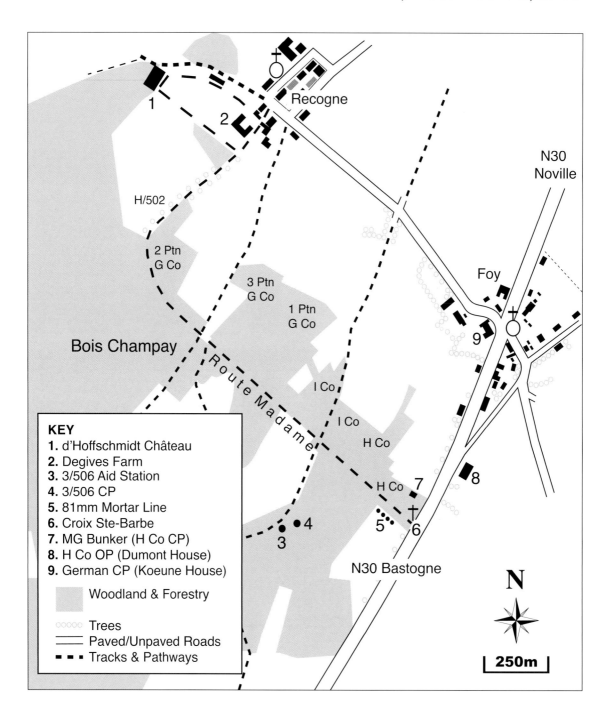

Recogne

N30
Noville

H/502

2 Ptn
G Co

3 Ptn
G Co

1 Ptn
G Co

Bois Champay

*Route Madame*

Foy

I Co

I Co

H Co

9

KEY
1. d'Hoffschmidt Château
2. Degives Farm
3. 3/506 Aid Station
4. 3/506 CP
5. 81mm Mortar Line
6. Croix Ste-Barbe
7. MG Bunker (H Co CP)
8. H Co OP (Dumont House)
9. German CP (Koeune House)

H Co  7

8

5  6

3  4

N30 Bastogne

Woodland & Forestry

Trees

Paved/Unpaved Roads

Tracks & Pathways

N

250m

"I was manning a .30cal with Private Vince 'Mike' Michael from G Company alongside a couple of bazooka teams when the tanks attacked the village and blew the roof off the house we were using. At that point everyone pulled back to the woods. As we were withdrawing, halfway between the house and a large rectangular barn, 'Mike' and I picked up an abandoned bazooka along with three rockets and decided to engage two Panthers that were by now only a short distance away on the road between Recogne and Foy. We were shaking in our boots as the first tank trundled closer but failed to spot us. Mike loaded and wired up the tube, and we waited until the tank was just past the building so that its turret would no longer be able to traverse in our direction. The bazooka round exploded into the engine compartment and a few seconds later the tank ground to a halt. As the second Panther drove up it stopped behind the one we'd just knocked out so at that point we decided to make a run for it and catch up with the others."

Corporal James A. Melhus – Machine Gun Platoon

"1 Platoon, G Company was forced to fix bayonets and fight hand-to-hand. At 0600hrs the order came for the company to withdraw into the woods. Before pulling out, Lieutenant Osborne asked our squad to remain behind and cover him with our machine gun. We held on for as long as we could before making our way back through heavy small-arms fire."

Sergeant Stanley B. Clever – 1 Platoon, G Company

"Pfc Ed Petrowski climbed out of his newly dug foxhole and ran over to one of the I Company guys [Bob Kangas] who was badly hurt. Ed was dragging the injured guy and just before they reached the tree line a mortar exploded close by, hitting Ed. Despite being injured, Petrowski made sure that he got the wounded man into a trench and lay on top, shielding the trooper from further harm. Several of us ran over to help load them both in the back of a jeep for evacuation. These guys were total strangers, yet Ed risked his life to save the other fellow because he felt it was the right thing to do. Sadly, we heard the following day that Kangas had died."

Sergeant Mario "Hank" J. DiCarlo – 1 Platoon, H Company

N30 was met with bazooka fire and some well-placed rounds from the two Sherman tanks still attached from the 705th Tank Destroyer Battalion. By first light, under a heavy mist, dozens of Volksgrenadiers along with tanks succeeded in entering Foy through the G Company defensive line. By 0600hrs the order came for the company to withdraw up into Bois Champay. Five hours later H and I followed suit and the MLR reorganized along the northern edge of Bois Champay between Foy and Recogne.

As the German armor was advancing toward the woods, Hank DiCarlo and his old buddy from Toccoa, Pfc Bill Briggs, nicknamed "The Undertaker," borrowed a bazooka and decided to engage the lead vehicle. The tank was now close enough for the two men to be under the traverse of the turret. A lucky shot penetrated the side plate and began to set off the ammunition inside.

Third Battalion dug in along the edge of Bois Champay and were somewhat envious of the Germans who now had the luxury of sleeping in the houses and barns below. Everyone did their best to insulate their frozen foxholes with layers of branches and ferns. However, rank definitely has its privileges ("RHIP"), as Captain Walker and the officers from H Company took over a small concrete pillbox overlooking the N30 that had been built by the Belgian Army during the 1930s. Rifle ammunition and food were still in short supply and the men took what they could from the dead.

Forward OPs were established in the east and west at the edge of two densely wooded fingers extending toward Foy and Recogne. At the time G Company was responsible for the largest section of woods and covered a front 800 yards wide running east, locking in with I Company. The eastern sector was shared equally between H and I and ultimately became the doorway into Foy for the regiment. Being the closest point overlooking the village, most of the forward OPs were located here.

The German probing attacks continued on and off throughout the day while the battalion did their level best to improve defenses against "tree bursts." A tree burst sent shrapnel of all shapes and sizes ripping through branches down into foxholes. Everyone started to cover up with logs, using soil to fill gaps, before pouring on water that would freeze to form an almost impenetrable barrier.

Back in the H Company area the crew of a 57mm antitank gun opened up on several German tanks at a range of about 500 yards, destroying two and damaging two more. The enemy response was overwhelming and a hail of tank and artillery fire tore into the H Company front lines. The first tree burst killed four men instantly (including three from the gun crew) and paralyzed another. Five minutes later, during another barrage, Private Ralph King was hit. Corporal Gene Johnson went over to help his friend and was horrified to see part of King's left shoulder had been torn away, exposing the bone. Grabbing hold, Gene dragged Ralph back to Route Madame and sat him against a tree before returning to help the others. In all, Johnson evacuated about ten guys to the medics who took them back to Bastogne.

H Company established their permanent OP in a house owned by the Dumont family diagonally opposite the concrete bunker on the eastern side of the N30. When the company took over, most of the animals except for a few chickens had already been killed by artillery.

One night, Sergeant Charles "Chuck" Richards, Pfc Dud Hefner and a couple of others from 3 Platoon were on duty at the house when two German soldiers came snooping around. One escaped while the other was killed. After dragging the body into the back garden, Chuck took the man's ID and left the corpse lying on its right side with one arm outstretched. In the morning, when Chuck turned the dead soldier over to check for unit insignia, the Volksgrenadier's frozen right arm extended upwards into the air. Of course, the guys found this "Nazi death salute" highly amusing. From then on it became a kind of ritual for the troopers to shake hands with the unfortunate man every time they arrived or left the house.

Raymond (son of owners Marcel and Julie Dumont) pictured shortly after the war outside his shattered family home. During the siege H Company used the various shell holes in the wall as observation points to observe down the N30 into Foy. The German soldier killed by Sergeant Richards and Pfc Dud Hefner was dragged into the garden at the rear of the property. (Ivonne Dumont via Joël Robert)

Located south of Route Madame in an old quarry behind H Company, the Third Battalion's CP was well hidden in Bois Champay. The natural bunkers soon became a safe haven for Colonel Patch and his staff. Another nearby pit was where Barney Ryan established the aid station. Casualties with early stage emersion foot or frostbite were stabilized inside the shelter by means of a coal-fired brazier before being sent back to their foxholes. With a diameter of about 25ft wide and over 10ft deep these two ancient works were ideal for the job, once cleared and covered by a thick layer of logs.

Sometime after midnight on December 21, a patrol from 2/506 discovered dozens of footprints near the railroad tracks and traced them back to a nearby patch of woods. The enemy troops were part of a spearhead whose job was to punch and consolidate a hole along the tracks, enabling the panzers a clear route into Bastogne. Finding their way blocked by the 501st and with daylight fast approaching, the Germans had decided to find shelter in a nearby woodland where the forest was scattered with trenches previously dug by the Belgian Army in 1940. At 0830hrs 2/506 heard German voices in the thick fog somewhere behind them and immediately formed a containment force with the 501st to block all possible escape routes. Thirty minutes later, First Battalion was mobilized and sent from Luzery to sweep the containment area and eliminate the enemy force. Led by Bob Harwick, A and C Companies pushed the Volksgrenadiers toward B Company, who were waiting in ambush. The forest here was so dense that it forced the Volksgrenadiers

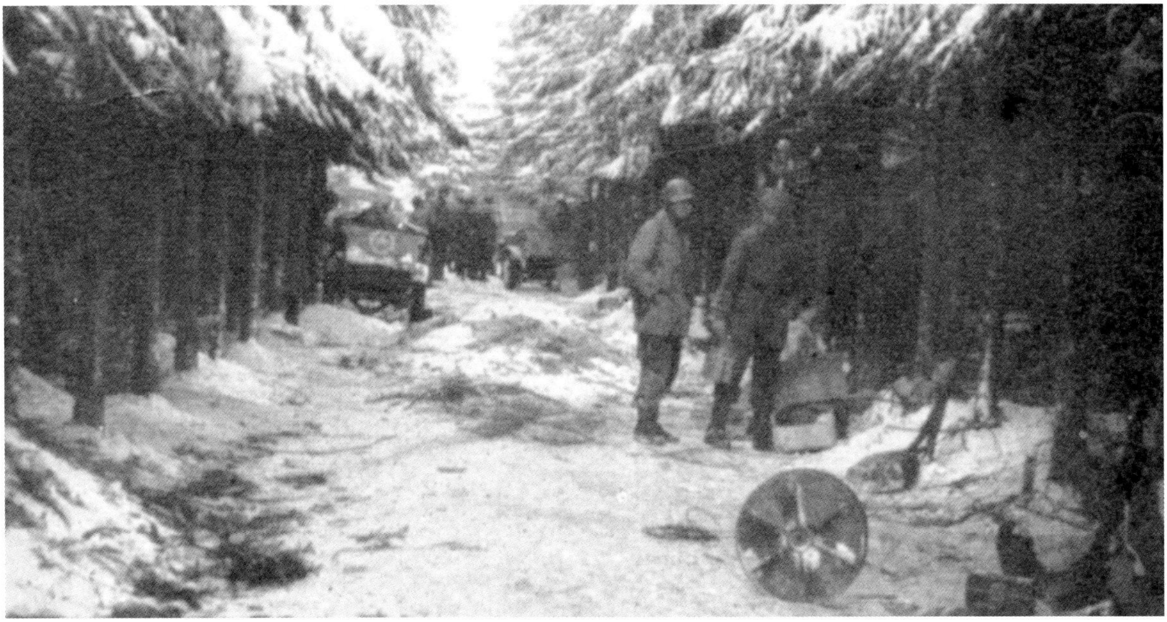

Post-Christmas view looking north through Bois Champay toward Route Madame and the Third Battalion MLR. The battalion aid station was located foreground (right) just inside the tree line.

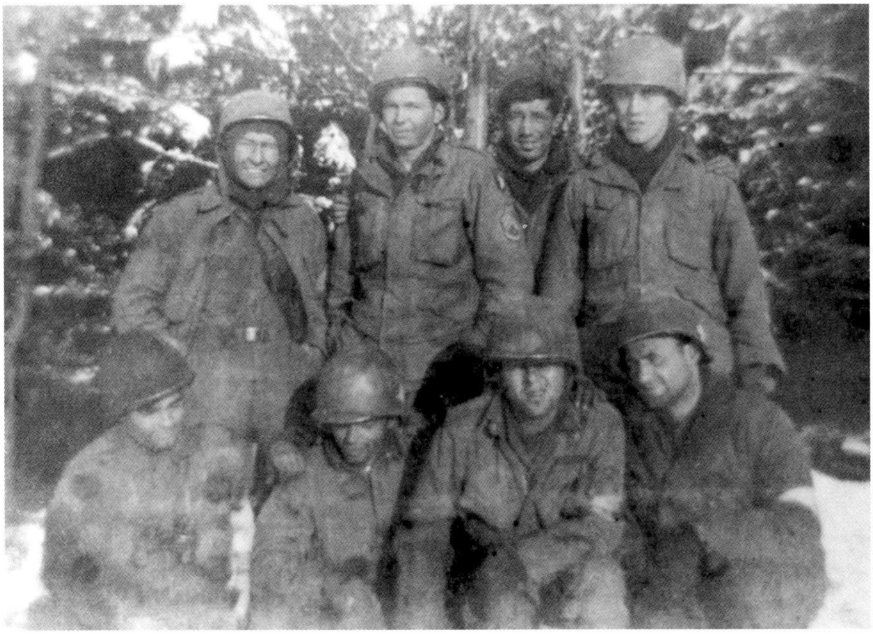

Christmas morning, Third Battalion's Medical Detachment posing on the track outside the aid station in Bois Champay. (Left to right, standing): Harold Haycraft, Talford Wynne, Walter Pelcher and John Eckman. (Left to right, kneeling): Gene Woodside, John Gibson, Robert Evans and Andy Sosnak. Robert Evans was killed on January 9, by artillery, and Andy Sosnak sadly took his own life after the war. (John Gibson)

to use the single-lane logging tracks that criss-crossed Bois Jacques. During the course of the morning, First Battalion, despite taking heavy casualties completely destroyed the substantially greater enemy force.

Back on the Third Battalion MLR, Joe Doughty had been surveying Recogne together with Lieutenant Sherman Sutherland. As the two officers were standing on

Some prisoners were organized into work parties, like these Germans seen here, to dig graves in the cemetery opposite the barracks. The burial details allowed extra rations so they were happy to volunteer. (NARA)

the edge of the woods, they came under an intense mortar barrage. Suddenly Sutherland fell, convulsing, to the ground. As Doughty was trying to revive his colleague, a piece of metal slipped from a gaping wound on the left side of the lieutenant's forehead. He died two days later. 2 Platoon suffered around a dozen casualties from the same bombardment.

One night Private Ray Calandrella was pulling guard duty and could not believe that somebody could be stupid enough to use a flashlight around the CP. Whispering angrily into the darkness, he asked for the man to immediately switch the light off and identify himself. It was Lieutenant John Williams, selfishly rooting around for a spare candy bar!

During the morning of the 22nd, DiCarlo was sent back by jeep to Bastogne with a detail to collect ammunition. Hank decided to look in on his friend Ed Petrowski, who was trapped with hundreds of other wounded at the seminary to see how he was doing. Ed had been wounded during the counterattack on Foy. Although he appeared to be in pain, he was still quite coherent and they talked for several minutes. Just as Hank was turning to leave, Ed grabbed Hank's sleeve and pulled him close. He handed him a set of rosary beads and a beautiful little medallion that he had "acquired" in Holland. These, he whispered, were to be given to his wife and baby girl if anything bad should happen. Hank accepted the items and held Ed's hand to assure him that everything was going to be fine. But that was not to be the case. A few hours later Ed Petrowski lost the fight and died quietly in his sleep.

Moving along the N30 on his way back to Foy, DiCarlo was passing by the back gate of the barracks when he noticed bodies being carried into the indoor range. Entering through a set of double doors, Hank found himself in the target store. Continuing down a short but steep flight of stairs, the ever inquisitive Hank arrived at the butts (enclosed brick walls with a sloping sand-filled area at the back of the range to stop the bullets that have been fired). The sight that greeted him was deeply shocking. Spread across the sand-covered floor and sloped bank were scores of dead bodies, American and German, plus dozens of amputated arms and legs. Just as they were about to leave the first of several German air raids began, forcing them to spend several more uncomfortable hours in the butts before it was safe to return.

At the same time that Hank was on his way back to Foy, a party of four Germans was approaching the American lines under a "white flag" of truce. Leutnant Helmuth Henke, who spoke English, pointed to the briefcase he was holding and explained that he had a "surrender" message for the American commander in Bastogne. Henke and another officer, Major Wagner, were both blindfolded and taken to one of the Glider Infantry command posts where their surrender demand was collected by the regimental intelligence officer. It was then taken to Bastogne, whereupon the famous answer of N-U-T-S was received. Several hours later Colonel Bud Harper, the CO of 327th Glider Infantry Regiment, gave Henke the good news. Henke and Wagner were naturally confused by the slang terminology, but once explained as "Go to Hell" they soon understood the "good news."

Capt Gene Brown and Lt Shrable Williams pictured at Littlecote in August 1944. Shrable (right) led the 101st Pathfinder mission on December 23, to initiate Operation *Repulse*, the first of several aerial resupply missions that changed everything for the besieged and encircled American forces at Bastogne. Gene took temporary command of I Company on January 12, 1945, after Andy Anderson was unexpectedly reassigned to battalion staff. (John Reeder via Roger Day)

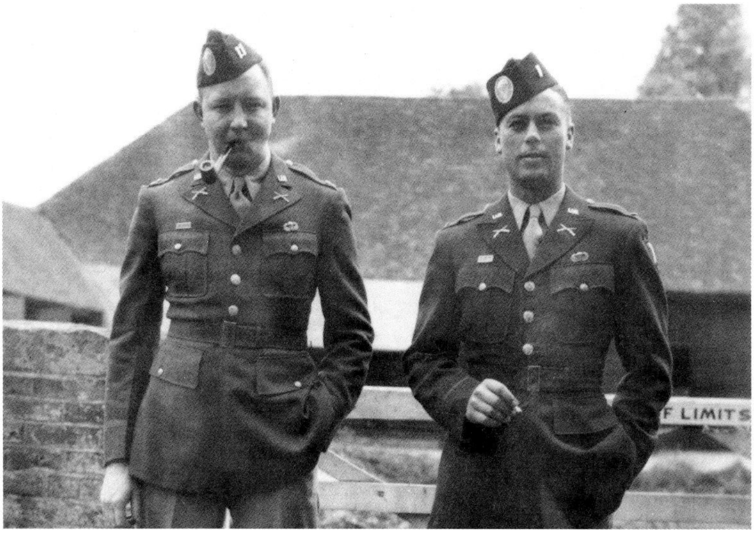
F LIMITS

December 23 dawned with a light covering of snow but the overcast weather began to disperse, and by early afternoon hundreds of vapor trails from Allied bombers began to appear in the clear blue sky bound for Germany. The first day of good weather also gave the Allies an unlimited ceiling and a free hand across the Bastogne battle area to wreak havoc. Air panels were displayed, marking friendly positions, while US and British ground attack aircraft went in for the kill. The improvement in the weather also brought in another surprise. The first of two ten-man teams from the 101st Pathfinder Company began dropping

First air resupply pictured coming in on December 23, 1944. In total, between December 23 and 27, 2,000 parachutes were dropped, carrying 481 tons of supplies. (NARA)

The drop on December 26, as seen from the parade ground at Caserne Heintz. Col Sink's CP was located in the last block on the right. Note the flag with a crucifix outside the temporary chapel. (NARA)

Paratroopers recovering equipment from a later supply drop. (Universal History Archive/UIG via Getty Images)

1 mile southwest of Bastogne. The Pathfinders were at the front of a huge stream of C-47s loaded with essential supplies. While the main body were preparing the Eureka signaling equipment, stick commanders Lieutenants Shrable Williams and Gordon Rothwell went straight to the barracks and established exactly where division wanted the supplies to be dropped. The Pathfinders were directed to set up their transmitters and signaling equipment on the high ground west of the city near Grande Fontaine. Within an hour of landing, the two teams established contact with the first 16 aircraft and Operation *Repulse* was now on. In total around 238 aircraft reached the target and dropped hundreds of bundles containing ammunition, food and medical supplies.

Every available truck and jeep was sent out to the drop zone to bring home the supplies. Everything was reused by the defenders, even the packing crates, felt and multicolored parachutes. More supply missions followed, but due to bad weather all flights were suspended on Christmas Day itself. The subsequent drops brought in a variety of items ranging from artillery shells and telephone cable to cigarettes, candy

"During the late afternoon, Captain Jim Morton visited our positions and stopped for a moment to speak with me. 'Jungle Jim' had been our original XO and knew me well. The captain told me that due to the shortage of officers in H Company he was now doubling up as temporary XO for Captain Walker. As we were discussing our individual hunger issues, he noticed the body of a German soldier lying out in front of my position. I couldn't believe what he said next – he suggested that we go out under cover of darkness and cut the backside out of the Kraut and fry it as a 'steak supper.' 'Sir,' I replied, 'surely you are joking?' He looked at me, smiled, and retorted, 'It's only a suggestion,' before disappearing back into the woods… I never did find out if he was being serious."

Pfc James H. Martin – 2 Platoon, G Company

"Before leaving Mourmelon, my parents sent me a package containing, among other things, a large tin of sweet peas along with a cryptic note saying, 'Do not open until your 22nd birthday,' which was… Christmas Eve. The guys in the platoon were always very liberal with their care parcels and everything was shared whenever possible. Everyone in the trench wished me a Happy Birthday as I punched a couple of holes in the tin and placed it to heat on our squad stove. As the can started to boil we noticed an odd smell, and it suddenly dawned on us that the container was actually full of liquor, so I poured a little into our cups before passing it around to the rest of the platoon. It certainly gave us something to smile about, and for once I toasted my dad for doing the right thing. Later that evening we got our first hot meal, which was brought up from Bastogne – so my birthday couldn't have been really any better!"

Staff Sergeant Ralph S. Bennett – 3 Platoon, H Company

"One night I led a group of around 15 soldiers out to a forward OP. They were all replacements of one sort or another and begged me not to leave them alone. They were so inexperienced and scared that I had to stay with them until it was time to return."

Sergeant Louis J. Vecchi – 1 Platoon, H Company

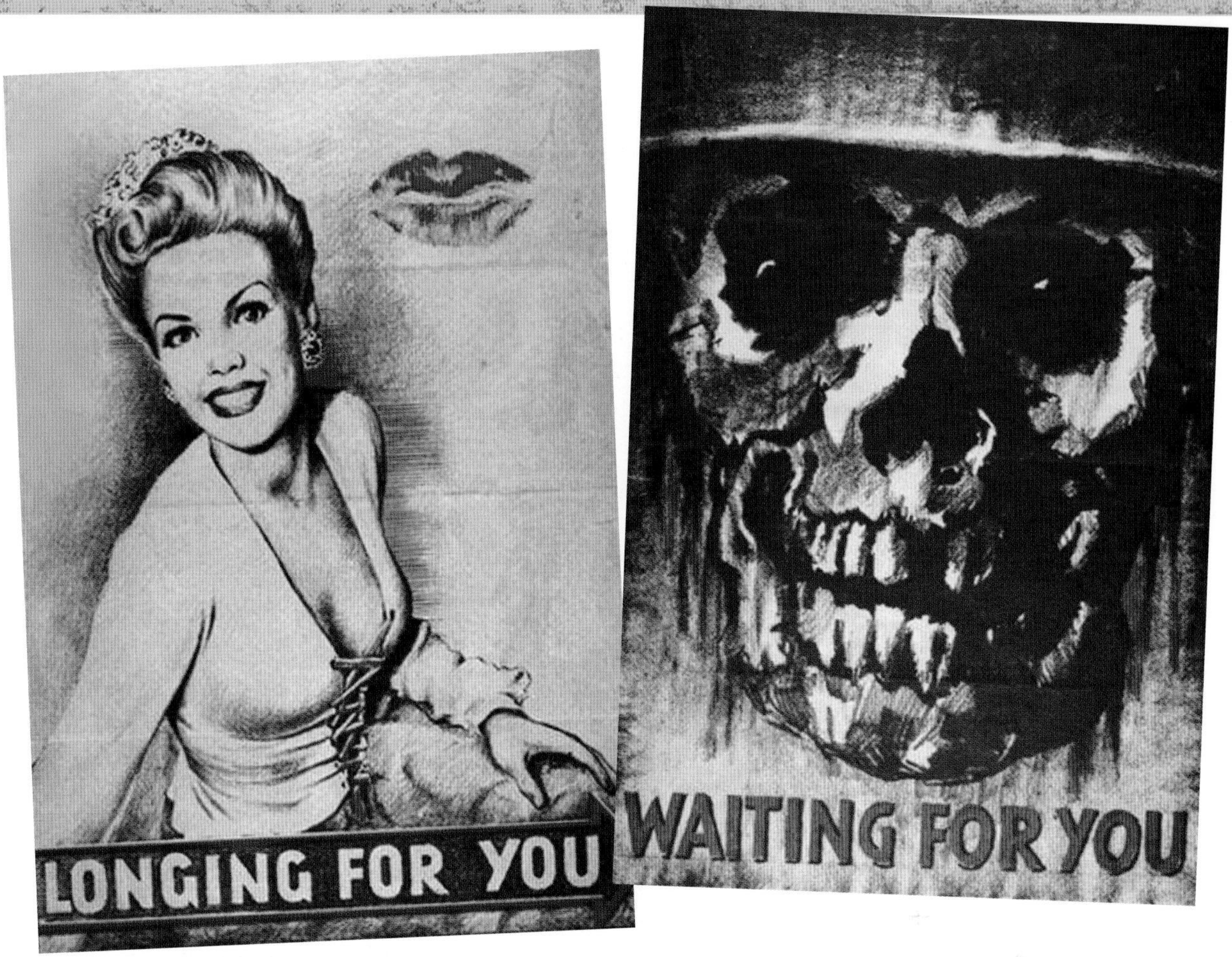
LONGING FOR YOU
WAITING FOR YOU

A German propaganda leaflet, front and back. (Mark Bando)

and mail. Doc Feiler organized work parties to gather up as many parachutes as possible and bring them back to the rifle range where they were used for blankets, bedding, and bandages.

By holding a tight and well-connected perimeter against the encirclement that became known as "the hole in the donut," the 101st Airborne was successfully able to keep the enemy infantry and armor well away from Bastogne. After the divisional defense force was regrouped, the 506th combat teams were further augmented by more AT and AAA batteries and tanks. Luckily, up to this point the Germans had not focused their attacks on any one particular place but instead had used smaller probing strikes to try to determine weak points. Despite the German ultimatum of surrender or face total annihilation, nothing really changed. However, the regiment did not know that the enemy had been building up strength in Recogne, Cobru, and, worryingly, on the eastern side of the MLR. At 0830hrs on Christmas Eve, the Volksgrenadiers launched a company-sized reconnaissance attack from their positions in Bois Jacques opposite 2/506. German casualties were heavy, and

Damaged caused by German air raids along Rue de Marche close to the railway bridge in Bastogne. (NARA)

Bastogne's bombed out town square during the early part of the siege. (Left – Reg Jans) (Right – Getty Images)

although the assault failed, it showed that the now scaled-down enemy force was still very active and ready to engage.

The first heavy snowfall came at midday on Christmas Eve. At the time only 50 percent of the division had rubber overshoes, and most of those (dropped in by air) never reached the front lines. As a stopgap, sandbags were issued and all available white cloth requisitioned for camouflage. Up until this point the men figured that the weather could not get any worse but they were in for a nasty surprise! The deep white blanket now forming was powdery, dry, freezing cold and even brought with it thousands of puerile German surrender leaflets packed into specially modified artillery shells. To counter the enemy propaganda, Lieutenant Colonel Kinnard

On Christmas Day the senior commanders took a few moments to contemplate the festive season at the barracks. (Left to right): William Roberts (CO Combat Command B, 10th Armored Division), Ned Moore (Division Personnel Officer), Gerald Higgins (Assistant Division CO), Tony McAuliffe (temporary Division CO), Thomas Sherburne (temporary Division Artillery CO), Harry Kinnard (Division Operations Officer), Carl Kohls (Division Supply Officer), Paul Danahy (Division Intelligence Officer) and Curtis Renfro (CO 401st Glider Infantry Regiment). (NARA colorized by Johnny Sirlande)

BELOW LEFT American convoy moving toward Bastogne (NARA)

BELOW RIGHT Midnight mass for the walking wounded in the barracks at Bastogne. Moments later a German air raid broke up the service. (NARA)

wrote a special Christmas message on behalf of General McAuliffe, stating: "The Allied troops are counterattacking in force. We continue to hold Bastogne. By holding Bastogne we assure the success of the Allied Armies. We know that our Division Commander General Taylor will say: 'Well done!' We are giving our country and our loved ones at home a worthy Christmas present and, being privileged to take part in this gallant feat of arms, are truly making for ourselves a Merry Christmas."

Due to the renewed activity within Bois Jacques, Third Battalion increased its night patrolling between Recogne and Foy. Hank DiCarlo's squad was down to eight men and they were starting to feel the effects of the last few days. At this point rations were becoming scarce again, forcing the men to scavenge. Most were rationing themselves to one tiny meal per day and they were beginning to lose weight at an alarming rate.

That afternoon elements of 1 and 2 Platoons, H Company, were ordered northwest toward the 502nd to find and identify suspected new enemy positions. The patrol had just stepped out from the tree line and moved forward about 100 yards when a machine gun opened up, wounding the lead scout. Back in the woods, medic Walter Pelcher removed his pack and bravely ran out into the snow and successfully retrieved the wounded man under heavy small-arms fire. Everyone who witnessed this act felt it had been suicidally brave but Walt simply shrugged and said it was all in the line of duty. When the mission started to unravel G Company rushed to assist. As they pushed down into Recogne, some 15 enemy tanks supported by infantry came from nowhere and attacked their left flank. The company were unable to hold against tank fire. The officers and NCOs were desperately trying to steady the line when Derwood Cann, then Operations Officer, turned up and by sheer weight of command inspired the starving and exhausted men to regroup and turn their attention back to the fight. As the situation escalated, DiCarlo and 1 Platoon ran through the woods to lend a hand. On approaching the G Company sector, they could hear the roar of tanks coming up the hill toward them. Using several dirt roads and logging tracks, the enemy armor had successfully managed to outflank G Company and circle around Château d'Hoffschmidt looking for a route into the western woods. The Panthers had split into smaller groups, each taking a different route toward the ridge. Totally

501st troopers searching German prisoners in front of the Gendarmerie stables in Bastogne before handing them over to the MPs and the Interrogation Prisoner of War (IPW) team. The nine-man IPW team had taken over several buildings surrounding the Gendarmerie where the MPs had established a POW cage. (NARA)

exposed, the German infantry were decimated by the 502nd, who were firmly entrenched to the west. A number of tanks then began to converge on a single-track road that crossed the Route Madame.

DiCarlo's small force, combined with the rearguard from G Company, began to neutralize the stragglers now trying to catch up with the Panthers. Upon crossing the MLR the enemy tanks were cut off by four Sherman tank destroyers, which forced a couple of them into an adjacent field and knocked them out. With their exit now blocked, the other tanks had no choice but to continue forward through the woods toward Savy, where they were picked off by antitank guns. Back in the field behind the MLR, the turrets flipped open, and rather than surrender, the crews ran toward the forest where they were cut down by the 502nd. Fighting was fierce around the château and the intense enemy bombardment that followed caused several deaths among the paratroopers.

Finally, around midnight on Christmas Eve, the gunfire subsided. High above the MLR, Sirius, the "Dog Star," brightly stood out in the night sky. Encapsulating the holy night, it was a sobering thought for those who had just participated in the

Vehicles clogging central Bastogne opposite the town square shortly after the breakthrough. (NARA)

last battle. Frank Kneller stood up and attempted to sing "Silent Night." Ken Johnson was not impressed, especially after one of the less compassionate enemy troops in Foy decided to take a pot shot. The bullet passed right between the two men, and Kneller was so angered by the response that he got on the radio and called for mortar fire. Ken watched as the shells exploded and a couple of German soldiers ran screaming into the open with their clothing ablaze.

Christmas Day in Bastogne began with another raid from the Luftwaffe. The bombing forced Colonel Sink to cut his losses and relocate to Luzery.

\*\*\*

On December 26, Doctor Ryan received several boxes of medicinal alcohol, which had been air dropped before Christmas. Barney had far more than he was ever going to use so as a gesture of benevolence he decided to distribute the excess among the men. The platoon sergeants were called over to the aid station and each allocated a number of the small bottles. Ryan stressed to everyone that because of the strength and purity only a tiny amount could be rationed to each person and even then it had to be drastically watered down. Ignoring Ryan's good advice, many hit the bottle so hard that they had to be temporarily removed from front-line duty with alcohol poisoning.

Patton's tanks slide along Rue de Clerveaux out of Bastogne toward Longvilly and Margeret. (NARA)

Over the next two days, dozens of gliders brought in heavier supplies and equipment, including a nine-man surgical team from Third Army. Their job was to operate on all the abdominal and chest patients to stabilize them for evacuation. Despite the weather conditions, three columns from Third Army simultaneously converged on Bastogne. By late afternoon on the 26th the first tanks had made contact with elements of the 326th Airborne Engineers. The following morning the road between Neufchâteau and Bastogne was officially declared open. Against the odds the airborne troops had survived the siege and reinforcements had finally broken through. The tankers were surprised to see the surrounding countryside littered with so much knocked-out German armor. Soon a convoy of trucks and ambulances arrived and evacuated over 250 priority patients.

The N30 (Rue du Seblon) through Bastogne jammed with vehicles heading for the northern perimeter. The seminary and Saint-Pierre church bell tower can be seen in the background. (NARA)

McAuliffe outside his HQ with General Taylor on December 27, 1944. Taylor had traveled in that morning from Neufchâteau after the road was opened. McAuliffe left Bastogne on January 9 and did a brief publicity tour before being posted to the 103rd Infantry Division in Alsace Lorraine. Two days before Tony's departure, Max Taylor relocated his Divisional HQ 2 miles southwest to Ile-le-Pré and Ile-la-Hesse. (NARA)

Despite bringing in reinforcements from Mourmelon, the regiment was still desperately short of manpower and began to draft in troops from other units such as the 327th and 401st Glider Infantry Regiments. The ground forces were now being actively supported by dozens of newly arrived heavy guns. Finally, Major General Max Taylor reached Bastogne himself and took back command of the division from Tony McAuliffe. Taking full advantage of the clear skies, Bastogne was bombed and strafed for the eighth time by the Luftwaffe and shortly afterwards the last remaining civilians were evacuated.

At exactly one minute past midnight on New Year's Eve, both sides welcomed in the New Year with several barrages of artillery and mortar fire. However, back in Berlin, Hitler had already begun to make plans for a new offensive in Alsace.

On January 2, 1945, a group of enemy soldiers, disguised as Americans, were captured in Foy. After all US night patrols had safely returned, the entire MLR went

German Panzer V, also known as the Panther, abandoned by its crew somewhere around the perimeter. Note: US M1 Carbine leaning against track nearest camera. (Johnny Gibson)

Pvt Duane Tedrick and Cpl Alvin Quimby from D Company strike a pose near the railway line at Bizory. Later in early January, D and E Companies would take a hammering from German rockets while reoccupying their old positions in Bois Jacques. (Mark Bando Collection)

onto high alert. This was followed by a two-hour timeframe, during which any unscheduled activity coming from no man's land could be targeted without challenge. Previously Lieutenant Joe Doughty had turned a blind eye to one of his sergeants, James West, making regular trips down to Degives Farm on the southern edge of Recogne. Although the farm had been abandoned two weeks earlier, the owner, Nester Degives, had left behind a well-stocked wine cellar. Despite the "lockdown," West and his friend Charles Hunton decided to ignore what was going on and carry on regardless. Route Madame was the boundary between Company G of the 506th and H Company of the 502nd. As usual, before he passed through, West informed the troops manning the OP what he was doing. However, while the two G Company men were relaxing down at the farm, the H Company, 502nd OP shift changed and the new guard was not updated with the facts. An hour or so later, as Hunton and West were returning along the beech-lined road, the soldier in the OP opened fire and killed both men instantly. After all that Third Battalion had been through it was a depressing way to ring in 1945. But they were not through the worst of it.

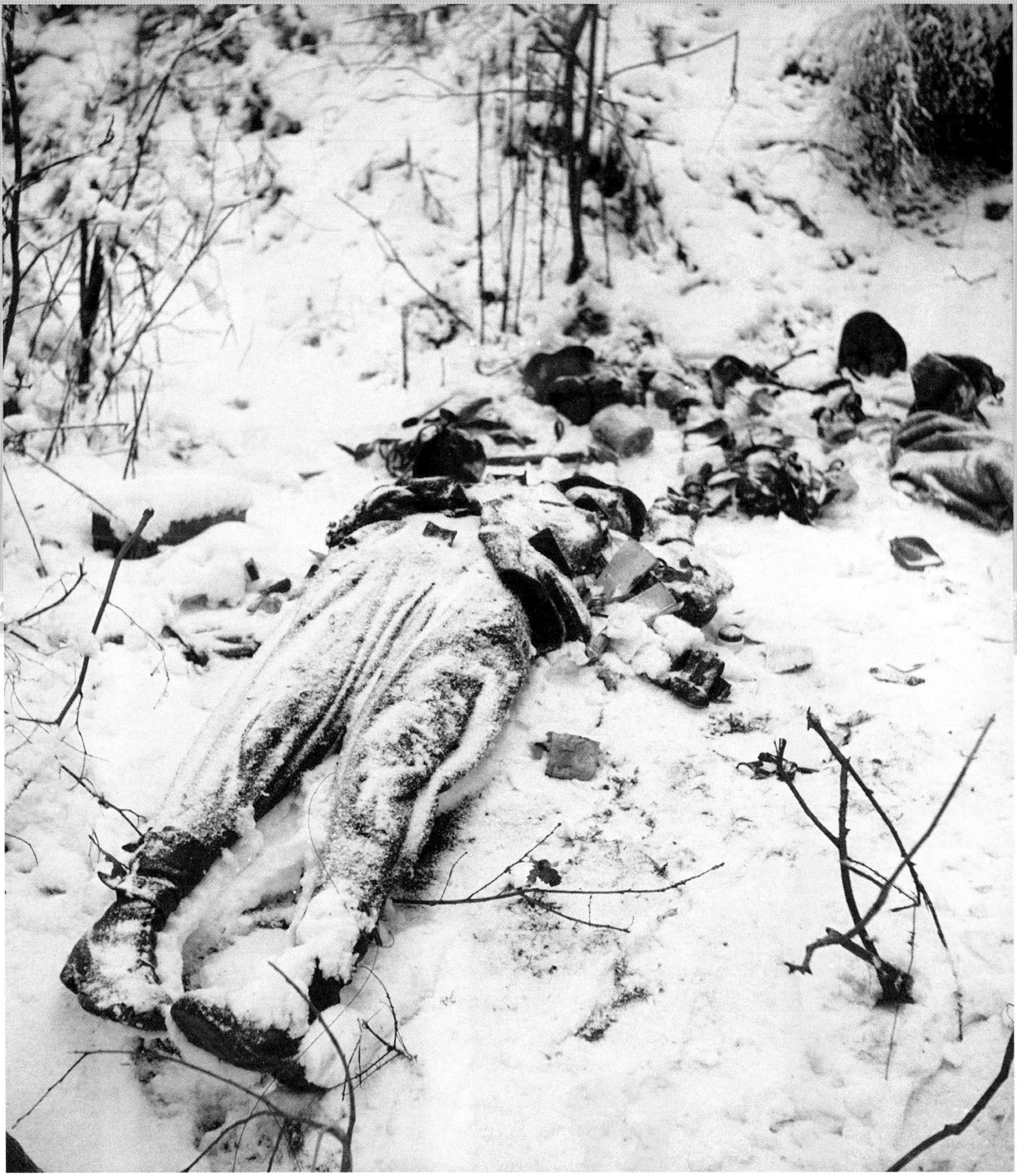

# Chapter 8
# DYING FOR A DREAM

## Hell Night and the Final Attack on Foy

### Attack into Bois Fazone, January 9, 1945

Since the siege was effectively broken on December 26, the regiment had been preparing for an all-out assault on the enemy lines. For the past week, General Patton's Third Army had been working hard to widen the main arterial road and clear a route. By January 5, the 506th had begun to step up its patrolling and small-unit activity in a determined effort to regain control of the hills and woods surrounding Bastogne. Over the next few days, in order to keep up with the fluid tactical situation, Bob Sink relocated several times before ending up at Lloyd Patch's CP in Bois Champay. After being relieved by 3/501 at 0500hrs on January 9, Patch and the Third Battalion moved southwest to an assembly area near Sonne Fontaine. A couple of hours earlier, Second Battalion had made a move north accompanied by tanks from Task Force Cherry. Their mission was to clear and occupy the woods at Fazone and the ground southwest of Vaux, in preparation for their forthcoming attack to reclaim Noville. January 9, 1945 would deliver some of the worst moments in just about everyone's military careers in the Third Battalion.

The body of a dead Volksgrenadier lies frozen in the snow. Some of the wounded enemy soldiers found in Bois Fazone by 3/506 on January 9 could not be dealt with there and then. By the following morning, more snow and even colder temperatures meant that many of these casualties simply froze to death where they fell. (Photo by John Florea/The LIFE Picture Collection/Getty Images)

Sgt Harold Stedman from 3 Platoon, I Company, pictured in 1942. (Harold Stedman)

Before midday, as the 501st were attacking Recogne, Third Battalion began their wide-sweeping parallel advance through fresh heavy snow toward Fazone. With 2/506 to the right and the 502nd supposedly on their left, Jim Morton and HQ Company came under intense and accurate mortar fire. The initial shelling killed Len Lundquist from the Machine Gun Platoon and seriously injured Lieutenant Ken Beard and runner Private Charles Coppala, along with six or seven others. Morton carried Coppala to the nearest protected place he could find, which was a concrete culvert. As they moved toward the ditch another shell exploded in the trees, knocking them to the ground. The intense blast tore away Jim's helmet, sunglasses and entrenching tool.

Earlier, while Morton had been saving Coppala, Bob Webb was at the end of his tether trying to maintain radio contact after all four of the battalion's SCR310 radio backpacks had their aerials blown off by the barrage. A soldier was crying out for his mother as Webb and Leroy Vickers frantically fought to re-establish communications. Nearby, a young replacement holding a bazooka took a direct hit and was blown to pieces, smattering Bob with blood and shredded flesh.

The Germans had booby-trapped most of the main pathways along which the battalion was now advancing. The men were constantly stopping to carefully step over tripwires. By now the temperature had dropped off the scale and the day was the coldest anyone could remember. Avoiding the booby-trapped logging tracks, H Company pushed ahead through the woods toward Cobru, the final objective, taking several casualties on the way due to friendly artillery fire. The ground on the edge of Bois Fazone slopes away in a long undulating curve toward the villages of Vaux and Cobru, which were still in German hands. Beyond the two hamlets on the high ground in the distance was the regiment's final prize – Noville.

The author in Bois Fazone on a snowy January morning in 2013. Back in 1945, the enemy booby-trapped many of these old logging tracks which they knew would be used by American tanks and infantry.

Unable to make contact with the 502nd, Jim Morton and one of his sergeants went on patrol to the western edge of the forest only to find the battalion's left flank completely exposed. Because of this, Colonel Patch halted the advance on the edge of Fazone and ordered the battalion to dig in. The shrieking crash of shells tore open the dense canopy, uprooting trees and anything else standing in their way. Shrapnel skipped through the branches, buzzing everywhere as soldiers cowered in their shallow, frozen holes. Between each barrage plaintive calls for "medic" could be heard, growing more piteous as the fear of being overlooked in the

# Attack into Bois Fazone, January 9, 1945

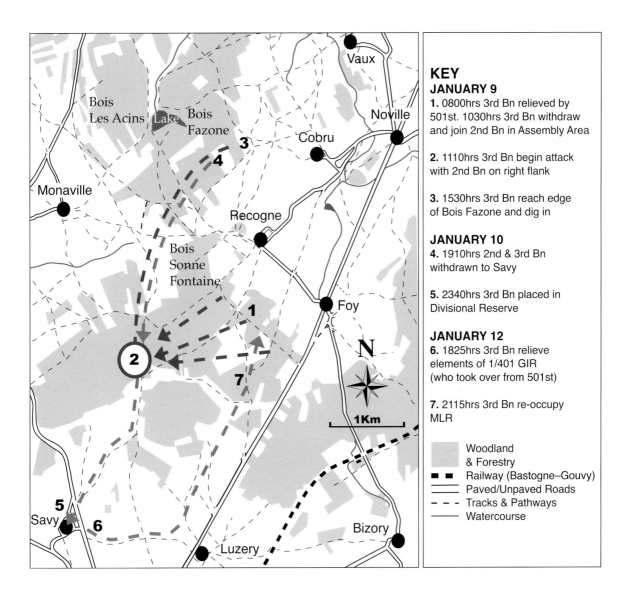

**KEY**

**JANUARY 9**
**1.** 0800hrs 3rd Bn relieved by 501st. 1030hrs 3rd Bn withdraw and join 2nd Bn in Assembly Area

**2.** 1110hrs 3rd Bn begin attack with 2nd Bn on right flank

**3.** 1530hrs 3rd Bn reach edge of Bois Fazone and dig in

**JANUARY 10**
**4.** 1910hrs 2nd & 3rd Bn withdrawn to Savy

**5.** 2340hrs 3rd Bn placed in Divisional Reserve

**JANUARY 12**
**6.** 1825hrs 3rd Bn relieve elements of 1/401 GIR (who took over from 501st)

**7.** 2115hrs 3rd Bn re-occupy MLR

| | |
|---|---|
| ▇ | Woodland & Forestry |
| ■ ■ | Railway (Bastogne–Gouvy) |
| — | Paved/Unpaved Roads |
| - - - | Tracks & Pathways |
| — | Watercourse |

1Km

View at dusk looking northeast from the edge of Bois Fazone toward Cobru. Many of the original foxholes dug by Third Battalion on January 9 are still in existence. It was here in the fields opposite that the German tanks appeared and pounded the woods at close range, causing many casualties including Jim Morton, Johnny Gibson, Harold Stedman and Bobbie Rommel.

growing darkness began to take hold. Between flares and flashes of gunfire, it was difficult for the senior NCOs to keep track of their men, let alone comprehend whether the enemy was advancing or retreating.

Doc Ryan and medic Harold Haycraft had just pulled a wounded soldier from his foxhole when they heard the sound of the first tank approaching. Swearing under his breath, Ryan turned around to see the Panther threshing up snow and practically looking right down their throats. Just as they were dragging the casualty away, the Panther put a round in but they managed to escape. It was getting dark and everyone except Jim Morton, Fred Bahlau and their HQ Company colleague

Medic Johnny Gibson (foreground on stretcher) en route to Paris after being wounded in Bois Fazone on January 9, 1945. The photo was probably taken at Massul near Luxembourg while in the care of the 429th Medical Collection Company. (Johnny Gibson)

Sergeant Dennis Wester had dug in. It was then that Morton reached for his shovel, only to find a torn remnant of canvas. The first tank round hit Wester and Morton as well as three or four others. Morton was still dazed when Medic Johnny Gibson ran across and found Jim face down in his unfinished hole. Fully aware of the risks, Johnny began cutting away at Morton's clothing. A large splinter of metal had penetrated Morton's left leg, leaving a 6in gash in the ankle and a gaping comma-shaped exit wound. Another, smaller, fragment had lodged next to the artery in his thigh. As John was

"There was more shelling up ahead, and while crossing an open clearing I came across a soldier sitting in the snow with his leg missing below the knee... The man's foot and part of his leg were still contained within his boot, which was lying on the ground no more than 20ft away. Although the casualty was pale and suffering from shock, he was able to support what was left of his leg with both hands. Taking out a large compression bandage and some sulfa powder, I bent down to dress the mangled stump, but the man refused treatment. Instead he requested a cigarette, so I grabbed one from his pocket, lit it, and placed it between his lips. Again, the trooper refused treatment but asked me if I would collect his severed leg. At that moment a patrol came by and I spotted a couple of medics and handed the guy over to them before leaving to catch up with the battalion. Trudging away, I turned around to see the casualty struggling physically with the medics who were desperately trying to treat his injury. Moving deeper into the forest the shelling seemed to intensify and shrapnel began to pick off our men, one by one. "

Corporal John W. Gibson – Medical Detachment

"Moving through the dense woodland with Fred Sneesby I bumped into my buddy Harold Stedman, who I'd known since high school in Modesto. Harold was standing in the snow with a 60mm mortar barrel slung over his shoulder, wearing an enormous Kraut greatcoat that went clear down to the ground. I mean, he looked so ridiculous that I had to laugh. Harold couldn't understand what I found so funny. Still laughing, I told Harold that I'd see him later, shook hands, and carried on to the edge of the wood with my two gun teams. As we were digging in, a Sherman came up behind us, which we knew was gonna get someone's attention. Predictably the artillery came in and the shells burst into the trees, covering us with snow. After digging ourselves out, a piece of shrapnel from another burst whizzed past, narrowly missing my knee. During the next barrage I wasn't so lucky and another tree burst, about 6ft above our heads, sent a chunk of shrapnel through my overshoes and boots, penetrating deep into the arch of my left foot. The pain was excruciating, and it felt like I'd been struck with a baseball bat. Guys were getting hit all around and hollering for medical attention. Incredibly, thinking they were going to be fed, the German prisoners who had been captured earlier were standing around holding their mess tins when another barrage hit the treetops, scattering the prisoners in all directions. I could only crawl, and as Fred Sneesby was such a little guy he struggled to support my weight. Fred ordered a couple of the Krauts to help carry me to the aid post where I was loaded into a jeep and taken to Bastogne.

Corporal Bobbie J. Rommel – Machine Gun Platoon

applying a tourniquet, another shell exploded overhead, perforating John's back with white-hot shrapnel. As he collapsed, another razor-sharp piece of steel penetrated his right lung and diaphragm. One of the fragments passed right through Gibson's body and lodged in Morton's thigh, tearing a hole the size of a teacup. Another medic, Andy Sosnak, arrived and went to work on both men, who were bundled away to be evacuated by jeep to Luzery along with an injured Bob Rommel from the Machine Gun Platoon. The next stop for Morton, Gibson, and Rommel was the regimental aid station in Bastogne, where the surgeon informed Jim Morton that his left foot was almost severed at the ankle and would probably need amputating. At the time Jim did not care one way or another. He was just glad to be alive.

Although still in reserve, Bob Harwick and First Battalion had been moving up behind 3/506 when they came under an intense artillery barrage. Bob did not hear the first shell – it was more like a pressure wave – but felt something hit him in the stomach followed by a sharp tearing pain to his side. Turning slowly as if in slow motion, he fell onto his knees and face into the snow, then crawled a few feet to a small tree. Resting against the trunk, snow from the branches tumbled down onto his face. Bob's Executive Officer Knut Raudstein was wounded at the same time and shouted across to see if he was OK. Bob tried to answer but could not get his breath and it was only then that he realized how badly he had been injured. After being stabilized by the medics, Harwick was placed on a stretcher and carried to an evacuation jeep. The ride through the woods along the logging tracks to the aid station was gut-wrenching due to the deep ruts churned over by the 30-ton Shermans. Shells were exploding all around. One mortar landed so close to the jeep that Bob instinctively covered his face. Shortly after arriving in Bastogne, Harwick was evacuated to Massul near Luxembourg. With First Battalion now completely leaderless, Charlie Shettle was temporarily reassigned from 2/506 to take command but was then also seriously wounded.

Throughout the night, mortar, artillery, and tank shells continually hammered into the woods, making medical evacuation next to impossible. Because of the exceptionally high wind chill factor, the temperature on January 9 dropped to -17 degrees Celsius (1.4 degrees Fahrenheit) and was the coldest night experienced during the campaign. At dawn the following morning Ryan's aid post looked like an image from hell. Barney had personally dealt with 15 severe cases including Charlie Shettle. Dead bodies were piled outside and trails of blood marked the snow in all directions where the wounded had desperately dragged themselves to seek treatment. Despite the chaos and confusion, the enemy had successfully been pushed further north beyond Cobru – which at least was something positive.

After spending the day on line at Fazone, the remnants of the battalion were replaced by 1/506, now under the command of Major Clarence Hester, who had

## The Final Attack on Foy, 0845–1100hrs, January 13, 1945

Foy
G Co
G Co
H Co
Route Madame
C 5
B
A
D
1
2
3
4
6
7
8
XXX
N
250m

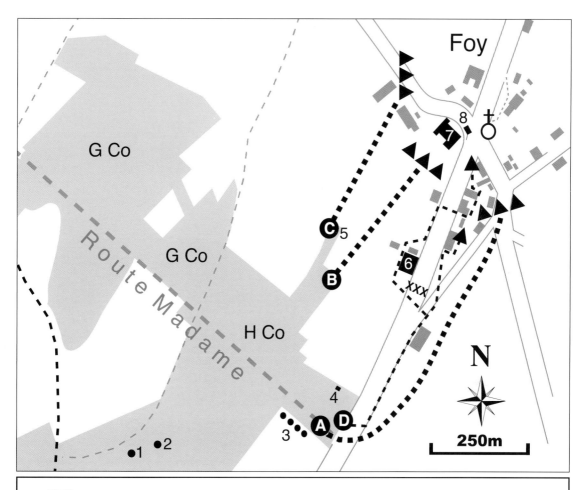

**KEY**

**A.** 0830hrs
2Lt Ed Shames & 3 Ptn E Co commence with a diversionary assault

**B.** 0900hrs
2Lt Jack Foley & 1 Ptn E Co

**C.** 1/Sgt Carwood Lipton & 2 Ptn E Co advance to form a Blocking Force
(NB: Assumed B & C line of attack)

**D.** 1015hrs
Capt Gene Brown & I Co

**1.** 3/506 Aid Station

**2.** 3/506 & 506th RHQ CP

**3.** 81mm Mortar Line

**4.** MG Bunker (H Co CP)

**5.** 81mm Mortar OP (1Lt Pete Madden)

**6.** Forward Aid Station established by Dr Barney Ryan at Albert Koeune's house (where Joe Madona was killed)

**7.** Jules Koeune's house used by Germans as a strongpoint and CP

**8.** Mk IV Panzer
(using dip in road for cover)

**XXX** German Minefield

taken over from Shettle. Withdrawn to Savy as divisional reserve, Bob Webb decided to carry on into Bastogne to look for some replacement radio aerials. He came across a road junction clogged with traffic and the last thing he remembered was running for a ditch as a shell exploded nearby. The battalion never got the radio antennas it so desperately needed as Webb was diagnosed with concussion and evacuated for treatment.

Meanwhile Bob Harwick was transferred to a hospital train at Massul and moved to Paris. In total, the regiment had sustained 126 casualties in what would become known as "Hell Night."

## The Final Attack on Foy 0845–1100hrs, January 13, 1945

Two days later, after relieving the 401st Glider Infantry Regiment on the ridgeline at Foy, Colonel Patch briefed what was left of his officers at the battalion CP. The idea was to secure the village without damaging the N30, enabling Shermans and M18 Hellcats from the 11th Armored Division to pass through unimpeded toward Noville. Due to the high number of casualties taken on January 9, the remaining senior NCOs were shuffled between rifle companies, which, for the most part, were down to fewer than 30 men each.

For the first phase, E Company would be attached to Third Battalion and join with I Company for the attack that was due to begin on January 13. As he had previously been working so closely with Lloyd Patch, the CO of Regimental HQ Company, Captain Gene Brown, was asked to take temporary command of I Company – Andy Anderson had himself gone over to H Company after Jim Morton

View north toward Foy around January 14 along the N30, showing one of the M18 Hellcats from 11th Armored Division.

had been hit. The company was split into two composite squads. The first was led by Lieutenant Roger Tinsley and the other by Sergeant Harley Dingman. The battalion as a whole was nothing more than an oversized platoon and Patch did not really know how he could effectively deploy them, but orders were orders. During the briefing, Lieutenant Pete Madden of the 81mm Mortar Platoon was told he would be providing mortar support to suppress a number of suspected enemy machine-gun positions dug in on the high ground beyond the village. During the early hours of the 13th, to be nearer to the fight, Colonel Sink relocated his HQ from Hemroulle to the Third Battalion CP along with reinforcements from Regimental HQ.

After a night of light enemy shelling, the American attack began as planned at 0900hrs. Pete Madden was waiting for the signal to commence his fire missions but it never came. He could see puffs of smoke coming from the German machine-gun nests and knew they were actively engaging the men from E Company who were spearheading the assault. Suddenly the radio crackled into life: "STAND BY – WAIT – OUT." Madden did not recognize the voice on the end of the line and called for clarification, and the reply came back, "THIS IS KIDNAP BLUE – HOLD YOUR FIRE MISSION." The radio chatter went back and forth several times before Pete asked for identification. When none was received, Madden immediately called all four batteries onto the pre-recorded targets.

As soon as the mortars opened up, Madden sprinted back to the battalion CP to advise that he thought the enemy must have tapped into the regimental communications network. Sink had no choice but to order complete radio silence, rendering command and control during the attack almost impossible. While this was happening, 1 and 2 Platoons from E Company had crossed their jump-off point and were now proceeding down into Foy. Earlier, Lieutenant Ed Shames and 3 Platoon of E Company had been sent across the N30 to the extreme western edge of Bois Jacques, where they were supposed to be the lead platoon in a diversionary attack. Shames' mission was to push down to the crossroads and draw the enemy forces away from the center of town. Simultaneously, keeping the main road on their right, the rest of E Company began their attack down the slope where they were to link up with Shames and form a blocking force along the road leading to Recogne.

Enemy forces had also established a firebase at the Koeune family house within Foy. Located at the strongpoint was a mortar fire controller who had all entry routes into the village covered. Machine guns located on the upper floors had uninterrupted views back toward the American lines. The guns were protecting a Mk IV Panzer parked directly outside the Koeune house. Here the road drops sharply away, leaving the turret barely visible from the main road. Together the tank and the well-established defenders would prove to be a formidable barrier to the men of the 506th from achieving their objectives.

## The Final Attack on Foy, 1100–1500hrs, January 13, 1945

Gene Brown had been tasked by Colonel Sink to lead I Company for the second phase of the assault. Assisted by Tinsley and Dingman, the idea was to advance down the right-hand edge of the main road and link up with Ed Shames' platoon at the crossroads. As the only medical officer available, Barney Ryan was attached to Brown along with two medics. Shortly after 1000hrs, as Brown's small force got to within sight of the crossroads, his drive came to an abrupt halt. Dozens of booby traps had been scattered by the Germans across the road. Moments later, the leading elements from I Company came under intense machine-gun fire, forcing Brown's men to grab their casualties and take cover behind the nearest house. Doc Ryan was immediately called forward and set up an aid station in a nearby property situated about 350 yards from the crossroads.

Bypassing the mines on the road and trying to outflank the tank, I Company quickly became pinned down by its machine gun. From here beyond an old blacksmith's shop the N30 dropped away to the crossroads where the Panzer IV had moved from its hiding place in the hollow onto the road. Although wounded, Private Al Cappelli managed to move close enough with his bazooka to get a clear shot. The rocket struck the tank, which immediately lost all power; minutes later, after running out of ammunition, the crew abandoned "ship," leaving the barrel of their 75mm gun pointing defiantly toward Bastogne.

After disabling the tank, a colleague helped Cappelli back across the street to the aid station. However, Al and the other casualties could not be evacuated by vehicle due to the minefield blocking the road diagonally opposite the aid post. Joe Madona, the newly promoted platoon sergeant for 2 Platoon, arrived and moved to the rear of the aid station with Doc Ryan, hoping to get a situation report from Captain Gene Brown. Brown had broken radio silence and was sheltering at the property behind a nearby barn. Ryan and Madona listened intently as Brown told Patch that he had hit a "hornet's nest" and needed immediate assistance. As Madona and Ryan walked back toward the doorway, they were hit by a sudden burst of machine-gun fire. Madona was killed instantly and crumpled to the floor. The burst ricocheted off the solid stone frame surrounding the door, striking Barney in the chest and Joe in the forehead. Ryan broke into a cold sweat,

This house, once owned by Albert Koeune (relation of Jules), became the Third Battalion Aid Station in Foy on January 13, 1945. Although the rear is a postwar extension, the fascia is original and still shows signs of battle damage. The Germans placed a chain of mines across the N30 a short distance away to the left. Upon entering the house, Barney Ryan discovered abandoned German equipment, including grenades and a Panzerfaust stashed in the kitchen. There were also a number of mattresses lying around which came in useful for the wounded.

## The Final Attack on Foy, 1100–1530hrs, January 13, 1945

Foy
8
7
G Co
G Co
Route Madame
F Co
D
5
6
XXX
4
E
F
3
1
2
N
250m

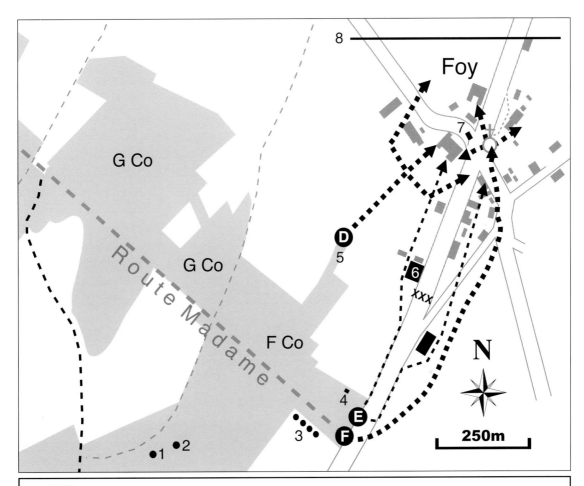

**KEY**

**D. 1100hrs Relief Group**
(In support of 1 & 2 Ptn E Co)
Capt Andy Anderson, HQ Co
& 2Lt Ben Stapelfeld 1 Ptn F Co plus
elements of HQ Co 2/506 – preceded by
1Lt Ron Speirs

**1100hrs – H Co Group**
(In support of 3 Ptn E Co & I Co)
**E.** Capt Jim Walker & 1 Ptn, 2 Ptn H Co
**F.** 1Lt Alex Andros & 3 Ptn H Co

**1.** 3/506 Aid Station
**2.** 3/506 & 506th RHQ CP
**3.** 81mm Mortar Line
**4.** MG Bunker (H Co CP)
**5.** 81mm Mortar OP
**6.** Forward Aid Station
**7.** Mk IV Panzer KO'd by I Co
**8.** 1530hrs New Defensive Line
**XXX** German Minefield

and although weakened, he managed to walk into the house and lie down beside the other wounded troopers.

> Blood had begun to trickle down my back as Eugene Woodside cut away my British tanker overalls, given to me on January 9 by Charlie Shettle, and applied a Carlisle bandage. Surprisingly I wasn't in that much pain so refused any morphine. I managed to get word to Captain Brown, who notified the regiment that the battalion needed another medical officer and Louis Kent was sent forward to keep things under control. Unbeknown to us, four Germans had been trapped in the cellar when we occupied the house. Uncertain of what to do next, they remained silent – that was until Walter Pelcher heard a German voice and sent someone down with a rifle to investigate. 30 seconds later the four young men appeared with their hands raised in surrender. I heard someone say, "Let's shoot the bastards." "Hell no!" I screamed. "We'll use them to carry the wounded back up to the MLR." (No doubt thinking of my own self-preservation at the same time!) Pelcher put the prisoners to work carrying the more severely wounded out on stretchers through roadside ditches to a hastily organized jeep collection point. I was taken to Bastogne before being evacuated by ambulance to the 60th Field Hospital at Neufchâteau. By the time I arrived, I was in deep shock and underwent immediate surgery. I awoke the next morning to find myself under the care of an old classmate from Med School, Larry Kilham, who presented me with a battered 7.92mm bullet that the surgical team had removed from my lung.

On the MLR, at approximately 1100hrs, in scenes reminiscent of the last-stand at the Alamo, Bob Sink and Lloyd Patch ordered Andy Anderson and Jim Walker to gather all available spare manpower and join forces with 1 Platoon, F Company, to relieve pressure on Gene Brown. The enemy shelled the woods while the composite group hastily assembled. The intense barrage delayed the relief mission and caused a number of casualties. Shortly before the relief force left the woods, Lieutenant Ron Speirs from 2/506 was sent ahead with a handful of troops to inform the commander of E Company, Lieutenant Norman Dike, what was about to happen.

After being attached to Third Battalion, F Company took over the positions vacated by H Company as Jim Walker ordered Alex Andros to take 3 Platoon and make a flanking movement across the main N30 road following the same route previously taken by Ed Shames. Before reaching the edge of the minefield, Walker's team came under heavy artillery fire and ran for cover. Down in Foy itself the situation was chaotic – Brown and Tinsley were now desperately trying to coordinate I Company as Walker's men battled to reach them. Brown was still taking fire near the aid station, although the enemy machine gun team that killed Joe Madona had been overrun and neutralized.

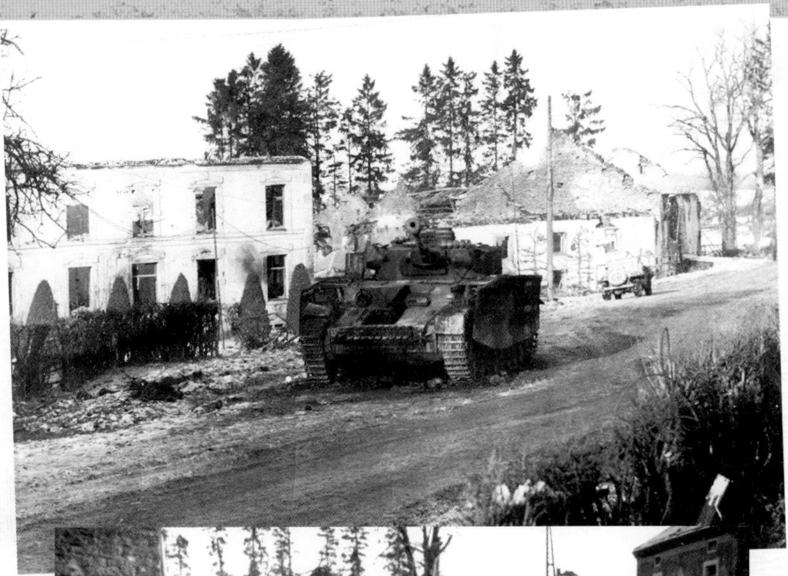

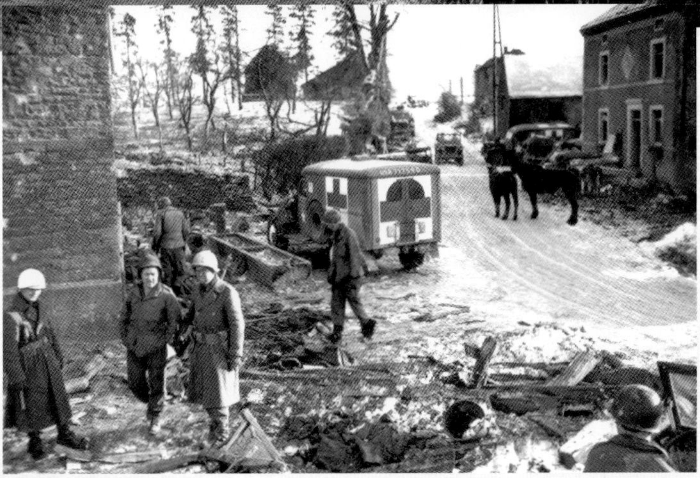

Most likely this is the Panzer IV disabled by Al Capelli from I Company on January 13, 1945. Initially the company became pinned down by machine-gun fire from this tank. Capelli, a bazooka operator with 2 Platoon, was called forward by Captain Brown to engage but was hit in the knee by shrapnel while moving into position. This did not deter him as the tank had to be neutralized at all costs. Limping across to the eastern side of the N30, a few minutes later Capelli found himself virtually opposite the village water well, and close enough to get a clear shot at the tank. (Al Krotchka via Mark Bando Collection)

Opposite view looking south from the crossroads in the direction of Bizory on January 14/15. (Johnny Gibson)

BELOW LEFT German prisoners marching down the N30 above Foy close to the 3/506 MLR on January 13, in the direction of Bastogne. These may well be part of the same group who were flushed out of the cellar of Jules Koeune's house at the crossroads by H Company during the closing stages of the battle. The tanks (on left) most probably belong or belonged to the 11th Armored Division. (NARA colorization by Johnny Sirlande)

BELOW RIGHT It is now believed that after the battle the Panzer IV knocked out by Al Capelli was pushed back to its original position outside Jules Koeune's house in order to clear the road, where it remained for at least a year and became a play area for local children. The tank is pictured here during the following winter looking east across the N30 to the burned-out village chapel. (Reg Jans)

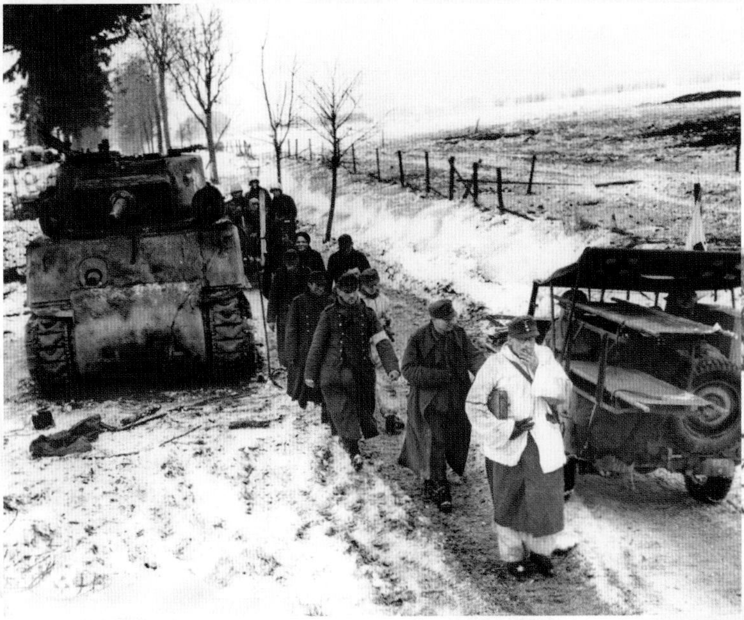

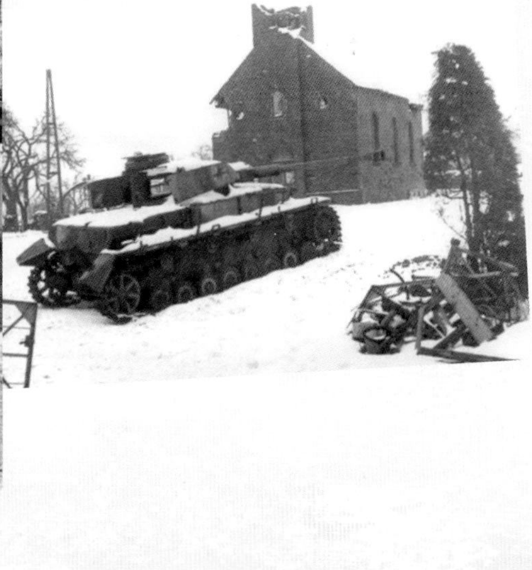

Hindered by the radio lockdown, Andy Anderson became embroiled in crossfire with E and I Companies plus the enemy. Both companies were now under such heavy mortar fire that they were struggling to maintain their individual missions. Something had to be done before somebody was killed by friendly fire. Taking a deep breath, Speirs ran across open ground and spoke directly with Tinsley, who immediately called for his men to stop firing. As Speirs was returning to E Company he looked around and saw Tinsley mortally wounded in the head and chest by a burst of enemy machine-gun fire.

2 Platoon from I Company came up against stiff resistance from one machine gun near the aid station, which was now clearly marked by a large Red Cross. Nowhere seemed safe from enemy machine-gun fire. Corporal Jim Brown was killed after being struck in the left eye by a bullet. Another, Wayman Womack, was also badly wounded. Eventually, one by one, the other enemy positions were silenced and I Company was able to join with H Company to complete the cleansing action around the aid station. Pumped with anger, those left standing from I Company took no prisoners. As I Company were still attempting to clear the houses along the southern edge of town, Alex Andros and his men were halfway around Foy.

After Jim Morton was evacuated, Captain Ed Harrell (G Company) took over command of HQ Company around mid-January 1945.

During the next hour or so, 1 Platoon from F Company played a vital role in mopping up, but further to the east Andros and his platoon came under heavy shellfire near the church. As Alex maneuvered to envelope the buildings on the western side of the road, the intense shelling suddenly lifted. It was at this point he realized that the enemy must have been communicating with their own artillery from the basement of the Koeune house at the crossroads. Several of the men ran forward and began firing through a 2ft-wide slit window near the entrance. The enemy troops in the basement fled back as the bullets tore into the walls and ricocheted across the ceiling adjacent to the door. Moments later, around 20 Germans emerged, hands on heads, and surrendered.

After Foy was back in American hands, radio silence was briefly lifted for H Company to call in air strikes. In total, around 70 prisoners were taken during the seven-hour operation. H Company secured an area around the center of the village, while I Company held the northern approaches near two concrete bunkers. The town was peppered with abandoned trenches and defensive positions full of lice and human feces. While checking that all the buildings were clear, Alex Andros came across a ruined barn containing dozens of frozen yet neatly stacked American and German corpses.

A heavy fog settled over the battlefield, providing cover not only for the assault pioneers who were clearing the main road of mines but also the handful of enemy

tanks that were now moving toward the village! Around 0400hrs the following morning, the Germans counterattacked. Sergeant Harley Dingman of I Company was hastily ordered to report to the forward CP, located near the crossroad. As Harley walked in, the "head-shed" were weighing up their options. Turning to Dingman, Gene Brown explained that he and his men were to cover a controlled withdrawal. It was not up for discussion. The rifle companies were then ordered to bring in all their remaining ammunition to the CP. After Dingman and his eight-man squad had "bombed up," he split the men into four two-man teams and allocated each to a house, forming a blocking line right through the center of Foy. Over the next two hours, the men kept up a continuous volley of small-arms fire as Dingman ran from house to house shooting in the air. Harley had his men moving between windows, firing randomly on a low trajectory toward the oncoming threat. The diversionary rearguard action worked but did not stop the enemy tanks from advancing.

As the battalion was reorganizing with 2/506 up on the ridgeline, the first American tanks began to move down into Foy. Second Battalion were diverted to an assembly area in the woods above Recogne in preparation for a hastily organized attack on Cobru, which they subsequently secured. At the same time Bois Champay came under heavy shellfire, but with the Allied armor now consolidating in Foy and Recogne, the last few remaining enemy tanks were destroyed. What was now left of Third Battalion was ordered northwest, hindered by sporadic friendly artillery fire, to the southern edge of Fazone near the lake to hook up with First Battalion and the newly formed 17th Airborne Division, who were scheduled to take over from the 101st. Bob Sink moved his HQ forward to Recogne and then Vaux after 2/506 bravely pushed the enemy from Noville. No sooner had the ruined town been recaptured than Sink began planning preparations for a combined regimental attack on Rachamps.

With all radio channels now reopened, full command and control was restored. Simultaneous moves to capture Rachamps, Wicourt, and Neuf-Moulin would be supported by two companies of tanks. The main attack designed to push the enemy forces away to the east began on January 16 and was spearheaded by First and Second Battalions. After Second Battalion reclaimed Rachamps, First and Third Armies were able to link up further north at Houffalize, spelling the beginning of the end of German actions in the Ardennes. By the time Third Battalion reached the high ground at Neuf-Moulin on the late afternoon of January 16, the Germans had seemingly just withdrawn, leaving most of their wounded behind. Walking away from the abandoned dugouts, Alex Andros headed to the edge of the wood to survey the valley through his binoculars. Across a shallow valley, Alex could see what looked like tanks in the trees. Suddenly there was a blinding flash and everything went black. A shell fragment had ripped through the upper part of his helmet, narrowly

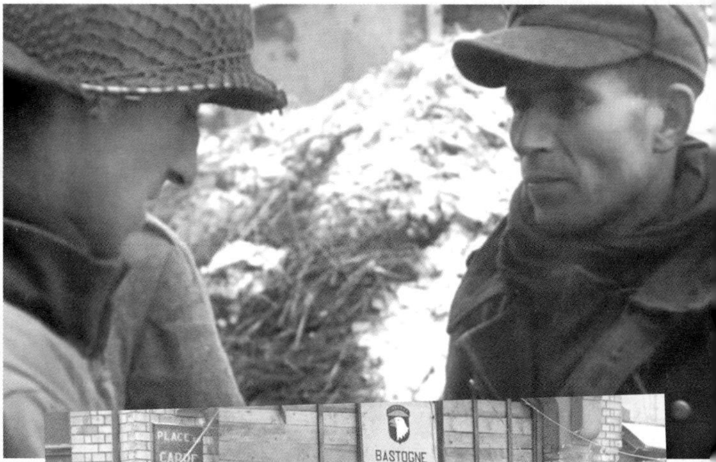

American "tanker" interviewing a captured German soldier. (NARA)

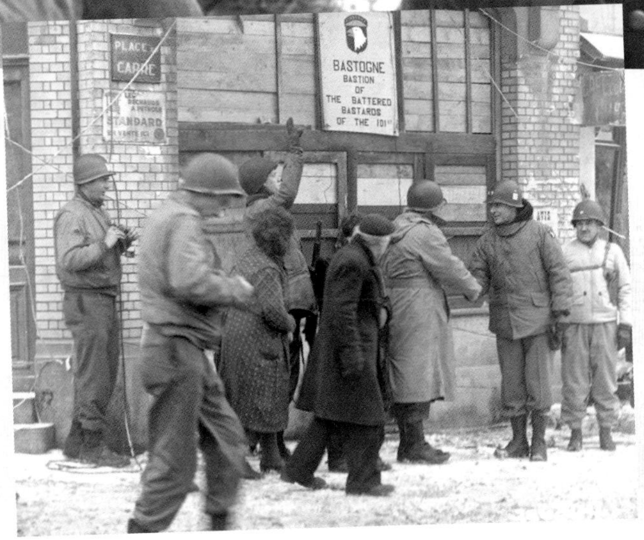
PLACE
CARRE
BASTOGNE
BASTION
OF
THE BATTERED
BASTARDS
OF THE 101

Silver Star Ceremony, Bastogne, January 18, 1945. Troy Middleton and Maxwell Taylor shake hands for the press as BrigGen Charles Kilburn (11th Armored Division) looks on. Coincidentally, the two civilians also pictured were the parents of nurse Renée Lemaire, a Bastogne native who was killed during the siege tending wounded soldiers and civilians. Also in attendance was mayor Leon Jacqmin, who after delivering a short but emotional speech, presented Taylor with a flag representing the official colors of the city. In total five men were honored, ranging from a private to a major. Before reviewing the troops, Middleton, Taylor, and assembled staff officers posed for press beneath a sign on the wall of a nearby building. The sign, posted close to the main road junction, aptly summed up the siege experience: "This is Bastogne, Bastion of the Battered Bastards of the 101st Airborne Division." (NARA)

OPPOSITE In 1945 a temporary burial ground was established at Foy and many local people were employed during its construction. Three years later, all the bodies were removed and sent to the official military cemeteries at Henri-Chappelle, Neupré and Hamm. (NARA)

missing the skull. Second Lieutenant Willie Miller took over after Alex was evacuated and he and Captain Walker were the only officers left from H Company. That night, during a battalion commanders' meeting, Colonel Patch got up and told the handful of officers who were left that he was planning a possible attack the following morning. Willie Miller was not impressed by the order and asked Patch just how he was supposed to do that with only 11 men at his disposal. Needless to say the ridiculous plan was abandoned.

Many of the soldiers had been ignoring symptoms of emersion foot because they did not want to leave their posts or let anyone down. Over the next seven days, the battalion would lose 50 percent of its remaining strength to non-battle-related injuries. I Company went into Bastogne with 150 men and came out on January 20 with 28. G and H companies fared little better. Over the past four weeks the 506th Parachute Infantry Regiment had suffered over 40 percent casualties: 119 killed, 670 wounded, and 59 missing – a total of 848.

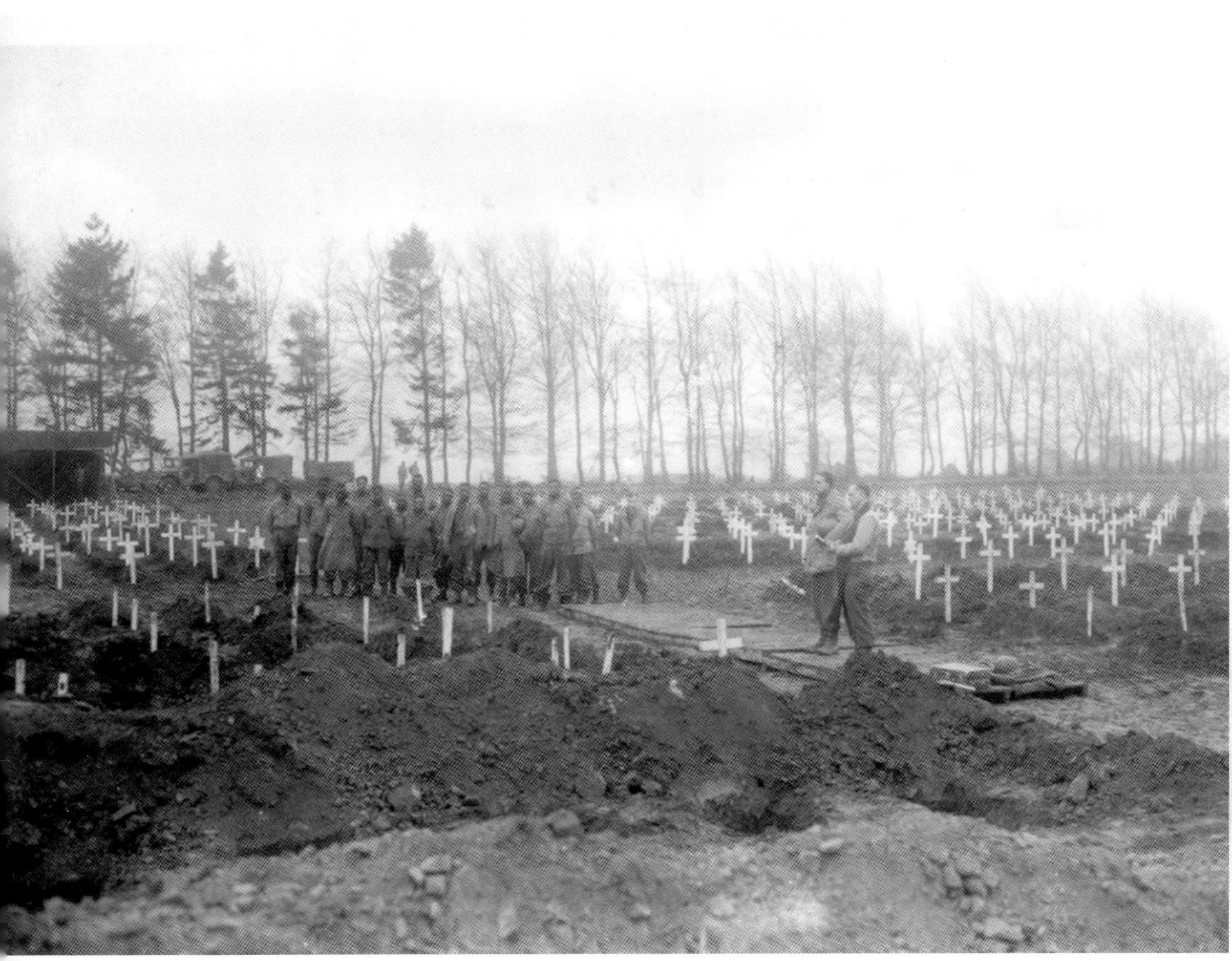

Finally, the entire regiment handed over control to the 17th Airborne Division, and the battalion spent their first stress-free night under cover in a warm barn at Luzery. Continuing bad weather hampered the First and Third Armies' advance, but by January 28, the enemy had been pushed back to the original point of departure and the thrust into the Ardennes was officially over. During the coming weeks and months, American and French forces attacked into Luxembourg and Germany. Although the war was by no means over, the Battle of the Bulge was arguably one of the most important events of World War II and signified the beginning of the end for Germany. The Wehrmacht had suffered some 110,000 casualties, while the overall American losses had risen to 80,000, of whom 19,000 had been killed. The devastation to the civilian population was also immense, with around 2,500 people dead, and dozens of small towns and villages all but destroyed.

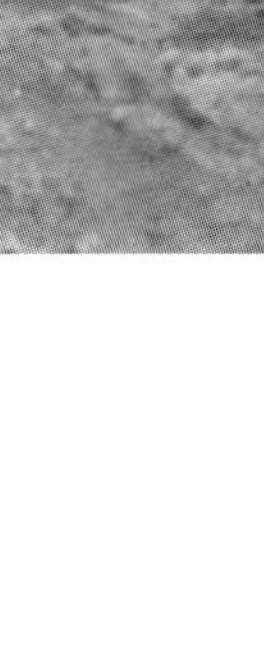
AIRBORNE

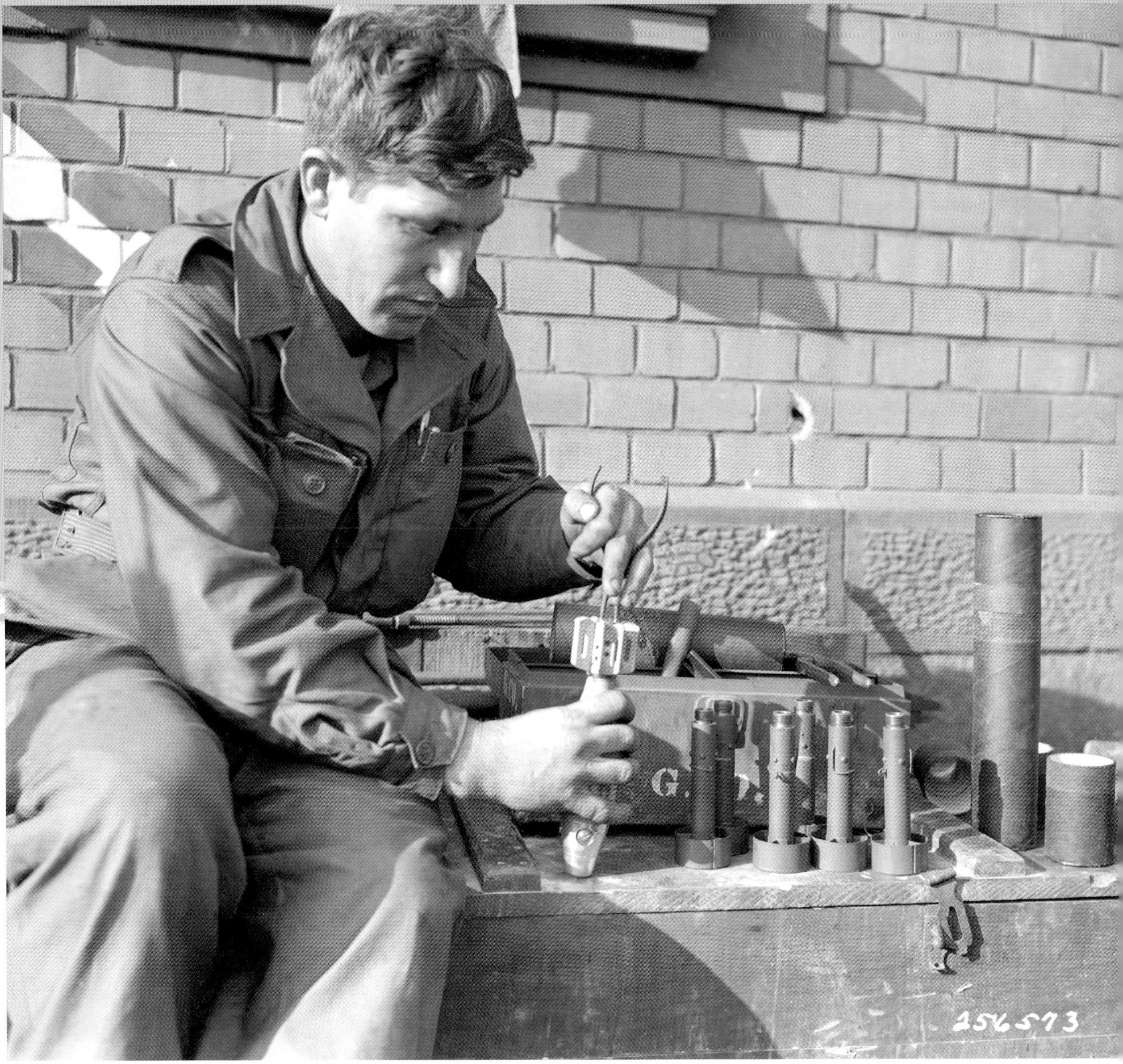
256573

During the Third Battalion's relative quiet time along the banks of the River Moder, many improvised explosive devices were launched across. The most successful is seen here with its creator Sgt Walter Kyle from G Company. With great ingenuity, Kyle adapted the standard tail fin of a rifle grenade to screw into the base of a 60mm shell, allowing it to be fired from an M1 rifle. (NARA)

Chapter 9

# DISTANT FLAGS

## Alsace and Lorraine, Western Germany and the Ruhr

Alsace and Lorraine are two separate regions in France's northeastern corner bordering Belgium, Luxembourg, Germany, and Switzerland. Historically, Alsace and Lorraine had both seen periods of either German or French control. In 1940, Hitler reoccupied the area and over the next four years conscripted around 130,000 Alsatian men into the Wehrmacht. By early 1945, the Western Front was divided into three army groups. Northernmost was the 21st, under Field Marshal Bernard Montgomery; General Omar Bradley and the 12th were situated in the middle, with General Jacob Devers' 6th Army Group to the south around Alsace Lorraine and the Swiss border. Devers' 6th Army Group was part of a joint force which encompassed the French First Army commanded by General Jean de Lattre de Tassigny.

Unlike some of the towns and villages further north, the French were initially unable to push the enemy back across the Rhine. Therefore, in late November 1944, the Germans had forced a bridgehead along the western edge of the Black Forest between the ancient towns of Pfaffenhoffen, Haguenau, Colmar, and Basel. Before Christmas the Nazi war machine began to threaten the rear of Patton's Third Army and also the Seventh Army. When Patton was redirected to the Ardennes, part of the

Seventh moved south to assist the French. During the early stages of the battle, the Germans tried desperately to break out and drive north to link up with their forces around Bastogne. The threat to the supply lines was real, and if the enemy had not been contained in Alsace then General Patton would have struggled to maintain his push to reach Bastogne.

So naturally it was here, in Alsace at the crossroads of Europe, that Hitler decided to reinstate his offensive on January 1, 1945. Operation *Nordwind* was similar in execution to *Die Wacht am Rhein* with its coordinated pincer attacks but with the one notable exception: Generalfeldmarschall Gerd von Runstedt, who had been the driving force behind the earlier Ardennes offensive, was completely opposed to this new plan. Subsequently, Hitler asked the commander of the SS, Reichsführer Heinrich Himmler, to take charge of the southern front with explicit instructions to ignore von Runstedt and report directly to him in Berlin. Hitler's idea was to cut off the regional capital, Strasbourg, with the two pincer movements striking from Haguenau in the north and further south at Colmar. Over the next three weeks, the attack shifted back and forth before finally grounding to a stalemate near Strasbourg.

\*\*\*

After being relieved by the 17th Airborne, the 506th was placed in reserve at La Petite Rosiére, a few miles south of Bastogne. On January 20, the 101st was instructed to take over one of the more peaceful sectors of the old Maginot Line along the Moder Valley in Alsace, allowing American forces a better chance to exploit their opportunities elsewhere. With 16in of snow on the ground, the journey for the 506th was once again cold and delayed by the icy road conditions. Ahead of the main force, billets were being secured in the villages of Diemeringen, Waldhambach, and Weislingen. Initially Third Battalion were sent to Diemeringen and stationed alongside Regimental HQ. Before the regiment reached Alsace information packs were handed out to remind everyone that although this was supposedly "friendly" territory the area contained many German-speaking civilians who were still sympathetic to the Fatherland.

By late January, the regiment had moved closer to the River Moder to take over from the 409th Infantry Regiment. From here the paratroopers were deployed along a 1-mile front overlooking the river between a set of partially demolished bridges between Pfaffenhoffen and Niedermodern. The basic plan was to send regular patrols across to the northern bank of Pfaffenhoffen and surrounding villages including Uberach, which nestled along the edge of the enormous Haguenau Forest. Other than that, this sector of the Siegfried Line, the almost 400-mile-long defensive line which had been Hitler's brainchild, was relatively peaceful. There was sporadic mortar fire, occasional enemy patrols and random salvos from a 15in rail gun hidden in the forest, appropriately nicknamed "Alsace Annie." Within a day or so, as the snow began to thaw, most of the forward outposts beyond the road overlooking the river had to be relocated because of flooding.

Before the week was out the battalion was withdrawn and sent east along the river to Haguenau. Their new job would be to assist VI Corps, who were going on the offensive north of Strasbourg. Haguenau was one of the largest towns in the region of Bas-Rhin. Straddling the meandering Moder, Haguenau had become a thriving industrial town with a wartime population of around 18,000 people, but with Germany on the backfoot most had fled by February 1945. From here the Moder twists and turns for around 10 miles before filtering into the mighty Rhine that marked the border with Germany.

Colonel Sink established his HQ to the southern side of the town in the former German Youth camp at Château Walk. At the center of the town, the river, which was now in full-flood, was overlooked on both sides by a number of tall, abandoned factory buildings. Over in the I Company sector the river was wider, the land open and dotted with small farms. Of course, the regular rations were still not enough, and the men had to scavenge anything and everything that could be cooked and eaten. Meanwhile, the rifle companies were overhauled as badly needed new blood began to arrive. The regiment ensured that each battalion now had at least three five-man patrols on 24-hour standby and one specified platoon trained to operate independently as a large-scale raiding party. Several communications cables had also been run across the river. The careful preparations and additional resources reaped benefits. Almost every patrol that went out came back with at least two prisoners. Most agreed that the old men and boys from the 245th Volksgrenadier-Division were mostly easy pickings, but discipline was still paramount, especially at night when any naked flame or light would be met by a substantial enemy response. But for the most part, the airborne troops couldn't shake the feeling that the war was very nearly over, as recalled by Sergeant Robert Webb:

> A large wine factory was nearby and kept us supplied with as much red and white wine as we could drink. HQ Company was billeted in a lovely bungalow that had a china cabinet with over 200 champagne glasses made from the finest crystal I'd ever seen. The owners had a fantastic cast-iron Aga stove in the kitchen, so we always had a hot brew on the go. By this time, I think we all realized the war was virtually over and we just wanted to stay alive to see the end.

By late February, the 506th started moving out by road to a rear holding area 50 miles away where they boarded boxcars at Saverne and returned to Mourmelon, most of which had now been taken over by a field hospital, with medical and

Capt Fred "Andy" Anderson, by this point the Third Battalion's XO, pictured at Mourmelon, March 1945. (The Anderson Family)

(Back row, left to right): Pvt James Baber, Cpl Ed Devine (Service Company) and Lt Piet "Pete" Luiten (Regimental IPW Team). (Front row, left to right): Pfc Paul Van Pelt and Cpl David Phillips. 22-year-old Piet Luiten was a civilian and came from the Stratum district of Eindhoven. Pete was one of many young Dutch kids who joined the Americans (and British) in Eindhoven to become what was known as "irregulars." Pete spoke several languages and initially worked with Second Battalion, 81mm Mortar Platoon, as their interpreter. By late September, he was promoted to "lieutenant" and reassigned to the IPW team before being wounded at Opheusden. After spending several months in hospital, Pete managed to hitchhike back to the regiment and rode down to Alsace where his excellent command of German and French would come in mighty useful. (John Phillips)

OPPOSITE PAGE

TOP LEFT Dave Phillips relaxing on the front balcony of the Negresco Hotel overlooking Rue d'Anglais, March 1945. (John Phillips)

TOP RIGHT Hank DiCarlo managed to "bum" a ride to Rome while on his furlough to Nice as he had relatives just outside of the city. But it was a far from uneventful trip. When the aircraft was rerouted on its final approach, DiCarlo managed to convince the crew chief and pilot to let him "borrow" a parachute and jump when they were 1,000ft over the air base. Unsurprisingly, he was greeted by MPs as soon as his boots hit the ground. But with Bastogne fresh in everyone's minds, the fact that he was from the now legendary 101st carried some weight, and he was let off with only a warning. (Hank DiCarlo)

BOTTOM LEFT Divisional Headquarters, Mourmelon, March 1945. (Mark Bando Collection)

BOTTOM RIGHT Lou Vecchi and his 506th compatriot Gordon Yates (left) strolling without a care in the world, along the seafront on Promenade des Anglais, Nice, March 1945. Lou was never much of a drinker, so he never spent that much money, unlike some of the other guys who went through $500 or more – an astonishing amount at that time! (Lou Vecchi)

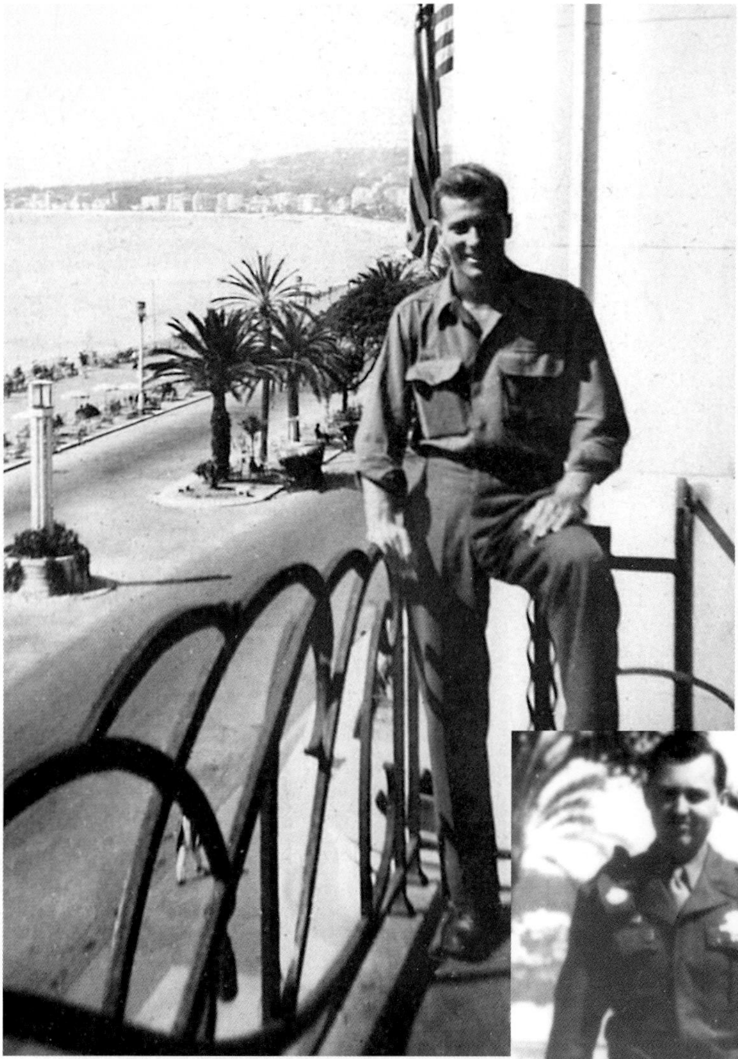

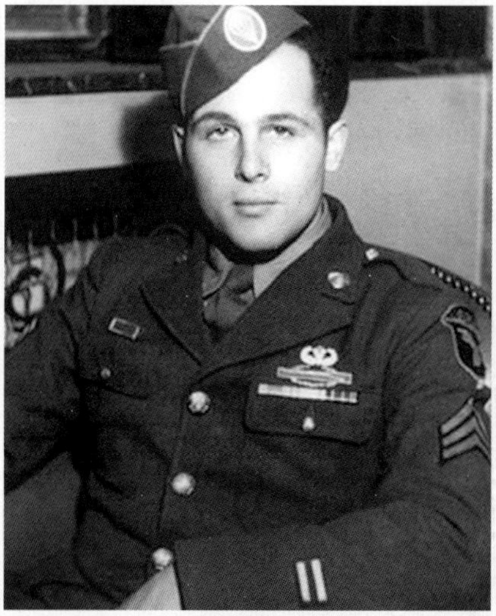

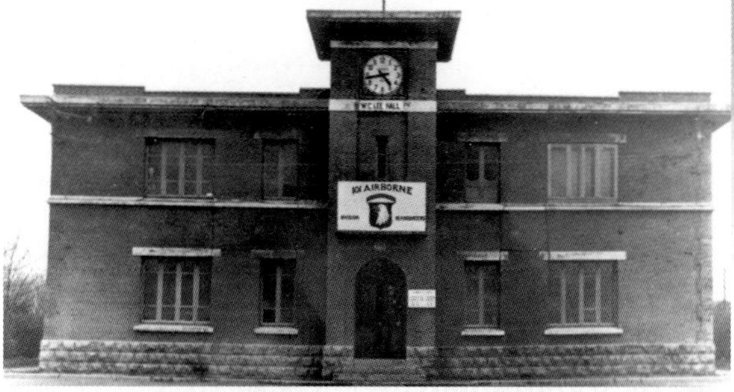
W.C. LEE HALL
AIRBORNE

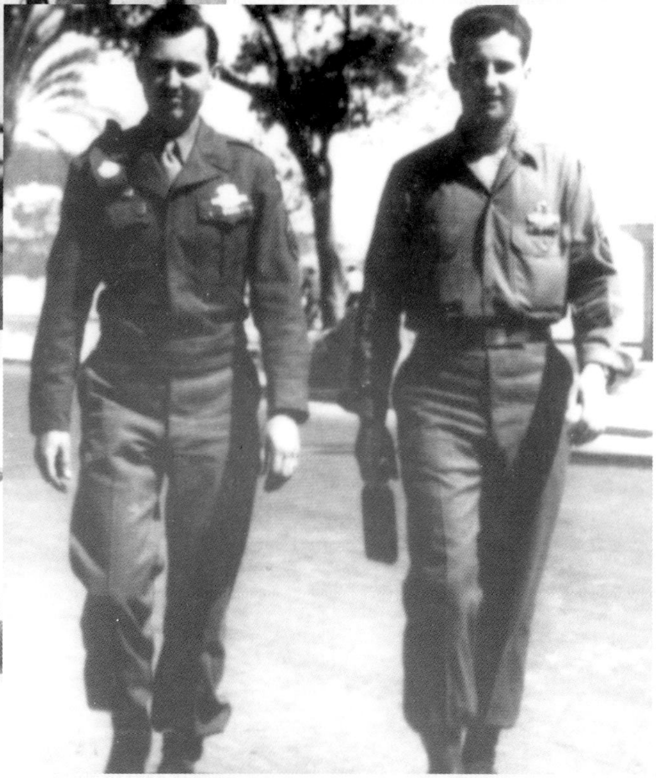

# Presidential Distinguished Unit Citation Award, Mourmelon, March 15, 1945

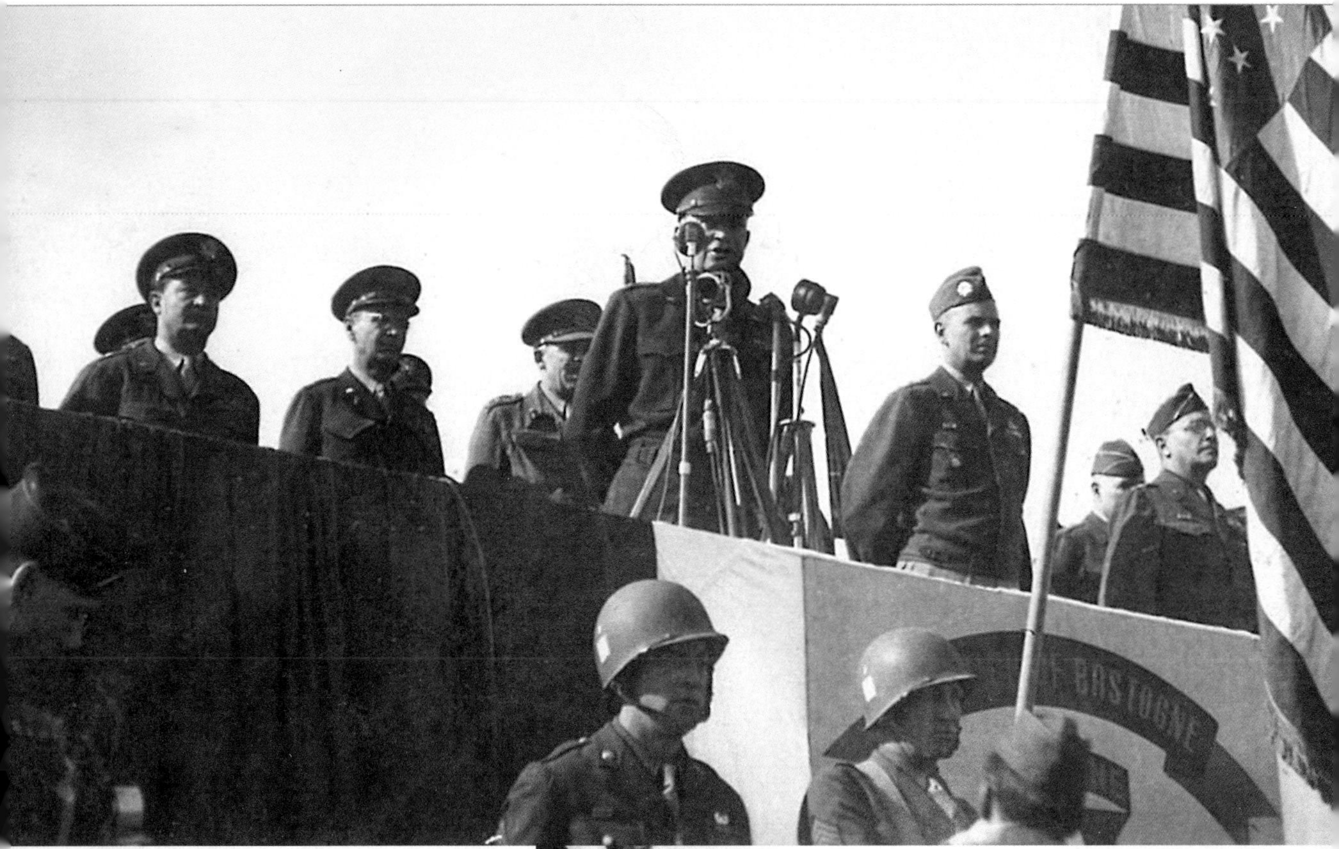
BASTOGNE

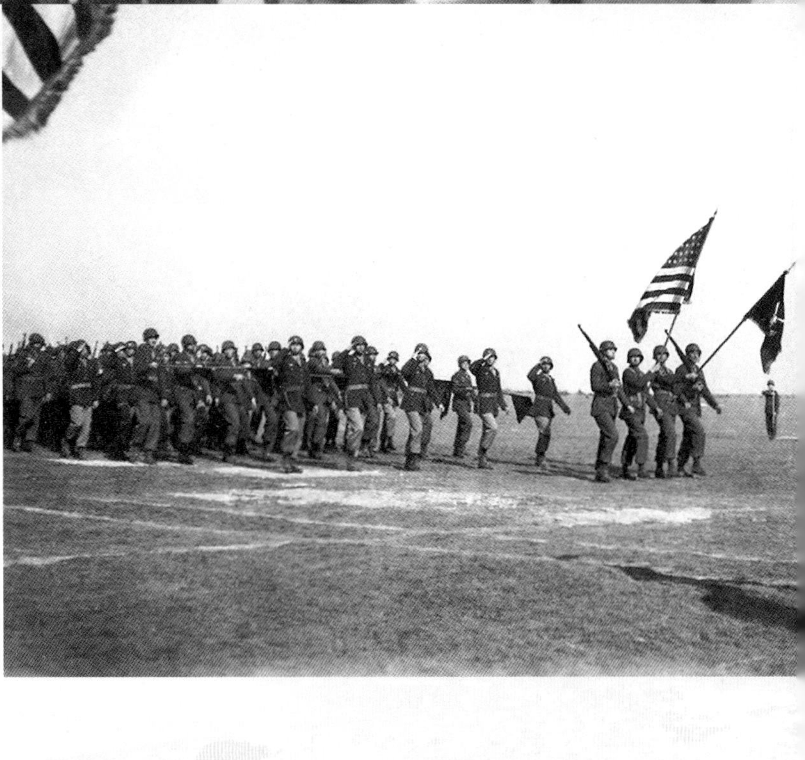

Eisenhower addresses the assembled 101st Airborne Division as it receives its Presidential Distinguished Unit Citation Award in Mourmelon, March 15, 1945. Absent from the podium was Anthony McAuliffe who had recently been promoted to major general. At the time McAuliffe and the 103rd Infantry Division were still fighting hard along the Siegfried Line west of Wissembourg in Alsace. (John Phillips)

The head of the seemingly endless column begins the long march past the reviewing stand. (John Phillips)

OPPOSITE TOP Marlene Dietrich talking with Assistant Chief of Staff LtCol Paul Danahy after the ceremony. At the time Dietrich was touring the European Theater and happened to be performing at Mourmelon in a USO show. (John Phillips)

OPPOSITE BOTTOM This wonderfully natural and relaxed snapshot taken by Dave Phillips shows General Eisenhower dragging casually on a cigarette as he prepares to leave. (John Phillips)

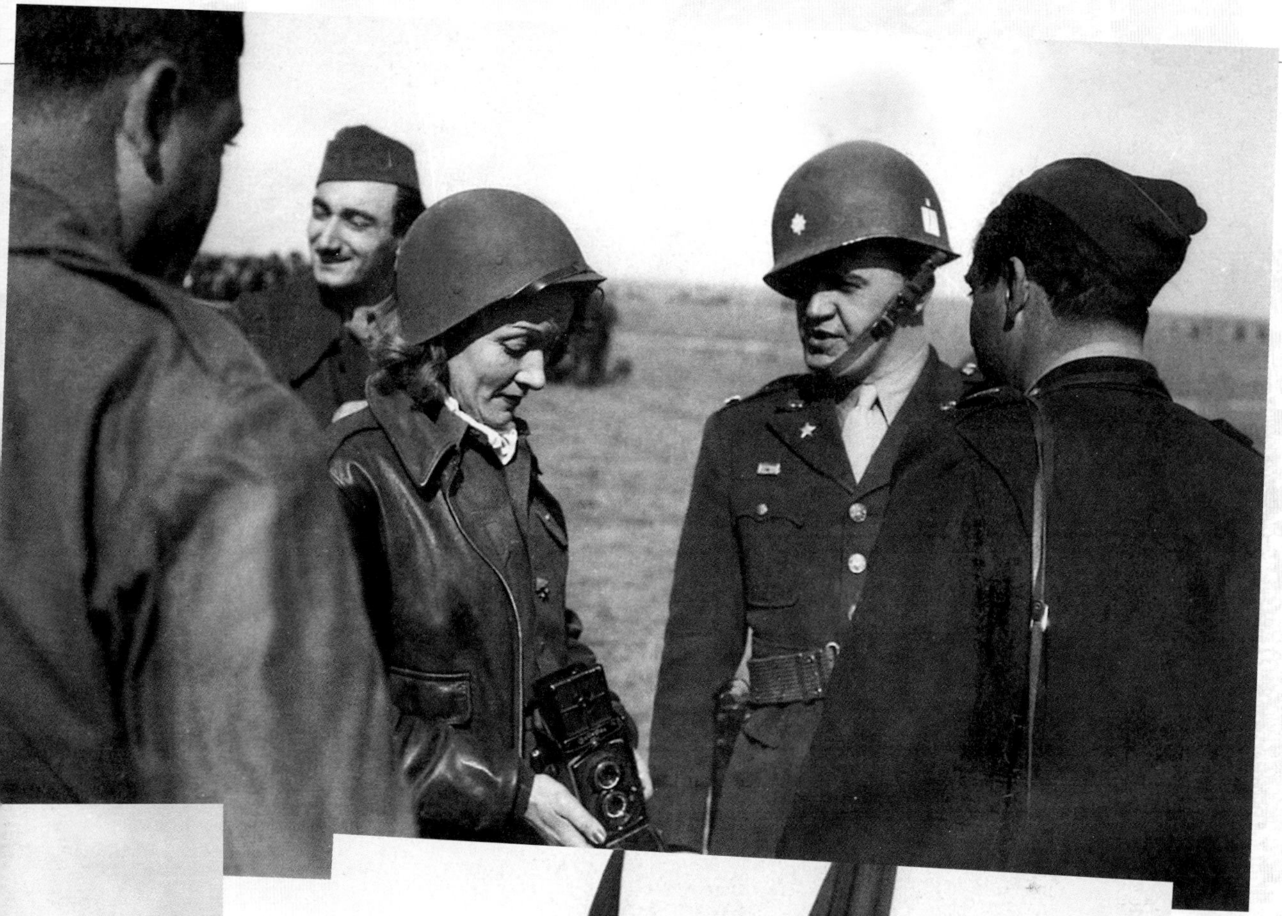

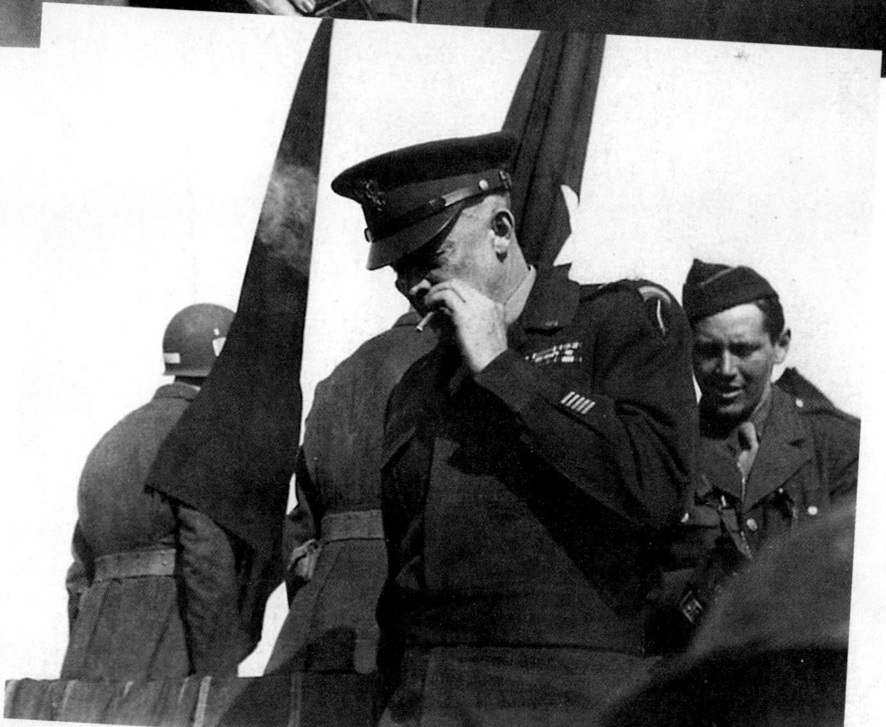

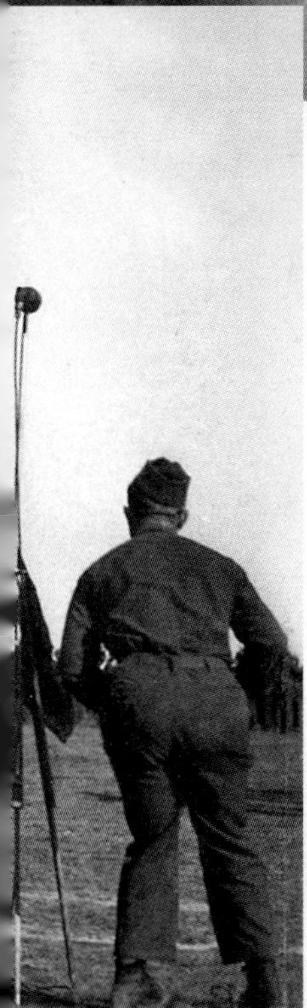

support staff occupying the permanent barracks that had previously been the home of the 101st. This meant that the men were now forced to live in a village of pyramid tents, but it certainly still beat the life they had been living in the Ardennes. Many were granted seven-day leave passes, and hundreds of troopers were flown down to the French Riviera each Sunday.

March 15, 1945 was a significant day in the history of the 101st Airborne when the division was awarded a second Presidential Distinguished Unit Citation. General Eisenhower himself presented the award "for extraordinary heroism" during the defense of the key communications center at Bastogne between December 18 and 27, 1944. The day was bathed in sunshine as 12,000 men stood sharply to attention along the edge of the airfield. Transport aircraft buzzed about busily overhead as Ike addressed them over the public address system:

> You in reserve were hurried forward and told to hold that position. All the elements of battle drama were there. You were cut off and surrounded. Only valor, complete self-confidence in yourselves and in your leaders and the knowledge that you were well trained and only the determination to win could sustain soldiers under those conditions. You were given a marvelous opportunity and you met every test. You have become a fighting symbol on which all citizens of the United Nations can say to their soldiers today: "We are proud of you." It is my great privilege to say to you here today, to the 101st Airborne Division and all its attached units: I am awfully proud of you. Just as you are the beginning of a new tradition, you must realize; each of you, that from now on the spotlight will beat on you with particular brilliance. Whenever you say you are a soldier from the 101st, everybody, whether it is on the street, in the city or in the front lines will expect unusual conduct from you. I know that you will meet every test of the future like you met in Bastogne. Good luck and God be with you.

Then the Supreme Commander stepped back from the microphone as the US Army band struck up a march and the troops began to move. For almost 70 minutes the men passed by the podium while Ike, Major General Maxwell Taylor and the other dignitaries proudly took their salutes. Directly afterwards, it was announced that the US Army would be introducing a point system which would ultimately lead to some of the "old timers" going home. In the meantime, all those who had been through Normandy, Holland and Bastogne would be entered into a lottery for a limited number of 30-day furloughs home to the US.

On the morning of March 24, the 17th Airborne Division took off from Mourmelon as part of Operation *Varsity* to assist Field Marshal Montgomery's 21st Army Group in their crossing of the Rhine. In just one day the joint force dropped 16,000 men onto a single DZ, dwarfing Normandy and Holland in

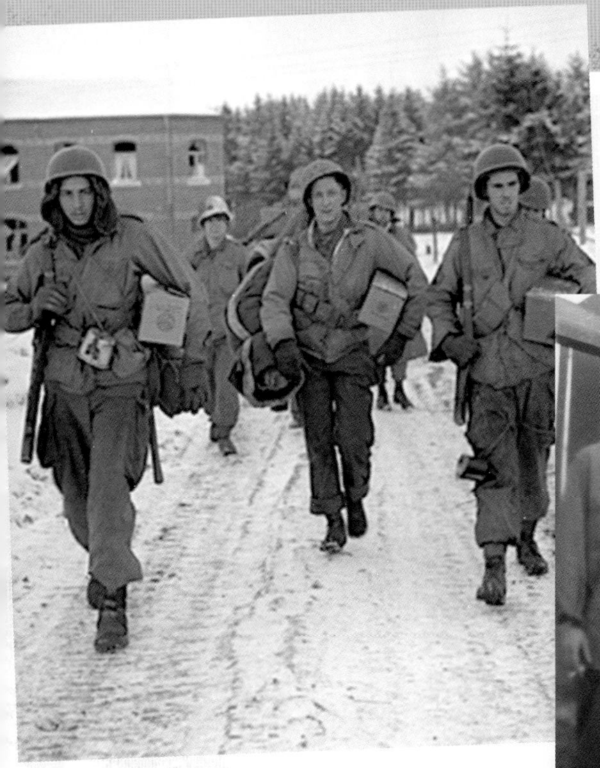

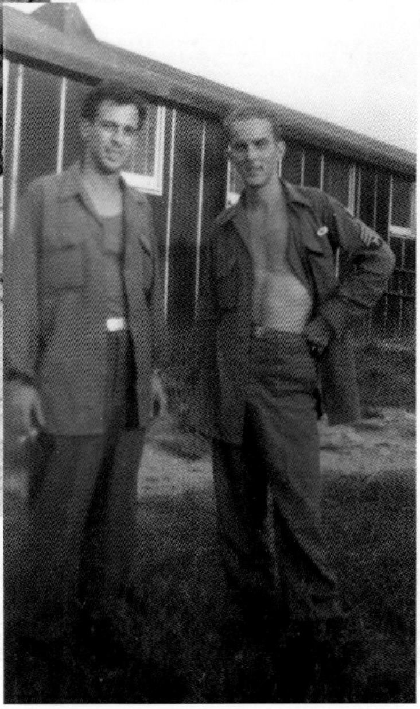

FAR LEFT This photograph appeared on the front cover of the March 1945 edition of *Yank* magazine. While relaxing over a coffee in the senior ranks' mess, Hank DiCarlo happened to pick up the magazine and nearly choked when he saw the front cover: "The picture showed some troops walking in the snow during the Battle of the Bulge and right up front with a big smile on his face was Sonny Sundquist. I can't tell you how much we despised that man. Sundquist had been transferred to First Battalion before Bastogne and was listed as 'Missing in Action' during the heavy fighting at Noville – that was until the S.O.B was picked up later in Marseille trying to blag his way onto a troopship!" (NARA)

LEFT Mourmelon, March 1945. Sgt Bill Pershing and Sgt Bob Webb enjoying the fine weather. Pershing was related to the famous military family and was a member of the bazooka platoon. (Bob Webb Jr)

sheer scope, and making *Varsity* the largest single airborne assault in military history. By the end of March all four US armies fighting in Western Europe were east of the Rhine, while First and Ninth Armies followed through to encircle enemy forces in the Ruhr. With the "Gates of the West" now firmly open, the 101st Airborne went on to provide security and establish military law wherever and whenever it was required.

At the end of March 1945, around 300,000 enemy troops, mostly belonging to Feldmarschall Model's reconstituted Heeresgruppe B, were encircled east of the Rhine along the Ruhr Valley in what quickly became known as the "Ruhr Pocket." After failing to destroy the vital bridge at Remagen, Model's army soon found itself outflanked and the "pocket" was reduced to a 25-mile front bordering the Rhine north from Cologne to Düsseldorf. Model, who had led the unsuccessful offensive in the Ardennes, was ordered by Hitler to destroy everything useable and turn the region into a fortress. Although he ignored the "scorched earth" directive, Model's attempts at defense ultimately failed when, in the middle of April, Heeresgruppe B was split in half by the Allies during their final penetration of the pocket. Unwilling to submit, Model discharged his youngest and oldest troops, while informing the remainder to either surrender or attempt to break out through the encirclement.

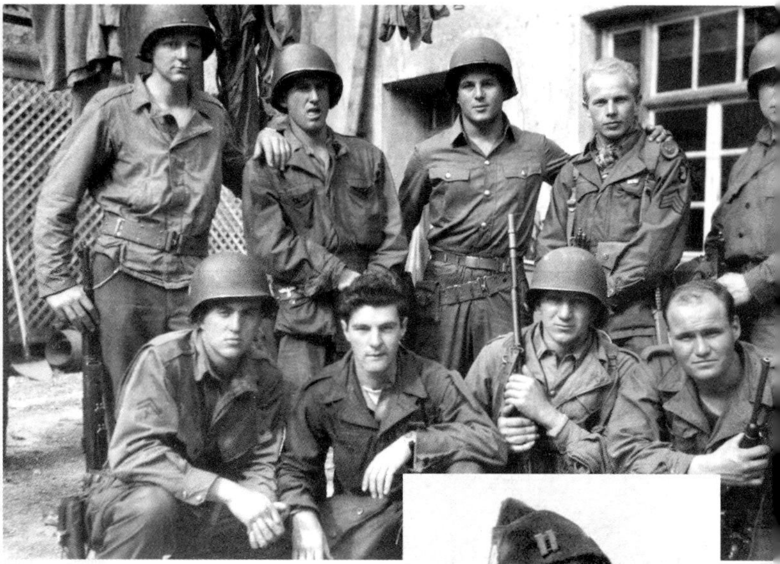

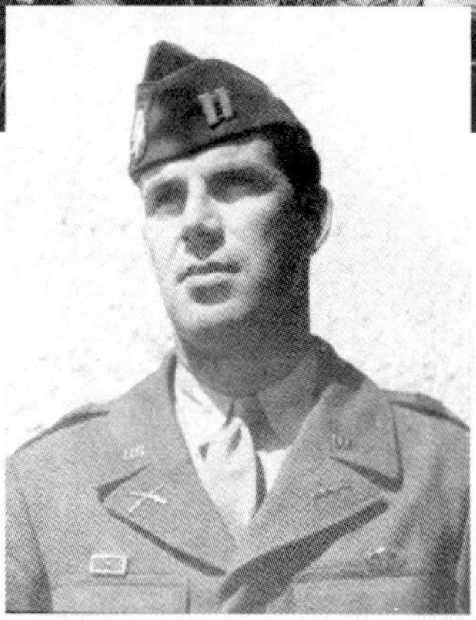

1 Squad, H Company, Nievenheim, Ruhr Pocket, April 1945. (Standing, left to right): Pvt Frank Parker, Pvt Carl Henson, Sgt Hank DiCarlo, Sgt Bob Hoffman (DiCarlo's assistant), Pvt Vernon Timm. (Kneeling, left to right): T/5 Jack Grace, Pfc Jimmy Igoe, Pvt Joe Novak, Pfc Wilber Johnson. (Hank DiCarlo)

Captain Jean Hollstein from Fayetteville, North Carolina, took over command of I Company from Gene Brown (who returned to Regimental HQ) in late April 1945.

OPPOSITE PAGE

While in regimental reserve, H Company ended up living in private homes around Nievenheim, and the boys from 1 Platoon happily posed for snapshots wearing German uniforms liberated from a local military outfitters. Here we have the commander of H Company, Captain Jim Walker (left), together with Lieutenant Bob Stroud who had just returned to 1 Platoon after being wounded four months earlier at Bastogne. (Lou Vecchi)

MIDDLE TOP Platoon Sergeant Lou Vecchi. (Lou Vecchi)

MIDDLE BOTTOM Sgt Luther Myers from 3 Squad striking a heroic pose! Myers too had been wounded at Bastogne. (Lou Vecchi)

FAR RIGHT Hank DiCarlo swapping his airborne uniform for some of the trappings of a Wehrmacht officer. (Lou Vecchi)

Berlin denounced Model and his army as traitors and ordered SS units within the pocket to seek revenge on any soldier or civilian refusing to stay and fight.

To help bolster up the military footprint, the 506th were called from Mourmelon on April 2 and traveled 200 miles by road to Düsseldorf to be deployed around the town of Nievenheim, close to the border with Holland and Belgium. Situated on the western tip of the Ruhr Valley, the ancient city of Düsseldorf straddles the Rhine. At the beginning of World War II, the city had become an important industrial center for the Nazi war machine. Colonel Sink established his regimental CP in the nearby town of Gohr and would be based there for the next three weeks. The MLR for the 506th was roughly a 10-mile front along the Rhine that meandered north from Worringen, through Himmelgeist, before reaching Düsseldorf. In addition, the three battalions were tasked with maintaining military government in their own specific areas. All the bridges across the Rhine in the regimental sector had been destroyed, isolating around 5,000 enemy troops from 176th and 338rd Volksgrenadier-Divisions. As part of the blocking force, Third Battalion were

allocated the northern sector and sent to Norf, where they were more than comfortably billeted in private homes and local farms.

Despite the chaos on the other side of the river, the first week in theater was quiet for the 506th, with many still being sent to the Riviera on leave. For the most part combat activity consisted of patrolling or crossing the Rhine to assess enemy strength and capture a few prisoners who preferred to surrender rather than fight. The only serious casualties sustained during this time were by returning patrols and tragically caused by friendly fire, including George Montilio from H Company and four men from Regimental HQ.

The last pocket of resistance at Düsseldorf did not stop fighting until Model committed suicide on April 21. By the end of the month, around 325,000 German troops had been taken prisoner. With the collapse of Heeresgruppe B, the German threat largely evaporated and the 506th was re-tasked to support the US Seventh Army. The mission was to protect Major General Lucian Truscott's flanks but also help stabilize southwest Bavaria behind Tony McAuliffe's 103rd Infantry Division.

Third Battalion staff at Götzenburg Castle, Southern Bavaria, late April 1945. (Left to right): Capt Fred "Andy" Anderson (Battalion XO), Lt Bruno Schroeder (S-2), LtCol Lloyd Patch (CO), Capt George Lancaster (Battalion Surgeon), Capt Joe Doughty (S-3), unknown, Lt Lloyd Wills (possibly). On April 22, Regimental HQ moved to Götzenburg Castle at Jagsthausen in the Heilbronn region situated midway between Würzburg and Stuttgart. A few days later the regiment was sent by train to Ludwigshafen, near Heidelberg, before moving out to Landsberg

Chapter 10

# A PRINCIPLE OF FAITH

## Southern Bavaria

At the end of April, the 506th Battle Group was travelling through Bavaria behind Seventh Army when they were ordered south toward the medieval walled town of Landsberg am Lech. The Germans had established a stop line, 15 miles long, west of the River Lech. As the name suggests, Landsberg am Lech straddles this powerful and mighty river which courses downhill through a series of impressive weirs and hydroelectric dams. Previously the town had played an important role in the development of National Socialism. Adolf Hitler had been imprisoned here in 1923, and while serving a five-year term for high treason, he had begun to write the first part of *Mein Kampf*, his twisted political directive for the future Nazi state.

Allied progress had been slowed somewhat by the destruction of road and rail bridges by the retreating German forces. However, on April 27 the 103rd Infantry Division, supported by the 10th Armored, attacked the southwestern edge of Landsberg.

While engaged in combat operations, the troops from Seventh Army began to notice a stifling odor permeating around the picturesque town and discovered three slave labor camps designated by the SS as "Kauferings" due to their close proximity to the railhead at Kaufering. These three facilities were KZ-I, III, and IV, but there were seven more waiting to be discovered. A total of ten labor facilities had been established in June 1944 to house 21,000 slave workers whose job it was to build three enormous factories (partially underground) west of the Lech.

With Seventh Army fast approaching, the order had been given by the SS to move all the prisoners. Those unable to walk were sent to the railway sidings at Kaufering where dozens of open boxcars were waiting to take them to Dachau. After the train had departed, most of the staff packed their bags and simply disappeared.

On the same day that the town of Landsberg capitulated, April 28, selected personnel from the 506th were sent to assist 12th Armored with their humanitarian clean-up operation at KZ-I. The semi-abandoned site was made up of around 60 wooden huts, and unsurprisingly the camp commandant and his staff could not be found. When the Americans arrived the gates were already wide open and those prisoners able to walk had already made their way into Landsberg to look for food. Members of RHQ were detailed to go after the starving inmates and bring them back where they did their best to provide care while waiting for the International Red Cross to arrive.

Meanwhile elements of H Company moved up to invest the southern edge of Landsberg behind L Company of the 411th Infantry Regiment. Before they could reach the last remaining hydroelectric dam over the Lech, L Company first had to neutralize the crew of a 20mm antiaircraft gun up on the hill above the dam and then clear the shallow valley below them of enemy forces. The GIs found a subterranean passageway through the dam, which enabled them to cross the river.

Once across they turned north and headed into Landsberg under harassing fire. Things were much quieter for Jim Walker, Bob Stroud and the rest of H Company

Emaciated bodies lie scattered among the burned-out huts of KZ-IV (Camp 4) at Hurlag near Landsberg, early May 1945. (NARA)

A postcard procured by Lou Vecchi while based in Landsberg seems idyllic and charming compared with the horrors of the surrounding camps. (Lou Vecchi)

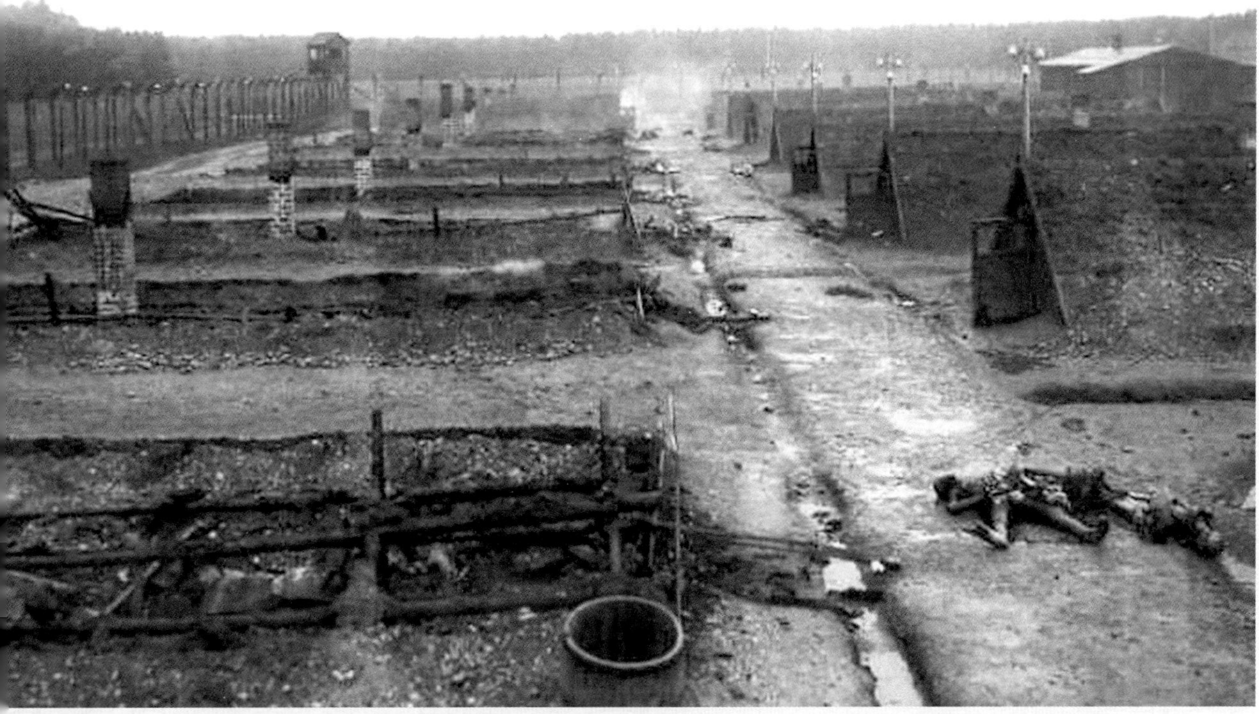

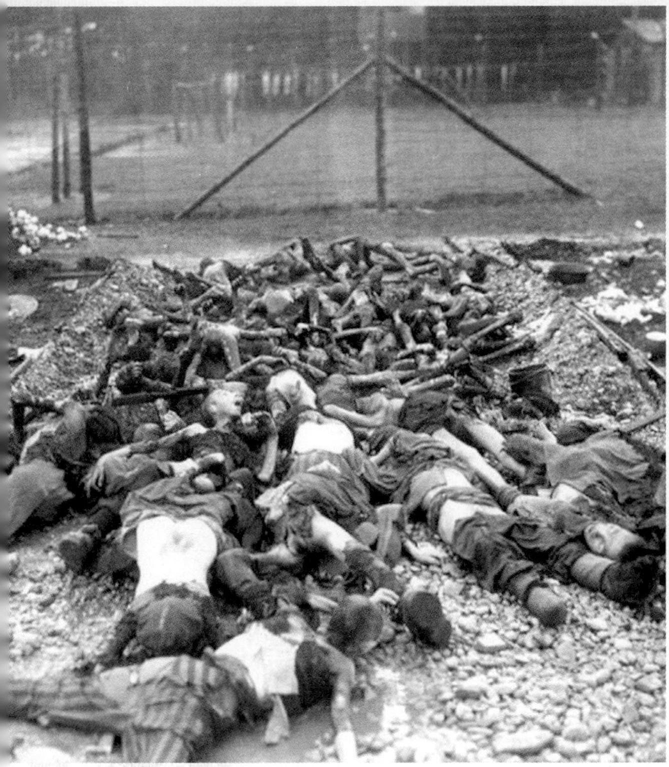

One corner of KZ-IV (Camp 4) at Hurlag shortly after being liberated. (NARA)

KZ-IV: these bodies were gathered between huts and soaked in gasoline before being torched by the SS. (NARA)

BELOW Looking at these charred bodies, it is easy to understand why H Company initially thought they were burning logs. This could quite possibly be KZ-VII – the same camp liberated by 3/506. (NARA)

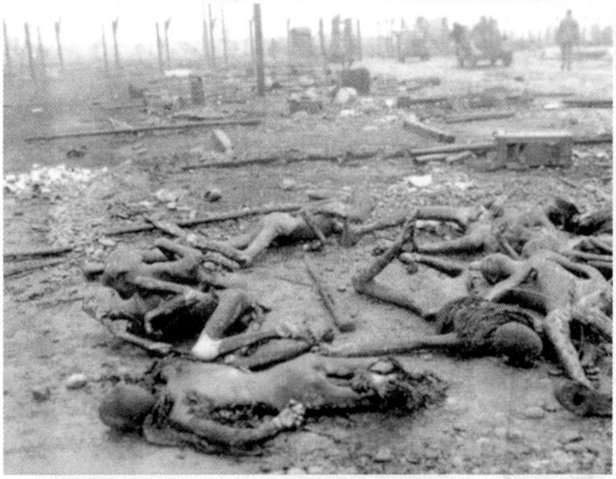

who were following on behind. Stroud had only just returned to 1 Platoon from hospital after being wounded at Bastogne. Hank DiCarlo and Private John Kelly went ahead and scouted a route down to the dam past the knocked out antiaircraft gun. Opening the access door to the dam, they could clearly hear the turbines humming away in the background. Upon closer investigation they followed a set of steps and quickly found their way into the deserted tunnel. Climbing to the top of the hill on the other side, they stopped to take stock. Ahead beyond the main highway they could clearly see a forest in the middle distance shrouded by several dense columns of rising black smoke. Surveying the rest of the landscape, they could also see a group of Volkssturm (a German home-guard organization mobilized to fight) handing over their weapons and armbands to members of L Company. On Jim Walker's orders, Hank DiCarlo and Ralph Bennett moved forward with two assault teams to investigate the smoke.

Advancing through the trees, the men began to choke on the stench of burning gasoline. Although they did not know it at the time, they were about to enter KZ-VII – one of the last remaining camps to be liberated. Reaching the main entrance, Bennett and DiCarlo saw a number of smoldering huts and buildings that appeared to be empty. Ralph took his men across the camp to investigate two huts that were still intact, while Hank approached several nearby piles of what he thought were charred logs. But he quickly realized that these "piles" had once been human beings. Tragically, one man still appeared to be alive but was in such a terrible state that he had to be put out of his misery. The remaining huts had both been doused in gasoline but not torched. Bennett broke open the first door and was shocked to find people inside. The other one seemed so overcrowded that some people looked to Ralph like they had died standing up. Ralph gestured for those remaining alive to come out, and when they realized he was friendly everyone began to weep. Ralph and his men were momentarily overwhelmed and did not know what to say. It was a life-changing moment for H Company. They then learned that the Volkssturm they had seen surrendering had entered the camp earlier and killed two SS men left behind to "clear" things up. About a dozen SS guards were brought back to the camp after being captured hiding out in the local area.

One of DiCarlo's men, Jack Grace, took the SS men aside and ordered them to dig a pit and had them stand in line while he mounted his machine gun on a tripod. Realizing what was about to happen, the Germans began begging for their lives. Jack was just about to close the top cover on a belt of ammunition when Lieutenant Ed Buss, who had recently been posted in from the States, came over and put a stop to the unfolding execution. Shortly afterwards Third Battalion moved into Landsberg, while the 12th Armored Division took control of the Kaufering camps and did an amazing job of sanitizing and saving the surviving inmates.

Upon orders from division, First and Third Battalions rounded up as many of the townspeople as possible and escorted them to KZ-IV and a couple of other camps so that they could witness for themselves the results of the atrocities committed by their fellow countrymen. After being liberated a number of the inmates joined the rifle companies as interpreters and/or cooks. It is incredible to note that by 1945 nearly 20,000 labor camps were scattered throughout the Third Reich but it would take a few more weeks before names such as Auschwitz/Birkenau, Buchenwald, Mauthausen, Flossenbürg, and Dachau would come to the world's attention.

Surrendered German troops near Munich.

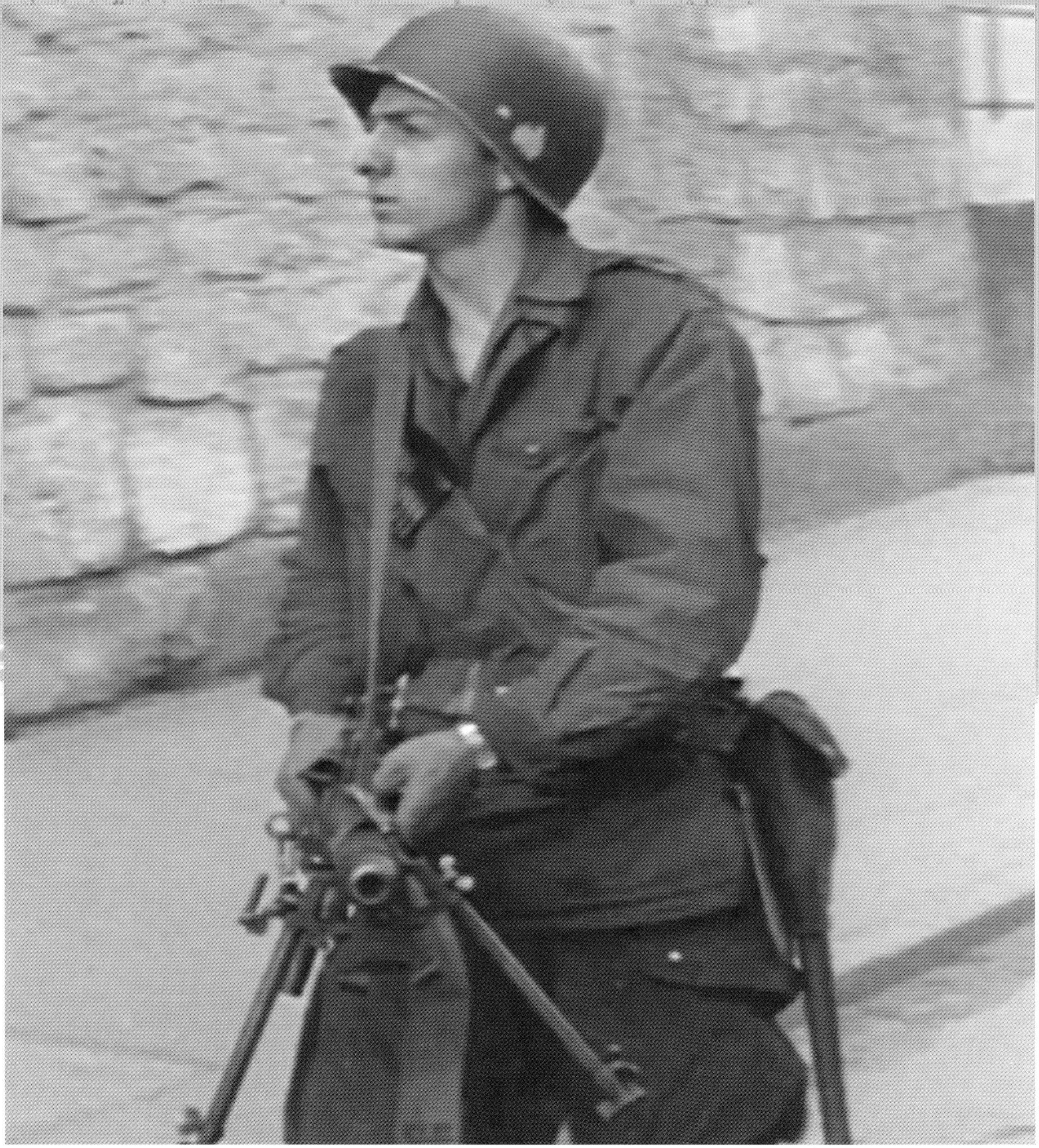

Soldier from 3/506 armed with a .30cal MG entering Berchtesgaden during the early evening of May 5, 1945. (NARA)

<br />

Chapter 11
# LIVING IN THE MACHINE
## Berchtesgaden, Austria and Joigny

It was probably May 3, in Miesbach, when Colonel Sink and the Regimental Combat Team were alerted for the move toward the Alps and the Austrian border. There was widespread expectation that the Waffen-SS would make a last stand around Hitler's Alpine resort, the Berghof, at Berchtesgaden. Highly favored by Hitler, Berchtesgaden was a beautiful place centered in the middle of three jagged mountain peaks. The fast-flowing River Ache courses its way through the eastern edge of the town before dividing into the Ramsauer and Königssee valleys. Dominated by the awe-inspiring twin peaks of the Watzmann Mountain, the nearby spa resort of Königsee nestles alongside a huge lake whose crystal-clear waters are among the deepest in Germany. Clearly, what makes it so beautiful also made it highly defendable throughout the war years.

Two weeks earlier, before abandoning his home in Berlin, 52-year-old Reichsmarschall Hermann Göring had sent a long telegram to Hitler, who was furious when he read: "In view of your decision to remain in the fortress of Berlin, do you agree that I take over at once the total leadership of the Reich, with full

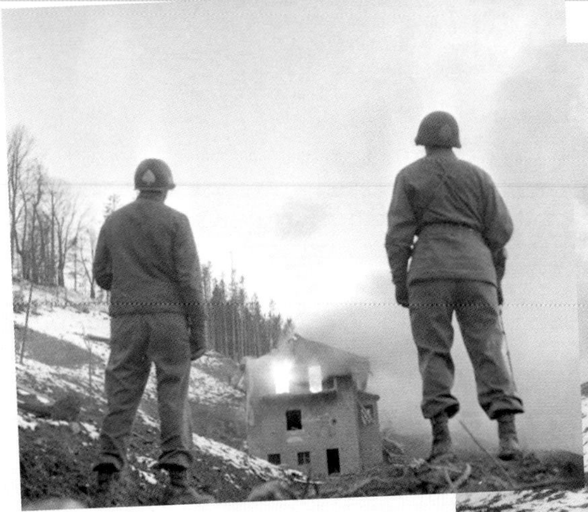

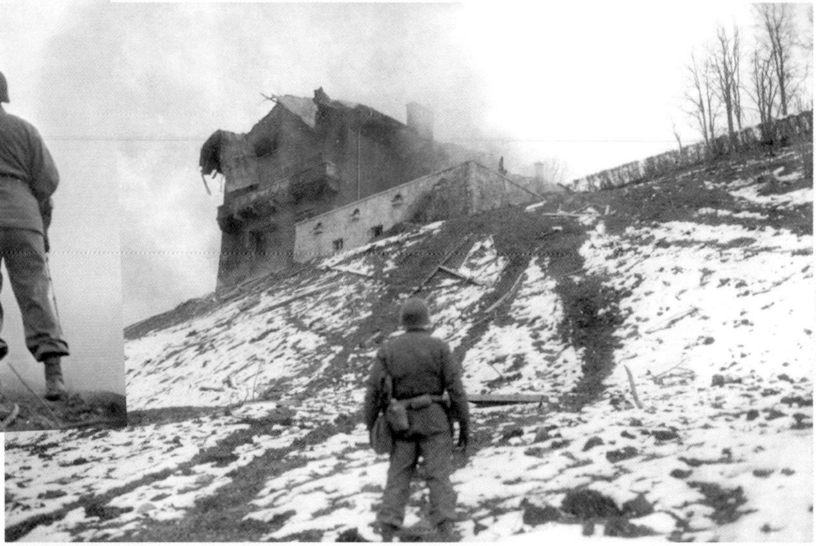

The Berghof, May 5, 1945 – bombed by the British, burned by the SS and then looted by the French. A soldier from 30th Infantry Regiment stands awestruck looking toward the famous picture window and garage. (NARA)

The Berghof is obscured by smoke as the SS annex erupts in flames. (NARA)

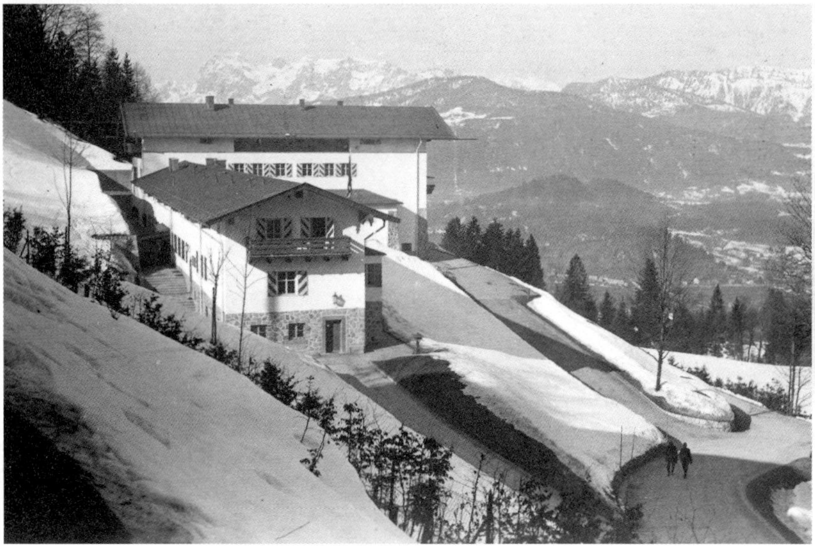

Hitler's Berghof complex looking toward the driveway of the SS annex with the main house behind. The annex belonged to the Führer's personal bodyguard unit – Leibstandarte SS Adolf Hitler. Directly behind the Berghof was the entrance to a 2-mile tunnel system. Heavily fortified, the main tunnel was accessed via the Leibstandarte annex and coursed northeast deep underground to Martin Bormann's private bunker and house. These tunnels also contained hundreds of art treasures and other precious objects. (Photo by Imagno/Getty Images)

freedom of action at home and abroad as your deputy in accordance with your previous decree? If no reply is received by 10 o'clock tonight, I shall take it for granted that you have lost your freedom of action and will act for the best interests of our country and our people." Hitler responded by accusing Göring of "high treason" and ordered his immediate arrest.

Blissfully unaware of Hitler's less than positive reaction, Göring headed south to Berchtesgaden with his family, personal adjutant, and a small protection force. Upon reaching the Alpine fortress, Göring and his staff were taken into custody by the SS based at Obersalzberg, which had just been bombed by the Royal Air Force. Because of the bomb damage, the SS were forced to move them further south into Austria. The Reichsmarschall's good fortune continued when he was rescued en route by a small contingent of loyal troops belonging to the Luftwaffe. On April 30, when news of Hitler's suicide reached Bavaria, Göring once again tried to take control and sought to negotiate directly with Eisenhower and SHAEF.

He was not the only one to make overtures to Eisenhower in these final days of the Third Reich. Feldmarschall Albert Kesselring, who had taken over from Gerd von Runstedt as Commander-in-Chief West on March 9, had sent a notice of possible surrender to SHAEF. Meanwhile, Heeresgruppe C surrendered on May 2, which meant that the Alps were now thrown wide open and the route to Berchtesgaden lay seemingly undefended. Kesselring subsequently sent a small delegation to Salzburg with a series of unworkable demands, while he made a personal approach to Eisenhower, who declined any dialogue that did not involve the total surrender of all German forces.

As such, on the morning of May 4, 1945, the 506th found themselves traveling east along the autobahn from Munich toward Berchtesgaden behind the US 3rd Infantry Division. Reaching Siegsdorf the battle group ran into the back of a massive traffic jam, causing Colonel Patch to send troops from G and I Companies southeast along a secondary road as an advance party. Attached to the 3rd Infantry Division was the French Armored Division Blindée, easily recognizable by their distinctive "Cross of Lorraine" insignia. Sergeant Manny Barrios and his squad from I Company decanted from their comfortable DUKW into several smaller vehicles before heading off along with a squad of engineers carrying collapsible boats. Twenty-five miles from

BELOW LEFT Fabulous views across the Nonntal area of Berchtesgaden from the Obersalzberg Road – note the twin spires which belong to the church of Sankt Peter und Johannes der Täufer with Watzmann Mountain towering in the background. (John Phillips)

A stunning vista northeast close to the zig-zag path across the "Eagle's Nest" from the top of Kehlstein Mountain. The shallow valley seen below (left) was the route taken by 3/506 on May 5, 1945, while the main body came in from the right. (NARA)

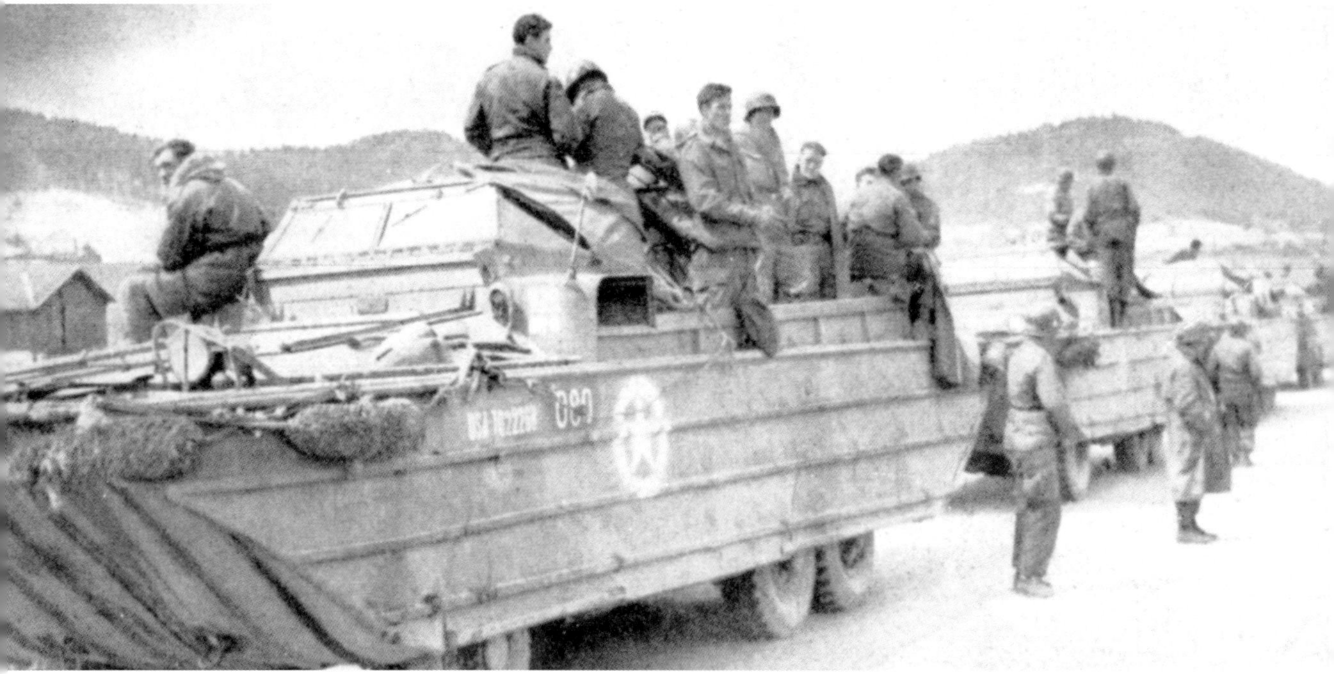

DUKWs transporting 506th troops toward Berchtesgaden.

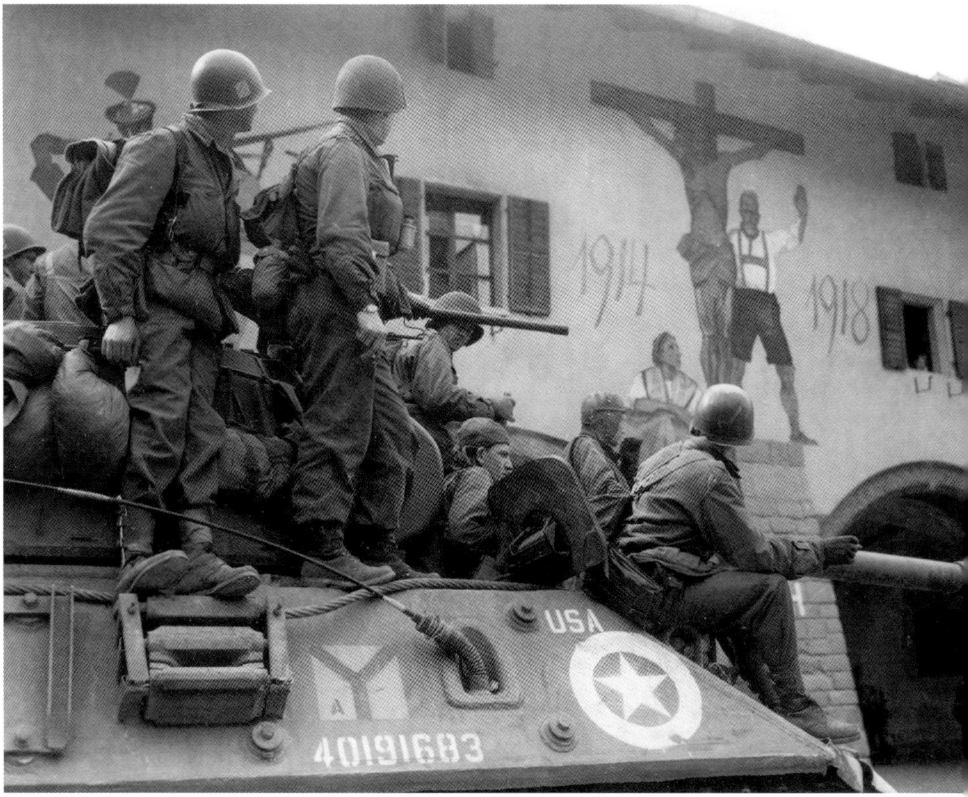
1914
1918
USA
40191683

Tanks and troops from 3rd Infantry Division were among the first American forces to reach Berchtesgaden and are seen here at Schlossplatz (the town square) opposite the World War I memorial. (NARA)

Ahead of the 506th were the French and elements of the 3rd Infantry Division (seen here) who had been traveling south from Bischofswiesen. This photo was probably taken on May 4, northwest of Berchtesgaden. (NARA)

Berchtesgaden, they came upon the rear elements of the 2nd French Armored Division at the town of Inzell on the River Rote Traun where the bridge had been demolished. As the 2nd French Armored Division had no bridging equipment, their tanks were stranded, although some had made it across before the bridge was blown. After reporting his location and situation to battalion headquarters, Manny was told to sit tight and await further instructions. It is somewhat unclear what happened next, but it seems likely that a squad from G Company was sent back in a liberated fire engine to scout an alternative route in from the west. Incredibly, the G Company team would go on to facilitate the surrender of over 1,200 German troops from Heeresgruppe G at Stockklaus.

Back at Inzell, Barrios was listening to the French engaging enemy forces across the river when the order came for them to advance and form a defensive perimeter on the opposite bank. The squad paddled over nervously and set up their arcs and waited. Early the following morning of May 5, the main body arrived and eventually crossed the river in DUKWs. Due to the increasing delays Bob Sink sent First and Second Battalions back to the autobahn with the intention of reaching Berchtesgaden via Bad Reichenhall – a huge detour of over 50 miles.

The previous afternoon, Karl Jacob, the district commissioner of Obersalzberg – a mountainside retreat for leading Nazis above Berchtesgaden – ran into a Sherman tank operated by Colonel John Heintges (CO of the 7th Infantry

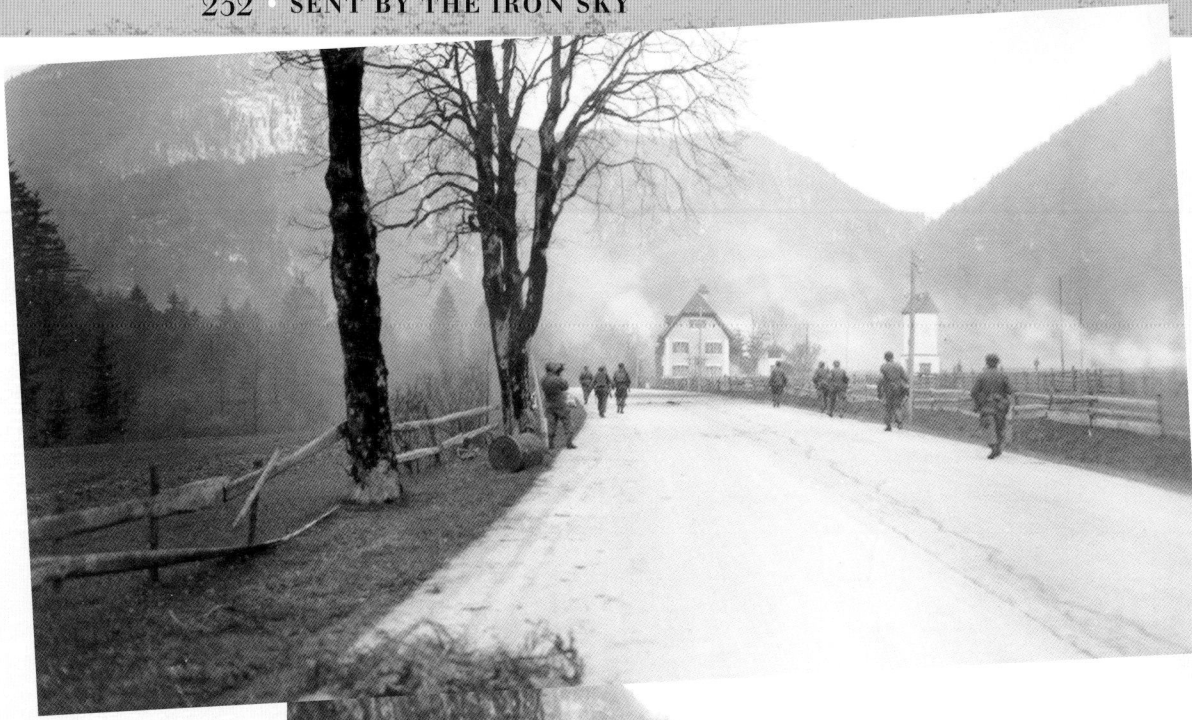

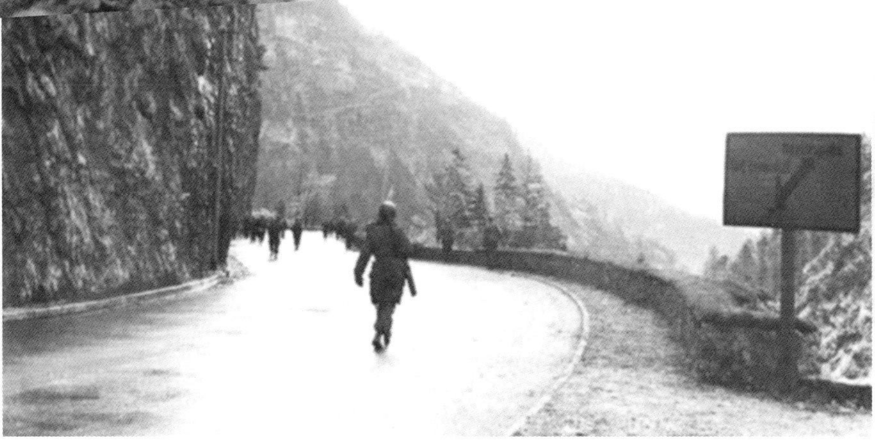

A blown bridge en route meant 3/506 were forced to de-truck and walk the last 6 miles to Berchtesgaden along the Ramsauer Valley. Consequently, they were the last unit from the 506th to arrive. (NARA)

Regiment), who ordered Jacob to lead him to Berchtesgaden. Thus the 7th Infantry Regiment became the first Allied unit to enter the town. Here in the shadow of the abbey and the World War I memorial, the colonel began negotiations for the full and unconditional surrender of the Alpine prize. At the same moment, east of the River Ache at Obersalzberg, the SS had set fire to what remained of the bombed-out Berghof.

After successfully crossing the river at Inzell, H Company, who had been designated as Battalion Assault Group, drove ahead in their DUKWs to clear the way along the Ramsauer Valley. The area was surrounded on both sides by tall, densely forested mountains, covered by a carpet of snow on the upper slopes. Along the route, patrols were sent out to clear isolated buildings, taking dozens of prisoners along the way. While herding a group of prisoners back toward the company, Hank DiCarlo and his squad came under artillery fire from the slopes high above them. Two members of his squad, Claude Rankin and Wilber Johnson, were directly in front of Hank as they double-timed behind the Germans. A shell came screaming in over their heads and exploded close to Rankin, who ran a few steps before falling to the ground. A large piece of shrapnel had ripped through Claude's upper body, killing him and the German soldier in front instantly. The shelling also killed another member of the squad, Nick Kozoroski, who together with Rankin were the last combat casualties sustained by the 506th in World War II.

The German artillery was quickly located and identified as a pair of 88mm antiaircraft guns. B Battery, from 321st Glider Field Artillery, who had been attached to the battalion, fired a barrage of phosphorus rounds at the 88s. Several four-man patrols from H Company were then sent to flank and neutralize the guns from behind. It transpired that the "men" crewing the 88s were in fact boys from the Hitler Youth who were quickly disarmed. Ironically, soon afterwards a message came through: "Effective immediately all troops will stand fast on present positions. German Army Group G in this sector has surrendered. No firing on Germans unless fired upon. Notify French units in the vicinity. Full details to be broadcast, will be issued by SHAEF."

Early evening, May 5; last troopers from 3/506 finally make it to Berchtesgaden. (NARA)

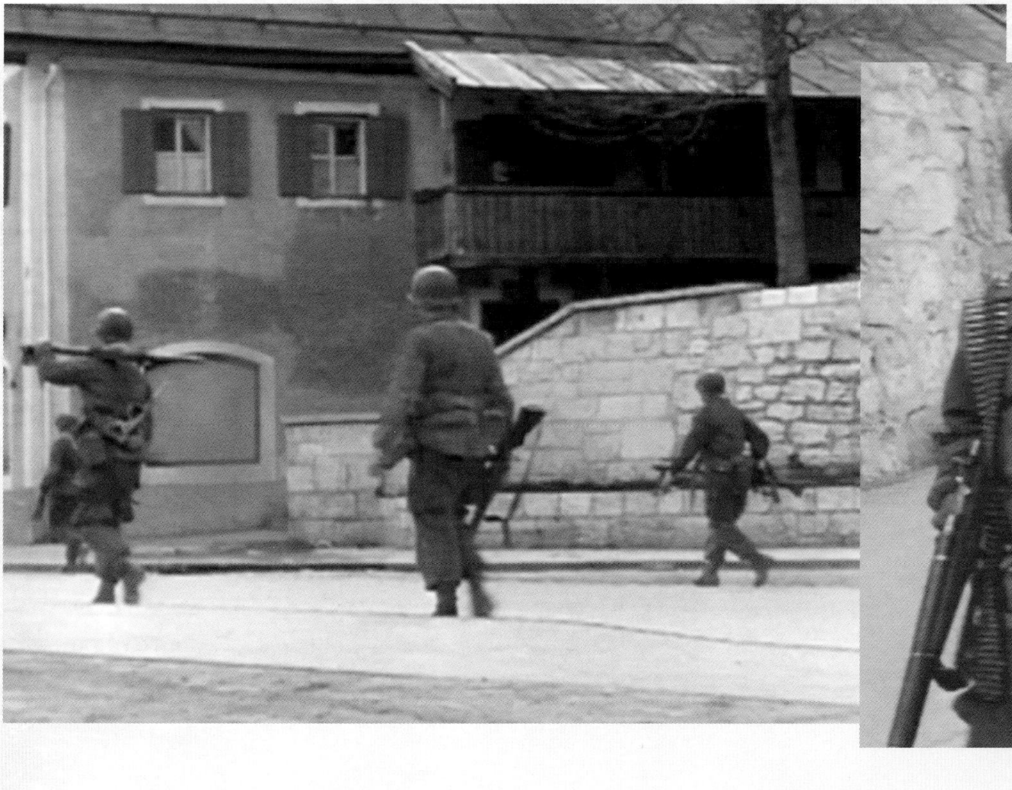

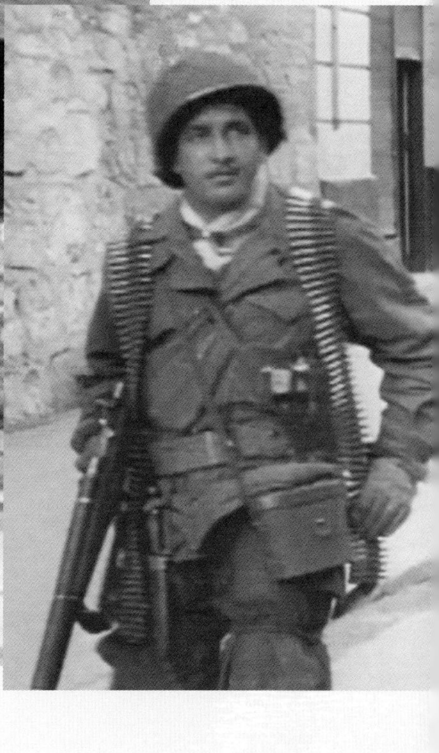

DER FÜHRER

Berchtesgaden
9 May 1945

Dearest Eileen and Bobbie,

This morning at one minute past midnight, the war came to an end. It is fitting that the 101st A/B should receive the surrender of Field Marshall Kesselring here at the heart of the Nazi Party.

I send you all my love and hope with all my heart to be with you once again. With victory I am suddenly very tired, very conscious of missing friends very anxious to be home.

Bob

Hotel

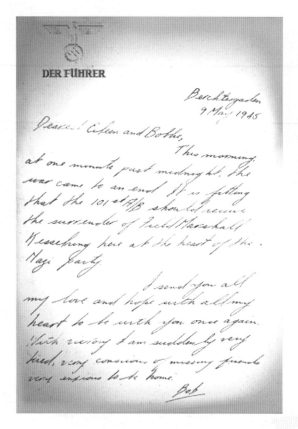

Bob Harwick, who had recently returned to active duty with the 501st PIR, wrote this note to his wife Eileen and daughter Bobbie on notepaper that had previously belonged to Adolf Hitler. (Denis & Donna Cortese)

TOP Hotel Geiger where Col Sink established his Regimental CP in Berchtesgaden. (Collection of G.A & G.R Walden)

BOTTOM The Berchtesgadener Hof Hotel on Hanielstrasse shortly before it was demolished in 2006. The hotel was well known for the view across the mountains and over the years had seen an impressive array of guests, including the Duke and Duchess of Windsor, Neville Chamberlain, and David Lloyd George, as well as many leading figures in the German government and military. (Collection of G.A & G.R Walden)

After being forced to de-truck at another blown bridge and continue on foot, the rest of the battalion advanced uphill past the beautiful 15th-century church of St-Sebastian at Ramsau. From here the road crossed back and forth over the River Ache as the valley ascended toward the southwestern edge of Berchtesgaden. There were only a few civilians left in Berchtesgaden itself and by then the French had moved across the Ache and were looting Obersalzberg. French execution squads brought a number of SS and regular soldiers down to the river for execution in the clear blue water. The 101st briefly turned a blind eye to most of this but it was then rumored that one of the French soldiers had raped a ten-year-old girl. Sink issued an immediate ultimatum to the French commander that if his forces did not leave Obersalzberg immediately, then the 506th would commence combat operations against them and thank goodness common sense on the part of the French commander prevailed. The battalion was divided up and billeted in various buildings around the resort, including the famous Berchtesgadener Hof Hotel. Sovereignty and control soon transferred to the 506th who then enforced a curfew. Schools were closed and all public amenities such as post, bus, and rail services stopped.

Waffen SS Obergruppenführer Gottlob Berger (left) seen here leaving the Berchtesgadener Hof Hotel. The white armband worn by the other officer signifies that permission had been granted by the 101st for him to carry his sidearm for protection. Forty-nine-year-old Berger was Heinrich Himmler's assistant and instrumental in the creation of the SS. Berger was responsible for the forced marches imposed on Allied POWs, which included many men from 3/506. (Johnny Gibson)

On May 7, the German Army formally surrendered and the first VE Day of sorts was quietly celebrated. General Theodor Tolsdorff, CO of Heeresgruppe G, together with a small party of senior officers from 82nd Armeekorps arrived at Hotel Geiger to formally sign a surrender deal with Colonel Sink. The next day Sink received a note from Max Taylor, short but to the point: "A German colonel has arrived at the HQ of 36th ID from Hermann Göring. The colonel has a letter that he is taking to Generals Devers and Eisenhower. He states that both Göring and Kesselring are present with a small staff just north of Bruck – go get them." Patrols were immediately sent out and roadblocks established, but although it was too late to capture Göring, the regiment did manage to snare Kesselring as well as Waffen-SS General Gottlob Berger who became temporary houseguests at the Berchtesgadener Hof.

US troops standing in the ruins of the Berghof's once magnificent picture window overlooking Berchtesgaden. (Photo by Keystone-France/Gamma-Keystone via Getty Images)

Due to the constantly changing attachments, the regiment struggled to

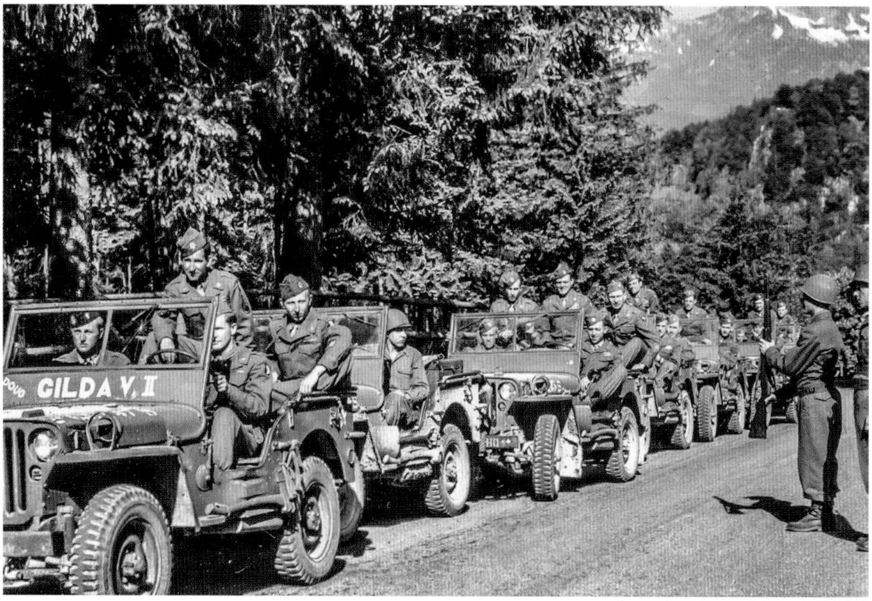
GILDA V. II

Members of the 327th Glider Infantry Regiment sightseeing around Berchtesgaden. (Universal History Archive/UIG via Getty Images)

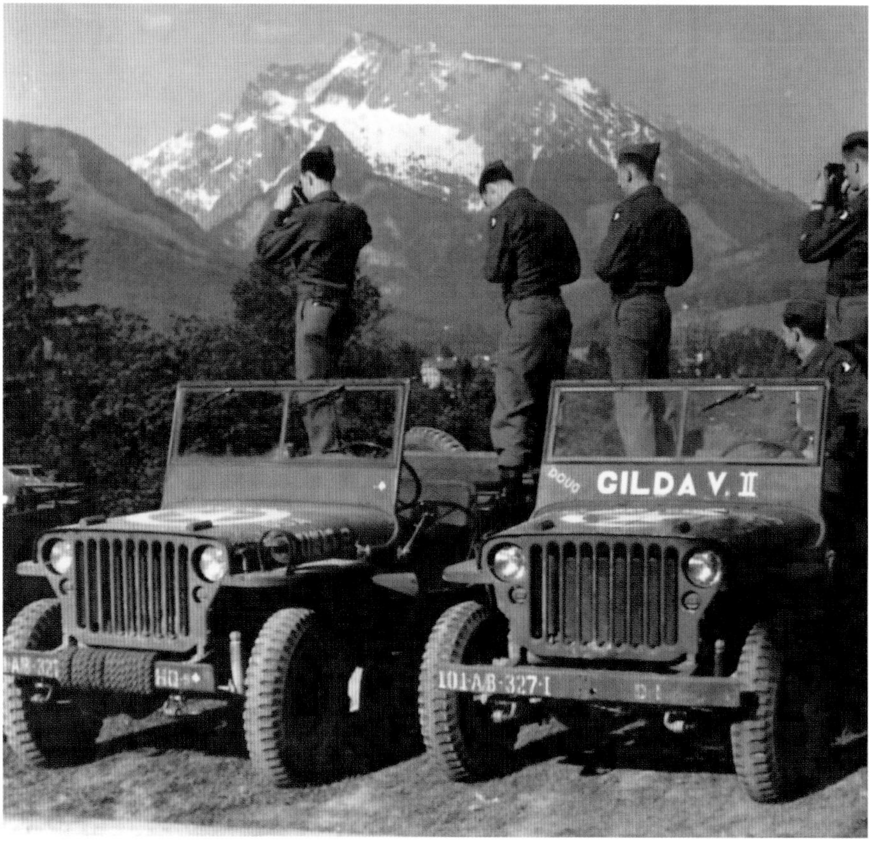
GILDA V. II
101-AB-327-I

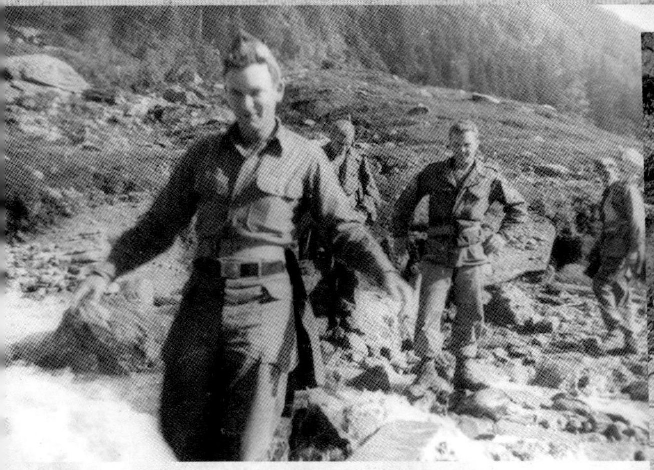

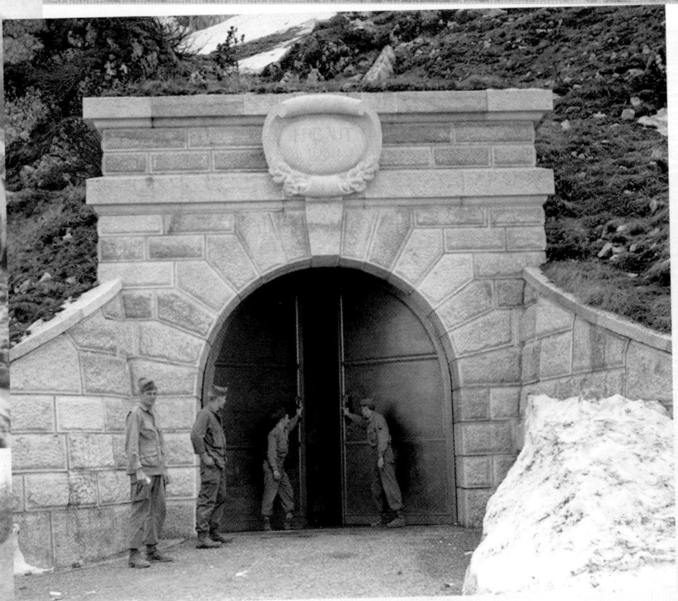

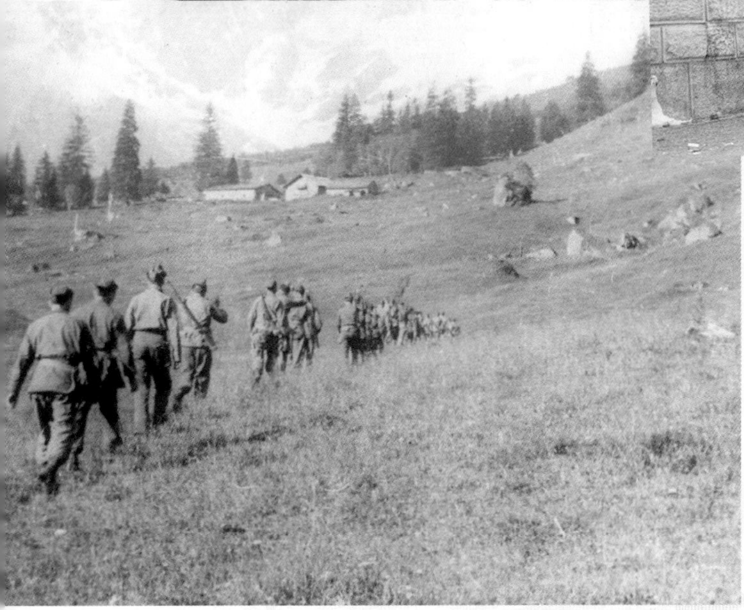

Carved into the mountain directly below the Eagle's Nest was an impressive stone archway. Beyond the bronze entrance doors (seen here) was a long tunnel leading to a circular domed waiting room where a brass-lined elevator, powered by a U-Boat engine, climbed vertically over 400ft to the nest itself. The entire complex had been staffed by SS troops and consisted of three levels, each serviced by the elevator. (Getty Image)

G Company on "patrol" in the mountains around Berchtesgaden. (Jim "Pee Wee" Martin)

2 Platoon, G Company, investigating a remote ski lodge northwest of Berchtesgaden. (Jim "Pee Wee" Martin)

get its correct ration allotments. Consequently, hunting parties were sent out to scour the surrounding high ground for food. Alcohol was not in short supply, however, as dozens of bottles of Cognac had been liberated from Göring's wine cellar before it was placed under heavy guard. G Company patrolled the surrounding mountains, looking for any "Werewolf" activity but there was none, meaning that they were free to enjoy the beautiful scenery.

Certain areas were placed under restriction, but many could not resist temptation. The drive up to Obersalzberg was comparatively short but nevertheless convoluted as the road climbed steeply to the ruins of the Berghof and surrounding SS buildings before turning off toward the famous Kehlsteinhaus or, as it became known to American forces, "The Eagle's Nest," which had been built upon the very summit of

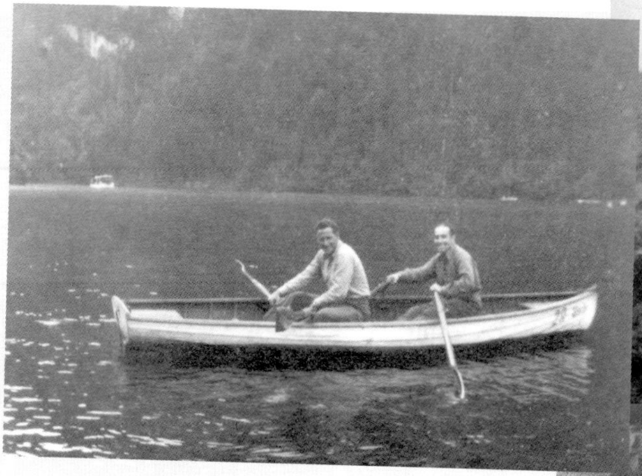

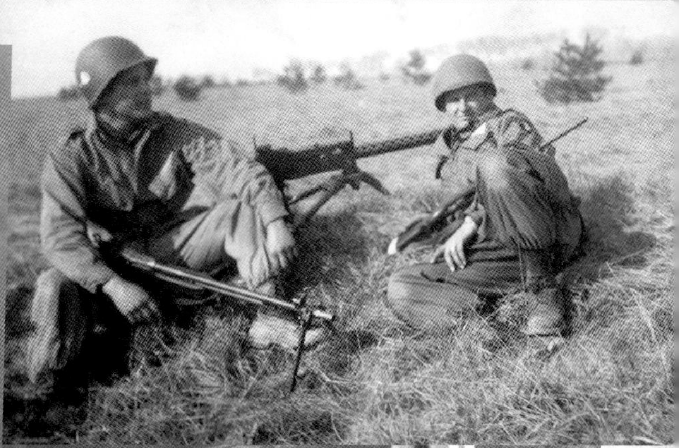

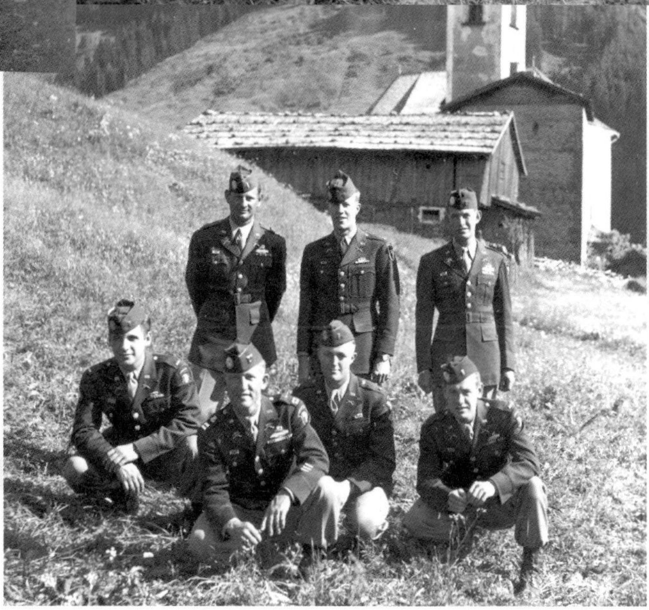

Bob Vann and Sharkey Tarquini after a few Bavarian beers on Lake Zeller See, Austria, July 5, 1945. (Lou Vecchi)

Hank DiCarlo and Lou Vecchi relaxing after a hard day on the ranges in Austria. (Lou Vecchi)

Saalbach, May 28, 1945. H Company officers pose for a photograph with the church of Heilige Nikolaus und Bartholomäus in the background. (Standing, left to right): 1Lt Willie Miller, 2Lt Don Barlow, 2Lt Harry Begle. (Kneeling, left to right): 1Lt Bob Stroud, Capt Jim Walker, 1Lt Ed Buss, 1Lt Alex Andros. (Lou Vecchi)

Kehlstein Mountain and used throughout the war to entertain high-ranking Nazi officials. The latter was so overwhelmed with "visitors" that guards were stationed at the tunnel entrance carved into the mountain immediately below with orders to allow only officers above the rank of major to enter. Everyone else still wanting to catch a glimpse of the Eagle's Nest had to traverse the steep winding path on foot to the top of the mountain. Staff Sergeant Ralph Bennett had been one of the lucky Third Battalion members who had been able to catch a ride in the elevator that had been installed at the base of the mountain within the tunnel up to the Eagle's Nest before it was declared out of bounds:

> Spencer Phillips and I were among the first members of Third Battalion to ride the "golden elevator" up to the Eagle's Nest where almost everything worth having had already been stolen by the French. We decided to walk back to the

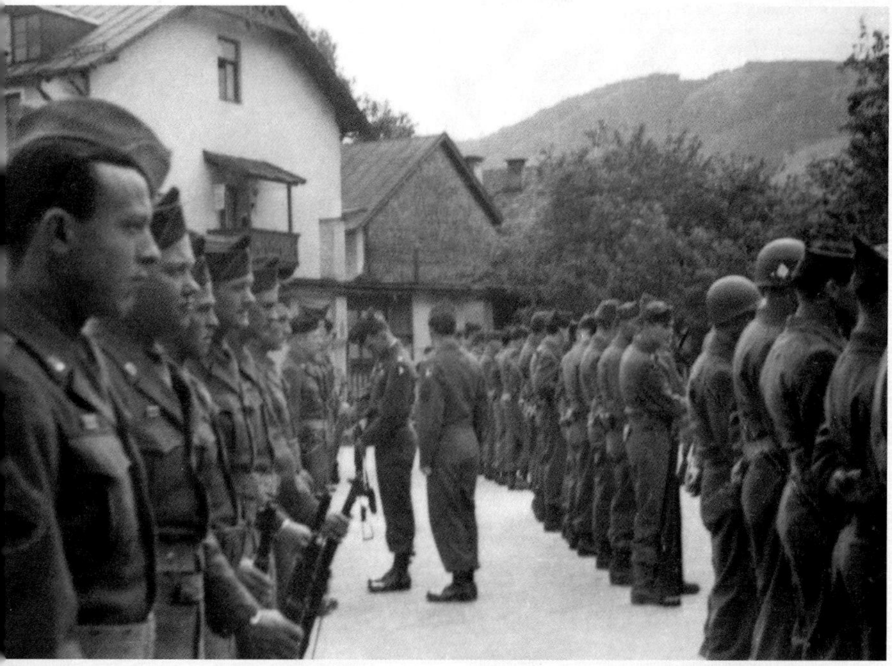

G Company being inspected at Saalfelden in June/July 1945. (Jim "Pee Wee" Martin)

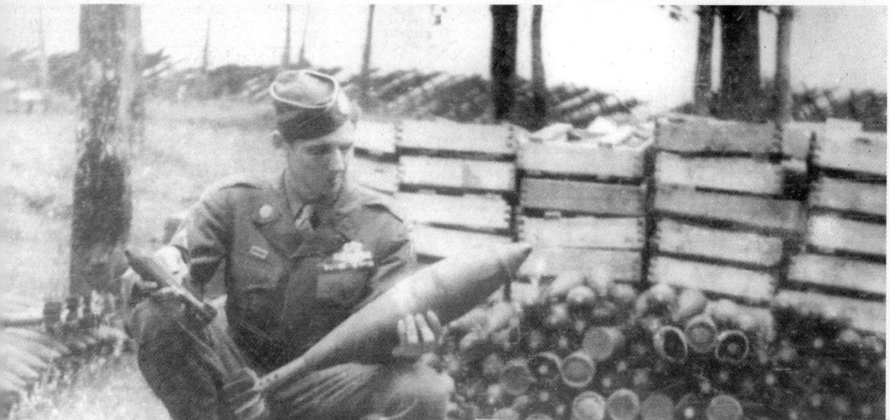

One weekend the guys visited a nearby ordnance depot and took as many explosives, flares and ammunition as they could carry into the foothills for a party and spent the day firing thousands of rounds, blowing up trees and anything else they could find. (Jim "Pee Wee" Martin)

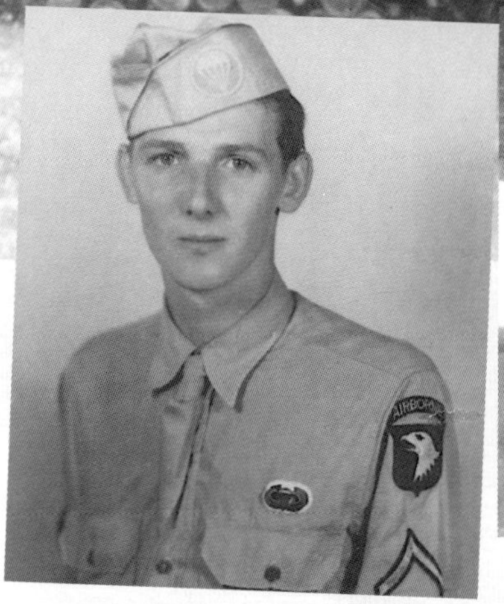

BELOW LEFT Jimmy Martin of G Company photographed while training back in the USA. "Our food supplies began to dry up and it became so bad that some like me in the company were on the verge of malnutrition. It didn't take long for us to find out that certain senior members of the QM Department, who were responsible for our rations, were in fact hauling them over the Alps from Innsbruck through the Brenner Pass down into Italy to sell at immense profit on the Black Market!" (Jim "Pee Wee" Martin)

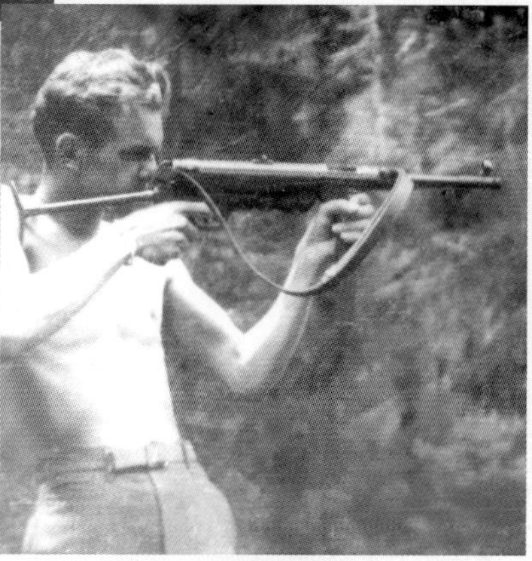

BELOW RIGHT Maurice Vaughan from G Company squeezing off a burst from a 9mm Schmeisser MP40 submachine gun in the hills above Saalfelden. (Jim "Pee Wee" Martin)

OPPOSITE PAGE

BOTTOM LEFT Fred Bahlau had discovered approximately 200 silver cups in Fischorn Castle while in Austria. Most likely they had originally been commissioned by an SS officer stationed there. Charlie Chase instructed Bahlau to employ a silversmith to customize around 40 of these dainty vessels by adding a pair of silver jump wings before individually engraving the names and campaigns of every surviving officer, including those with battlefield commissions, such as Fred and Ed Shames, who had taken part in combat operations with the 506th beginning with Normandy. (Sarah Shames Ehret)

BOTTOM RIGHT
S/Sgt Ralph Bennett married June Earl, whom he had met while based at Ramsbury, at Saint Mary's Parish Church, Church Street, in Slough. The wedding took place on August 15, 1945 – the day Japan officially surrendered. Ralph's colleague from the 506th, Spencer Phillips, was supposed to be his best man but he had disappeared on a seven-day bender to celebrate the end of World War II and didn't bother to turn up. The wedding cake looked stunning, but as it was made with powdered eggs, it had gone off, and was inedible. But Ralph and June did not care; they were together and that was all that mattered. Although Ralph returned home in November, it would be another year of waiting before he and June were reunited in the States. (Ralph Bennett)

tunnel entrance via the zigzag path situated just to the left of the Eagle's Nest. On the way down we came across a dining set all marked with an eagle sitting on a swastika between the initials "A-H." I picked up the solid silver service and was on my way back to Göring's house when we were stopped by a major in a command car who asked, "What have you got there, sergeant?" I told him it was a souvenir, but he snapped back, "Nope, that's loot; you know the rules – hand it over!" As Spence and I were sheepishly walking away another officer, a colonel, approached the major and did exactly the same thing. RHIP: Rank Has Its Privileges. No doubt about it.

On May 10, the regiment handed over control to a new governing body before moving to Zell am See in Austria to support Third and Seventh Armies. Each battalion was allocated a specific sector, which was then subdivided by company. Roadblocks were the key factor to controlling and monitoring all military and civilian traffic while disarming and directing German soldiers to the discharge centers where they would be processed. Over the occupation period the 506th apprehended around 50 people wanted for war crimes.

The regiment was deployed along two glorious steep-sided Alpine river valleys located either side of the Kitzbühel Alps, covering a total patrol footprint of some 430 square miles. Colonel Patch established the Third Battalion CP at the five-star Grand Hotel in the spa town of Zell am See. The hotel even had its own private beach on the lake shore, so conditions were certainly far more luxurious than had been the norm in the preceding months and years. H Company was billeted further afield in a spacious ski lodge near the small town of Saalbach in the mountains, while 2 and 3 Platoons were split between surrounding hotels and private homes throughout the designated area.

For the most part the men were able to simply do they own thing, whether that was fishing, skiing or hunting, with any deer they came across butchered and shared with the locals. Despite being ordered to surrender, many SS men absconded to the mountains, only to be hunted down over the coming weeks under the automatic arrest policy.

Initially elements of G Company were sent to nearby Uttendorf in the Pinzgau Valley below the hydroelectric power plant to guard an enormous POW enclosure. The prisoners mainly consisted of troops whose hometowns were now in the Russian occupied zone and many were put to work rebuilding local infrastructure such as roads and power lines. It was easy work with picturesque surroundings, but things became tougher once they were relocated to Saalfelden. Here G Company soon found themselves desperately short of food and many of the men became painfully thin. The problems with the food supply chain were soon rectified once it became clear that the Quartermasters Department had been redirecting their rations to Italy to sell on the black market.

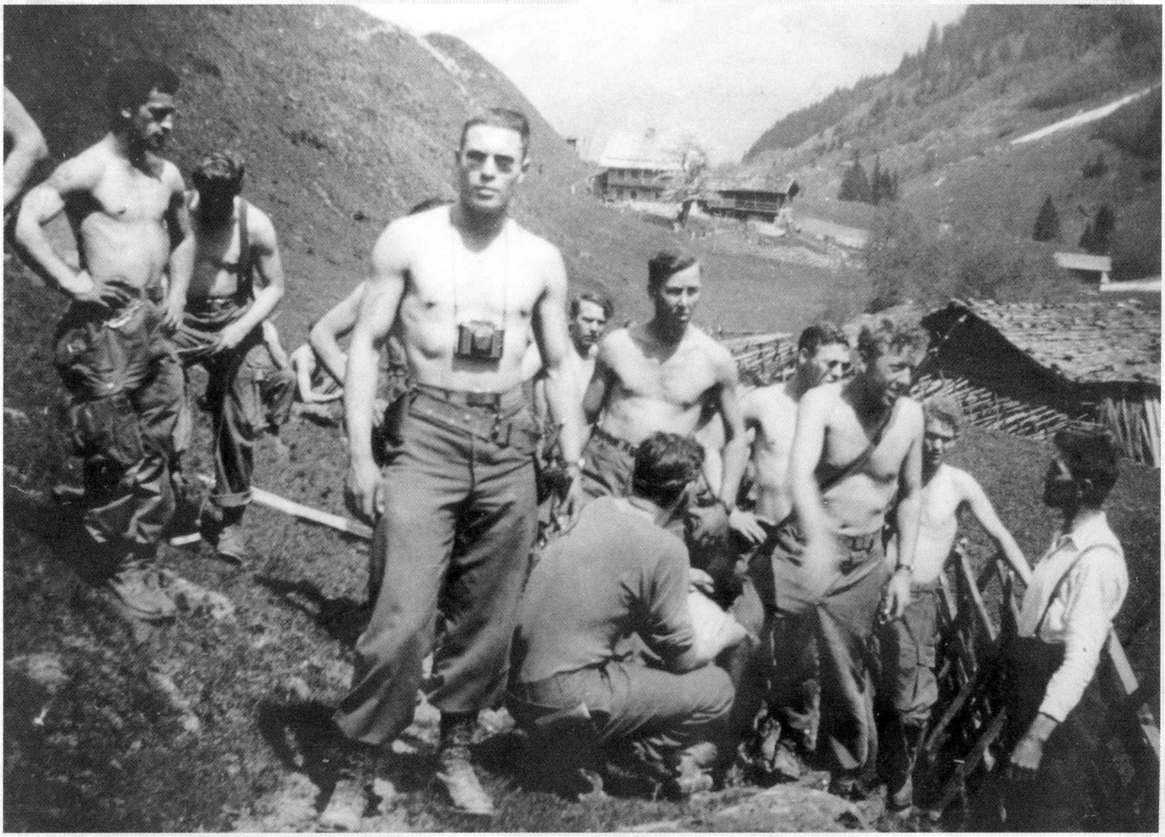

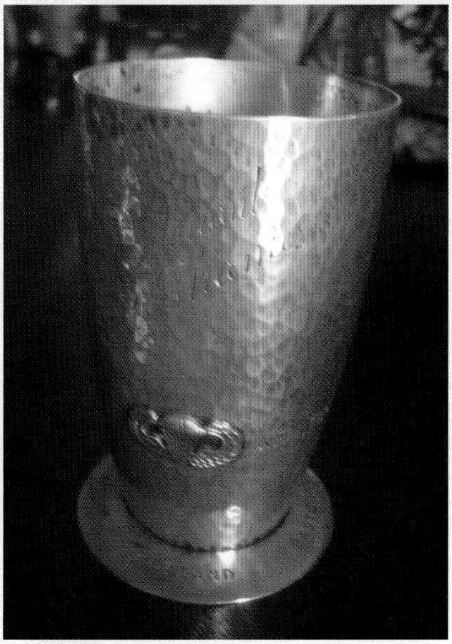

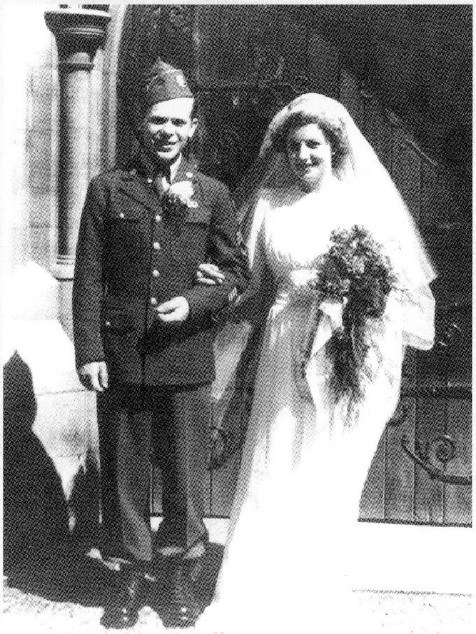

ABOVE Lieutenant Fred Bahlau (now an officer in C/506) enjoying the sunshine with his platoon in the foothills above Bruck prior to the regiment's departure to France. (Fred Bahlau via Mark Bando Collection)

Soon the division began to construct rifle ranges and introduced a regular training program. Inter-company athletic competitions took place, while the men anxiously waited to hear if they had accrued enough points to go home. At the core of the US Army Demobilization Plan was the point system. Points were awarded for the number of years and months spent overseas, medals, commendations, campaign battle stars, and other factors such as Purple Hearts, Presidential Unit Citations, and even number of children. General Taylor took it upon himself to address the regiment as a whole regarding their future role:

> We have reached another critical point in our lives and in the life of the division. It is time to face the prospect of future action in the Pacific. This commitment is only probable – not possible. So, the future for most of you low point men at this stage is unknown. I cannot see why a top-notch division like this should be allowed to remain in the States but that is entirely up to General MacArthur. Back home this division tops the hearts of the nation and the eagle patch is recognized everywhere. The American civilians haven't relaxed their efforts because of VE Day and everyone is anxious to see Japan crushed. Those of you with 85 points or more will be leaving soon for America and I will see you later to say goodbye. I am sure that the men from the 506th would earn the same fine reputation on the shores of Japan that you made on the shores of Normandy and the battlefields of Belgium.

By late June around 400 men with a minimum of 85 points were alerted for transfer to the 501st PIR, which was to be the first regiment scheduled for deactivation. At the same time the 501st reassigned its low-point troopers back to the 506th. Colonel Sink gave the "Old Boys" a moving and heartfelt speech, telling them of his pride, and thanked everyone for what they had done for their country over the last two years.

The regiment then received orders on July 31 for a move to Auxerre in Burgundy, France. Over the next two days the unit established itself in the crumbling garrison towns of Joigny and Sens. Meanwhile, most of the high-point enlisted men had already been transferred out and sent to Nancy; from there they traveled to a transit camp near Marseille. Some, such as Ralph Bennett and Vince Michaels, then traveled by boat to England to meet up with and marry their respective sweethearts.

Around September 1, Jimmy Martin, along with Manny Barrios, Hank DiCarlo, Bob Webb and dozens of other "high-pointers" from Third Battalion, set sail from Marseille for America on the troopship SS *Manhattan* and arrived at Camp Shanks, Orangeburg, New York – ironically the exact same place from where the regiment had departed in September 1943. Shortly after arriving, the men boarded different trains that took them back to the military camps from where they had originally enlisted.

SS *Manhattan* dockside at Marseille. (Jim "Pee Wee" Martin)

Bob Webb on his way home to Texas. (Bob Webb Jr)

SS *Manhattan* arriving in New York, September 1945. (Bob Webb Jr)

Since June 1944, the division had spent an astonishing 214 days in combat. During that time over 2,000 men had been killed and over 8,000 wounded or missing.

The 101st Airborne Division was now part of Supreme Headquarters Reserve and Third Battalion was posted to Joigny. But after Japan formally surrendered, the prospect of the division seeing any further action quickly faded away. Shortly afterwards Max Taylor handed over command and returned to the United States to take up a new role at West Point. In September, it was announced that every parachute-trained individual had to make one last clean fatigue jump to qualify for "Para Pay." During the next four weeks over 5,000 descents were carried out in near

RIGHT The Belgian Government awarded the Fourragére lanyard to the 101st Airborne Division during a special ceremony in Auxerre, France, on November 7, 1945. (NARA via Jacqueline Rickards Andrews)

BELOW Members of H Company 'chuted up for the last jump in September 1945 at Joigny. (DF Pratt Museum Fort Campbell via Mark Bando Collection)

perfect weather conditions. A delegation from the House of Representatives was sent over to observe and assess the future of the division.

Soon afterwards, the powers that be decided to shut down the 101st in favor of the 82nd Airborne Division. Now having the correct number of points, Harley Dingman was held back and ordered to organize the formal Honor Company for a parade on November 7, to mark the award by the Belgian Government of the Fourragére lanyard. This braided orange lanyard was presented to the division to honor its service in France and Belgium. When the 506th was officially deactivated on November 30, 1945, Dingman and the remainder of the regiment were

LEFT Harold Stedman finally made it home and just in time for Christmas. This wonderful color photo shows Harold back home in Modesto outside the No. 2 Firehouse (where his father was the Fire Chief) with twin brothers Ernest (left) and Everett (right) on December 22, 1945. The twins had been air gunners in the USAF and were both heavily decorated for their service. Harold is sporting his orange Fourragére lanyard on his right shoulder. (Harold Stedman)

BELOW This photograph was taken in October 1945 shortly after Marty Clark (left) and George "Doc" Dwyer had been discharged early from the Army. They left Fort Benning on October 14 and drove across the country to Doc's home in California, stopping at numerous addresses on the way to pay their respects to the families of friends who had been killed in Europe. (Bob Webb Jr)

sent home on the fast cruise liner SS *America*. After the ship reached Boston on December 18, Harley was sent back to Camp Miles Standish, where annoyingly he was given the job of a temporary administrative NCO. After a frustrating week of office work, he simply typed his own name on a discharge list and left! Dingman got home just in time for Christmas. Trudging through the snow, heavy barracks bag over his shoulder, Harley's folks were waiting for him on the bridge into Carthage. It was only then that he could truly believe that the war was over.

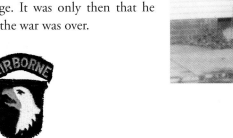

Outside one of the entrances to the Muehlebach Hotel.(Left to right): Forrest Troxel (HQ Company), Vince "Mike" Michael, Billy Bowen and Oscar Saxvik from G Company; George Rosie (head down facing camera), Jim Morrow (back to camera) and Charles "Chick" Stewart all from HQ Company. At the end of the war Company G ended up with three men in its ranks all named Billy Bowen, which got very confusing for the new officers. Vince, Oscar, George and Chick were all original Toccoa men. Vince married an English girl from Ramsbury who came to the reunion. A member of the 81mm Mortar Platoon, Stewart had been badly wounded on D-Day, while his colleague Rosie had been in the same stick for Normandy as medic Johnny Gibson. Both were captured during the same ambush. Only a handful of people like Oscar Saxvik chose to stay on and make the army their career. Oscar was commissioned in Paris in the late summer of 1945. (Bob Webb Jr)

Chapter 12

# THOUGH OUR
# PICTURES FADE

On Wednesday June 5, 1946, around 50 survivors from 3/506 traveled to Missouri to gather as per Bob Wolverton's last wishes at the Muehlebach Hotel in Kansas City. On the eve of D-Day, Wolverton had designated the Midwest's most prestigious hotel as their meeting point. Bob's wife Kay along with Helen Briggs arranged the reunion to honor her late husband and the 200 men from Third Battalion who had lost their lives since that fateful night.

Mr and Mrs Kangas were also in attendance, remembering their son Bob of I Company who died defending Foy. Only recently released from hospital, Johnny Gibson drove from Tucson with his girlfriend Pearle. The reunion centered on the Muehlebach's beautiful ballroom with its polished wooden floor, enormous mirrors, 25ft-high ceiling and ornate art deco moldings. A memorial service was also held in a local chapel, where Kay read aloud her husband's pre-D-Day prayer followed by an alphabetical roll call of the dead. Gibson was already tearful but then began to weep uncontrollably when Kay began with his friend Private Philip D. Abbey. Phil's death had occurred at sunrise on June 6, 1944 and had been witnessed by Johnny and George Rosie, who was standing beside him at the church. The faces and personalities of those who did not come back were still raw in the minds of the people who were there. And this, probably the first reunion of its kind, was a clear indication of the close bonds that had been forged under the leadership of Lieutenant Colonel Robert Lee Wolverton.

***

With the deactivation of the 506th many began to wonder if the sacrifice of their kin had been worthwhile. For others it would take 50 years or more to accept the time spent in Europe as being a positive experience, but time was and still is a great healer. Some stayed in touch after the reunion, while others simply got on with their postwar lives, raised families, and never saw or spoke to each other again. Andy Anderson eventually married Kay Wolverton on July 19, 1947. Shortly before tying the knot, Anderson adopted Wolverton's son Lach as his own and they eventually shared another three children. Kay and Andy remained very close to the Sinks especially after they retired, and even after Bob and his wife Margaret's early demise, they continued to visit Bob's mother in Charlotte, North Carolina. Although Andy was a caring father to all his children, he only ever talked about the amusing things that happened during the war and never spoke of the many dark days and nights he had endured with his brothers-in-arms. Like Bob Harwick, Andy died long before his time, after returning from a pilgrimage to Normandy in 1985… he had hoped for many more.

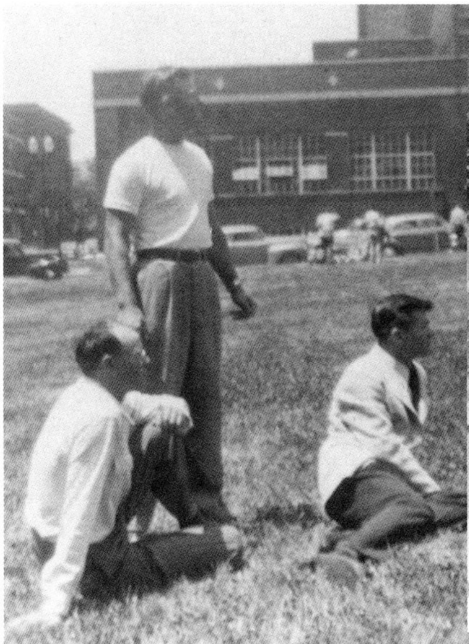

RIGHT John Allison, Jim Bradley and "Chick" Stewart were members of the 81mm Mortar Platoon. Allison, by then a California Highway Patrolman, rode 1,500 miles from Los Angeles on his motorcycle with Bradley. Bradley and Stewart both jumped from 1st Lt Howard Littell's plane in Normandy. On June 6, Chick was seriously wounded and Bradley captured. Miss-dropped miles away, Allison was also captured; although wounded, he escaped and returned to American lines. Littell himself was killed-in-action on June 7. (Bob Webb Jr)

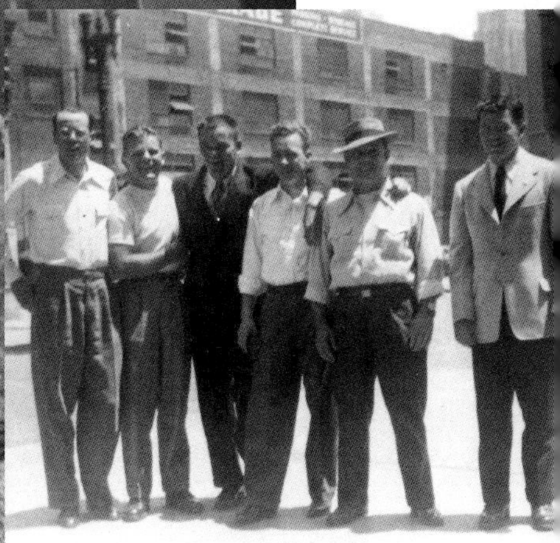

FAR RIGHT Mortarmen John Allison, Jim Bradley, George Rosie, Ivan Glancy, E.E. Lee and "Chick" Stewart. Rosie was captured on D-Day and remained a POW for the duration of the war. Glancy was seriously wounded in Normandy. (Bob Webb Jr)

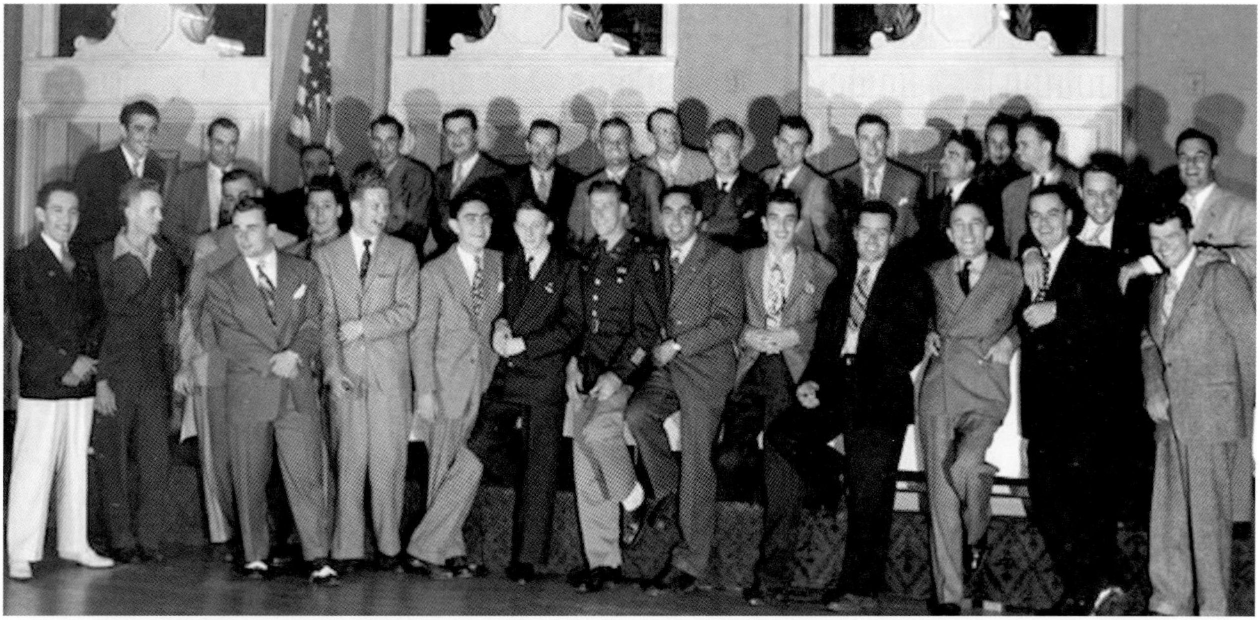

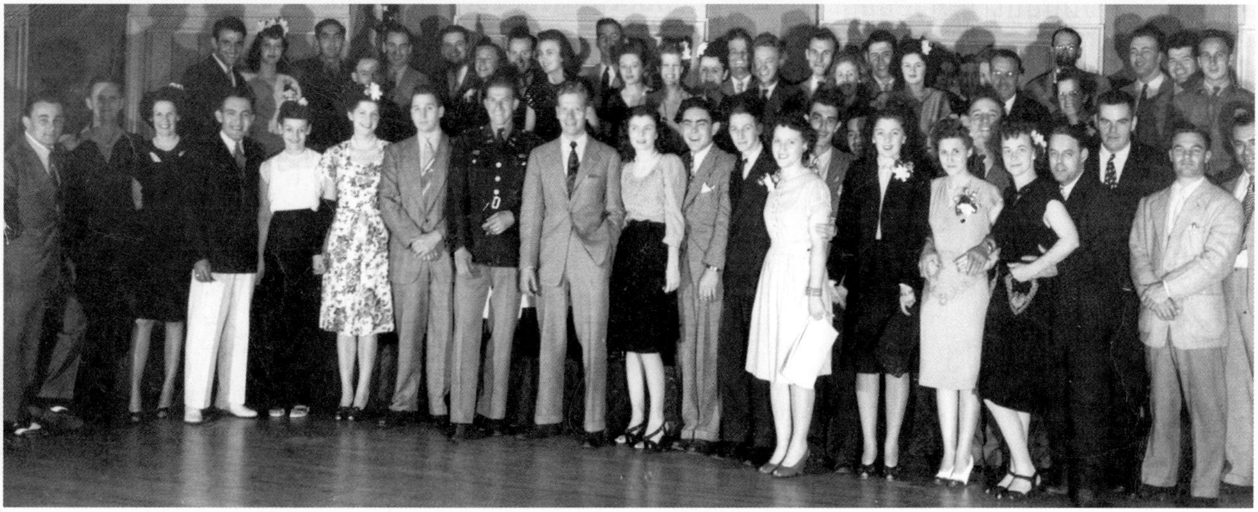

TOP All the boys together with their company designation listed next to their name. (Left to right, rear): James DeRoin (visitor), Bob Harwick (H), Dominic Nazzalorso (H), Dud Hefner (H), Daniel Seasock (G), Harold Johnson (I), Jim Bradley (HQ), John Allison (HQ), Ivan Glancy (HQ), Audrey Lewallen (HQ), Fred Bahlau (H & HQ), John Luteran (I), Walter Lukasavage (I), Ray Calandrella (HQ). (Left to right, front): Bob Nash (I), Forrest Troxel (HQ), Dick Campbell (visitor from the 502nd), Ed Austin (I), Ed Shames (I, HQ & E), Jim Morrow (HQ), Bill Bowen (G), Jim Martin (G), Oscar Saxvik (G), Sam Snobar (G), Vince Michael (G), Norm Capels (G), Cecil Hutt (G), George Rosie (HQ), E.E. Lee (HQ), "Chick" Stewart (HQ), Johnny Gibson (Med Det). (D-Day Publishing Collection)

BOTTOM The entire gang gathered together with Kay Wolverton and Helen Briggs back row center. (Bob Webb Jr)

Kay Wolverton was invited on November 10, 1946 to the West Point Military Academy by Maxwell Taylor (who had recently been appointed as its superintendent) to receive the prestigious Legion of Merit on behalf of her late husband. Immediately after the war Taylor invited a handful of his most trusted friends and colleagues from the 101st, West Point graduates themselves, to bring their families and work alongside him at the academy. For a while, the academy became known as the "101st on the Hudson" and Sink, then a brigadier general, was given the responsibility of organizing and commanding its garrison unit. It certainly seemed as though the academy was a good place for rest, restoration, reward and camaraderie after a bloody war.

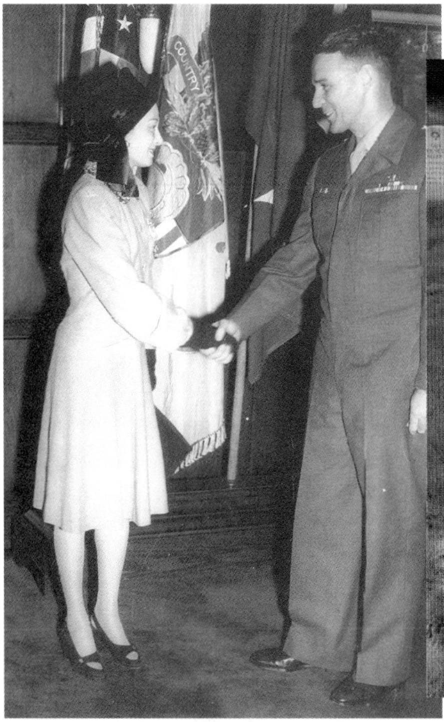

Before shipping overseas Bob Wolverton had left a request with his father Wayne, that if killed in action his remains were to be returned to the USA and buried at West Point. Bob's body was eventually repatriated, and he was buried with full military honors in October 1948. (Clayton Gaskill via Bob Webb Jr)

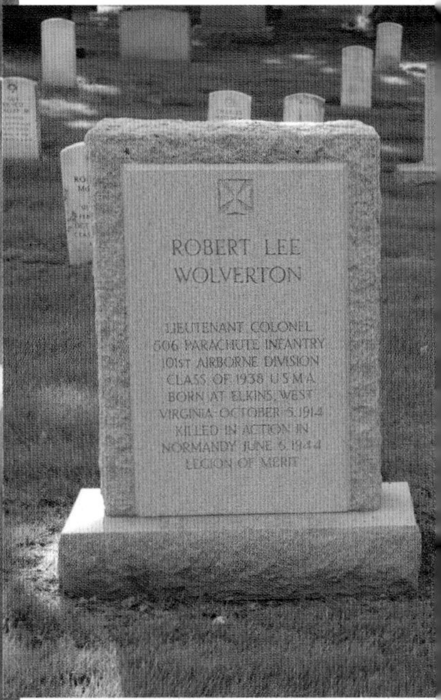
ROBERT LEE
WOLVERTON
LIEUTENANT COLONEL
506 PARACHUTE INFANTRY
101st AIRBORNE DIVISION
CLASS OF 1938 U.S.M.A.
BORN AT ELKINS, WEST
VIRGINIA OCTOBER 5, 1914
KILLED IN ACTION IN
NORMANDY JUNE 5, 1944
LEGION OF MERIT

Here Kay Wolverton is pictured in the center with Taylor to her left, and Harry Kinnard and Bob Sink immediately alongside. (The Wolverton Family)

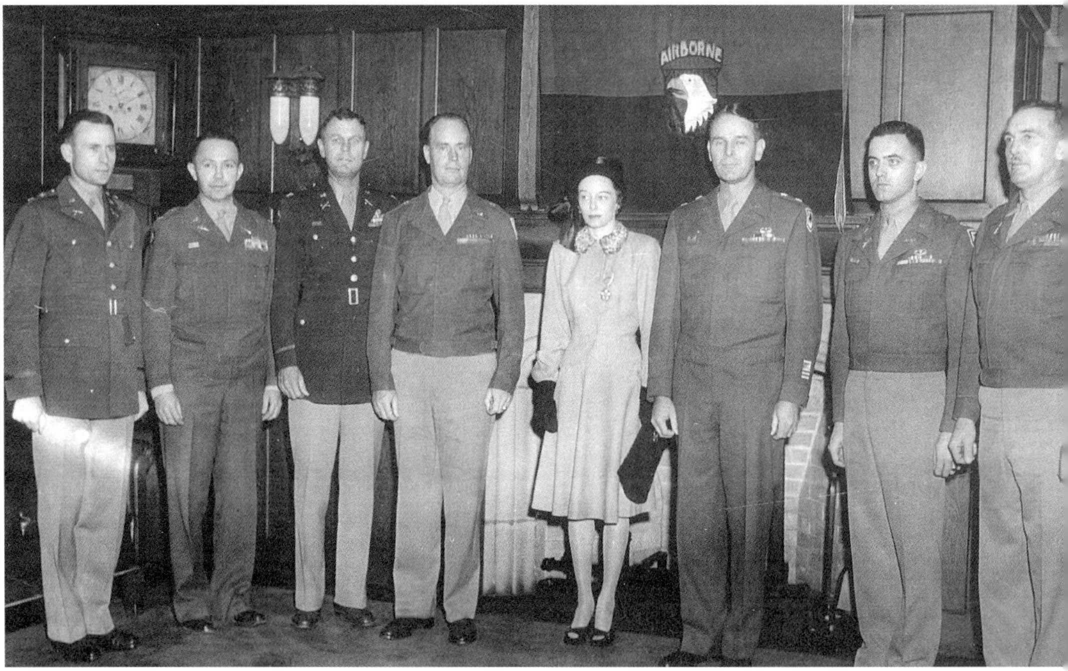
AIRBORNE

# BIBLIOGRAPHY

Listed below are the works that I have consulted during my research over the last 14 years. To their authors I offer my sincere thanks.

## Books and papers

Ambrose, Stephen E., *Band of Brothers* (Simon & Schuster Classic Edition, 2001)

Bando, Mark A., *The 101st Airborne at Normandy* (MBI, 1994)

Bando, Mark A., *101st Airborne: The Screaming Eagles at Normandy* (MBI, 2001)

Baumgardner, Randy, *101st Airborne Division – Screaming Eagles* (Turner Publishing, 2nd Edition, 2001)

Brotherton Marcus, *Shifty's War, The Authorized Biography of Sergeant Darrell "Shifty" Powers, the Legendary Sharpshooter from BAND OF BROTHERS* (Penguin Books Ltd, 2011)

Burgett, Donald R., *As Eagles Screamed* (Bantam Books, 1979)

Burgett, Donald R., *The Road to Arnhem* (Dell Publishing, 2001)

Day, Roger, *Ramsbury at War* (self-published, 2004)

DeTrez, Michel, *American Warriors* (D-Day Publishing, 1994)

DiCarlo, Hank and Westphal, Alan, *Currahee Scrapbook* (506th PIR, 1945)

Forty, George, *Patton's Third Army at War* (Ian Allan Printing Ltd, 1978)

Gardner, Ian and Day, Roger, *Tonight We Die as Men* (Osprey Publishing, 2009)

Gardner, Ian, *Deliver Us from Darkness* (Osprey Publishing, 2012)

Gardner, Ian, *No Victory in Valhalla* (Osprey Publishing, 2014)

Gutjahr, Major Robert G., *The Role of Jedburgh Teams in Operation Market Garden* (thesis presented to the US Army Command and General Staff College, 1978) c/o Tom Timmermans

Hannah, Harold W., *A Military Interlude, Cornfields to Academia to Parachutes* (self-published, 1999)

Heaps, Leo, *The Grey Goose of Arnhem* (Futura Publications Ltd, 1976)

Höjris, René, *Anthony "NUTS" McAuliffe* (Roger Publishing House, 2004)

Hoyt, Edwin P., *The Invasion Before Normandy* (Robert Hale, 1985)

Kesselring, Albert, *The Memoirs of Field-Marshal Kesselring* (William Kimber, 1974)

Killblane, Richard and McNiece, Jake, *The Filthy Thirteen* (Casemate, 2003)

Koskimaki, George E., *D-Day With the Screaming Eagles* (101st Airborne Division Association, 1970)

Koskimaki, George E., *Hell's Highway* (101st Airborne Division Association, 1989)

Koskimaki, George E., *The Battered Bastards of Bastogne* (Casemate reprint, 2011)

Laurence, Nicole and Léonard, Michel, *Saint-Côme-du-Mont Témoins d'hier* (Eurocibles, 2005)

Levit, Sergeant Saul, "The Siege of Bastogne," *Yank Magazine* (1945)

Margry, Karel, *De bevrijding van Eindhoven (The Liberation of Eindhoven)* (September Festival Foundation, 1982)

Marshall, S.L.A., *Night Drop* (Atlantic Monthly Press, 1962)

McAuliffe, Kenneth J. Jr, *NUTS! The Life of Anthony C. McAuliffe* (self-published, 2011)

Mehosky, Ivan Paul, *The Story of a Soldier* (Rutledge Books, Inc., 2001)

Nekrassoff, Philippe R., and Eric Brissard, *Magneville Ce jour Lá* (Park Printing, 2000)

Norton, G.G., *The Red Devils: From Bruneval to the Falklands* (Leo Cooper, 1984)

Pöppel, Martin, *Heaven & Hell – The War Diary of a German Paratrooper* (Spellmount, 2000)

Ramsey, Winston G. (ed.), *D-Day Then and Now, volumes 1 and 2* (Battle of Britain Prints, International Ltd 1995)

Rapport, Leonard and Northwood, Arthur Jr, *Rendezvous with Destiny* (Infantry Journal Press, 1948)

Ross, Donald C., *He beat the Odds – WW2 Autobiography* (self-published, 2004)

Sigmond, Robert and Van den Bosch, Cees (ed.), *Escape across the Rhine, Operations "Pegasus" I and II, October/ November 1944* (Airborne Museum, Hartenstein, 1999)

Taylor, Thomas H., *The Simple Sounds of Freedom* (Random House, 2002)

*Terrify and Destroy: The Story of the 10th Armored Division* (*The Stars & Stripes*, Paris, 1944/45)

Van Hout, Jan, (ed.), *Aangeboden Door De Gemeente Eindhoven, Herinneringen Aan September 1944 (Memories of September 1944 – presented by the Municipality of Eindhoven)* (self-published, 2004)

Webb, Robert, *Freedom Found* (self-published, 2000)

Reports and personal letters

436th Troop Carrier Group After Action Reports, Holland 1944

440th Troop Carrier Group After Action Reports, Normandy 1944

Air Support Requests 101st A/B Division 20–26 September 1944

"Buck" Taylor letter to Dick Winters (December 14, 1992), c/o Joe Muccia

Eindhoven Fire Brigade Reports 13–19 September (1944), c/o Tom Timmermans

G Co Morning Reports 1942 to 1945, c/o Tim Moore

Headquarters 3rd Bn 506th PIR Combat Report for Neptune (1944), *Utah Beach to Cherbourg June 6–27, 1944,* The Historical Division (US Army World War II)

Headquarters VII Corps Exercise *Tiger* Reports, US National Archives

Headquarters 506th PIR "After Action Report" – Operation "Market" (1944)

Headquarters 506th PIR Citation "Operation Pegasus 1" – Operation "Market" (1944)

Headquarters 506th PIR Statistics: 17–26 September (1944)

Headquarters 506th PIR Unit Journal for Operation "Market" (1944)

Headquarters 506th PIR "After Action Reports" (17 December 1944–August 1945)

Headquarters IX Troop Carrier Command Operation: "Linnet," "Comet" and "Market" (1944)

Interview Notes from War Crimes Investigation Team, October 1945, c/o Gerhard Roletscheck

Memoir of C. Carwood Lipton, "Experience at Bastogne" (April 1990, revised February 1991) c/o Reg Jans

Memoir of John van Kooijk "Experiences with 2nd BN, 506th PIR during Market Garden, Bastogne, Alsace, Germany and Austria" (1990), c/o Joe Muccia

Memorandum to Lt Van Horn from Colonel Sink about Operation "Pegasus 1" (23 August 1945) c/o Joe Muccia

Memoir of Maarten van den Bent "Pegasus I" – Airborne Museum Hartenstein, c/o Daan Viergever

Missing Aircrew Report June 7, 1944, US National Archives c/o Denis van den Brink

Medical History of Normandy Campaign, 506th PIR Medical Detachment (1944)

Operation "Neptune" – 506th PIR Regimental Journals May 28, 1944–June 27, 1944

Participation of the 101st Airborne Division in Exercise Tiger (1944), US National Archives

Paul Rogers letter to Walter Gordon (August 2, 1992), c/o Joe Muccia

Pegasus Memorial Battlefield Tour Guide, 12 September 2008, c/o Daan Viergever

Personal Letter of Carwood Lipton, c/o Reg Jans

"Shifty" Powers Letter to Stephen Ambrose (May 24, 1992), c/o Joe Muccia

Tactical Operations of the 101st A/B Division 17–27 September (1944)

Tactical Study HQ XVIII Corps Airborne Operation "Market" (1944)

US Army Military History Institute, George E. Koskimaki Collection: personal letters and documents, including 101st Divisional After-Action Reports (December 1944), 101st Signal Company, 321st GFA Battalion, Troop Carrier and Glider Information

# INDEX